Instant HTML

Second Edition

Alex Homer
Chris Ullman
Steve Wright

Wrox Press Ltd.®

Instant HTML *Second Edition*

Second Edition 1997
Updated June 1998

Published by Wrox Press Ltd., Arden House,
1102 Warwick Road, Acocks Green,
Birmingham. B27 6BH. UK.

Printed in USA

ISBN 1-861001-56-8

Trademark Acknowledgements

Credits

Authors
Alex Homer
Chris Ullman
Steve Wright

Additional Material
Richard Harrison
Dan Kohn

Editors
Anthea Elston
Jeremy Beacock
Dan Maharry
Sonia Mullineux

Technical Reviewers
Jon Bonnell
Rick Kingslan
Diana Castillo
Alex Federov
Brian Francis
Richard Harrison
Simon Oliver
Mark Richer

Design/Layout/Cover
Andrew Guillaume

Index
Simon Gilks

Cover image by David Maclean. Digital processing by Andrew Guillaume.

About the Authors

Alex Homer

Alex Homer is a software consultant and developer, who lives and works in the idyllic rural surroundings of Derbyshire UK. His company, Stonebroom Software, specializes in office integration and Internet-related development, and produces a range of vertical application software. He works with Wrox Press regularly.

Chris Ullman

Chris Ullman is a computer science graduate who's not let this handicap prevent him becoming a programmer fluent in Visual Basic, Java and SQL. Currently interested in all things web-based, he's trying to figure out how to design a web-bot which drags off every mention of his favourite soccer team, Birmingham City, from the web and displays it within an IE4 desktop component without him lifting a finger.

Steve Wright

Steve is a proprietor of Business Machine Services, a supplier of office machines specializing in photocopiers and facsimiles. As well as office machines, he and his company also develop leading edge web sites for local as well as national and international companies.

Table of Contents

Chapter 11: Dynamic HTML in Navigator/Communicator 4 ... 219

Chapter 12: Dynamic HTML in Internet Explorer 4 ... 247

An Introduction to HTML

HTML stands for **Hyper Text Markup Language** and is the publishing language of the World Wide Web.

The concept of the World Wide Web, or simply the Web, was born in 1983 at the CERN laboratory in Geneva, when Tim Berners-Lee was looking for a way of disseminating information in a friendly, but platform-independent, manner. The scheme he devised was placed in the public domain in 1992, and the World Wide Web was born.

Most of the activity in developing the many standards and technologies that go into making the World Wide Web function have now been transferred from CERN to the World Wide Web Consortium (W3C). Their web site at `http://www.w3.org/` is always a good starting place for discovering more about the Web. Here is the home page of the World Wide Web Consortium:

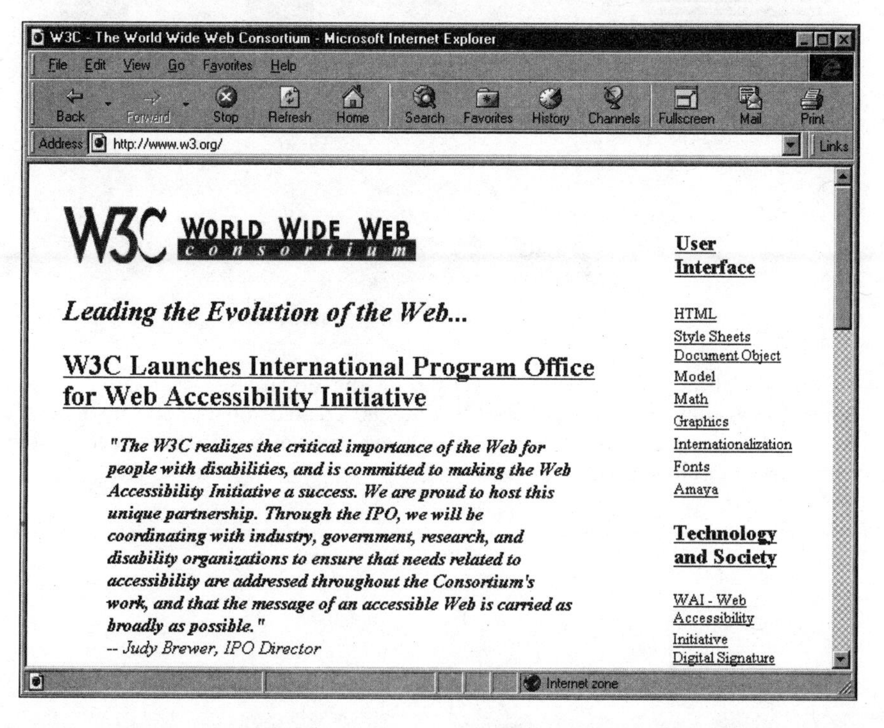

How the World Wide Web Works

In this book, we won't spend a lot of time examining how the World Wide Web works, but it is important to understand the basics of the technology that make it possible. There are three parts to this technology:

- The **server** that holds the information
- The **client** that is viewing the information
- The **protocol** that connects the two

Documents, including text, images, sounds, and other types of information are held on a server, viewed on a client, and transferred between the two using the HTTP (Hyper Text Transfer Protocol).

When a client (the computer or workstation being used by the person that wishes to view the document) makes a request to the server, it uses the HTTP protocol across a network to request the information—in the form of a URL—from the server. The server processes the request and, again, uses HTTP to transfer the information back to the client. As well as transferring the actual document, the server must tell the client the type of document being returned. This is usually defined as a MIME type. The client must then process the information before it presents it to the human viewer.

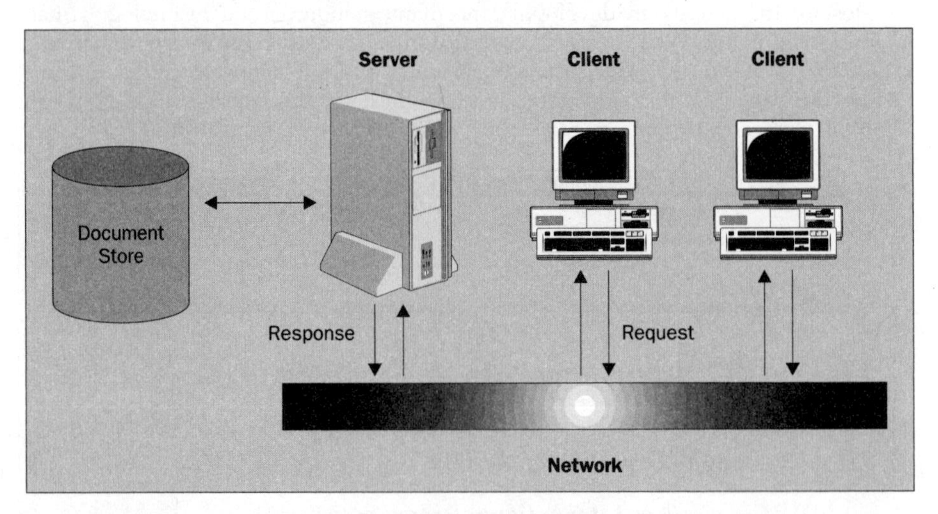

In this simplified diagram, we have shown the documents as fixed; however, in some cases, they can be dynamic documents, created 'on the fly' by the server as the client requests them. The simplest example of a dynamic document is the 'hit counter' that appears on many pages.

Some Terminology

Before we go any further, it's perhaps a good idea to define some terminology.

RFC (Request For Comments)—this is something of a misnomer, as almost all of the protocols and conventions that make the Internet function are defined in documents called RFCs. For example, RFC1725 defines POP3, the protocol often used for retrieving Internet mail, and HTML 2.0 can be found in RFC1866. All RFC documents can be found on the Internet.

URL (Uniform Resource Locator)—this is a way of specifying a resource. It consists of a protocol name, a colon (`:`), two forward slash characters (`//`), a machine name, and a path to a resource (using `/` as a separator). For example, the Wrox Press home page can be found at **`http://www.wrox.com/`**. URLs are the way that all resources are specified on the web. Note that URLs can specify more than just web pages. For example, to retrieve RFC1866 using FTP, we could specify **`ftp://ds.internic.net/rfc/rfc1866.txt`**. URLs are often embedded inside web pages, to provide links to other pages, as we shall see later.

SGML (Standard Generalized Markup Language)—a standard for defining markup languages. More about this in a moment.

DTD (Document Type Definition)—a set of rules on how to apply SGML to a particular markup language. Again, more in a moment.

HTML (Hyper Text Markup Language)—the subject of this book!

MIME (Multimedia Internet Mail Extensions)—this was originally intended as a way of embedding complex binary documents in mail messages, but is now used much more widely. When a server passes web information to a client browser, it first tells the client the type of information it is going to send using a MIME type and a subtype. The browser can then decide how it wishes to handle that document type. It may choose to process it internally, or invoke an external program to handle the information. MIME types consist of a main type and subtype. For example, plain text is 'text/plain', but 'image/mpeg' specifies an image stored in mpeg format.

HTTP (Hyper Text Transfer Protocol)—this is the protocol used to transfer information between the client and server computer. Although vital for the operation of the Web, it isn't generally necessary to know any details of HTPP to provide information across the Web, so we will not consider it further here.

Now we have defined some terminology, we can look in more detail at how HTML is defined.

Introduction to SGML and the HTML DTD

The original documents used in the World Wide Web were in a new format called HTML—Hyper Text Markup Language. The two most important features of this were that a basic HTML document was simple to create, and that HTML was almost totally platform and viewer independent.

HTML is a markup language that tells the client, in general terms, how the information should be presented. For example, to define a heading in an HTML document, you might write:

<H2>This is a heading</H2>

This tells the client that the text "This is a heading" should be displayed as a level 2 heading, but leaves it up to the client to decide the most appropriate way of displaying it. As HTML develops, this original scheme is being diluted, and more and more specific display information can be passed to the client, such as fonts, point size, and colors.

An interesting side-effect of this way of defining documents is that it allows people with visual disabilities to use special browsers that render the document in a form which they are better able to comprehend.

The first version of HTML was a fairly loosely defined standard. Not until version 2 of HTML was it more rigorously defined in terms of another standard, known as SGML.

SGML

SGML is the abbreviation for 'Standard Generalized Markup Language'. This language, or meta-language as it should be called, was defined by International Standards in 1986 as ISO 8879:1986.

The purpose of SGML is very simple. At the time it was developed, there were several 'markup languages', none of which were particularly portable between platforms or even software packages. The purpose of SGML is to allow a formal definition of markup languages that can then be used to give complete flexibility and portability of information display between applications and platforms.

It is tempting for the newcomer to SGML to view it as a markup language in its own right—defining a set of tags, etc., and providing meanings for those tags. This is not the case. SGML is a theoretical language (i.e. one that you can't program in or compile—it only exists in paper format) for describing other languages. What SGML *does* do is describe the relation of components within a document. As such, SGML is not a competitor with the likes of TeX or Postscript which define such things as layout, but a way of describing what the document 'is' rather than how it should be 'rendered'.

A markup language consists of a set of conventions that can be used to provide a way to encode text. A markup language must also specify what markup is allowed, what markup is required and how the markup is distinguished from the text of the document. SGML does all this—what it doesn't do is specify what the markups are, or what they mean.

XML

Another language, XML (Extensible Markup Language) has emerged, derived from SGML. It's a programmable version of SGML, albeit a very simplified one. It can be used to create languages in the same way that SGML can. It's important that you don't confuse with it HTML, as they are very different. XML is like the rules of grammar, an overall structure for defining language; HTML is the vocabulary, the actual words that you use.

Currently the most common application of XML is in Internet Explorer 4—in the Channel Definition Format, or CDF for short. Channels are a new method of retrieving information, where the server appears to broadcast the information to the receiver, IE4, which acts like a television or radio set. CDF is the language used to create channels. CDF is an application of XML, in the same way that HTML is an application of SGML. CDF is in fact an HTML-like language itself. You can use tags, you can set attributes: it's all very familiar. In fact, unless you look closely at CDF and you already know some HTML, you probably wouldn't be able to tell the two apart.

So, SGML and XML are like templates for creating languages. What SGML actually produces is a DTD.

The DTD

DTD stands for Document Type Definition. Its purpose is to define the legal productions of a particular markup language. A simple DTD would do nothing more than, say, define a set of tags that can be used by a particular markup language.

The HTML 4.0 standard is a formally defined SGML DTD. In other words, the definition of HTML 4.0 is itself specified using the SGML meta-language. This allows HTML specifications to be rigorously defined.

To fully define HTML 4.0, two different specifications are required. The first is the relatively small SGML definition that defines general features, such as the character set and size limits. The main information is contained in the DTD, which defines the detail, such as the tags and attributes, which we will learn more about later. The HTML 4.0 DTD can be found at the following address: `http://www.w3.org/TR/PR-html40/`

HTML Standards and Specifications

HTML 4.0 is the latest recommendation. This has led to some confusion over what is now a standard and what isn't. The HTML standards have to go through three stages before they become standard and can be officially termed **recommendations**.

The first stage is the draft, where the proposals are made public and are open to large-scale review and change. Once the proposals have been available for a length of time, the draft moves forward and becomes known as a **proposed recommendation**. During this 6-week period members of W3C vote on whether the recommendation should be adopted as the final standard. It is possible for them to accept the standard fully, to accept it with minor changes, to return it to draft status for further consultation or to reject it completely. If the vote is for one of the two former options, then the standard becomes a recommendation and is finally adopted by W3C.

The confusion stems from HTML 3.0, which was never an official recommendation, but always only a working draft. The Web developed so rapidly, with vendors implementing proprietary tags all the time, that the draft HTML 3.0 specification was left looking dated before it could even be issued. The consortium decided that, rather than continue work on HTML 3.0, they would move immediately to HTML 3.2. The HTML 3.2 standard incorporates all of HTML 2.0 (with some very minor changes) plus many of the proposals that were in the HTML 3.0 draft, and additional features such as tables and applets.

Since the 3.2 standard was completed, additions continue to be made to new browsers—over and above the requirements to meet the standard. The proposals for HTML 4.0 were created with input from both Microsoft and Netscape. HTML 4.0 is not *that* different from HTML 3.2, but there are several subtle changes that require a new standard to be defined.

Hopefully there should be less need for new tags and new attributes as a general framework has been established and changes might only need to be made to the scripting languages from now on. Only once there is a stable standard that the major companies adhere to, do we have any chance of achieving a fully standardized and platform-independent way of viewing information.

What You Need to Use this Book

To create an HTML document, all you need is a text editor that is capable of saving files in ASCII format, and a browser such as Netscape's Navigator or Microsoft's Internet Explorer. The latest version of both these browsers can be downloaded to your system via the Internet from the following sites:

Netscape Navigator (the browser section of the Communicator 4 suite)
`http://home.netscape.com/comprod/mirror/index.html`

Internet Explorer
`http://www.microsoft.com/ie/`

The examples and screenshots in this book were taken from PCs running Windows 95 and Windows 98 using Windows Notepad as the text editor. However, HTML is a platform-independent language, so you can just as easily use a Macintosh or other operating system with the same results.

The past several months have seen many HTML editors come onto the market. Some of these do a very good job of adding tags, in-line images, etc., and presenting the page in a WYSIWYG format. By all means, try these editors out, they certainly make the task of adding tags much easier and quicker. For the purposes of this book, however, it is suggested that you stay with a plain text editor as there are some tricks and techniques that even the most powerful HTML editor can't handle.

So, let's get started....

Creating an HTML Document

HTML is incredibly easy to learn. If you have done any surfing at all, you will have seen just how much can be achieved with this simple language. In this chapter, we will look at what you need to lay the foundations of an HTML document.

Web Page Authoring

HTML isn't the only language you can use when creating web pages, but it is the one you'll need to start with. Throughout this book we'll mention other languages that work with HTML, and before we go any further we will differentiate between these languages, and explain the functions of each one.

HTML

HTML(Hyper Text Markup Language) is a language that consists of a set of predefined tags that are included along with the text. These tags tell the browser whether the text is to be a paragraph, a heading, an image, a table, etc. At the same time, the tags also allow a certain amount of formatting information to be included, such as alignment of images with respect to text. It is the basic language that you'll use to create web pages.

Scripting Languages

Scripting languages were in existence long before web browsers, but only concern us since their introduction into browsers, from Netscape Navigator 2.0 onwards. Netscape had originally developed a scripting language, known as LiveScript, to add interactivity to their web server and browser range. With the release of Navigator 2, they joined forces with Sun in the creation of the language, and added it to the browser. In the process, they changed its name to **JavaScript**.

While HTML creates basic, static web pages of text and graphics only, scripting languages add the extra dimension of being able to accept information from a user, and return results that depend on the user's input. They allow the user's web pages to come alive and be interactive in a way not previously possible. Three scripting languages are commonly used to do this, although two of them are effectively the same language.

JavaScript

JavaScript is the original browser scripting language, and is not to be confused with Java. Java is a complete application programming language in its own right. JavaScript borrows much of its syntax and basic structures from Java, but has a different purpose—and evolved from different origins (LiveScript was completely different to Java).

For example, while JavaScript can control browser behavior and content, it isn't capable of drawing graphics on the HTML document. Java on the other hand can't control the browser as a whole, but it can do graphics and perform network and threading functions. They make a useful combination, but JavaScript is much simpler to learn. It is designed to create small, efficient programs which can do many things—from performing repetitive tasks, to handling events generated by the user (such as mouse clicks, keyboard responses, etc.).

Microsoft introduced their own version of JavaScript, known as **JScript**, in Internet Explorer 3.0. It has only minor differences to the Netscape version of the language.

VBScript

In Internet Explorer 3.0, Microsoft introduced their own scripting language, **VBScript**, which was based on their Visual Basic programming language. Because JavaScript borrowed from Java, which in turn borrowed from C++, JavaScript isn't the simplest language to learn. Visual Basic is a lot easier to learn than C++, so in turn VBScript is a simpler language to use than JavaScript. In terms of functionality, there isn't much to choose between the two, it's more a matter of personal preference. The biggest drawback is that Netscape Navigator doesn't support VBScript without the aid of a proprietary plug-in, so you'll find that JavaScript is much more widely used and supported.

ECMAScript

With two different scripting languages being employed by the two main browsers, and two versions (albeit not that different) of JavaScript, the cross-platform compatibility of the Web is being compromised by the rivalry of Microsoft and Netscape. The European Computer Manufacturers Association (ECMA) is a standards body that took on the task of producing a single scripting language for everybody to use. They chose JavaScript as the basis, and since then Microsoft have brought JScript 3.0 into line with the ECMA proposals, while Netscape have made sure that JavaScript 1.2 is fully compliant as well.

In the future, it's quite feasible that ECMAScript (or JavaScript) will become the sole scripting language, and indeed Microsoft are already changing many of the samples on their web site from VBScript to JavaScript.

Dynamic HTML

This is a set of extensions to HTML that make use of some of the new properties in the HTML 4.0 standard. Microsoft and Netscape have both adopted the term to describe the set of techniques which make many of the elements in a web page accessible to scripting languages. On top of that, these techniques allow you to position elements exactly, and move them around without a page refresh. This was previously impossible, even with VBScript or JavaScript. However, Dynamic HTML isn't (as you might expect) a set of new tags or attributes. It's more a way of providing hooks from elements to your script code, allowing it to get at the document that is visible on the screen.

It does this via the innovation of a **Document Object Model**. This is a representation of the web page or **HTML document** as it is known, which organizes the content and style of the page in a way that is easily accessible to the scripting code. The document object is made up of properties, methods and events, which can be accessed directly and executed by script code. This power allows the web page to become 'dynamic', hence the name.

Predictably, Microsoft and Netscape versions of Dynamic HTML vary so much as to be almost totally incompatible. In version 4, Internet Explorer's interpretation of Dynamic HTML is closer to the HTML 4.0 standard than the Dynamic HTML found in Navigator 4.0. Netscape has promised full compliance with HTML 4.0 in the next release of their browser suite, Communicator 5.

Which Language Do I Use?

This is a book about HTML, so we're looking primarily at this language. However, there are elements which enable us to use scripting languages, and in turn Dynamic HTML, in our pages. So we will, in later chapters, be looking at how the different languages link together. For the time being, all we need to consider is HTML.

The Different Components of HTML

We'll now take a look at the components that go to make up the language.

Tags and Elements

There are two basic parts to any web page: the **head** and the **body**. Both parts use **HTML elements**. Elements are defined in a page using **tags**—these are what you actually see in the page. Each structural part of the document is referred to as an element. So, paragraphs, tables, forms, images, lists, etc. are all examples of elements. The elements are created using tags.

Tags are normally typed in CAPITALS, but browsers are case-insensitive—you can use lowercase or mixed case if you prefer. Using capitals makes the tags stand out, and therefore makes your life a lot easier when you come to alter the code in several months time. However, HTML 4.0 recommends using lower case, because this often allows better compression of the document, as the content is likely to contain more lower that upper case text.

You'll also find that using capitals helps to distinguish HTML from scripting code, because it is commonly written in lower-case (However, you won't come across any script until chapter 10). We have used capitals for tags in this book to help you see how the pages are constructed.

Start and End Tags

In HTML, there are two types of tags: **start tags** and **end tags**. Both are placed inside angled brackets, e.g. `<H1>`. End tags are the same as start tags, except that they are preceded by a forward slash, e.g. `</H1>`. The combination is used to indicate where the effect of the tags start and finish.
For example, if you type the following code into a text editor:

```
<HTML>
<HEAD>
<TITLE>Instant HTML</TITLE>
</HEAD>

<BODY>
<H1>An Introduction to Tags</H1>
In HTML tags are used to add special effects to plain text.
</BODY>
</HTML>
```

then save it as a file with an `htm` extension (or `html` if your system isn't constrained by the 8.3 naming convention) and view it in a browser via the File | Open menu options, you will see:

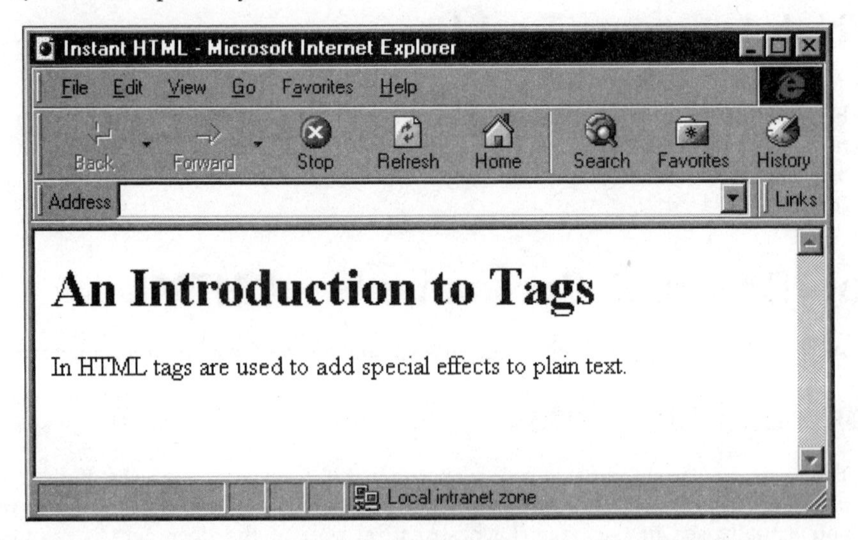

Most elements have a start and end tag, but not all. If you think of the end tag as 'switching off' the start tag, it will seem logical. For example, the `<P>` element (new paragraph) does not require a corresponding end tag, although you can use one if you wish. Other elements simply don't have an end tag at all, for example, `<IMG>` (insert an image). Elements with both start and end versions are often referred to as **enclosures**.

Nesting Elements

Most elements can be nested. In other words, you can have elements inside other elements. The order of nesting is important. For instance, this is legal:

```
<B>This word is <I>emphasized</I></B>
```

though this isn't:

```
<B>This word is <I>emphasized</B></I>
```

Although the above line of code is illegal, most browsers will still render the text as you would expect—it just makes your code harder to understand!

Attributes

Attributes allow you to extend the capabilities of elements, and are placed within the opening tag. You can use attributes to control fonts, border spacing, text alignment, etc. For example, the **`<H1>`** element, which prints text on a separate line and in a larger font (as a level 1 heading), has an **`ALIGN`** attribute, which affects the positioning of the heading on the screen.

So, as you might expect,

```
<H1 ALIGN=CENTER>An Introduction to Tags</H1>
In HTML tags are used to add special effects to plain text.
```

will result in:

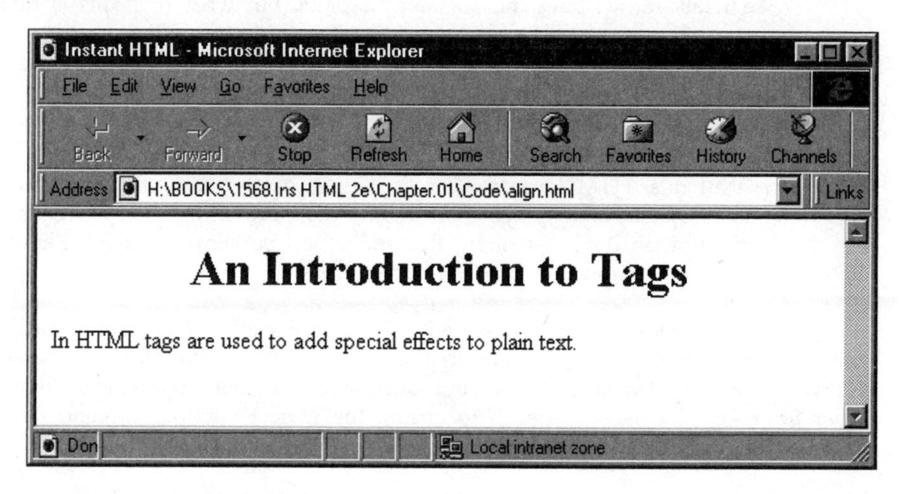

The syntax for attributes is as follows:

`<TAGNAME ATTRIBUTE=`*value***`>`**

Note that if the value contains anything other than letters, numbers, hyphens, or periods, it must be contained within quotes.

Creating an HTML Document

When writing HTML, the first thing you need to understand is that it is almost impossible to format a page so that it will look exactly the same on every client (or browser). Indeed, the original HTML idea was specifically based on not telling the client exactly how the page should look.

There are several good reasons for this:

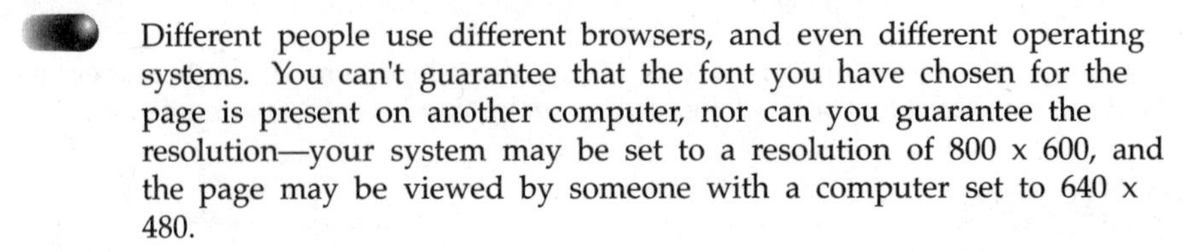

- Different people use different browsers, and even different operating systems. You can't guarantee that the font you have chosen for the page is present on another computer, nor can you guarantee the resolution—your system may be set to a resolution of 800 x 600, and the page may be viewed by someone with a computer set to 640 x 480.

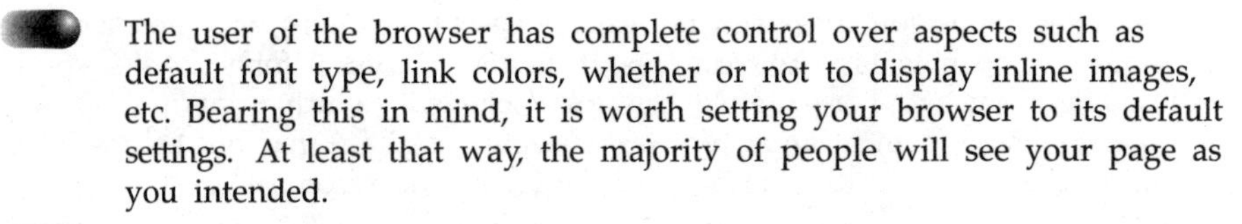

- The user of the browser has complete control over aspects such as default font type, link colors, whether or not to display inline images, etc. Bearing this in mind, it is worth setting your browser to its default settings. At least that way, the majority of people will see your page as you intended.

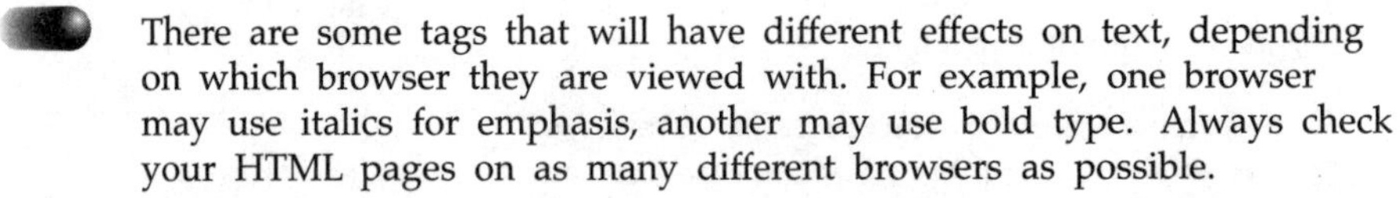

- There are some tags that will have different effects on text, depending on which browser they are viewed with. For example, one browser may use italics for emphasis, another may use bold type. Always check your HTML pages on as many different browsers as possible.

- Different browsers support different extensions to the HTML standard. We'll talk more about this in later chapters, but what it means is that if you want your pages to be readable to as wide an audience as possible, you should stick to the standard syntax. Compromise is the order of the day! Staying with the standard tags and attributes will mean that as many people as possible will be able to view your pages.

Having said all this, HTML's great strength lies in its flexibility. For instance, if a browser is incapable of displaying an image, then providing the HTML has been properly written, text describing the image can be shown instead; likewise, static images can be shown in place of video, etc.

When an HTML viewer is presented with a tag it doesn't understand, it usually just skips past that tag. This means that it's possible to use vendor extensions to HTML, providing you ensure that your document still looks reasonable with other browsers. The best approach to ensure the widest possible audience for your HTML is to stick to the standard.

There are several elements that should be included in all HTML documents. These define the structure of the document and allow browsers to correctly interpret the content. Have a look at this code:

```
<!DOCTYPE>

<HTML>

<HEAD>
```

```
<TITLE> A description of the page </TITLE>
Other head elements
</HEAD>

<BODY>
Body elements go here
</BODY>

</HTML>
```

This is the basic form that every HTML document should take. Let's have a look at each of the elements.

The <!DOCTYPE> Element

The **<!DOCTYPE>** element is used to declare the type of document in which it appears. This is most useful for parsers, as it declares what version of HTML the document is written in, and thereby allows the parser to interpret the coding correctly. A rigorous HTML-checking program will reject any document which does not include this tag—most browsers are not so fussy, and so most of the documents on the web do not include this tag, even though it is required by the HTML 4.0 standard. This tag should be the first item in any proper HTML document.

For documents that conform to the HTML 4.0 standard, the declaration should be as follows:

```
<!DOCTYPE HTML PUBLIC "-//W3C//DTD HTML 4.0 //EN">
```

*The word **Draft** was suggested in HTML 3.2, as a modifier in **<!DOCTYPE>**, to distinguish between draft and final standards and indeed HTML 4.0 has only just moved out of draft status, to become a proposed recommendation. However this keyword was deemed ineffectual and has since been dropped.*

Remember that, although this tag is required by the HTML standard, if your document includes vendor specific extensions or deviates from the standard in any other way, it should be left out. Otherwise, you may get unpredictable results.

The <HTML> Element

This tag signals the beginning of the HTML document. Although **<!DOCTYPE>** appears first, this is the tag that defines the beginning and end of the HTML content, and encapsulates everything that is supposed to be parsed as HTML. Closing this tag with **</HTML>** ends the document—anything appearing afterwards is supposed to be ignored by browsers.

From HTML 3.2 onwards, this tag was no longer required, but it is strongly recommended; browsers that do not understand the **<!DOCTYPE>** declaration will act strangely if you don't include **<HTML>**.

The <HEAD> Element

This tag signals the document header, which is used to contain generic information about the document—such as the title, the base URL of the document, what the style of the document is, and so on. From the HTML 3.2 standard onwards, it is no longer strictly necessary to include a **<HEAD>** tag, but most browsers will behave oddly if you omit it—so we recommend using it at all times. The **<HEAD>** tag can take, according to the HTML 4 standard, a number of attributes:

```
DIR     PROFILE       LANG
```

There are also three IE 4 only attributes. Before we look at these attributes, we should note that there are a number of **universal** attributes, which are attributes that can be used with most, if not all, elements.

Universal Attributes

Although there are no truly universal attributes that *all* elements share, there are six attributes that most of them use, and that are defined within the HTML 4.0 standard as being universal. Some of these universal attributes have particular functions, which we will examine later in the book—particularly the **STYLE** and **CLASS** attributes, which are used by style sheets. We will describe what each of these elements does here and then just list them, without explanation, with later elements (unless something is different about them). The six attributes are:

```
ID  DIR  TITLE  LANG  CLASS  STYLE
```

There is one further universal attribute, **LANGUAGE**, which is found in IE4—but which isn't in HTML 4.0. This attribute sets the default scripting language for the element, as either JavaScript or VBScript. The script interpreter will use this attribute if a **<SCRIPT>** tag is included with no **LANGUAGE** attribute.

We'll look briefly at each attribute here. You'll find more details about how you use them with the individual elements in later chapters.

ID

Specifies a unique name or identifier for an element in a page or style sheet. The syntax is:

ID=*string*

DIR

Specifies a direction for text to flow in, when surrounded by elements of text which flow in differing directions. This attribute has not been implemented in either IE4 or Navigator 4. The syntax is:

DIR=LTR|RTL

TITLE

An advisory title for the element in which it is set. This information is often displayed as a tool tip, in a help query or while the element is loading. The syntax is:

TITLE="*string*"

LANG

The ISO description of the language for the element. The syntax is:

LANG=*string*

CLASS

Specifies the class of element, and is used to associate an element with a style sheet. The syntax is:

CLASS=*classname*

We'll look at how you can specify classes in more detail in chapter 3.

STYLE

Specifies style information for the element, in the form of a property or set of properties. The syntax is:

STYLE="*string*"

All the style information is enclosed in quotes as a single string, for example:

```
<H2 STYLE="font-family:arial">This is a heading</H2>
```

We'll look at how you can specify style information in more detail in chapter 3.

Attributes of <HEAD>

As five (including the IE 4 only) attributes of **<HEAD>** are universal, this only leaves one to discuss.

PROFILE

Specifies the location of a **meta-data profile**. This is used in conjunction with the **<META>** tag, which is discussed later in this chapter. A meta-data profile is used either as a globally unique name, which a browser can assume things about and perform activities for the profile without the actual profile being accessed or as a link where the browser can actually use properties defined within the profile.

PROFILE=*url*

Elements That <HEAD> Can Enclose

As well as having a set of attributes, **<HEAD>** can also enclose other elements, which provide similar capabilities to its attributes. These are:

TITLE BASE ISINDEX LINK SCRIPT STYLE META

We'll look at these now.

The <TITLE> Element

Every valid HTML 4.0 document must have a **<TITLE>** element. The title is usually (but not always) displayed by the browser in the title bar. Note, however, that you can't include any other HTML inside the **<TITLE>** tag. If you do, this will be rendered on-screen, rather than applied as a title. The title should be a meaningful description of the page, since it is usually the title that is used as a bookmark by browsers. **TITLE** takes two universal attributes **LANG** and **DIR**.

__Bookmarks__ (or __Favorites__ as they are known in Internet Explorer) are used to build up a list of sites and pages that you visit often. You can normally bookmark any page that you are currently viewing, and come back to it later.

The <BASE> Element

This element defines the base URL, or original location, of the document. Without **<BASE>**, if the document was moved somewhere, relative links (i.e. links that do not include the entire server and directory path) may no longer work. This is because the base URL would be defined as the new, current URL for the document. If **<BASE>** is included, the URL it specifies is used to create absolute addresses for any relative ones. **<BASE>** takes the following attributes:

HREF **TARGET**

HREF

The entire URL of the page as a string. The syntax is:

HREF=*URL*

An example is:

```
<BASE HREF="http://this-server.org/inthisdir/filename.html">
```

TARGET

Specifies the window or frame into which the new page should be loaded. The syntax is:

TARGET=*window_name* **| _parent | _blank | _top | _self**

Note that some older browsers do not support the use of **<BASE>** though others will use it as the URL to 'bookmark'.

In Chapter 4, we look at the whole concept of relative and absolute addresses, or URLs.

The <ISINDEX> Element

This element indicates that the document creates a search string which will be sent to the server. This means that you can send keywords back to the server via the document you are reading. It does not mean that the document itself is searchable. If you include **<ISINDEX>**, your document will automatically display the following text:

You can search this index. Type the keyword(s) you want to search for:

and this will be followed by a text box for user input.

Submitting a search in this way appends the keywords you enter to the document's URL. They are then sent to the server for processing, provided that the server has been set up to do so. This is a somewhat clumsy way of performing a search, and the search will only apply to the current document. Forms are now the preferred way to instigate a search and the tag has been deprecated in HTML 4.0.

The <LINK> Element

This defines the current document's relationship with other documents, and can convey relationship information between documents to be used in different ways—such as to create a toolbar with a drop-down list of links, or a glossary or index of links. Here is a list of attributes that the **<LINK>** tag can contain:

CHARSET	**CLASS**	**DIR**	**HREF**	**HREFLANG**	**MEDIA**	**METHODS**
REL	**REV**	**STYLE**	**TARGET**	**TITLE**	**TYPE**	**URN**

Descriptions of each non-universal attribute follow:

CHARSET

Specifies the **character encoding** of the resource designated by the link.

CHARSET=*charset*

Character encoding is a method of converting a stream of bytes(what the browser receives data as) into a stream of characters(what the user will hopefully understand).

HREF

The entire URL of the linked file as a string. The syntax is:

HREF=*url*

HREFLANG

Specifies the language of the resource designated by **HREF** and can only be used when **HREF** is also defined.

HREFLANG=*langcode*

MEDIA

Indicates the output device to be used for the document. The syntax is:

MEDIA=SCREEN | PRINT | PROJECTION | BRAILLE | SPEECH | ALL

METHODS

This provides information about the functions that a user can perform on an object. This is new to HTML 4.0 and isn't supported in either IE4 or Navigator 4. The syntax is:

METHODS=*string*

REL

The 'forward' relationship between this document and the one specified by the **HREF** attribute. This is also known as the 'link type'. The syntax is:

REL=*relationship*

where *relationship* can be:

ALTERNATE	Defines substitute versions for the document in which the link occurs.
STYLESHEET	References an external style sheet. See chapter 3 for details.
CONTENTS *or* **TOC**	References a document serving as a table of contents.
INDEX	References a document providing an index for the current document.
GLOSSARY	References a document providing a glossary of terms for the current document.
COPYRIGHT	References a copyright statement for the current document.
START	Points to the first document of a series of documents.
NEXT	Points to the next document of a series of documents.
PREV *or* **PREVIOUS**	Points to the previous document of a series of documents.
HELP	Points to a document offering help. This is aimed at helping users who have lost their way.
CHAPTER	Points to a document which acts as a chapter in a collection of documents.
SECTION	Points to a document which acts as a section in a collection of documents.
SUBSECTION	Points to a document which acts as a subsection in a collection of documents.
APPENDIX	Points to a document which acts as an appendix in a collection of documents.
BOOKMARK	Provides a means for orienting users in an extended document. Several bookmarks may be defined in each document.

REV

Defines a 'reverse' relationship, i.e. the relationship between the document specified by the **HREF** attribute and this document. The syntax is:

REV=*relationship*

where *relationship* can be the same values as for the **REL** attribute.

TARGET

Specifies the window or frame of where the new page should be loaded. The syntax is:

TARGET=*window_name* **| _parent | _blank | _top | _self**

TYPE

Specifies the MIME type for the link. The syntax is:

TYPE=*MIME-type*

We look at MIME-types later in the book.

URN

The **Uniform Resource Name** for the target document. This is new to HTML 4.0 and this isn't supported in IE4 or Navigator4. The syntax is:

URN=*string*

The <STYLE> Element

The **<STYLE>** element plays a vital part in styles and style sheets, by providing the web page author with a means of including style sheet information within the head of an HTML document. If your browser doesn't support the **<STYLE>** element, the contents must be hidden from the browser. We'll discuss style sheets and the **<STYLE>** element in detail in Chapter 3.

The <SCRIPT> Element

The **<SCRIPT>** element is used to place script within a document. Scripts can be specified within the head or body of an HTML document or in an external file. You can specify more than one script, throughout the head or body. We'll look at scripting and the **<SCRIPT>** element in Chapter 10.
bit confusing when the browser attributes are intended to be read by web search robots.

The <META> Element

The **<META>** element is used to provide information about the HTML document. This **meta-information** can be extracted by web servers to identify, index, or perform other specialized functions. One of the most useful functions of the **<META>** element is that you can use it to provide information to search engines and to the users of search engines. Quite often when you supply details to a search engine, and you get information returned in an incomprehensible format. This is because in the absence of a description in the **<META>** tag, the search engine will return the first couple of lines of text available on the page.

You can also add details such as who the author of the document is and when the document should expire by. The **<META>** tag can be used in conjunction with the meta-data profile set up in the **<HEAD>** tag. Properties defined by the profile can have their values set in subsequent **<META>** declarations.

There are nine attributes for the **META** tag:

DIR	**LANG**	**TITLE**	**SCHEME**	**NAME**
CONTENT	**HTTP-EQUIV**	**CHARSET**	**URL**	

Three of the attributes **DIR**, **LANG** and **TITLE** are universal. Internet Explorer also supports the **URL** and **CHARSET** attributes. **CHARSET** was only supported by IE3, so we won't discuss it further while **URL** specifies the address in the **META** tag.

NAME

Used to specify the name of a property for your web page, such as author, date, company, etc. The syntax is:

NAME=*metaname*

This can be set to **DESCRIPTION** or **KEYWORDSCONTENT**. Specifies the value for the **NAME** property. The syntax is:

CONTENT=*metacontent*

HTTP-EQUIV

Maps the tags and their respective names to an HTTP response header for processing. The syntax is:

HTTP-EQUIV=*string*

SCHEME

The **SCHEME** attribute will be used to specify a scheme which will be used to interpret the property's value. This is new to the HTML 4.0 standard and hasn't been implemented in IE4 or Navigator 4. The syntax is:

SCHEME=*string*

Using the <META> Element

The **<META>** element must include the **CONTENT** attribute. It should also contain either the **NAME** or **HTTP-EQUIV** attribute. **<META>** elements with the **NAME** attribute are usually intended for interpretation by the browser, while those with the **HTTP-EQUIV** attribute are intended for the server. This can sometimes be a bit confusing when the browser attributes are intended to be read by web search robots.

So that you understand the tag, we'll take a look at a few examples of how it is used.

Providing Information to Search Engines

The **NAME** attribute can be assigned several values to help make your site more visible, to make it's description more user friendly, and to make sure that it turns up on more lists when hit. For instance when you search on a site the description, if you set **NAME** to **DESCRIPTION** then the information contained within the **CONTENT** attribute, is the text that a search engine will return.

```
<META NAME ="description" CONTENT=" Wrox Press Limited publishes computer
programming books, written for programmers by programmers.">
```

Of course what's there to stop you writing a thesis on your web site within the description tag, or supplying (as some insalubrious web sites do) every keyword under the sun? Well there is a practical limit to the number of characters you are allowed to supply in your description. If you supply more than the recommended 200 characters, you will find that the search engine will cut your description off there.

If you set **NAME** to **KEYWORDS**, then you can specify all of the keywords that you wish to be associated with your web page. So when a user types in one of the keywords, if you have submitted your page to the search engine, you page will be returned along with a list of all of the other matches.

```
<META NAME ="keywords" CONTENT=" Web-Developer, Community, Visual Basic,
VBScript, JScript, JavaScript, IE, Navigator, Netscape, Browser, Scriptlets,
Internet, Intranet, Java, IIS, IIS3, IIS4, NT4, NT5, NT Server, SQL, Access,
Microsoft, VB, Wrox, Books, Programming, Computer, Developer, Professional">
```

This means that your site will be categorized more effectively, which means more 'hits' (or people visiting your site). Remember that a web site's effectiveness is measured mainly by the number of visitors it attracts. You can supply up to a maximum of 1000 characters worth of keywords. If you supply too many then this is considered **spamming**, and many search engines carry a penalty for spamming, typically not indexing your site at all.

Not all search engines support the **<META>** tag, so if you wish to supply a description to the engines that don't, then you need to supply the contents of the **DESCRIPTION** attribute in comment tags as follows:

```
<!-- Wrox Press Limited publishes computer programming books, written for
programmers by programmers.-->
```

Redirecting the Browser to Another Page

If the element was:

```
<META HTTP-EQUIV="REFRESH"
      CONTENT="5;URL=http://www.server.org/next.html">
```

then after five seconds, the browser will load the next page. This is very useful if you change the location of the page, because it will automatically be loaded from the new location.

Specifying the Expiry Date

If you include:

```
<META HTTP-EQUIV="Expires" CONTENT="Tue, 24 Oct 1996 17:45:00 GMT">
```

it ensures that, if the page is reloaded by the user after the expiry date, a fresh copy is fetched from the server, rather than the browser displaying a cached copy. This is useful if you want your readers to get the latest version of your documents.

About Ratings

The `<META>` tag can also be used to declare a rating for your page. If you don't include a rating, certain browsers may prevent access to your site.

The method of associating labels with the content of a web page is known as PICS or **Platform for Internet Content Selection**. Originally PICS was designed for use by parents and teachers to effectively control what could be viewed on the Web by minors, whilst protecting everyone's right of free speech. New uses for PICS are, however, being developed all the time; these include privacy and code signing. PICS does not provide a rating system itself, it merely provides the ability to apply ratings to content. Comprehensive information on the PICS specification can be viewed at:

`http://www.w3.org/pub/WWW/PICS/`

The actual rating information is known as the **rating label**. The label appears in a Web document as part of the HTML code and each part of the content that is rated has its own label.

To include ratings within your code, you specify the rating as part of the `<META>` tag in this general form:

```
<HTML>
<HEAD>
<META HTTP-EQUIV="PICS-Label"
      CONTENT='(PICS-1.0 "http://www.rsac.org"
labels on "1996.11.05T08:15-0500"
until "1999.12.31T23:59-0000"
for "http://www.rsac.org/index.html"
by "RSAC"
rating (language 2 nudity 0 violence 1))'>
</HEAD>
```

For more information on how to rate your own content, go to:

`http://www.rsac.org/`

The <BODY> Element

The body section is where the meat of your HTML goes. The `<BODY>` and `</BODY>` tags marks the beginning and end of the body section. Here, you add the text you want displayed in the main browser window, tags and attributes to modify that text, hyperlinks to other documents, etc. You can also set the color of the text, background, etc., for your document.

There are many attributes that can be used with the `<BODY>` tag. We'll break them down into three sections, the HTML 4.0 standard attributes, the deprecated attributes, and the browser-specific attributes.

The HTML 4.0 <BODY> Attributes

The only attributes `<BODY>` supports fully in HTML 4.0 are the universal attributes:

```
CLASS    ID    DIR    LANG    STYLE    TITLE
```

Deprecated Attributes of <BODY>

Some attributes are marked as **deprecated** in the HTML 4.0 standard. Deprecated attributes are those that are still present in the standard, but have been marked for removal and will disappear in later versions of the standard. This is generally because there are alternative and better ways of achieving the same presentation, either with other attributes or style sheets. We briefly consider the issue of deprecation in conjunction with style sheets in chapter 3. The deprecated attributes in `<BODY>` are:

```
BACKGROUND    BGCOLOR  ALINK  LINK  VLINK  TEXT
```

BACKGROUND

Specifies a background picture. The syntax is:

BACKGROUND=*url*

where *url* is the address of the picture to display. The picture is tiled behind all images and text.

BGCOLOR

Sets the background color of the page. The syntax is:

BGCOLOR="#*rrggbb***"**

where *rrggbb* are pairs of hexadecimal numbers for the red, green, and blue content, respectively (for example, **FFFFFF** would be white, and **000000** would be black. We'll discuss this in detail a little later). **BGCOLOR** can be used in conjunction with **BACKGROUND**. If the background is a large image, you might set the color of the page using **BGCOLOR**, so that this color will be displayed by the browser while the image is loading. This is useful if, for example, you are using white text over a dark background image: set a dark background color so that the text is visible even before the image loads.

ALINK

Sets the color of an active hypertext link. A hypertext link is active only while the mouse is clicked on the link. The syntax is:

ALINK="#*rrggbb***"**

where *rrggbb* are hexadecimal values for red, green, and blue. Some browsers do not provide an active state for hypertext links

LINK

Sets the color of hypertext links that have not been visited. The syntax is:

LINK="#*rrggbb***"**

where *rrggbb* are hexadecimal numbers relating to red, green, and blue.

VLINK

Sets the color of visited hypertext links. The syntax is

VLINK="#*rrggbb***"**

where *rrggbb* are hexadecimal numbers relating to red, green, and blue.

TEXT

Sets the color of normal text on the page. The syntax is:

TEXT="#*rrggbb***"**

where *rrggbb* are hexadecimal numbers relating to red, green, and blue.

Internet Explorer Extensions to <BODY>

There are also seven extensions for the **<BODY>** element found in Internet Explorer, but not in Navigator:

BGPROPERTIES	LANGUAGE	BOTTOMMARGIN	LEFTMARGIN
RIGHTMARGIN	TOPMARGIN	SCROLL	

BGPROPERTIES

Sets a watermark. The watermark is the background picture, previously set with the **BACKGROUND** attribute. It remains 'fixed' in place and doesn't scroll with the rest of the page. The syntax is simply:

```
BGPROPERTIES=FIXED
```

BOTTOMMARGIN

Specifies the bottom margin for the page. The syntax is:

```
BOTTOMMARGIN=n
```

where *n* is a numeric value expressed in pixels. If *n* is set to 0, the bottom margin will be on the bottom edge of the page.

LEFTMARGIN

Specifies the left margin for the entire page. The syntax is:

```
LEFTMARGIN=n
```

where *n* is a numeric value expressed in pixels. If *n* is set to 0, the left margin will be exactly aligned with the left edge of the page.

RIGHTMARGIN

Specifies the right margin for the entire page. The syntax is:

```
RIGHTMARGIN=n
```

where *n* is a numeric value expressed in pixels. If *n* is set to 0, the right margin will be exactly aligned with the right edge of the page.

TOPMARGIN

Specifies the top margin for the page. The syntax is:

```
TOPMARGIN=n
```

where *n* is a numeric value expressed in pixels. If *n* is set to 0, the top margin will be on the top edge of the page.

SCROLL

Turns the scrollbars on and off on the screen.

```
SCROLL=YES | NO
```

Colors

When creating web pages, you will want to use colors to make the page attractive, and to draw the user's eye to certain parts. With HTML, you express the color you want to be displayed as a six digit hexadecimal value, which represents the individual red, green, and blue components of the color. The first two digits are the red component, the second two are the green component, and the last two are the blue component. Setting a value to `00` means the component is 'off', in other words has an intensity of zero. A value of **`FF`** means the component is fully 'on', i.e. is at full intensity. Different colors are achieved by 'mixing' different intensity levels of the three components. White is all three components fully 'on', represented as **`FFFFFF`**; black is all components fully 'off', represented as `000000`.

Note that hexadecimal RGB colors are exactly the same as the RGB colors used in most graphics editing programs—the only difference is that they are expressed in hexadecimal, not decimal.

As an example, to display normal text in red, you would use the **`TEXT`** attribute of the **`<BODY>`** element:

```
<BODY TEXT="#FF0000">
```

If you're confused by hexadecimal notation, don't worry. There's a much easier way of defining the color you want. Both Netscape and Internet Explorer support the use of color names: you can replace the hexadecimal value with a name—which is somewhat easier to remember:

```
<BODY TEXT="midnightblue">
```

There are over 200 color names supported by both Navigator and Explorer. A full list is supplied in Appendix D.

An Example Page

Let's put some of this into practice. Type the following, exactly as shown:

```
<!DOCTYPE HTML PUBLIC "-//W3C//DTD HTML 4.0 //EN">
<HTML>
<HEAD>
<TITLE>Welcome to The Global Coffee Club</TITLE>
</HEAD>

<BODY BGCOLOR="#FFFFEA" TEXT="#0000A0" LINK="#FF0000"
      VLINK="#808080" ALINK="#008040">
<H1>The Global Coffee Club welcomes you to its Web-Site!</H1>
<H2>We hope you enjoy your visit</H2>
News flash! You can now
<A HREF="taste.html">taste our range of beans on-line</A>
</BODY>
</HTML>
```

> **The <A HREF="..."> tag defines a hypertext link. We'll be looking at this in more detail in chapter 5.**

Save the file as **index.html** and view it. It should look like this:

If your page doesn't look exactly as above, don't worry. There are many reasons why your browser may be rendering the page differently. What you should see, though, is that all the text is in blue (the color of the hypertext link could be different), and the background is an off-white. At the moment, of course, the hypertext link doesn't lead anywhere, because we have yet to create the **taste.html** document. Clicking on the link may result in an error message, or maybe nothing at all: it depends on your browser.

Let's look at this example more closely. The first line

```
<!DOCTYPE HTML PUBLIC "-//W3C//DTD HTML 4.0 //EN">
```

is where we define the standard that this particular document conforms to. Next, we have:

```
<HTML>
<HEAD>
<TITLE>Welcome to The Global Coffee Club</TITLE>
</HEAD>
```

The **<HTML>** tag indicates the beginning of the HTML document, and within the **<HEAD>** section, we have just one element: the **<TITLE>**.

Now we come to the document body. The **<BODY>** tag is where we set the color attributes for the rest of the document.

```
<BODY BGCOLOR="#FFFFEA" TEXT="#0000A0" LINK="#FF0000"
      VLINK="#808080" ALINK="#008040">
```

Note that we could just as easily (in fact, more easily) have used color names instead of the hexadecimal numbers. The rest of the code looks like this:

```
<H1>The Global Coffee Club welcomes you to its Web-Site!</H1>
<H2>We hope you enjoy your visit</H2>
News flash! You can now
<A HREF="taste.html">taste our range of beans on-line</A>
</BODY>
</HTML>
```

The first two lines format the text to be rendered as different sized headings. Then comes some ordinary body text, in which we specify a hypertext link. We're getting a bit ahead of ourselves here, but don't worry, it's just been included to make the usage of the **<BODY>** element's color attributes clearer. The code ends by closing the body section of the document and then the HTML document itself.

Adding Comments

Adding comments to your documents is as good an idea in HTML as it is in other languages. Comments allow you to re-acquaint yourself with the code when you come to alter it months later. Anything between the `<!--` and `-->` tags will be ignored by the browser, and forms a comment:

```
<!-- This text will be visible only to someone viewing the
source code -->
```

Note that this comment spans two lines—comments can be multi- or single-line; they will still be ignored by the browser.

Revision Numbers

In keeping with general programming practice, it's a good idea to add revision numbers to all your documents. The majority of visitors to your site will want to know when the last revision was made, and it's common practice to add the current date to the bottom of a document. Many authors just put the following:

```
<P ALIGN=RIGHT>Last Revision : Oct 25 1997 by Chris Ullman</P>
```

Remember that the World Wide Web is a global entity. Avoid using country or regional-specific syntax such as 10/25/97.

Summary

This chapter has introduced you to the basics of HTML. We talked about the difference between elements, tags and attributes, and how these together create the effects you see on all web pages. We looked at the elements you must include in a valid HTML document, and at others that you can use to enhance its appearance. Remember that your documents will not necessarily appear the same to all users; you should get into the habit of testing your pages on different machines and using different browsers.

In the next chapter, we'll go on to look at creating text documents—using different formatting and styles.

Formatting Text

The basis of any HTML document is the information you are trying to get across. More often than not, this comes in the form of text. In this chapter, we will look at how you can manipulate the text of your document to use styles, alter layout, and add special effects.

Text Layout

One way of enhancing the text on your page is to lay it out well, so that the user can easily follow what's written. You can do this by breaking the text up into paragraphs and sections, by grouping related information together in lists, and by breaking the information up into separate pages where appropriate.

Headings

There are six levels of headings. They can all be defined via the **<H*n*>** tag.

The <H*n*> element

n can be a value between 1 and 6, where level 1 is the largest and level 6 is the smallest. Most browsers allow the user to alter the relative sizes of headings, so don't be surprised if you find that checking your site on another system shows a level 1 heading at the same size as a level 3 heading on your system. The corresponding end tag **</Hn>** must be used.

```
<H2> This is a second level heading</H2>
```

Under HTML 2.0, headings had no associated attributes, under HTML 3.2, only the **ALIGN** attribute was permitted, but under HTML 4.0 there are now a total of seven permitted attributes.

ALIGN   CLASS   DIR   ID   LANG   STYLE   TITLE

Six of these are universal, so won't be further discussed here—refer back to Chapter 1 for details of what they do.

ALIGN

The **ALIGN** attribute has been deprecated under HTML 4.0.

ALIGN=LEFT | RIGHT | CENTER

The default here is **LEFT**.

*It's possible to create different size headings using the **<FONT>** tag, but be warned—not all browsers will display the attributes of **<FONT>**, so you risk your headings not appearing as you want them to for some users. Also, some search engines use words that appear in higher level headings as items to index.*

Breaking up Text

You can't use carriage returns to create new paragraphs or to break lines in HTML, since they are ignored by browsers. Have a look at the following code:

```
<HTML>
<HEAD>
<TITLE>Examples of line breaks</TITLE>

<BODY>
This line has a carriage return here,
but it is ignored by the browser.
</BODY>
</HTML>
```

The carriage return after the word **here** is ignored by the browser. It's the width of the window that determines where lines break, not the carriage returns you put in your code.

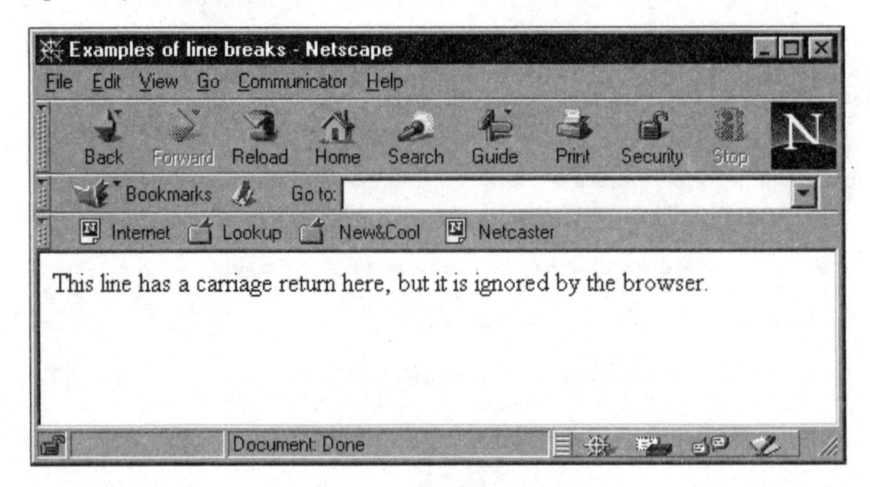

To break text up, you must use special tags.

The <P> (Paragraph) Element

Paragraphs are defined with the **<P>** tag. The use of the end tag **</P>** is optional. The rule for paragraphs is that the next **<P>** tag ends the previous paragraph. **<P>** has seven attributes.

ALIGN CLASS DIR ID LANG STYLE TITLE

Again, six of these are universal, so won't be further discussed here.

ALIGN

The **ALIGN** attribute has been deprecated under HTML 4.0. The syntax is:

ALIGN=LEFT | RIGHT | CENTER

The
 (Line Break) Element

Line breaks are achieved by using the **
** tag.

In some browsers, including Internet Explorer and Netscape, you can use consecutive **
** elements if you want to space out blocks of text:

```
<BR><BR><BR>
```

It isn't valid HTML to use consecutive **<P>** *elements. By definition, a paragraph can't be empty. If you do use consecutive* **<P>** *elements, some browsers will add the space, some will ignore all but the first* **<P>** *and some will complain about the use of invalid HTML.*

The **
** tag takes five attributes. Four of them are universal.

CLASS CLEAR ID STYLE TITLE

CLEAR

The **CLEAR** attribute can be used with the **
** tag to extend the wrapping options of text around images. When **CLEAR** is used in text that's wrapped round an image, it ensures that any subsequent text begins below the image.

```
<HTML>
<HEAD>
<TITLE>Example of the CLEAR attribute</TITLE>
<BODY>
<IMG ALIGN=LEFT SRC=wrox.gif>
This text would normally continue to wrap around the right hand side of the
image, but the clear
attribute here,<BR CLEAR=LEFT>means that text will continue here instead.
</BODY>
</HTML>
```

This code would have the following effect:

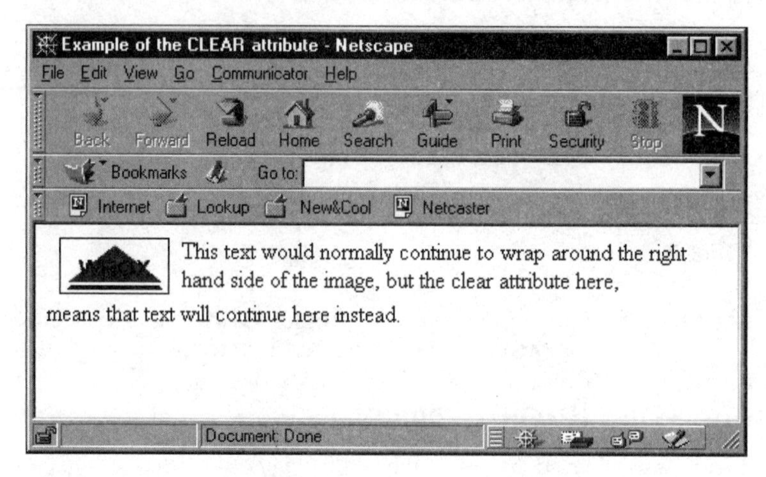

The syntax is:

```
CLEAR=LEFT | RIGHT | ALL | NONE
```

LEFT means that the text will appear at the first clear left margin position. **RIGHT** means the text will appear at the first clear right margin position. **ALL** means that both margins have to be clear before text will appear.

If, on the other hand, you don't want a line of text to be broken, you can use the Netscape extension **<NOBR>**, like this:

```
<NOBR>Here's a line of text I don't want broken ... here's the end</NOBR>
```

This attribute has been deprecated in HTML 4.0.

Lists

Lists are used to organize information in a clear and easily understood format. There are three main types of list that you can set up in a document:

- Unordered, or bulleted, lists (using **<UL>**)
- Ordered, or numbered, lists (using **<OL>**)
- Definition lists (using **<DL>**)

<UL>, **<OL>**, and **<DL>** are the tags that define the type of list. They are all container tags—in other words, they must have a corresponding end tag. The list entries themselves are defined by **<LI>** in bulleted and numbered lists, and by **<DT>** and **<DD>** in a definition list.

The <UL> (Unordered List) Element

The purpose of `<UL>` is to produce an unordered list, which is the same as a bulleted list that you would type in a word processor. The syntax for unordered lists is:

```
<UL>
<LI>first list item</LI>
<LI>second list item</LI>
<LI>third list item</LI>
<LI>etc.</LI>
</UL>
```

The closing `</LI>` tag is optional, and usually omitted. The list would be displayed as follows:

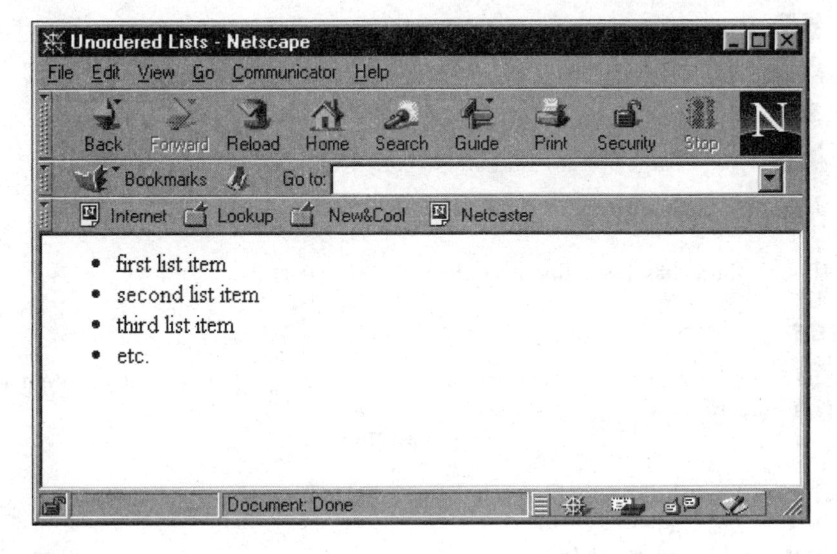

The `<UL>` tag has eight attributes:

CLASS	COMPACT	DIR	ID	LANG	STYLE
TITLE	TYPE				

COMPACT

This tag has now been deprecated under HTML 4.0 and isn't supported in IE4. `COMPACT` tells the browser to fit the list into a smaller space. This is usually achieved by removing white space from between each list item. However, the browsers that don't support `COMPACT` will just ignore it.

TYPE

The `TYPE` attribute allows you to change the appearance of the bullets.

```
TYPE = CIRCLE | DISC | SQUARE
```

This attribute has now been deprecated in HTML 4.0.

The <LI> (List Items) element

This is used to define each of the bullet points within the list. It's typically used with the **<UL>**, **<OL>** or **<DL>** tags and can take two attributes.

TYPE VALUE

plus the universal attributes of **CLASS**, **DIR**, **ID**, **LANG**, **STYLE** and **TITLE**.

TYPE

The **TYPE** attribute specifies the type of numbering used. The syntax is:

TYPE=*n*

where *n* is one of the following:

- 1 Arabic numerals (default)
- A Capital letters
- a Small letters
- I Large roman numerals (I, II, III)
- i Small roman numerals (i, ii, iii)

This attribute has been deprecated in HTML 4.0.

VALUE

Specifies the number of the current list item, even if the current list item is non-numeric.

VALUE=*n*

This attribute has been deprecated in HTML 4.0.

Using <UL> and <LI>

The following example displays a compact, unordered list with square bullets:

```
...
<UL COMPACT TYPE=SQUARE>
<LI>First list item
<LI>Second list item
<LI>Third list item
</UL>
...
```

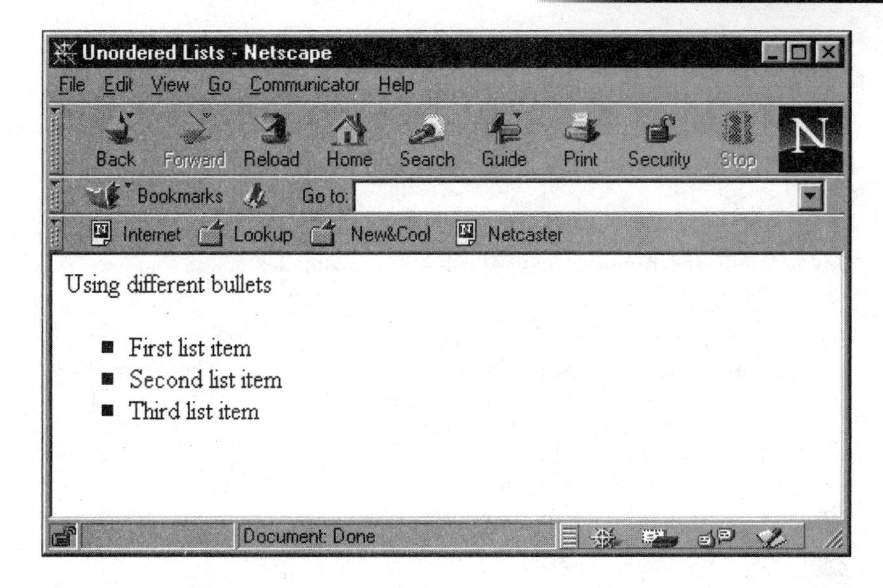

The <OL> (Ordered List) Element

`<OL>` will produce an ordered list numbered in a style of your choice. The default style is 1, 2, 3, but you can choose various other styles such as a, b, c, or i, ii, iii, etc. The syntax is:

```
<OL>
<LI>First item
<LI>Second item
<LI>Third item
<LI>And so on...
</OL>
```

This is displayed as:

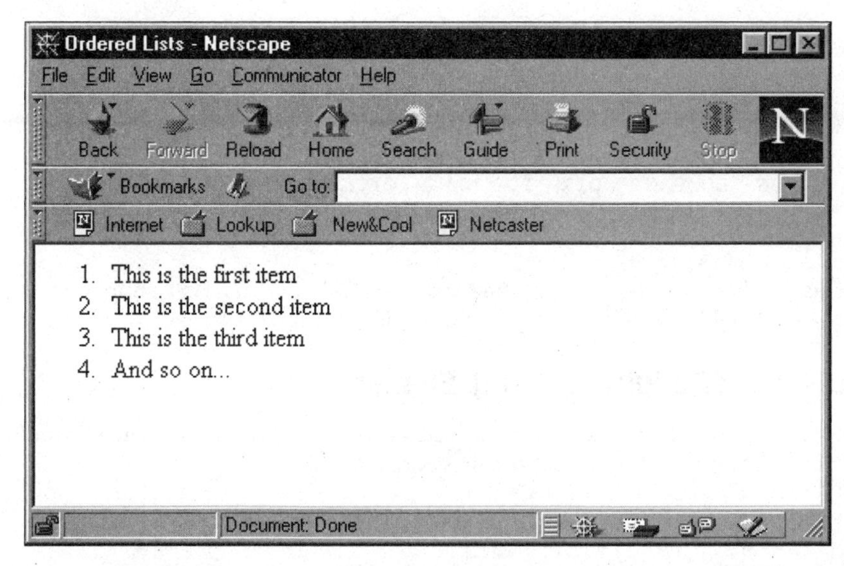

Note how the numbers have been inserted for you by the browser. Allowable attributes for are **<OL>**:

```
CLASS  COMPACT  DIR  ID  LANG  TITLE  TYPE START  STYLE
```

COMPACT

This tag has now been deprecated under HTML 4.0 and isn't supported in IE4. **COMPACT** tells the browser to fit the list into a smaller space.

TYPE

The **TYPE** attribute specifies the type of numbering used. The syntax is:

TYPE=*n*

where *n* is one of the following:

- 1 Arabic numerals (default)
- A Capital letters
- a Small letters
- I Large roman numerals (I, II, III)
- i Small roman numerals (i, ii, iii)

This attribute has been deprecated in HTML 4.0.

START

Alters the number that the list starts with. The syntax is:

START=*n*

where ***n*** specifies the new start number, e.g. 3, C, c, III, or iii. This attribute has now been deprecated in HTML 4.0.

The <DL> (Definition List) Element

Definition lists are used when you want to include a description for each list item. Allowable attributes for are **<DL>**:

```
CLASS  COMPACT  DIR  ID  LANG  TITLE STYLE
```

COMPACT

This tag has now been deprecated under HTML 4.0 and isn't supported in IE4. **COMPACT** tells the browser to fit the list into a smaller space.

The <DT> (Definition Term) Element

This used to define a term with a **<DL>** element. **<DT>** is restricted to in-line content. Allowable attributes for are **<DL>**:

```
CLASS   DIR   ID   LANG   TITLE   STYLE
```

The <DD> (Definition Description) Element

This used to specify a description within a **<DL>** element and is usually indented from the list. Allowable attributes for are **<DD>**:

CLASS **DIR** **ID** **LANG** **TITLE** **STYLE**

Using <DL>, <DT> and <DD>

You could use a definition list to produce, for example, a glossary of terms, using **<DT>** for the definition term and **<DD>** for the description. The closing **</DT>** and **</DD>** tags are optional:

```
<DL>
<DT>HTML
 <DD>HyperText Markup Language
<DT>HEAD
 <DD>The first part of an HTML document
<DT>BODY
 <DD>The main part of an HTML document
</DL>
```

This would be displayed as follows:

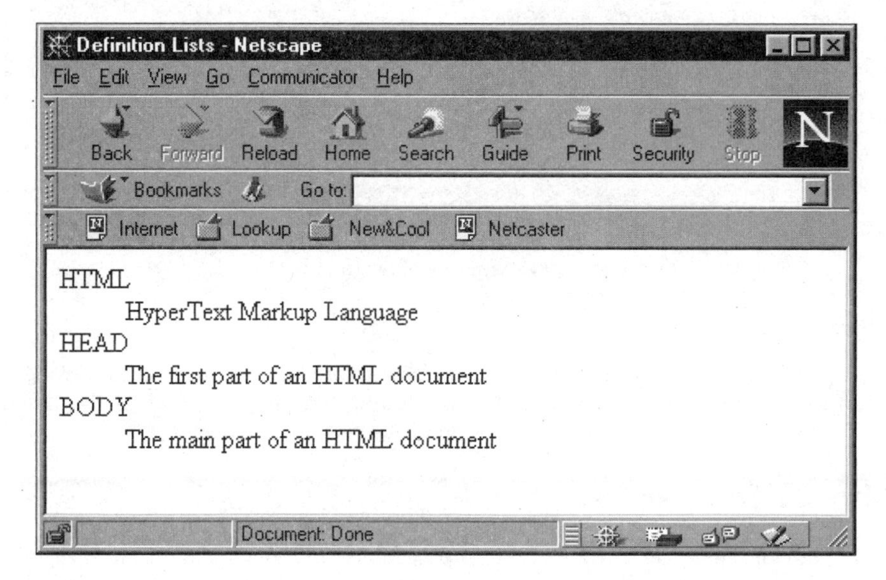

Nesting Lists

Lists can be **nested,** as can most elements within HTML. Nesting means placing a set of tags or elements inside another set. The nested list is independent of the outer list, so if it is numbered, it will start again from 1 (unless you explicitly change this).

```
<OL TYPE=i>
 <LI>first list item
 <LI>second list item
 <LI>third list item
        <OL TYPE=i>
                <LI>fourth list item
                <LI>fifth list item
                <LI>sixth list item
        </OL>
</OL>
```

A nested list would be displayed as follows:

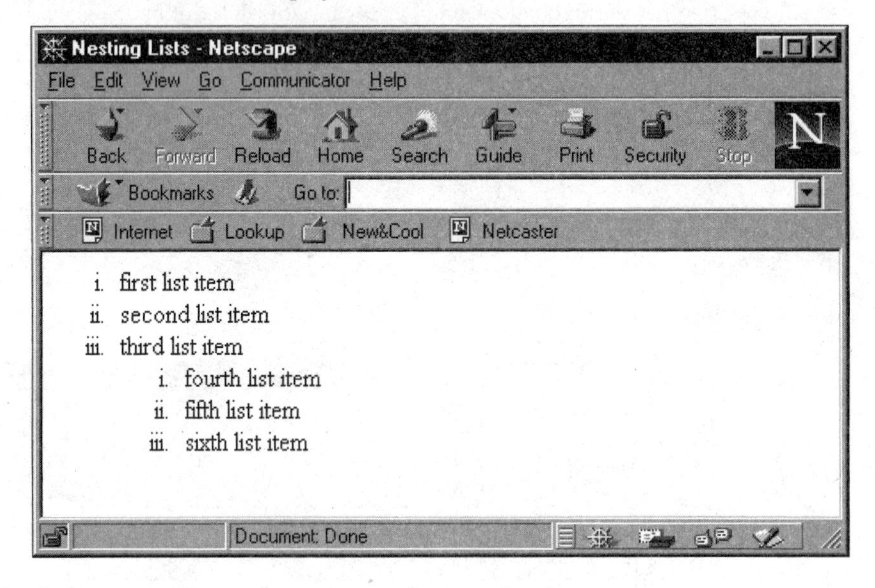

Don't forget to close each start tag when nesting lists.

Other Types of List

As well as the types of list discussed above, you can also use **<MENU>** and **<DIR>** for lists. You can use **<LI>** with both, and each will indent the items in the list. These tags are likely to become obsolete in the future.

The <HR> (Horizontal Rules) Element

Horizontal rules are used to break up sections of a document from each other. You place a horizontal rule using the **<HR>** element. As this isn't a container element, no end tag is required or allowed.

Allowable Attributes

Allowable attributes for **<HR>** are:

ALIGN	CLASS	COLOR	DIR	LANG	NOSHADE
SIZE	SRC	STYLE	TITLE	WIDTH	

ALIGN

Specifies the position of the rule. The syntax is:

```
ALIGN=LEFT | RIGHT | CENTER
```

The default value is **CENTER**. This attribute is deprecated under HTML 4.0.

NOSHADE

NOSHADE means the rule is displayed without any 3-D shading effects. This attribute is deprecated under HTML 4.0.

SIZE

Sets the height of the rule. The syntax is:

SIZE=*n*

where *n* is the height in pixels. The default value is 2.

WIDTH

Sets the width of the rule across the browser window. The syntax is:

WIDTH=*n*

where **n** is the width in pixels. To express the width as a percentage of the window's width, add **%**, e.g. **WIDTH=50%**.

Internet Explorer Specific Attributes

IE4 also supports two non-standard attributes; **COLOR** and **SRC**.

COLOR

Specifies the color that the rule is displayed in. The syntax is:

COLOR="#*rrggbb***"**

where **"#***rrggbb***"** is a hexadecimal number defining the amount of red, green, and blue that makes up the color, or a color name. The default color is based on the background.

SRC

Specifies the external file to use as a source for the element.

SRC=*url*

Using Horizontal Rules

Have a look at the following example:

```
<!DOCTYPE HTML PUBLIC "-//W3C//DTD HTML 4.0//EN">
<HTML>
<HEAD>
<TITLE>An example of a horizontal rule</TITLE>
</HEAD>
<BODY>
```

```
<HR ALIGN=CENTER SIZE=5 WIDTH=70%>
<HR ALIGN=CENTER SIZE=10 WIDTH=80%>
<HR ALIGN=CENTER SIZE=2 WIDTH=50% NOSHADE>

</BODY>
</HTML>
```

This gives:

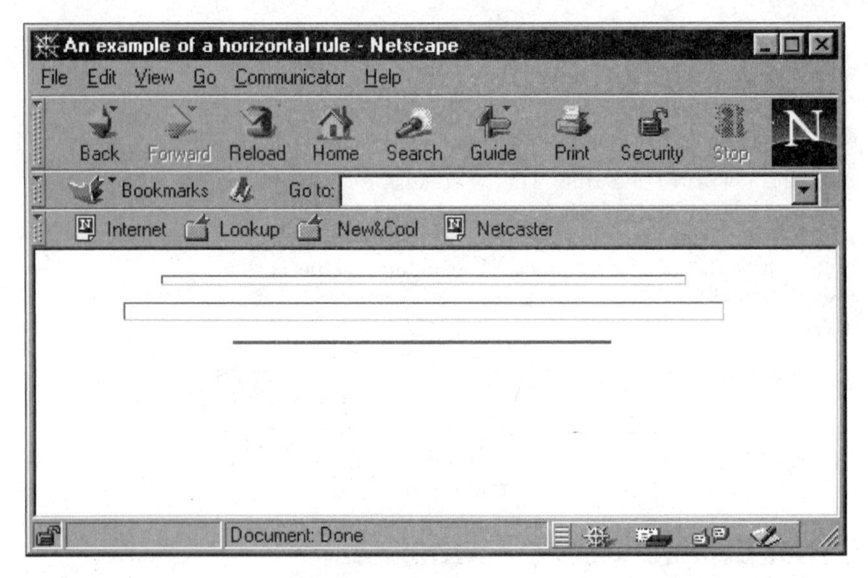

Note that the first two horizontal rules appear in 3-D, whereas the last example is flat, because we've used the **NOSHADE** attribute. This is particularly useful when the background color is very light, as the 3-D shading won't show up very well.

Text Emphasis and Style

There are many different tags for emphasizing and styling text. One of the major methods of doing this is to change the font of a piece of text. We'll look at how you can do that now.

Fonts

Most documents on the web are in the default font, which can be set by the user of the browser. Until recently, it wasn't possible to define the font in a web document. The main reason for this is that you can't guarantee that the font you define for the text is installed on the user's system. However, with the current rate of advance in computers and software, this is becoming much less of issue. Most Windows platforms have several standard fonts such as Arial, Courier or Times New Roman.

Microsoft and Netscape have both worked on the embedding of fonts into web documents. This means that the font is transferred to the user's system at the same time as the rest of the page downloads. In Netscape the technology is known as dynamic fonts and we look at them in more detail in chapter 11. IE4 also allows for the possibility of downloadable fonts.

However, if you want to specify the font type, the most popular method is still the **<FONT>** tag.

The <FONT> Element

This element and each of its attributes have become deprecated under HTML 4.0. Nevertheless it is still the easiest way to apply a font. It has become deprecated mainly due to the introduction of **style sheets**. Style sheets are a list of display rules that can be applied to different HTML elements. They are becoming the recommended way to apply fonts and styles. This is because it is preferable that there should only be one method with which to specify style information, otherwise conflicts could arise within the code. We look at style sheets in Chapter 3.

The tag defines the appearance of the text it encloses. Allowable attributes are:

```
CLASS    DIR    ID    SIZE    FACE    COLOR    LANG
STYLE    TITLE
```

SIZE

Specifies the size of the lettering. The syntax is:

SIZE=*n*

where *n* is a number 1 through 7; 1 is the smallest, 7 the largest. The actual size of the font is relative to the **<BASEFONT>** element (see next section). The **SIZE** attribute can be used on its own with the **<FONT>** element. This will result in the default system font being displayed, but at the size you've specified. **SIZE** can also be used to set font settings relative to the previous font size using the + or – modifiers. **SIZE="+2"** would make the font two sizes larger, **SIZE="-1"** would make the font one size smaller.

FACE

Specifies the font you want to use.

FACE="*fontname1*, *fontname2*, *fontname3*"

When **FACE** is used to specify a list of fonts, if the first font in the list isn't present on the user's system, the second will be tried, and so on. If none of the specified fonts exist on the user's system, the default font will be used.

Microsoft recently announced a list of special TrueType web fonts, that anyone can download from their web site. The idea is that you code your pages with the relevant fonts, and then put a link to Microsoft's site so that the user can download the fonts for use on their system. To check the latest details on this, go to:

http://www.microsoft.com/truetype/fontpack/win.htm

If you're wondering what fonts to use, a general guideline is to use sans-serif fonts (like Arial) for headlines and serifed fonts (like Times) for large portions of text.

COLOR

COLOR specifies the color that the font will appear in. This can be displayed as a hexadecimal number or a color name.

Some interesting typographical effects can be achieved with these attributes, for example:

```
<!DOCTYPE HTML PUBLIC "-//W3C//DTD//HTML 4.0//EN">
<HTML>
<HEAD>
<TITLE>An example of the FONT element</TITLE>
</HEAD>
<BODY>
<P>
<BASEFONT SIZE=2 FACE="VERDANA" COLOR=BLACK>

<!--If the Arial font isn't installed, Verdana will be used instead. If neither
are available, the default font will be used-- >

<FONT SIZE=5 FACE="ARIAL" COLOR=BLUE>T</FONT>he first letter of this sentence
should be three sizes larger than the rest of the sentence. The first letter
should also be displayed in blue rather than black.

</BODY>
</HTML>
```

The result of this code is as follows:

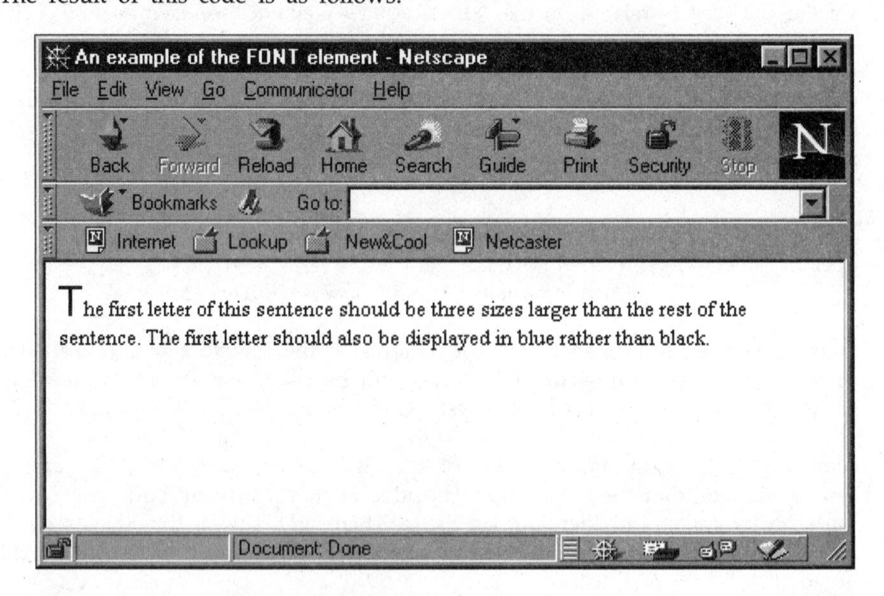

Navigator 4 Specific Attributes

There are two attributes particular to Navigator 4 that aren't part of the HTML 4.0 standard. These are **WEIGHT** and **POINT-SIZE**.

WEIGHT

Specifies the weight of the font used to display the text. It can be a string such as **BOLD**, or a number.

WEIGHT=*string* | *number*

POINT-SIZE

The size (absolute or relative) of the font.

POINT-SIZE=*string* | *number*

The <BASEFONT> Element

Notice that, in the code above, we used an element called **<BASEFONT>**. This element sets the default attributes for any text that has not been formatted with the **<FONT>** element or a style sheet. This has also been deprecated under HTML 4.0. Allowable attributes are:

```
CLASS  SIZE  FACE  COLOR  ID  LANG
```

The **SIZE**, **FACE** and **COLOR** attributes all function in the same way as for the **FONT** tag. The values for the attributes are the same as for **<FONT>**. The default value for the **SIZE** attribute is 3. You can specify the value for the **<FONT> SIZE** attribute, relative to the **<BASEFONT> SIZE**, like this.

```
<HTML>
<HEAD>
<TITLE>Relative font sizes</TITLE>
</HEAD>

<BODY BGCOLOR="#F9FFFF">

<BASEFONT SIZE=4 FACE="ARIAL">
<P>
<FONT SIZE=-1>This text is one size down from the basefont size.</FONT>
<P>
<FONT SIZE=+2>This text is two sizes larger than the basefont size.</FONT>

</BODY>
</HTML>
```

The result of this code is:

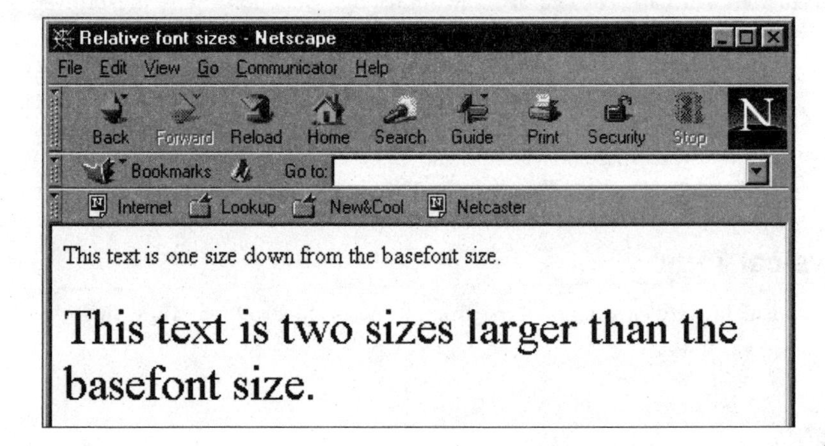

The simple addition of a minus or plus sign before the value means that the size becomes relative to the **<BASEFONT> SIZE** attribute. Unfortunately, you are still constrained where 1 is smallest, 7 is largest limit. Choosing values outside this range won't work:

```
<!-- This is acceptable -->
<BASEFONT SIZE=1>
<FONT SIZE=+6>This will work as 1 + 6 = 7 </FONT>
```

```
<!-- This is wrong. The font size won't change -->
<BASEFONT SIZE=2>
<FONT SIZE=+6>This won't work as 2 + 6 = 8 </FONT>
```

When a + or - is used, the **<FONT> SIZE** attribute is always relative to the **<BASEFONT> SIZE** attribute, not the last **<FONT> SIZE**.

*The **<BASEFONT>** element should generally, appear in the **<HEAD>** of the page, but always before any **<FONT>** elements.*

Physical and Logical Style Tags

Fonts aren't the only way you can affect the appearance of a piece of text. There are many different tags which can be used to italicize or bold the text. These tags can broadly be split into two categories:

 Physical style tags

 Logical style tags

HTML distinguishes between two groups of character-formatting tags: logical character-attribute tags and physical character-attribute tags. It may help to think of physical character-attribute tags as closely related to the direct formatting you could apply to text from a word processor, e.g. bold. The appearance of HTML text formatted with physical character-attribute tags is more likely to remain constant from one browser to another. Logical character-attribute tags in HTML can be thought of as like 'styles' in a word processor—the appearance of text formatted with a style, in a word processor, depends on how the style is defined in that word processor. Similarly, the appearance of HTML text formatted with logical character-attribute tags depends upon the browser's interpretation of that logical character-attribute tag.

The idea behind logical styles is that they can be rendered in the best way for that particular platform. For example, if you want to emphasize a word, <EM> might produce italics in a browser, but on a text-to-speech system, it could be rendered by increasing the volume slightly.

Physical Tags

Physical tag styles do not vary from browser to browser. They include:

- **<B>** Bold
- **<I>** Italic
- **<U>** Underscore—deprecated under HTML 4.0
- **<TT>** Typewriter
- **<S>** Strikeout—deprecated under HTML 4.0
- **<DFN>** Definition
- **<BLINK>** Blinking text (Netscape specific)

and are rendered as follows:

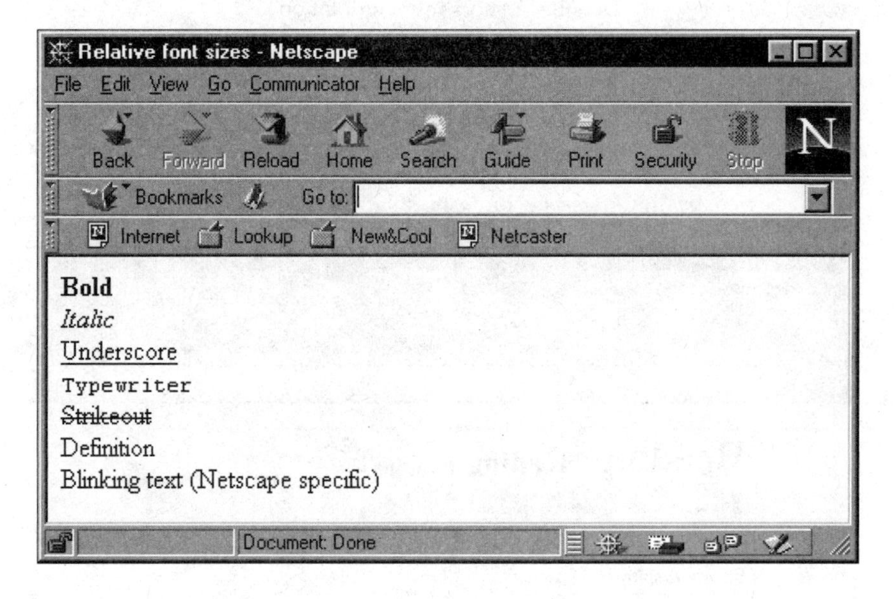

Logical Tags

One of the things you should remember when building web pages is that HTML was designed to specify the relationships between the different parts of the document. Many tags are logical tags, and HTML does not specify how they should be represented. Logical style tags take on the preferences set for them within the browser, as well as being rendered differently depending on the browser vendor. For example, many browsers will let the user specify which size and shape of font will be used to display the **<H1>** tag. It will usually be larger than the **<H2>** tag, but you can't even be sure of that! Logical tags include:

- **<Hn>** Headings
- **<EM>** Emphasis (usually italic)
- **<STRONG>** Strong (usually bold)
- **<ADDRESS>** Usually italic
- **<CITE>** Used for quoting text (usually italic)

- **<CODE>** Monospaced font (usually Courier)
- **<SAMP>** Monospaced font (usually Courier)
- **<KBD>** Monospaced font (usually Courier)
- **<BIG>** Makes text one size larger
- **<SMALL>** Makes text one size smaller
- **<SUP>** Renders text as superscript
- **<SUB>** Renders text as subscript
- **<ABBR>** Logically denotes abbreviations and acronyms
- **<Q>** Denotes a short inline quotation
- **<VAR>** Denotes a variable name, usually rendered in italics

<CODE>, **<SAMP>**, and **<KBD>** (keyboard) are particularly useful if your document contains actual code that you are trying to explain to your reader.

When viewed by the Netscape browser, relative tags appear as follows:

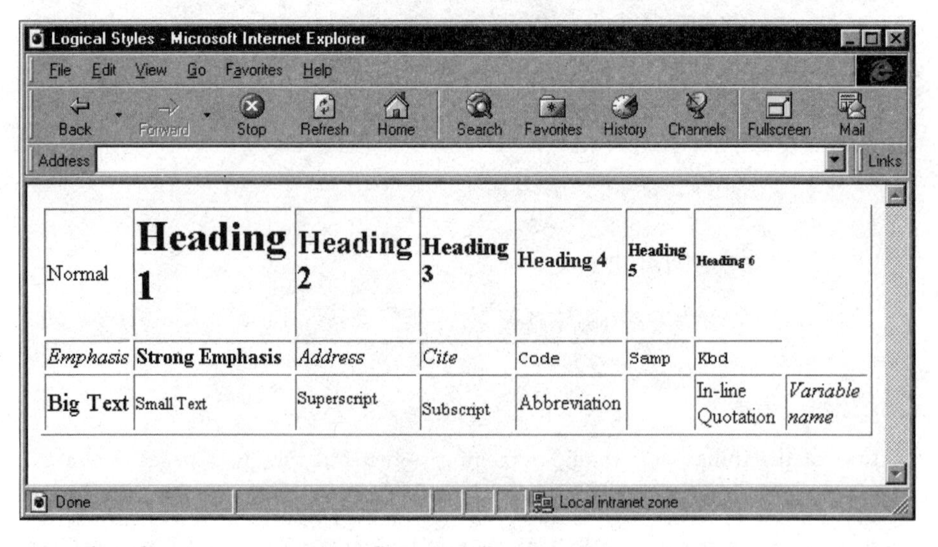

Note that the above style types have all the universal attributes associated with them. The **<Hn>** tag also allows the **ALIGN** attribute to be included.

When deciding which type of tag to use, bear in mind that it's probably better to stick with the physical styles—at least, that way you can be sure that the page will be viewed as you intended.

The <MARQUEE> Element

Finally one interesting, but definitely non-standard element that Internet Explorer supports is **<MARQUEE>**. This is used to produce scrolling text messages, which otherwise might require complex scripting or Java code. Its attributes are:

ALIGN	**BEHAVIOR**	**BGCOLOR**	**CLASS**
DATAFLD	**DATAFORMATAS**	**DATASRC**	**DIRECTION**
HEIGHT	**HSPACE**	**ID**	**LANG**
LOOP	**SCROLLAMOUNT**	**SCROLLDELAY**	**STYLE**
TITLE	**TRUESPEED**	**VSPACE**	**WIDTH**

Note that the **DATASRC**, **DATAFLD** and **DATAFORMATAS** attributes are all used to enable data binding which is discussed in Chapter 12.

ALIGN

Aligns the marquee. The syntax is:

ALIGN=*alignment*

where **alignment** is one of **TOP**, **MIDDLE**, or **BOTTOM**. This attribute aligns the marquee with the top, middle, or bottom of the surrounding text.

BEHAVIOR

Indicates how the marquee will move across the screen. The syntax is:

BEHAVIOR=*type*

where **type** is **SCROLL**, **SLIDE**, or **ALTERNATE**. **SCROLL** means the marquee will start completely off one side, scroll all the way across and off the other side, and then start again. This is the default. **SLIDE** will commence with the marquee completely off one side, it will then scroll in, stop when it reaches the far margin and then start again. **ALTERNATE** will bounce the marquee back and forth between the margins.

BGCOLOR

Sets the background color of the scrolling text. The syntax is:

BGCOLOR="#*rrggbb***"**

where *rrggbb* are hexadecimal values for red, green, and blue. You can also use predefined color names, such as **Blue**, **Red**, **Yellow**.

DIRECTION

Sets the direction that the marquee scrolls in. The syntax is:

DIRECTION=*direction*

where **direction** is **LEFT** or **RIGHT**. The default is **LEFT**, which means the text scrolls to the left from the right.

HEIGHT

Sets the height of the marquee. The syntax is:

HEIGHT=*n*

where *n* is the height of the marquee in pixels, or as a percentage of the screen height. To express the value as a percentage, you must append a **%** sign to the end of the value.

HSPACE

Sets the width of the left and right margins of the marquee. The syntax is:

HSPACE=*n*

where *n* specifies the amount of space in pixels.

LOOP

Determines how many times the marquee will scroll across the screen. The syntax is:

LOOP=*n*

where *n* specifies the number of times. If the value for *n* is set to **-1** or **INFINITE**, it will loop indefinitely.

SCROLLAMOUNT

Specifies the number of pixels between each successive draw of the marquee text. The syntax is:

SCROLLAMOUNT=*n*

SCROLLDELAY

Specifies the number of milliseconds between each successive draw of the marquee text. The syntax is:

SCROLLDELAY=*n*

TRUESPEED

Indicates if the exact scroll delay should be used, otherwise values smaller than 60 are rounded to 60ms.

TRUESPEED

VSPACE

Specifies the top and bottom margins of the marquee. The syntax is:

VSPACE=*n*

where *n* is the amount of space in pixels.

WIDTH

Sets the width of the marquee. The syntax is:

WIDTH=*n*

where *n* is the width of the marquee, expressed in pixels or as a percentage of the screen width. To specify a percentage, a % sign must be appended to the end of the value.

If you have Internet Explorer installed on your system, you can try the following example:

```
<MARQUEE DIRECTION=RIGHT BEHAVIOR=SCROLL SCROLLAMOUNT=10 SCROLLDELAY=200>This
is a scrolling marquee!</MARQUEE>
```

Summary

This chapter has shown you how to format and layout text. You have seen how to break text up into manageable sections, and how to apply formatting to make particular words or phrases stand out. However, as we have hinted, all this is changing with HTML 4.0. There are many different tags and attributes that can all be used to apply the different/conflicting formats. The advent of style sheets may achieve a uniform way for specifying style information. So while many of these tags and attributes work now, tags such as **<FONT>** have already been deprecated and will probably be omitted from future HTML standards. So you should prepare for future standard amendments by learning about style sheets *now*. This is the subject of our next chapter.

Styles and Style Sheets

As we've seen, one of the original aims of the Web was to separate information from presentation. HTML is a semantic markup language, and is concerned with the meaning of formatting in a document—not its visual representation. Contrary to popular belief, this is not a 'limitation' in HTML—it has some very important advantages, not least of which is the ability to define document appearance locally.

However, as the Web has grown in popularity, the concept of a semantic markup language has been perceived as limiting. Authors want higher and higher levels of control over the appearance of their web documents, and aren't content to restrict themselves to the basic HTML constructs. This demand is, in many ways, responsible for the state of HTML today; it is precisely the reason why the early Netscape extensions to HTML were adopted so rapidly. However, the newest way to give authors control over document appearance, without simultaneously sacrificing the content/presentation separation, is through style sheets.

Using Styles and Style Sheets

There are currently two main ways to implement style sheets. Both Netscape Navigator and Internet Explorer implement style sheets by using **Cascading Style Sheets Level One**, or **CSS1**.

The new updated version of the standard, Cascading Style Sheets Level Two (CSS2) has just been accepted as a recommendation by W3C. New features include positioned elements, downloadable fonts and enhanced printing facilities. You can find details at **`http://www.w3.org/TR/WD-CSS2/`**. *Some elements of CSS2 have already been implemented in both Internet Explorer 4 and Netscape Navigator 4, however for the most part the two browsers adhere mainly to CSS1.*

CSS1 is the de facto standard for Web style sheets, since the major browsers support it and W3C have supported it from HTML version 3.2 onwards. The W3C proposals for HTML 4.0 have extended style sheets by adding some new attributes, but continue to omit some style properties implemented by Netscape in Navigator 4.

CSS1 is designed to be easy to use and implement. By contrast, the alternative, **DSSSL-Online**, although more comprehensive, is rather more difficult to use and isn't supported by Internet Explorer or Netscape Navigator.

> ***DSSSL-Online*** *is the web version of* ***Document Style Semantics and Specification Language****, a remarkably large and complex standard supported by the ISO. There is now a practical implementation of DSSSL-Online being created, in the form of XSL, however as it is used to display XML documents rather than HTML ones, it is beyond the scope of this book. You can find more details in the Wrox Press book Professional Style Sheets for HTML and XSL – ISBN 1-861001-65-7.*

Netscape Navigator 4 itself offers another form of style sheet, which allows styles to be defined using simple JavaScript statements within `<STYLE>` tags. Using JavaScript style sheets you can define styles for all HTML elements of one type, just as you can with Cascading Style Sheets(CSS). We'll look at JavaScript style sheets later in the book in chapter 11, as they're unique to Netscape Navigator 4.0.

What are Style Sheets?

A style sheet is essentially a declaration of display rules, specifying the display attributes of particular HTML elements or groups of elements.These rules are easy to write, consisting of combinations of tags, property names and values.

Advantages of Style Sheets

There are three main advantages of using style sheets. The first is their universality of application. This means that we can develop a style sheet and then apply it to any document or group of documents, by simply setting them so that they refer to the style sheet we have just created. This universality can also have an added benefit: we can change the appearance of all our pages by simply changing the style sheet, when the style sheet is stored as a separate file.

The next advantage is that style sheets can convey greater typographic control than is normally possible. CSS provides a number of properties that can be used to create effects like drop-caps, overlapping text, shadowed text and so on.

The third benefit is that style sheets, unlike other methods of display control, retain the content/presentation split. So, style sheet information is separate from the actual text information. This can result in smaller file sizes—five 1K documents can reference one 5K style sheet, instead of having five 6K documents, each containing their own style information. Furthermore, the split allows the content to be altered without having to have the document re-formatted with the correct HTML tags.

Why use Style Sheets?

Why use style sheets at all? In the last chapter we looked at how the **<ALIGN>**, **<B>** and **<I>** tags allow us to format text. It might seem a lot simpler to use these tags rather than learning a whole new technique for presentation. However, style sheets do simplify the job of HTML markup and can relieve HTML of the burden of presentation. If you're in any doubt, consider this, if you wanted to specify that a certain piece of text was formatted in bold type, then you could specify this style information in the <B> tag, or as the **WEIGHT** attribute of the **<FONT>** tag, or even as a style sheet. If you specified contradictory information in each technique, what would the final result look like? And would that result be consistent on all browsers?

HTML 4.0 is trying to lay down a uniform way of specifying style information, so that all content can be displayed in a similar way, across browsers and across browser platforms. You'll find that tags such as **<FONT>** are now **deprecated** as the standard moves towards embracing the CSS1 recommendations.

Deprecated means that while the tags themselves haven't actually been removed, they've been marked up for removal in future versions of HTML.

The recommendation doesn't actually go as far as saying you should use CSS1, but it does use CSS1 in all of its examples, and W3C handles both the HTML 4.0 and CSS1 standards

Why are Style Sheets more important in HTML 4.0?

Style sheets have gained greater importance with the advent of HTML 4.0, as they can now be used to connect the elements in a page to scripting code in the version 4.0 browsers. This is because the HTML 4.0 recommendation proposes that all style properties are stored separately as properties in an object model. This would allow all of the elements on the page to be addressed via a scripting language. If styles are stored in such a way, (and in IE4 they're stored within a style object), it allows you to achieve clever effects such as being able to update the position of elements on the page without the aid of a page refresh.

New style properties in HTML 4.0 provide the user with a greater degree of control over the positioning of elements on the page. You can now specify positions of text or graphics to pixel-point accuracy, using x and y coordinates, something not previously possible. In version 3.0 browsers, elements such as images were positioned in terms of alignment to the side of the screen or relative to other elements.

However, style information isn't yet accessible to scripting languages in Netscape Navigator, so you can't dynamically update styles in it. Nevertheless, as both browsers support most of the CSS1 recommendations, we'll look at how style sheets work in both browsers now, and then consider separately in later chapters how they go about making the elements come alive!

Style Sheets in Action

We'll start by taking a look at an example of CSS in use. The following picture is all text, with no bitmaps (the word 'emphasized' appears in red type).

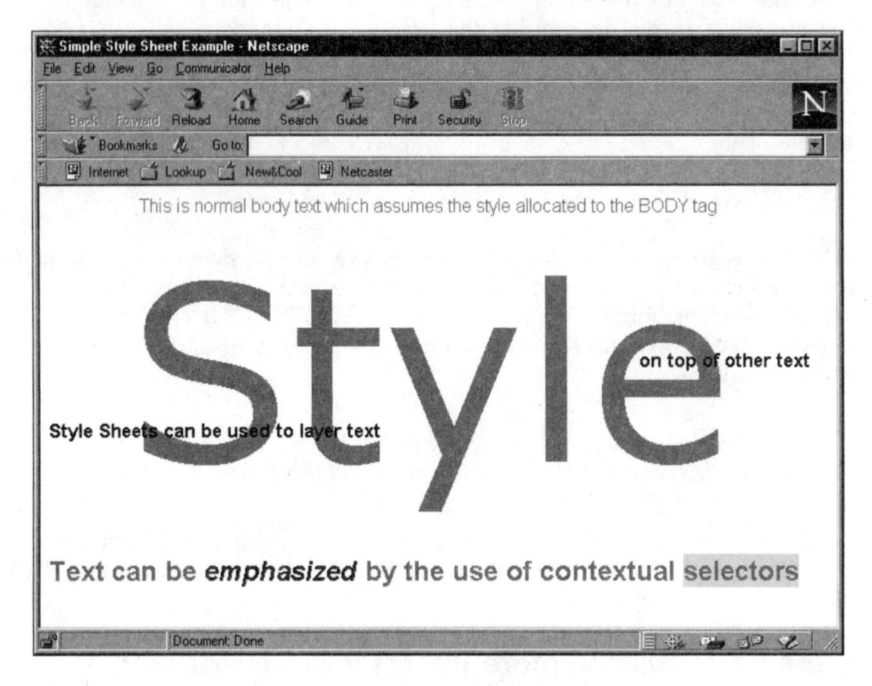

You can run this page, called Simple Style Sheets, from our Web site at:
http://rapid.wrox.co.uk/books/1568

The actual HTML file that generates this page is:

```
<HTML>
<HEAD>
 <TITLE>Simple Style Sheet Example</TITLE>
<STYLE TYPE="text/css">

BODY     {color: mediumseagreen;
 font-family: arial}

H2       {margin-top: 140px}

H2 I     {color: red}

H2 B {background: yellow}

.style1 {color:black;
 margin-top: -80px;
 font-family: arial;
 font-weight: bold;
 font-size: 18px}

.style2 {font-family: verdana;
 font-size:212px;
 margin-top: 20px;
 text-align: center}
```

```
</STYLE>
</HEAD>
<BODY>
This is normal body text which assumes the style allocated to the BODY tag
<SPAN ID=Span1 class=style2>
Style</SPAN>
<DIV ID=Div1 ALIGN=LEFT class=style1>
Style Sheets can be used to layer text </DIV>
<DIV ID=Div2 ALIGN=RIGHT class=style1>
on top of other text</DIV>
<H2>Text can be<I> emphasized </I>by the use of contextual <B>selectors</B></
H2>
</BODY>
</HTML>
```

Creating Style Sheets

We'll start by looking at how you specify the rules that make up a cascading style sheet.

Syntax

When designing a style sheet, you only need to know a little HTML and understand the meaning of some basic terminology. For example, all CSS declarations are known as **rules**. An example rule to change all text contained between `<H1>` and `</H1>` tags to white would be as follows:

```
H1 { color: white }
```

Rules are broken up into two parts:

 the **selector** (the element to which the rule applies)

 the **declaration** (the part which defines what style the text should be)

The declaration itself is further split into two parts, the **property** of the text which is being affected, and the **value** to which it is being set. So looking back at our example line of code, H1 is our selector, the declaration is {color: white}, the property being affected is the color of the text and the value of the property is set to white.

All rules follow the same format:

```
TAG { property: value }
```

For example, to set all level 1 headings to white, we could use either of the following rules:

```
H1 { color: white }
H1 { color: #FFFFFF }
```

Both of these lines declare that everything enclosed by an `<H1>` tag will have the color white (or hex #FFFFFF) applied to it.

There's a list of the color names and values in Section D at the back of this book.

We can apply a single property to multiple tags by grouping those tags in the selector statement. In this example, we've set all three headings to display in black:

```
H1, H2, H3 { color: #000000 }
```

As well as grouping tags, we can also group properties by enclosing our multiple property declarations inside the curly braces and separating them with semicolons:

```
H2 {
 color: #000000;
 font-size: 14pt;
 font-family: monaco;
    }
```

This example will display all level 2 headings in 14 point Monaco, in black. Note the use of a semicolon after each declaration to divide one property from another. In our example, we've spread the selector across multiple lines to make your code easier to read. It has the same effect as placing it all on one line. In both cases, though, don't forget the closing brace.

Inheritance

One of the best features of CSS is the ability to have one tag inherit the properties of an enclosing tag. This means that we don't need to specify every possible tag; if we neglect to set a property for **<EM>** it will simply acquire the characteristics of whatever tag encloses it. Consider the following:

```
<H3>Section Four: <EM>Colossal</EM> Widgets</H3>
```

If our style sheet specified that all **<H3>** items were to be in green, but didn't say anything about **<EM>**, then Colossal would be green, just like the rest of the line. If, on the other hand, we carefully specified that **<EM>** was blue, it would appear as such. This system of inheritance follows through all of the possible properties, allowing us to set default values. We then only need to worry about the exceptions to our rules (the best way to do this is to set all default properties for **<BODY>**, and then change things for all the usual tags where necessary).

Even better, we can specify that one property will have a value that is relative to its parent property:

```
P { font-size: 14pt }
P { line-height: 120% }
```

In this instance, line height is defined as a percentage of font size, which will ensure that the paragraph is easy to read. This is useful when we come to revise the styles later, since it automatically ensures that our line heights will instantly change whenever we change the font size. If we explicitly declared the line height, we would need to change it manually—easily forgotten in the heat of designing a site.

Contextual Selectors

Another useful feature of inheritance is that it can be used to apply styles contextually. For example, we can not only set **<H3>** to green and **<EM>** to blue, but we can also set all instances of **<EM>** that occur in **<H3>** as yellow, without affecting either of other declarations. This is remarkably easy to achieve:

```
H3 EM { color: yellow }
```

Here the style sheet is specifying that any instance of **<EM>** that occurs inside **<H3>** will be shown as yellow. This does not affect any other instance of **<EM>**. You must be careful to omit the comma between the tags when using this method, or the selector will be interpreted as meaning that both **<H3>** *and* **<EM>** should be yellow.

This technique can be applied in great detail: it's possible to specify that all emphasized words are in red, in small print, but only when they appear in a listing that is itself enclosed by **<I>**. This is what we've done in our main example.

These types of declaration are termed **contextual selectors,** since they select values based on their context. It is also possible to specify values for several contextual selectors in a single statement by dividing them with commas. For example:

```
H3 EM, H2 I { color: yellow }
```

is the same thing as:

```
H3 EM { color: yellow }
H2 I { color: yellow }
```

Pseudo-classes and Pseudo-elements

By now you may have noticed that CSS1 hasn't really addressed some of the more commonly customized elements of HTML for example, what color the links are on a page. Fortunately, CSS1 not only lets you control that, it actually adds on all of the additional control that it provides for other elements.

The mechanism for doing this is by **pseudo-classes**, which can be used to apply formatting based on link status (visited, not visited, active) and can be applied to normal classes as well. For example:

```
A:link { color: green }
```

breaks down like this: A indicates that the selector applies to an anchor element, Link indicates that the properties will apply for an unvisited URL (other possible values are visited and active) and the rest will set properties as usual.

Pseudo-elements on the other hand allow a relatively fine level of control over commonly used typographical elements. For example, they can be used to set special characteristics for the first letter in a paragraph, for the first line, and so on. They are relatively simple to use. In the following example, we set the first letter of any paragraph to appear in red:

```
P:first-letter { color: red }
```

However pseudo-elements aren't yet supported by either of the main browsers in their version 4 incarnations, and so we'll have to wait until future releases to be able to use them.

Creating for Cross Browser Compatibility

Of course if you could create one style sheet and guarantee that it would look the same in both Internet Explorer 4 and Netscape Navigator 4, you'd be laughing. However, as you might have guessed this isn't as easy as it seems. It certainly isn't impossible though as long you stick to these common rules.

To Hyphenate or Not to Hyphenate?

If you turn to Appendix G you'll see that there's a list of all of the Cascading Style Sheet Properties. If you flick through it for long enough, then you'll probably realize that a lot of the properties are hyphenated. However underneath you'll find their equivalent scripting properties aren't. Indeed you could enter a property such as **fontsize** instead of **font-size** into your style sheet, and Netscape Navigator 4 would know what you mean and would display the style sheet correctly. Internet Explorer on the other hand wouldn't understand it. So for properties such as **font-size**, always remember to include the hyphen.

One Mistake Breaks Everything

Secondly you'll find that Netscape Navigator 4 is pretty intolerant of mistakes. So if you entered the following:

```
H2 {
 color: #000000;
 font-size: 14pt;
 font-family: monaco;
 font-wait: bold;                                   ' incorrect line
   }
```

You'd find that Internet Explorer 4 would display the text with all of the other stipulated properties apart from the incorrect **font-wait**, but that Netscape Navigator 4 would not display any of the styling information.

Units of Measurement

Some Cascading Style Sheets properties for fonts and margins require a numerical value such as **font-size**. It may seem perfectly acceptable to you to enter just a numerical value, but Netscape Navigator 4 also requires you to specify the unit of measurement afterwards. If you entered the following:

```
H4 {
 color: blue;
 font-size: 14;
 font-family: sans-serif;
    }
```

then Internet Explorer would assume that you meant pixels for unit of measurement and would display you style sheet with a **`font-size`** of 14 pixels. Netscape Navigator 4 is unable to assume a default unit of measurement and would fail to apply any style (including color) whatsoever to the text.

You need to beware of all of these minor problems otherwise your style sheets when viewed in one browser might not look the same as in another.

How do Style Sheets Cascade Anyway?

One of the most impressive capabilities of CSS is the ability to have style sheets that **cascade**—hence the name **Cascading** Style Sheets. This means that compliant browsers allow multiple style sheets to have control over the same document at the same time. It is possible, for example, to have three separate style sheets trying to format a document at once.

The idea is this: when authors set up documents and refer to style sheets, they are expressing their preferred mode of display. Browsers have a 'default style' of their own that they prefer to use when displaying pages. As the browser interprets documents on the Web, it will display them in its default style. If, however, it runs across a document that uses CSS, it will give way to the preferences stated in that style sheet. The basic idea appears to be that 'normal' HTML documents have nothing to lose by being formatted according to browser preferences, but that documents using CSS ought to be displayed the way the author intended (or else they wouldn't have been formatted that way in the first place).

Which style sheet 'wins' is determined on a selector-by-selector basis, so that the browser can win sometimes, and the author others. The method that browsers use to determine which instructions will be used is basically as follows:

- Determine if the settings for any element actually conflict. If not, any inherited values (from 'parent' tags) are used instead. If there aren't any, the default values are used
- If there is a conflict, the values are sorted by origin (author values are higher than reader values)
- Sort by specificity: if two values conflict, and one applies only to the situation at hand, but the other applies in all cases, then the restricted value will win

Notice that this system allows for the possibility of having effects from multiple style sheets all appearing at once on the page. This is actually a benefit, since it allows you to create multiple focused style sheets, and then apply them in different combinations to different documents. Unfortunately, however, this is neither particularly easy to do nor very intuitive, and requires careful use of the correct **implementation tags** within the document.

Cascading Style Sheets Example

Here's an example which allows you to link three separate style sheets (from the same server) to a document and then apply the different styles to the text, on the page. Of course, in this case, it would probably be easier to combine the three style sheets, but for the purposes of our example and with larger style sheets, the benefits should soon become obvious.

```
<HTML>
<HEAD>
<TITLE>Cascading Style Sheet Example</TITLE>
<LINK REL=STYLESHEET TYPE="text/css"
 HREF="http://rapid.wrox.co.uk/books/1568/style1.css">
<LINK REL=STYLESHEET TYPE="text/css"
 HREF="http://rapid.wrox.co.uk/books/1568/style2.css">
<LINK REL=STYLESHEET TYPE="text/css"
 HREF="http://rapid.wrox.co.uk/books/1568/style3.css">
</HEAD>
<BODY>
<DIV ID=Div1 CLASS=style1>
Cascading
</DIV>
<DIV ID=Div2 CLASS=style2>
Style
</DIV>
<DIV ID=Div3 CLASS=style3>
Sheets
</DIV>
</BODY>
</HTML>
```

The result would be that a different style sheet is applied to each separate word on the page.

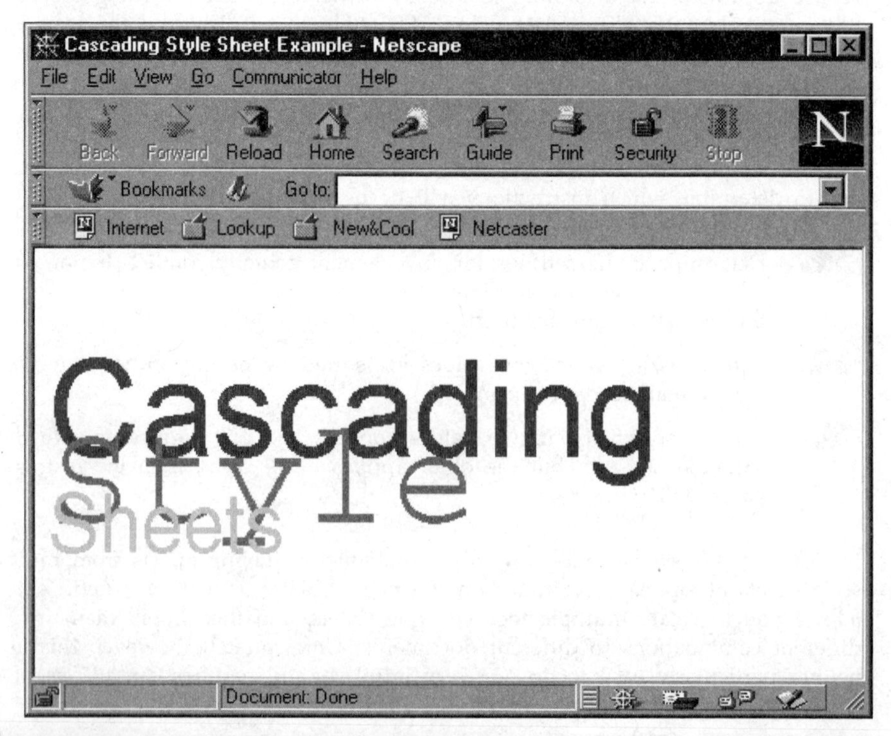

You can run this page, called Cascading Style Sheets, from our Web site at:
http://rapid.wrox.co.uk/books/1568

Next, we'll examine how to link a style sheet to our document.

Linking Style Sheets to your Document

There are three ways to do this and they each have slightly different effects. It is important to decide which method suits your purpose, since they're not functionally identical.

<LINK>

The first method is a special use of the **<LINK>** tag. This can be used to reference alternative style sheets within the HTML code. To use the **<LINK>** method, we place the following in the **<HEAD>** of our document:

```
<LINK REL=STYLESHEET TYPE="text/css" HREF="http://rapid.wrox.co.uk/books/1568/
style.css" TITLE="Style">
```

This provides a link to external style sheet file, specified in the **HREF** attribute. Style Sheets are normally saved in files with the **.css** extension. No extra information is required in the style sheet file, other than the information you'd typically place between the opening and closing **<STYLE>** tags. So a typical style sheet file could look just like this:

```
.style1 {margin-top:44px;
         font-family: arial;
         font-size: 80px;
         color: darkolivegreen}
```

Obviously, you can also change the **HREF** to point to your own style sheets. This means you can apply style sheets that reside on completely different servers. This can be particularly useful in an Intranet situation, where one department can set up several 'approved' styles for all documents to use.

The <STYLE> Element

The next way to use style sheets is to use the special **<STYLE>** tag. The idea here is to enclose the style sheet data in the **<STYLE>** tag, so that it can be parsed and applied as the document is loaded. To this end, we use the following code, placed in the **<HEAD>** of our document:

```
<STYLE TYPE="text/css">
...style info goes here...
</STYLE>
```

This seems quick and easy (and indeed we used it in the earlier example) but there are a few things you should be aware of. The first problem is that older browsers will ignore the **<STYLE>** tag, and will try to handle the style data as if it were normal text. This can be avoided by enclosing the whole line in HTML comment tags, as follows:

```
<STYLE TYPE="text/css">
<!--
...style info goes here...
-->
</STYLE>
```

Style-aware browsers will still find the style information and handle it appropriately.

More problems that arise from using the **<STYLE>** tag are due to the fact that we are required to include a complete style sheet in every document. This not only increases the time needed to create a document, but also increases the file sizes and makes it more difficult to change a complete site's appearance as well. In effect, this method erases two of the three advantages conferred by style sheets, and should be avoided if possible.

The **STYLE** tag takes the following attributes:

DIR	**MEDIA**	**ID**
LANG	**TITLE**	**TYPE**

Netscape Navigator 4 also allows use of the **SRC** attribute which can be used to specify an external file with a set of style sheet definitions. This is used to compensate the lack of a working **@import** notation.

MEDIA

This specifies the mode of output for the style definitions. Possible values are:
MEDIA=SCREEN | PRINT | PROJECTION | BRAILLE | SPEECH | ALL

TYPE

This specifies the MIME type allowed for the style sheet.
TYPE=*string*

Currently allowed for cascading style sheets is:

```
TYPE='text/css'
```

and for JavaScript style sheets is:

```
TYPE='text/javascript'
```

In Netscape Navigator, if you don't specify the **TYPE** then, while Netscape should default to CSS, what actually happens is that Navigator acts erratically, and only recognizes the names of styles that are specified in JavaScript styling, i.e. without hyphens. So you should always specify the **TYPE** when creating your pages if you want both browsers to respond as expected.

@import

While the **<LINK>** element references alternative style sheets that the reader can select, the reader can import style sheets which are automatically merged with the rest of the style sheet using a special notation in CSS1:

```
@import url (http://rapid.wrox.co.uk/books/1568/style.css);
```

This notation tells the browser to get the style sheet 'style' from the server at **rapid.wrox.co.uk**. If we place this line in a **<STYLE>** section in the **<HEAD>** of our document, the style will automatically be retrieved and applied before our document is displayed. Even better, we can override the imported style by simply declaring any changes in the document itself, using the CSS1 description format we'll be covering shortly (this lets us set up a 'baseline' style sheet, from which individual documents can diverge).

Unfortunately this notation has only been realized in IE4. It still isn't implemented in Navigator 4. None of the older versions of either browser support the format.

Applying Cascading Style Sheets

Once you've linked the style sheets into the document, you still need a way of identifying the text to which you wish to apply the style. This is done using classes.

Classes

You might have noticed that we used the **CLASS** attribute to apply a pre-defined style to an element in our previous examples. A **class** can be a defined as either a property or a set of properties. A class can be a subset of a previous declaration. We can specify properties on a class-wide basis, with any properties of that class applying to all instances of that class—even when used with different tags. Declaring the properties of a class is easy. In our first example we define the class **style1** as follows:

```
.style1 { color:black;
          margin-top: -80px;
          font-family: arial;
          font-weight: bold;
          font-size: 18px}
```

Notice the period that appears before **style1**—this establishes that we are naming a class and defining its properties. We then use the **CLASS** attribute of the **<DIV>** tag to apply it solely to the text Style Sheets can be used to layer text:

```
<DIV ID=Div1 ALIGN=LEFT class=style1>
Style Sheets can be used to layer text
</DIV>
```

We can also create a subset of a previous declaration. For example, if we specify that **<H3>** is blue, uses the monaco font and is size 14,then we can create a subset of **<H3>** that is white. This subset will retain any other properties we've given the parent, and must be referenced by name (in order to separate it from the parent.) The following code demonstrates this by creating a new class named **second** to apply to **<H3>** tags:

```
H3 { font-size:14pt; font-family: monaco; color: #0000FF }
H3.second { color: #FFFFFF }
```

To implement our newly created class, we must call it explicitly like this:

```
<H3 CLASS=second> This is in white fourteen-point monaco </H3>
<H3> This is in the default color and fourteen-point monaco </H3>
```

The advantage of defining a class as a property rather than as a subset is that if we define it as a property, as follows:

```
.second { color: #FFFFFF }
```

we can then apply the properties of **second** wherever we call it, without having to set up every conceivable combination of tag and class:

```
<H1 CLASS=second> Level One </H1>
<EM CLASS=second> Emphasis </EM>
```

In this example, both items of text will be in white, and each will have whatever characteristics were previously defined, without having to explicitly define the properties of **H1.second** and **EM.second**.

As **CLASS** is a universal attribute, you can deduce that you're able to add style sheets to just about every tag. However most tags provide formatted output of their own. To be able to apply a style to a section of the page without adding other formatting, there are two specific tags that are used with style sheets. We'll look at them now.

The <DIV> Element

This tag was introduced in the HTML 3.2 standard. It is used to define an area of the page, or **document division**. Anything between the opening and closing tag is referred to as a single item. The **<DIV>** tag doesn't allocate any particular style or structure to the text, it just allocates an area. This tag was used in our style sheets example to enclose each of the separate lines of text and to allow them to be layered on top of one another. **<DIV>** is a block level element, it can be used to group other block-level elements, but it can't be used within paragraph elements.

```
<DIV ID=Div1 ALIGN=LEFT class=style1>
Cascading Style Sheets can be used to layer text
</DIV>
<DIV ID=Div2 ALIGN=RIGHT class=style1>
on top of other text
</DIV>
```

The current standard bars the attributes of **<DIV>**, other than **<STYLE>**, from controlling the display in any way (all information should be set in the style sheet), apart from using the **ALIGN** attribute.

DIV can take the following attributes:

ALIGN	CLASS	DIR	ID
LANG	STYLE	TITLE	

We're ignoring IE4's **DATAFLD**, **DATASRC** and **DATAFORMATAS** attributes as they aren't supported in HTML 4.0 and are explained separately in chapter 12. Also Navigator 4 supports **NOWRAP** which indicates whether or not the browser should perform automatic word wrapping.

ALIGN

Specifies where the element should be positioned in relation to the rest of the page. This is now deprecated in HTML 4.0, as positioning of elements via the style sheet makes it redundant.

ALIGN=LEFT | RIGHT | CENTER

The <SPAN> Element

Microsoft originally introduced this tag, but it is now present in the HTML 4.0 standard. It's been adopted in Navigator 4 as another way of applying style sheets to an area of text. The way this is done is very similar to the **<DIV>** tag. The **<SPAN>** tag defines localized style information, and anything between the open and closing tags is referred to as a single item. According to the HTML 4.0 standard, the difference is that the **<DIV>** tag groups blocks together, which **<SPAN>** is an in-line element and can only be used within paragraphs when you wish to group together words and apply styles to them.

SPAN can take the following attributes:

CLASS	**DIR**	**ID**
LANG	**STYLE**	**TITLE**

Again, we're ignoring IE4's **DATAFLD**, **DATASRC** and **DATAFORMATAS** attributes as they aren't supported in HTML 4.0 and are explained separately in chapter 12.

Using the STYLE attribute with Individual Tags

One final way of specifying CSS1 information is in the **STYLE** attribute of the tag we want it to affect. For example:

```
<P STYLE="color: green">This paragraph will be green</P>
```

This is extremely flexible and easy to use, but we do need to specify each tag individually. If you want to specify more than one style property, then each property must be separated by a semi-colon. For example:

```
<P STYLE="color: green; font-size: 18"> This paragraph will be green and size
18</P>
```

In HTML 4.0, all text and graphics tags now support the **STYLE** attribute and the new properties. However, only in IE4 do most of the tags actually support the **STYLE** attribute. Specifying styles like this does remove the major benefit of style sheets, namely being able to alter information from one location. If one particular style needed changing, you'd have to go back and alter each affected tag's **STYLE** attribute and this could rapidly prove burdensome.

Summary

Style sheets are exceedingly useful, if used in moderation. They not only give the developer control over the display, they also provide the basis for manipulating the elements you see on the page. We've stopped short of showing you how you might use style sheets to expose the properties of text and images on the page, because this is another topic that's dealt with differently by the two major browsers. Instead we've focused on how style sheets were used to give the developer much more control over the display. We broke it down into four main steps:

- Creating a Style Sheet
- Linking your style sheet into your HTML code
- Applying your style sheet to specific text
- Applying styles to single elements

It is vital to know how style sheets can be used to enhance your pages when using many aspects of HTML, not least in the next chapter, which considers how you can go about inserting images into your pages.

Images and Inclusions

The ability to display images of various types on the web is one of the biggest attractions for many people, and probably the main reason for its rapid growth rate. Images also present the biggest problems. As this area could easily cover several large books on its own, we'll concentrate on the aspects that are important in relation to download times and the image formats available, and show you some examples of their uses.

What are Inclusions?

Traditionally, images have been inserted into a document using the **<IMG>** tag. Just looking around the web will reveal all sorts of amazing graphical effects that can be achieved with the use of this simple element. However, the world has moved on since the beginnings where the ability to include a static image was the main way of spicing up your pages. There are lots of new and exciting techniques now coming along.

HTML 4.0 proposes a more general technique for inserting images and other items into HTML documents, called **inclusions**. The reason for this is that more and more types of objects are becoming available for use in web pages. Many of these are graphical in nature, but are not actually plain images of the type we've got used to using. For example, it's now quite common to find animated images, video and audio streams, and small embedded programs running within a page. Modern browsers can also often display other types of documents within the browser window, such as a word-processor or spreadsheet file.

In current and third-generation browsers these kinds of objects were handled in different ways, by a series of different HTML elements. Amongst these were **<OBJECT>**, **<APPLET>**, **<EMBED>**, **<BGSOUND>**, **<MARQUEE>** and, of course, **<IMAGE>**. The intention in HTML 4.0 is to replace all these with one single element: **<OBJECT>**.

However, that's the future. At present no browsers support the **<OBJECT>** element fully in the ways that are envisaged by HTML 4.0. In this chapter, we'll be looking at how we insert images the 'old-fashioned' way using an **<IMG>** element, and then, in Chapter 9, explore the proposals for the **<OBJECT>**

element. Bear in mind that the `<IMG>` tag is deprecated and won't be used in future versions of HTML. Before we look at how to insert images, however, we'll take a quick overview of the common graphics formats used on the Web.

Image Files and Formats

At present there are only two graphic formats that are widely supported on the Web; GIF image format and JPEG image format. However, it's likely that one of the new formats; PNG, will be added soon (some applications already support it)—and we may even see browsers supporting other platform-specific formats. For example, Internet Explorer may soon provide native support for the vector-based Windows Metafile format (WMF).

The GIF Image Format

GIF (Graphics Interchange Format) is the most widely supported graphics format. It is capable of displaying images in black and white, grayscale or color. The one drawback of the GIF image format is that it is limited to displaying a maximum of 256 colors or gray scales. When you save an image in GIF format, the software searches for the 256 colors that best represent the colors in the image, creates a palette or color table containing these colors, and stores it with the image.

One of the reasons for the success of the GIF format is that it stores images in a highly compressed state. Because of the type of compression used, it is particularly effective for large areas of a single color, such as icons, company logos, etc. However, the compression technique it uses is not ideally suited to photographic images—in this case, it is invariably better to use the JPEG format (covered later on).

The Right Number of Colors

Images destined to be downloaded over the web should be as small as possible. The physical size of the image when displayed is not significant. What is significant is the size of image file—the larger the file, the longer the download time. The easiest way to reduce the file size for a GIF format image is to reduce the number of colors that it contains.

The reduced number of colors has another advantage, because many computer users have their system set up to display only 256 colors at one time. While the browser will quite happily display one GIF image containing 256 colors, it can lead to problems if it tries to display two GIF files at the same time. If they both use 256 colors, but these aren't the *same* 256 colors, the browser will 'dither' the colors—in other words, it will find the best compromise between the two images. This can result in a real mess, with neither image looking the way you expected it to.

Transparent GIFs

There are two versions of the GIF format: GIF87 and GIF89a. The second of these, GIF89a has the advantage of being able to make a single color within the image transparent. This can lead to some stunning effects if used creatively. For instance, you could have a background image with a transparent GIF format image on top so that the background shows through, like this:

Interlaced GIF Images

Another useful feature of the GIF 89a image format is its ability to produce an **interlaced** image. Normally, as a browser loads an image, it appears in horizontal bands starting from the top and 'growing' down to the bottom. On a slow connection, the user will not see the whole image until it has completely downloaded. With interlaced GIF files the whole image is displayed at once in a very low (blocky) resolution. This then builds up to a high resolution as the rest of the file downloads. Although the time taken for either file type to download is the same, the interlaced file appears to load faster because the whole image can be seen at once. Many programs and utilities that can produce interlaced (and transparent) GIF format files are available on the Internet.

Animated GIF Files

Finally, an increasingly useful technique with GIF files is to produce animated images. The GIF file format is not just a 'single-image' one. The header section of a GIF file contains all kinds of information about the file, such as its color palette, size, and even comments. More than that, it also allows multiple images to be stored in a single file. These individual images can be rendered into an animation sequence.

Even though the GIF89a standard has been around for more than seven years, some browsers do not support animated GIFs. These older browsers will display only the first image in a GIF animation sequence.

Standard image-editing packages usually can't manage animated GIFs directly, but you can use them to create the individual images that make up an animated GIF. Then a special-purpose utility is used to package the images together into one file, and edit the control information within the file. For example, the next screenshot shows a shareware package called the GIF Construction Set 95, which lets you easily see the final structure of the file:

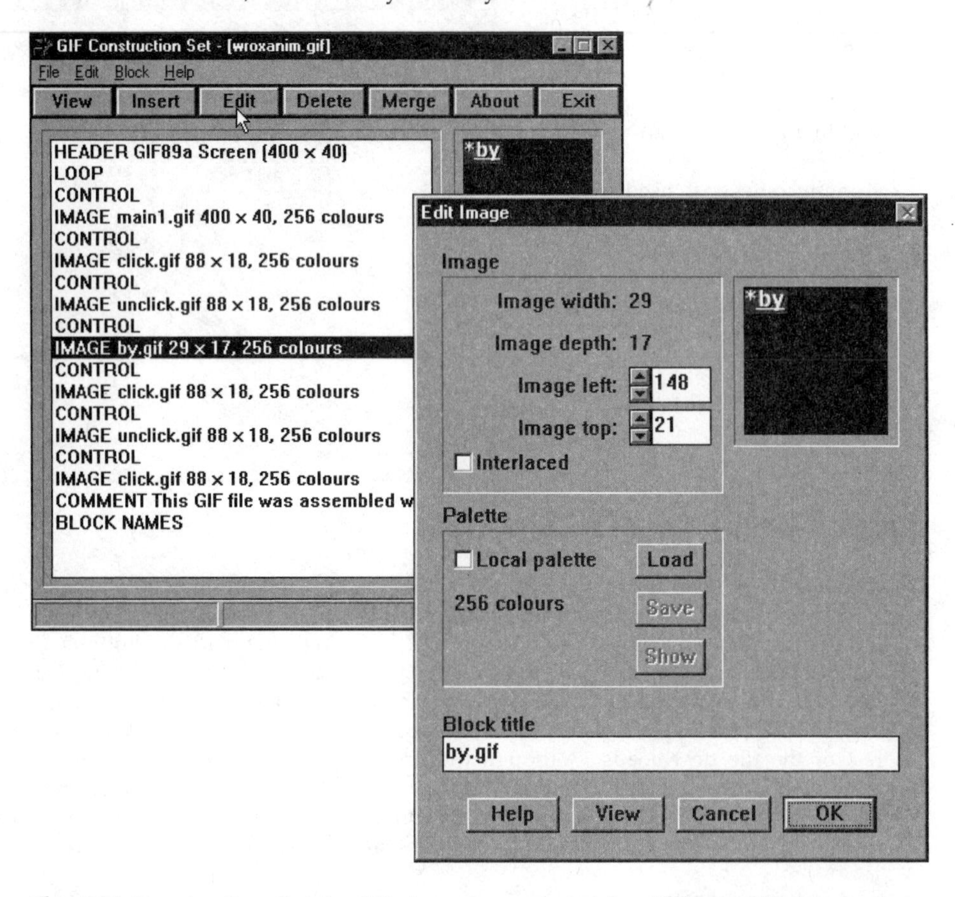

The GIF Construction Set for Windows is produced by **Alchemy Mindworks Inc., Canada**. Their Web site is at `http://www.mindworkshop.com/alchemy/alchemy.html`

Resources

You can get a whole range of image-editing and animation tools from sources on the Web. You might like to try the PhotoImpact and GIF Animator applications from `http://www.ulead.com`, and PaintShop Pro from `http://www.jasc.com`. Both of these are available on a free 30-day trial. Microsoft also produce a GIF animator utility, and include it in their FrontPage application along with other image editing software. In fact, there are literally hundreds of other image editing packages available—depending on your operating system and personal preferences.

The JPEG Image Format

The JPEG (Joint Photographic Experts Group) image format (pronounced **jay'peg**) was designed specifically for storing photographic images at a range of different compression rates. The compression is achieved through a **lossy** technique. This means that the higher the compression ratio, the more of the fine detail is abandoned. There is then a greater chance of the image not looking like the uncompressed version, as parts of it are lost from the original, and then 'made up' on the fly when it is displayed—according to special algorithms. However, this is not visible to the eye for most images except at very high compression levels.

The JPEG image format is capable of storing images in millions of colors as opposed to the GIF format's 256, though they are slower to compress and decompress. Interlacing and transparency are not supported by JPEG itself, but Netscape have introduced the Progressive JPEG format, which produces a similar effect to interlaced GIF.

> **Note that JPEG is *not* a good format for text, or images with hard edges. You should also be aware that some older browsers do not support the use of inline JPEG images.**

The PNG Format

A relatively new format that is rapidly gaining in popularity is PNG (Portable Network Graphic). In comparison to GIF, this format produces smaller, faster loading files that can be viewed on different platforms without loss of quality. It produces interlaced images, displaying the first image preview when just 1/64 of the image data has been downloaded (GIFs produce the first preview after 1/8 of the image data has been downloaded). PNG images will therefore display the first impression of the image much more quickly than GIFs.

Another advantage is that you can include meta-information within the file which will, for example, allow the image to be located with a search based on its description rather than its file name. Although the PNG format is not suitable for photographic images, it can handle images that are a lot more complicated than GIF images, including ray-traced scenes.

Working with Images

When you insert an image into your page it is loaded into the browser at the same time as all the other elements, and is effectively treated the same way as a block-level text element such as `<P>` or `<LI>`. Care must be exercised, however, if you expect your audience to print or save your pages. Images are not saved with the rest of the document, and many users turn off images to speed up download time on slower lines, therefore, the document must be understandable without the images.

While images can make your pages look a lot more attractive, don't be tempted to overdo it. Large images take a long time to download and frustrate users who have only a slow connection. Because many people may have graphics 'turned off' in their browser, or be using a browser or other application that can't display images, you also need to provide an alternative where the image is an important part of the informational or navigational content.

Remember that one of the aims of HTML 4.0 is to widen the appeal and usability of the Web to people who may be disadvantaged—particularly those with visual disabilities. Browsers are available that can magnify the text on a page, or output the content as spoken text. They won't do very well with your pages if the entire information content is contained in the images.

In general, you should take advantage of the ability of the **<IMG>** and **<OBJECT>** elements (discussed in chapter 9) to display alternative text and captions, plus pop-up 'tooltips' in the **TITLE** attribute. These can be translated by non-visual applications. Also, where possible, provide a text version of the menus on your site, or a separate text-based 'site map' page, to assist users in navigating to the pages they want.

The <IMG> Element

The **<IMG>** element is the traditional and most widely supported way to insert images into your pages. The attributes for the **<IMG>** element are:

SRC	**ALIGN**	**ALT**	**BORDER**	**HEIGHT**	**WIDTH**	**HSPACE**
VSPACE	**ISMAP**	**USEMAP**	**LONGDESC**			

plus the usual HTML 4.0 attributes **ID**, **CLASS**, **STYLE**, **DIR**, **LANG** and **TITLE**. The **<IMG>** element also supports a range of events that can be used in **scripting**. We look briefly at this topic in chapter 10.

Of these attributes only **SRC** is *required*, while the others are implied by the image itself or the surrounding parts of the page.

SRC

This specifies the **SouRCe**, or URL of the picture or image to include. The syntax is:

SRC="*url***"**

where *url* is the absolute or relative path of the image file. It's possible to specify a source file from anywhere—just put the full URL as the **SRC**:

```
<IMG SRC="http://www.mysite.com/pics/mydog.gif">
```

ALIGN

Use this attribute to align the image within the page and the surrounding elements. The syntax is:

ALIGN="*alignment***"**

where *alignment* is one of:

TOP	Text outside the image is aligned with the top of the image.
MIDDLE	Text outside the image is aligned with the middle of the image.
BOTTOM	Text outside the image is aligned with the bottom of the image.
LEFT	The image is aligned along the left border of the browser window, and text and other elements flow around it to the right.
RIGHT	The image is aligned along the right border of the browser window, and text and other elements flow around it to the left.
ABSBOTTOM*	The image is aligned so that the bottom is in line with the absolute bottom of the surrounding text. The absolute bottom is the baseline of the text minus the height of the largest character descender.
TEXTTOP*	The image is aligned so that the top is in line with the absolute top of the surrounding text. The absolute top is the baseline of the text plus the height of the largest character ascender.
ABSMIDDLE*	Text outside the image is aligned with the middle of the image, using the midpoint between the **ABSBOTTOM** and **TEXTTOP** of the surrounding text.
BASELINE*	The bottom of the image is aligned with the baseline of the surrounding text.

* *Note that not all browsers support the last four values*

In HTML 4.0, the ALIGN attribute is deprecated, and only maintained for backward compatibility. You should instead use cascading style sheets (see chapter 3) for future compatibility.

ALT

This attribute specifies a text alternative for the image if the browser or application cannot display images. The syntax is:

ALT="*text***"**

where *text* is a word or phrase relating to the image specified by the **SRC** attribute. The importance of this attribute cannot be over-emphasized—remember that many people turn off graphics, or use an application that cannot display them. Many browsers will also display the **ALT** text while waiting for the image to download, and some will use it when printing hardcopy versions of the page.

BORDER

Specifies the width of the border around the image. The syntax is:

BORDER=*n*

where *n* is a numerical value in pixels.

The value `0` turns the border off. The default for images is generally `0`, unless they are used as a hyperlink—see chapter 5 for details. Note that this attribute is deprecated in HTML 4.0, and you should use style sheets instead.

HEIGHT and WIDTH

Specifies the height and width that the image is to be displayed at. The syntax is:

WIDTH=*n* HEIGHT=*n*

where *n* is the width and height in pixels. Images are scaleable. That is, you can use the **WIDTH** and **HEIGHT** attributes to specify the size of box that you want the image to fit into, and the browser will scale the image to suit. Using **WIDTH** and **HEIGHT** with the **<IMG>** element helps the page to load faster, because the browser can get on with laying out the rest of the page as it knows the dimensions of the image before loading it.

Another advantage is that if the user has images turned off in their browser, a 'missing image' area the same size as the image will be displayed instead. This way, the formatting of the rest of the page is left unchanged. If the attributes are missing, and images turned off, a default icon will be shown. As this is unlikely to be the same size as the image, text flow and other formatting will not be what you intended.

> **Note that although using WIDTH and HEIGHT will scale the image size to the required dimensions, the image file size remains the same. The attributes are useful for making minor adjustments to the image size, but should not be used for large changes. If you want to significantly reduce the size of an image, do so using an image editing program. Otherwise the reduced image will take the same amount of time to load as the larger version.**

HSPACE and VSPACE

These attributes are used to control the white space around an image. The syntax is:

HSPACE=*n*

where *n* is a numerical value in pixels. Other elements next to, or above and below the image, will be moved away by the specified number of pixels.

ISMAP and USEMAP

ISMAP and **USEMAP** are used with image maps, which are discussed in chapter 5. **ISMAP** indicates to the browser that the image is a server side image map, while **USEMAP** is used with client side image maps and indicates to the browser which map file to use.

LONGDESC

This is a new HTML 4.0 attribute that allows you to add a link to another document that describes the image in more detail. The syntax is:

`LONGDESC=`*url*

where *url* is the address of the other document or resource. This is useful for providing extra information about an image that the user can see if they wish, without cluttering up the page. It is also designed for use in non-visual applications. It is not supported in current browsers, however.

Extensions to the <IMG> Element

Both Internet Explorer (from version 4) and Navigator (all versions) support the **`LOWSRC`** attribute, and both also add the **`NAME`** attribute in their respective version 4 releases. Neither of these are part of the HTML standards, however.

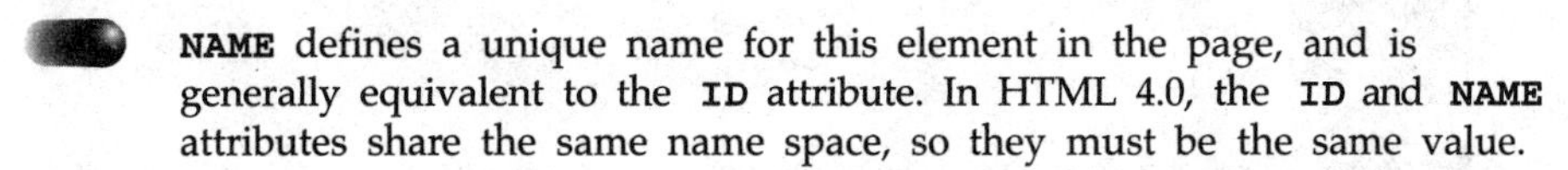

- **`NAME`** defines a unique name for this element in the page, and is generally equivalent to the **`ID`** attribute. In HTML 4.0, the **`ID`** and **`NAME`** attributes share the same name space, so they must be the same value.

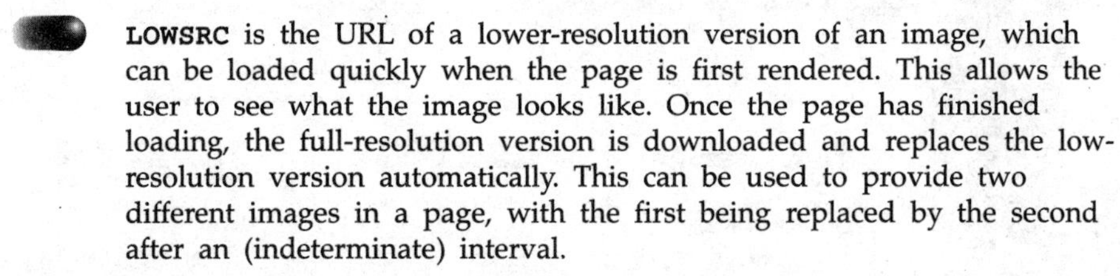

- **`LOWSRC`** is the URL of a lower-resolution version of an image, which can be loaded quickly when the page is first rendered. This allows the user to see what the image looks like. Once the page has finished loading, the full-resolution version is downloaded and replaces the low-resolution version automatically. This can be used to provide two different images in a page, with the first being replaced by the second after an (indeterminate) interval.

Internet Explorer <IMG> Extensions

Internet Explorer adds other attributes to the **`<IMG>`** element:

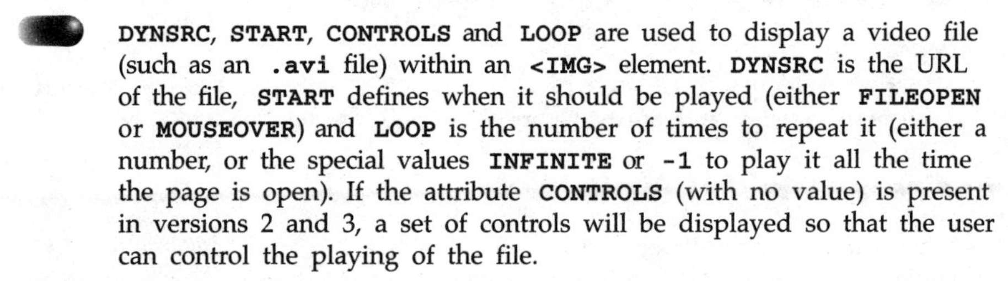

- **`DYNSRC`**, **`START`**, **`CONTROLS`** and **`LOOP`** are used to display a video file (such as an **`.avi`** file) within an **`<IMG>`** element. **`DYNSRC`** is the URL of the file, **`START`** defines when it should be played (either **`FILEOPEN`** or **`MOUSEOVER`**) and **`LOOP`** is the number of times to repeat it (either a number, or the special values **`INFINITE`** or **`-1`** to play it all the time the page is open). If the attribute **`CONTROLS`** (with no value) is present in versions 2 and 3, a set of controls will be displayed so that the user can control the playing of the file.

- **`DATAFLD`** and **`DATASRC`** are used to connect the **`<IMG>`** element to a client-side cached data source in Internet Explorer 4, in a technique called **data binding**. We look briefly at this in chapter 12.

Some Examples of Using Images

To end this chapter, we'll see some ways in which the **`<IMG>`** elements can be used.

Using the <IMG> Element

The 'welcome' page on our Web-Developer site uses a selection of small and quick-to-load images to brighten it up, make it look attractive, and provide clear visual clues to visitors as to what's going on:

The main Wrox Web-Developer logo in the white section of this page is a GIF file, and is inserted into the page with the following code;

```
<IMG SRC="wd_images/WDLogoLg.gif" WIDTH=355 HEIGHT=48
     ALT="Wrox Web-Developer">
```

Notice that we specify the **WIDTH** and **HEIGHT** to help the browser lay out the page more quickly and neatly before the image finishes loading.

Adding a LOWSRC Attribute

If we had a low-resolution version of this image, we could load it first by adding the **LOWSRC** attribute to the element:

```
<IMG SRC="wd_images/WDLogoLg.gif" WIDTH=355 HEIGHT=48
     LOWSRC="wd_images/WDLogoLowRes.gif"
     ALT="Wrox Web-Developer">
```

Using the ALT Attribute

The Books and Samples link is important in our page, because that's what a lot of people are looking for when they come to our site. We've included the **ALT** attribute, which provides a pop-up 'tooltip' when their mouse hovers over it.

This will be used if their browser doesn't support graphics, or can't display the image for any reason:

Here's the code that produces this image element:

```
<IMG SRC="wd_images/booksamp.gif" WIDTH=114 HEIGHT=112
     ALT="Books and Samples Pages">
```

Using Transparent GIFs

We've also used some transparent GIF files on our page. The following code inserts the image for the Ultimate HTML Database button:

```
<IMG HSPACE=5 SRC="wd_images/HtmlDB.gif" WIDTH=136 HEIGHT=20
     ALT="The Ultimate HTML Database">
```

This image is shaped like a button with rounded ends, but we can only use images that are in fact rectangular. By making the background transparent, the page shows through. If our page had a different background pattern or color (other than white), you'd still be able to see this through it:

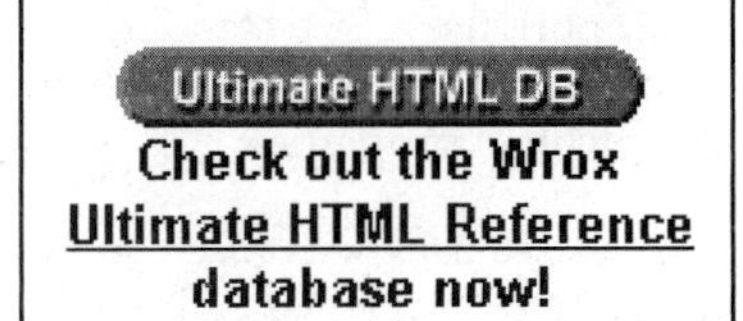

Wrapping Text Round an Image

We can also wrap text around an image. In the following example, we've placed a series of images in a page. The one on the left has the text wrapping around it, while the ones on the right are placed separately from the text:

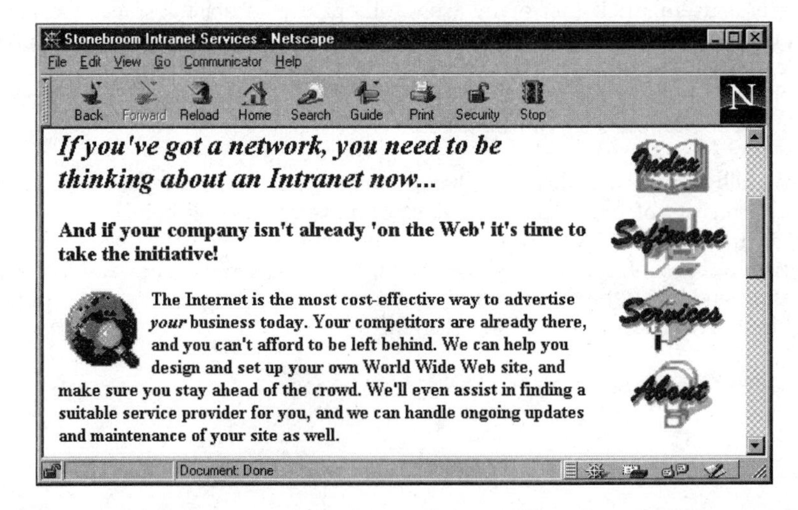

In fact this page uses a table to separate the page into two sections. We'll look at how tables work in chapter 6. In the meantime, the important line is the one that inserts the left-hand image:

```
<IMG SRC="world.gif" ALIGN="LEFT" WIDTH=75 HEIGHT=73>
<B>The Internet is the most cost-effective way to
advertise <I>your</I> business today ... etc
```

You can see that we've used the value **"LEFT"** for the **ALIGN** attribute (the quotation marks are in fact optional, because the value is a single word with no spaces). This causes the image to be aligned with the left margin, and the text wraps to the right of it. If it appears to be too close, we could use the **HSPACE** and **VSPACE** attributes to give it more room, although in our case we wanted it to wrap as closely as possible.

Using the HTML 4.0 'float' Style Property

Of course, we should be using the new HTML 4.0 style sheets standards to place our image, instead of the attributes of the **<IMG>** element directly:

```
<IMG SRC="world.gif"
     STYLE="float:left; width:75; height:73; >
```

Here, the CSS1 **float** property is used to move the element to the left margin of the page, and wrap the text round it. This will only work in browsers that support the CSS1 standard, but you could always take the 'belt-and-braces' approach and include both the direct attributes and the style attribute with the matching properties:

```
<IMG SRC="world.gif" ALIGN="LEFT" WIDTH=75 HEIGHT=73
     STYLE="float:left; width:75; height:73; >
```

The only problem now is that the behavior may be erratic in browsers that partly support CSS1. If they don't handle it properly, and it takes precedence over the direct properties (as it should), the results could be less than appealing.

The Single Pixel GIF Trick

This is a useful trick that many web authors use to achieve precise control over layout and formatting. It's a little out of date now, because you should be using style sheets (see the previous chapter) to control the placement and alignment of all the elements in your pages. However, until more browsers fully support the style sheet proposals, it can be useful.

It basically works like this. You have an image, in this case **dot_clear.gif**, which consists of one pixel. The pixel color is defined as being the invisible one, a trick that GIF version 89a files can achieve. When you want to add a precise amount of space across or down, you insert the image and use the **HSPACE** and/or **VSPACE** attributes to move the following elements around as required. The code is something like this:

```
<IMG SRC="dot_clear.gif" HSPACE=x VSPACE=y>
```

where x is the number of pixels horizontally, and y is the number of pixels vertically. This makes a clear rectangle of any size, which you can use as a spacer to move things about. Here's an example:

```
<HTML>
<HEAD>
<TITLE>Single pixel GIF trick</TITLE>
</HEAD>
<BODY BGCOLOR=WHITE>

<IMG SRC=dot_clear.gif HSPACE=10 VSPACE=10>
This paragraph starts indented because<BR>
we have utilised the single pixel GIF<BR>
trick.<BR>

<IMG SRC=dot_clear.gif HSPACE=30 VSPACE=30>
This paragraph also starts with an<BR>
indent, but the indent is larger because<BR>
the value of HSPACE has been increased.<BR>
The gap between the paragraphs has also<BR>
been increased by setting VSPACE to 30.

</BODY>
</HTML>
```

This is what it looks like in the browser:

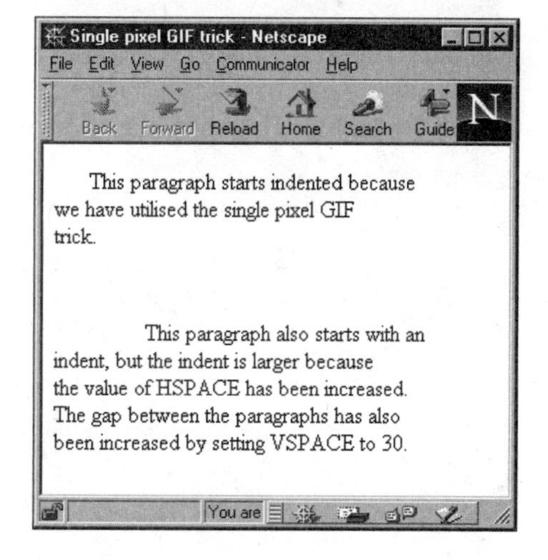

HTML purists will no doubt tell you that this is a workaround that wastes bandwidth. Technically, they're correct—but the image is extremely small and will be cached by the browser, so it will only be downloaded once and then loaded from the user's cache when required.

Summary

In this chapter, we have explored how you can brighten up your web pages using images. We looked at the traditional techniques using the **<IMG>** element and its attributes. HTML 4.0 proposes to use the generic **<OBJECT>** element instead. This provides a whole new way to provide better support for all kinds of **inclusions**, and we cover this in chapter 9.

We also discussed the different graphic file formats that are widely supported by browsers, such as GIF, JPEG and PNG, looking at the advantages of each one. We also briefly outlined how you can create animated GIF images for your pages.

Finally, we looked at some examples of the `<IMG>` element in use.

Linking to Other Files

The heart of any HTML document is its hypertext links. These give your visitors the ability to retrieve or display a different document from your own or someone else's site simply by clicking the mouse on a word, phrase or image. They can also be used to send an email message to someone, or to download a resource other than an HTML page—such as a zip file. The abbreviation HTML itself means HyperText Markup Language, indicating the important position that hypertext links hold.

Your site will probably consist of several documents and other resources connected together via hypertext links. No single document should be so long that the reader has to constantly scroll up and down to find the information they need. Where possible, break large documents down into smaller parts to limit the amount of scrolling. This also has the advantage of reducing download time if the reader is interested in just part of the document. In this chapter we look at the different ways that you can use hypertext links

Creating Hypertext Links

To include a hypertext link within your document that loads another page, or resource all you need to know is that target document's unique address and how to include an **anchor** element in your HTML code. The anchor element is defined by an `<A>` tag, which can be used in a variety of ways. It's also possible to use other elements such as `<META>`, `<AREA>`, and `<LINK>` to reference other pages, as well as including the `<BASE>` element to define how the values in these attributes are used.

Uniform Resource Locators

Every single document or resource on the Internet (or your local Intranet or Extranet) has its location defined by a unique address. This is known as a **Uniform Resource Locator** or **URL**. URLs are made up of the server's communication protocol; the domain name of the server that holds the resource, and the document or resource path and filename:

```
protocol://server_domain_name/path/filename
```

The most common protocols are:

`http:` **Hypertext Transfer Protocol**; the protocol used for HTML documents and other resources on the World Wide Web.

`https:` A special version of HTTP where a secure connection has been established, and information is encrypted when being transmitted.

`ftp:` **File Transfer Protocol**; normally used to transfer files between special applications and a server. It provides file manager-like capabilities to the client when accessing the server.

`telnet:` A protocol used to transmit instructions and receive information from the server, as though the client were acting as a terminal on the network.

`gopher:` A protocol used for searching for and retrieving files. This has generally been superceded by HTTP and modern search engines.

`file:` This is used by most browsers to indicate that the source of the page is a local file, either on the local machine or on the network, that was loaded without using an Internet protocol—i.e. by double-clicking on it in a file manager application. If the file is on a network, it will be loaded via the default network transport protocol.

`mailto:` This is not really a true protocol at all either, but a way of indicating to the browser that it should prepare to send an email message.

The Type and Format of URLs

Some examples of URLs, or 'addresses' as they are sometimes known, are:

```
http://www.mycompany.com/docs/mydocument.html
http://www.wrox.com/books/
```

The first of these addresses is known as an **absolute** URL. This leaves nothing to chance because it includes all the parts of the URL format—protocol, server, pathname and document name. The second example is similar, but doesn't refer to an exact file, just a directory name. In this instance the server will return a previously configured default file, usually `index.html` or `default.htm`.

One other optional part of a URL is the **port number**. This defines the 'port' on the server that the particular protocol is attached to, and listening on. The default for HTTP is port `80`, and you rarely see other ones specified. However, it is required if the server has been configured to use a different port instead. An example is `http://www.secret.com/myfile.htm:800`.

*Note that the server will generally be configured with **alias** directories so that the path and filename in the address will not correspond with a physical directory on the server. For example, the URL `http://www.wrox.com/books/` may actually refer to the directory `G:\INET\ROOT\WEBSITE\BOOKS\` on the server.*

Secure Connections

Secure connections allow the information to be protected from prying eyes, and are often achieved through a technology called the **Secure Sockets Layer** (SSL). This is generally indicated in the browser with a message box and a 'lock' symbol in the status bar.

```
https://www.securesite.co.au/order.htm
```

This URL specifies the `https` protocol to a site that can establish a secure connection.

Server-side Scripts and Applications

These URLs specify pages that are not normal HTML files. They are generally scripts or applications that will be executed on the server, and which dynamically produce a page that is sent back to the browser.

```
http://myserver.co.uk/scripts/newstuff.pl
http://myserver.co.uk/scripts/newstuff.asp
http://myserver.co.uk/scripts/newstuff.exe
```

The file extension normally indicates the type of file, such as `.pl` for a Perl script, `.exe` for an application, and `.asp` for an Active Server Pages file.

Files for Downloading

If the server has the ability to provide a File Transfer Protocol service, the browser can download a file using this by specifying the FTP protocol:

```
ftp://ftp.shareware.com/pub/interesting.zip
```

This causes the server's FTP service to send the file `interesting.zip` back to the client machine, where it is stored as a file on the local system.

Sending Email

You can provide a hypertext link in your pages that is used by the viewer to send email. This depends on the browser having a suitable mail application installed, but generally works fine on most modern browsers:

```
mailto:feedback@wrox.com
```

Notice that there are no double 'slashes' in the address this time, because it is not a protocol, just an instruction to the browser to open the email application and insert the address after the colon into the 'To' box.

Most browsers have other installed applications available, or can handle some file types themselves, so that referencing a file of a suitable type will actually display the file, rather than downloading it and storing it on the client system. For example the URL `http://www.mysite.com/images/mydog.gif` *will usually display the image directly in the browser. Browsers may provide the user with the option to display various types of file, or to download them to a local or network disk.*

Relative URLs Inside an HTML Document

Inside an HTML document we can use an additional type of reference. Because the URL of the currently displayed document becomes the default address for the browser, we can use **relative** URLs to specify other documents or resources. The browser automatically calculates the full (absolute) URL and uses this to request the document.

For files in the same server directory as the current document, we just use the file name, or we can specify a subdirectory or the parent directory just as we would when providing a filename in ordinary local operating system environments:

```
mydog.html
dogs/yourdog.html
../images/mydogpic.jpg
```

The first of these is a reference to a file in the same server directory, the second to a page in the `dogs` subdirectory (below the current directory), and the third is a reference to a page stored in the `images` subdirectory of the parent directory.

It's a good idea to use relative URLs where possible because it allows you to move all the files to a new server without having to change any of the hyperlinks to specify the new server and/or domain name.

Anchors Within A Page

Finally, we can also include an anchor within a page so that, when we load the page, that part of the document is automatically scrolled into view. The anchor name is added to the URL after a hash `#` sign:

```
http://www.mysite.com/dogs/dogs.html#dalmation
```

This will load the page `dogs.html`, and scroll it to the section about Dalmatians, where an anchor tag has been placed with the name `dalmation`.

The HyperText Elements

In this section of the chapter, we'll examine the two main elements that are used for creating and executing hypertext links: the `<A>` and `<BASE>` elements.

The <A> Anchor Element

The `<A>` element is used to define both the source and destination of a hypertext link. Anything that appears between the start tag `<A>` and the end tag `</A>` becomes 'active' within the page, therefore, allowing the user to click on that area to load another page or resource. Hypertext links are not just limited to text. You can also use images as hyperlinks by placing the image between the anchor tags in the same way that you would place text.

The attributes supported by the **<A>** element are:

ACCESSKEY	**CHARSET**	**COORDS**	**HREF**	**HREFLANG**
NAME	**REL**	**REV**	**SHAPE**	**TABINDEX**
TARGET	**TYPE**			

plus the usual HTML 4.0 attributes; **ID**, **CLASS**, **TITLE**, **STYLE**, **DIR** and **LANG** as described in Chapter 1. In HTML 4.0, the **<A>** element also provides a series of **events** that can be used in scripting. (See Chapter 10 for more information about using script in your pages).

ACCESSKEY

This attribute specifies a keyboard character that can be pressed to activate the link and load the resource it references. The syntax is:

ACCESSKEY="*key***"**

where *key* is the keyboard character—such as **"J"**, which is pressed in conjunction with the *Alt* or *Command* key (depending on the client system). The value *key* is case-insensitive. This attribute is defined in HTML 4.0, but only implemented by Internet Explorer 4 at present.

CHARSET

This attribute defines the character encoding of the document that the hypertext link references, i.e. the page that will be loaded. The syntax is:

CHARSET="*character_set***"**

where *character_set* is a string containing a valid character set type. The default is "ISO-8859-1" (Latin) if not specified. It allows the browser or viewer to select a suitable language page without having to download it. This attribute is defined in HTML 4.0, but not implemented in current browsers.

COORDS

If the element is used with an image map, this attribute defines an area within the image and the URL it will reference when clicked. The syntax is:

COORDS="*coordinates_list***"**

where *coordinates_list* defines the area as a set of coordinates. We'll look at image maps and the associated attributes later in this chapter.

HREF

This indicates that the element is a hypertext jump, and specifies the URL of the resource that it references. The syntax is:

HREF="*url***"**

where *url* is the URL or address of the resource that will be loaded when the element is clicked.

HREFLANG

Specifies the language of the resource designated by **HREF** and can only be used when **HREF** is also defined.

HREFLANG= "*langcode*"

NAME

Indicates that the element is an anchor within a page that will allow other hypertext links to jump to it. The syntax is:

NAME= "*name*"

where *name* is a unique name within this document. The position of the element indicates the part of the document that will be scrolled into view when the browser references the element. We'll look at this in more depth later.

REL

Specifies a relative forward relationship between this document and the resource specified in the **HREF** attribute. The syntax is:

REL= "*relationship*"

where *relationship* is a string value defining how the two documents are connected. For more information on using relationships, refer to the **<LINK>** element in Chapter 1.

REV

Specifies the reverse relationship, in other words, the opposite of **REL**. The syntax is:

REV= "*relationship*"

where *relationship* describes the way that the two documents are related. For more information on using relationships, refer to the **<LINK>** element in Chapter 1.

SHAPE

If the element is used with an image map, this attribute defines the shape of the area that it references. The syntax is:

SHAPE= "*shape_name*"

where *shape_name* can be **DEFAULT**, **RECT**, **CIRC** or **POLY**. Some browsers also accept **RECTANGLE**, **CIRCLE** and **POLYGON** for this attribute. We'll look at image maps and the associated attributes later in this chapter.

TABINDEX

Indicates the position within the tabbing order of the page for this hypertext link. The syntax is:

TABINDEX=*number*

where *number* is the position in the tabbing order. When the user presses the *Tab* key, the input focus moves through all the elements that can receive it in turn, in the order they are declared in the HTML source. By setting the **TABINDEX** value you can change this order. Setting it to **-1** removes the element from the tabbing order altogether.

TARGET

Indicates that the document referenced by the **<A>** element should be loaded into the specified window or frame. The syntax is:

TARGET="*window_name***"**

where *window_name* is the name of an existing frame in a frameset (see Chapter 7), or a separate browser window. If a window or frame with this name does not exist, a new separate browser window is opened and the page is loaded into it. This allows you to open documents in a separate window, so that the user can browse that page and follow any links, then close the window and return to the original document.

The value for *window_name* can also be one of four special values:

_blank	Loads the link into a new browser window. This window is not named.
_parent	Loads the document into the immediate parent of the current document if there is one, or into the whole window if not.
_self	Loads the document into the current window.
_top	Loads the document into the main browser window.

> **To appreciate why some of these values are useful, you need to know about using frames in a browser. We'll cover frames in Chapter 7.**

TYPE

Specifies the MIME type for the link. The syntax is:

TYPE=*MIME-type*

Internet Explorer <A> Extensions

Internet Explorer adds three extra attributes to the **<A>** element:

DATAFLD and **DATASRC** are used in Internet Explorer 4 to link the element to a value from a data source cached on the client. This technique is known as data binding. We look briefly at this in Chapter 12.

METHODS provides information about the kind of information that the link references, in a similar fashion to the way that the **CHARSET** attribute supplies information about the referenced document's character set. For example, future browser may be able to chose different ways of displaying the link, perhaps it may get a different icon.

The <BASE> Element

When the browser requests a new page in response to a click on a hypertext link, it first checks to see if the URL in the link's **HREF** attribute is an **absolute** or **relative** link. If it's a relative link (i.e. doesn't include the protocol, server domain name and path) the browser uses default values for these parts of the URL to create the final URL for the request. These defaults are those of the currently loaded page.

Also, by default, the returned document is loaded into the same window or frame as the document that contained the hypertext link—unless a value for the **TARGET** attribute is specified in the **<A>** tag. However, we can specify different defaults for all these using the **<BASE>** element. It supports two attributes:

HREF **TARGET**

HREF

This attribute specifies the URL that will be used as the default. Generally you shouldn't include a filename, just the path required. The syntax is:

HREF="*url***"**

where *url* is the URL or address with which the browser will calculate absolute URLs for all the relative ones in the page. See the **<A>** element for more details.

TARGET

Indicates the window or frame in which all new documents will be loaded, unless the hypertext link specifies a different target. See the **<A>** element for more details.

The <BASE> element must be placed within the <HEAD> section of the page.

Other Linking Elements

There are two other elements that can be used to link pages together, and to load other pages. It's also possible to load another page using **scripting**, a subject we'll be covering in Chapter 10.

The <LINK> element (which we first met in Chapter 1) can provide information to the browser about where this page comes within the structure of other pages on your site. For example, if you have several pages that are normally read in order, you can indicate which is the previous one and which is the next one. You can also provide a link to the contents, and to other pages.

For example, adding the following to the <HEAD> section of **page3.html** provides this information:

```
<LINK REL="Next" HREF="page4.html">
<LINK REL="Previous" HREF="page2.html">
<LINK REL="Contents" HREF="contents.html">
<LINK REL="Copyright" HREF="mycompany.html">
<LINK REL="Help" HREF="helpindex.html">
```

The <LINK> element can also identify your page in the 'reverse direction', using the **REV** attribute. For example, the page **helpindex.html** may contain:

```
<LINK REV="Help" HREF="page3.html">
```

The other useful element is the <META> element, which provides many useful features. One of these is the ability to load another page after a pre-defined period. This can, for example, provide a slide-show type of effect, or just redirect visitors to a new version of your site:

```
<META HTTP-EQUIV="Refresh" CONTENT="30;URL=page4.html">
<META HTTP-EQUIV="Refresh" CONTENT="0;URL=http://www.newsite.com">
```

The **CONTENT** attribute in this case specifies the number of seconds to wait, followed by the URL of the page to load.

> **The <LINK> and <META> elements must be in the <HEAD> section of a page, and are used for several other tasks as well. They are both described in more detail in Chapter 1.**

Hypertext Link Examples

Have a look at the following example. This uses text as the hyperlink, and specifies the <BASE> that will be used to calculate the full absolute URL of the new page:

```
<HTML>
<HEAD>
<TITLE>A hypertext link</TITLE>
<BASE HREF="http://mysite.com/testpages/">
</HEAD>
<BODY>
Clicking <A HREF="nextpage.html">right here</A> will open
the page named nextpage.html that we created earlier.
</BODY>
</HTML>
```

If you open this in a browser, you see the following. The text within the <A> element is underlined and colored blue to indicate that it's 'clickable' and will load another page. Clicking on the words right here causes the browser to request the file **nextpage.html** and open it:

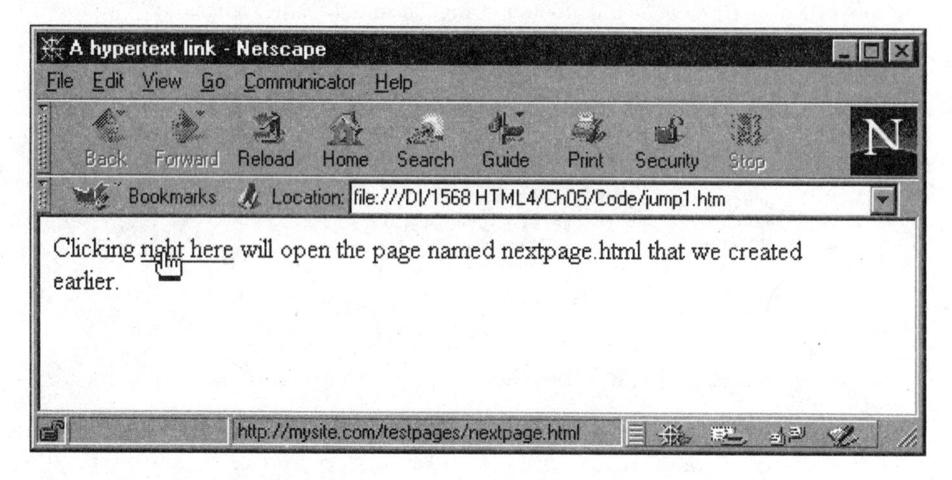

Specifying a Default URL

Notice how the browser indicates the presence of the link in other ways. The cursor changes to a hand (in Navigator) or another type of pointer, and the status bar shows the URL of the document that will be loaded.

It's here that you can see the results of the **<BASE>** element in the page. The browser's Location bar shows that the current page is a local file on the disk, namely **D:\1568HTML4\Ch05\Code\jump1.htm** (each browser displays local files in a different way, but usually with the **file:** dummy protocol). In the HTML source of this page, we only specified the name of the new file:

```
Clicking <A HREF="nextpage.html">right here</A> will open ...
```

The browser takes the **<BASE> HREF** which we specified in the **<HEAD>** section of the page:

```
<BASE HREF="http://mysite.com/testpages/">
```

and creates the new URL **http://mysite.com/testpages/nextpage.html**. We could, of course, have got the same effect by just specifying the **HREF** attribute as:

```
<A HREF="http://mysite.com/testpages/nextpage.html">right here</A>
```

Formatting and Positioning <A> Tags

One thing to watch out for is that all the text and content between the opening and closing **<A>** tags is rendered as a hypertext link. If we place the **</A>** tag after the space following a word, we get an extra lump of underline, which looks untidy:

```
Clicking <A HREF="nextpage.html">right here </A>will open
```

This can easily be avoided by always placing the tags directly before and after the first and last characters you want to include as 'active' text. It can also happen when we use other content for the element; an image, for example.

The other point to watch our for is that you can quite easily change the formatting of the text in a hyperlink using the `<FONT>` tag, the attributes of the `<BODY>` tag, or (more correctly in HTML 4.0) **styles** in a cascading style sheet. If you remove the underline and change the color it makes it difficult for your viewers to see what they can click on, and what they can't. The same applies if you format non-hyperlinked text using underlines and different colors.

Using Anchors in Your Pages

Now that we've seen how we can load another page, we'll see how we can use the `<A>` element to jump to specific parts of a page. Look at this HTML code fragment:

```
<HTML>
<HEAD><TITLE>The NAME attribute</TITLE></HEAD>
<BODY>

<H1> <A NAME="intro">List of contents</A> </H1>
<A HREF="#chapter1">Go to Chapter 1</A><P>
<A HREF="#chapter2">Go to Chapter 2</A><P>

<H2>Introduction</H2>
Part 1<BR>
Part 2<BR>
Part 3<BR>
Part 4<BR>
<A HREF="#intro">Back</A> to the top of this list<P>

<H2> <A NAME="chapter1">Chapter 1</A> </H2>
Part 1<BR>
Part 2<BR>
Part 3<BR>
Part 4<BR>
<A HREF="#intro">Back</A> to the introduction<P>

<H2> <A NAME="chapter2">Chapter 2</A> </H2>
Part 1<BR>
Part 2<BR>
Part 3<BR>
Part 4<BR>
<A HREF="#intro">Back</A> to the introduction

</BODY>
</HTML>
```

In it we have three main sections of content on a page, with the headings `Introduction`, `Chapter 1` and `Chapter 2`. The top of the page has the heading `List of Contents`. When viewed in the browser, it looks like this:

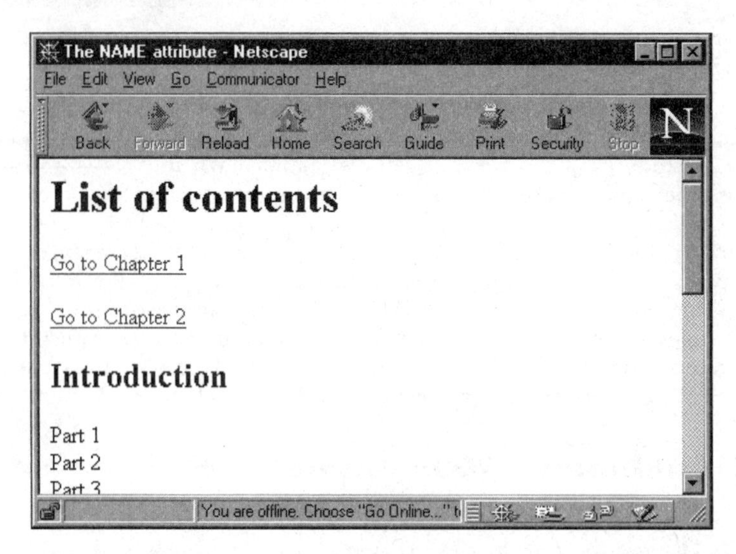

OK, so we have a small-sized window here, but we're simulating the situation where each section is considerably longer than our example code. Obviously, the reader will have to scroll the page to read it all. The two links at the top, however, allow them to go straight to either of the chapters.

At the end of each section, there is a corresponding link that scrolls the page back to the top again:

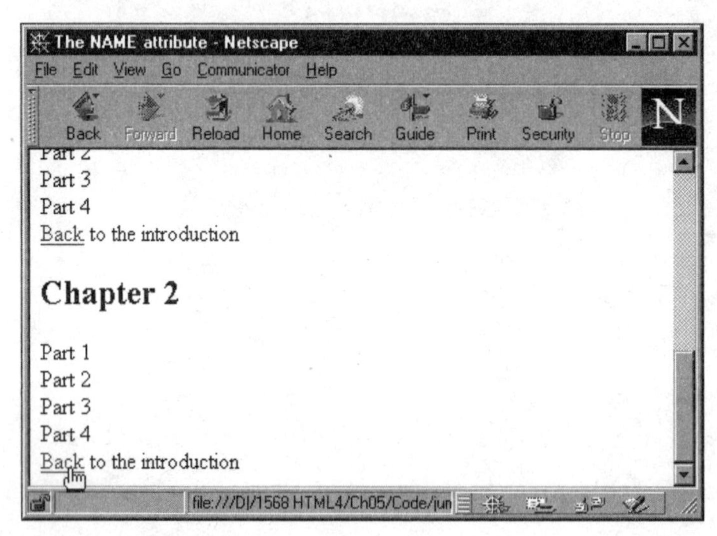

How the Example Works

This example shows the two ways that the `<A>` element can be used. At the top of the page is an anchor element that contains just the **`NAME`** attribute with the value **`"intro"`**. This connects the name **`intro`** with this point in the document, and we can then use it as a target to jump to. Notice that the content of the element (the words List of contents) is not rendered as a hypertext link, but in its normal format:

```
<H1> <A NAME="intro">List of contents</A> </H1>
...
```

The next two lines use the <A> element in the same way we did in the previous example—to create a hypertext link. The only difference is that now the **HREF** is the name of the anchor we want to jump to:

```
...
<A HREF="#chapter1">Go to Chapter 1</A><P>
<A HREF="#chapter2">Go to Chapter 2</A><P>
...
```

Here's the end section of the document, showing the anchor for the Chapter 2 link, and the hypertext link that jumps back to the list of contents:

```
...
<H2> <A NAME="chapter2">Chapter 2</A> </H2>
Part 1<BR>
Part 2<BR>
Part 3<BR>
Part 4<BR>
<A HREF="#intro">Back</A> to the introduction
```

Anchors in Different Pages

We aren't limited to jumping to an anchor in the same page. The **HREF** we used above—**"#intro"**—is simply a relative URL. Because the current page is the default URL for all the links it contains, we just get the same page again if we don't specify a different one in the **HREF** attribute. So **"#intro"** on the page **http://mysite.com/pages/mypage.html** is just a relative address that the browser expands to "**http://mysite.com/pages/mypage.html#intro**". If we provide a different page as the main part of the URL, the browser will load that page instead, then look for the anchor named **"#intro"** in it.

So, we could create pages that each contained three chapters of our 150 chapter book, and then go direct to any chapter by specifying the filename of the HTML page containing that chapter, and the name of an anchor element in the page at the start of the chapter. We could even create lots of anchors in each chapter to provide a kind of index.

More Techniques with Anchors

Most browsers will accept an empty anchor tag, and even one with no closing **</A>** tag:

```
<A NAME="chapter 1"></A> Chapter 1 ...  <- not recommended
<A NAME="chapter1"> Chapter 1 ...       <- illegal syntax
```

However, you should always include content and the closing **</A>** tag to ensure maximum compatibility for your pages. HTML 4.0 defines the closing tag as always required.

Of course, if the **<A>** tag describes a hypertext jump using the **HREF** attribute, it must have *some* content, otherwise, there is nothing to click on. And omitting the closing **</A>** tag in this case will cause the remainder of the page (up to the next **</A>** tag) to become part of the link.

It is possible to use both the **NAME** and **HREF** attributes in the same **<A>** element, if it needs to act as an anchor as well as a link:

```
<A HREF="#chapter2" NAME="intro">Go to Chapter 2</A><P>
...
...
<A HREF="#intro" NAME="chapter2">Back</A> to the introduction
```

Finally, the **ID** attribute can be used instead of the **NAME** attribute to assign a name to an **<A>** element:

```
<A ID="intro">Go to Chapter 2</A><P>
```

This is not widely supported, but there is no reason why you shouldn't include it anyway, together with the **NAME** attribute—just make sure that they are the same, and that this value is unique on the page:

```
<A ID="intro" NAME="intro">Go to Chapter 2</A><P>
```

Using Images as Hyperlinks

Using images as hyperlinks is easy once you know how to use text as a link. One important thing to remember is that the image needs to look as if it's 'clickable' (unless you are providing a page where you want the user to explore and discover disguised hyperlinks). The browser will normally add a border to an image, of the same color as the underline it provides for text, when it's used as a hyperlink. However, this can often spoil the appearance, especially when using transparent GIF images where the background shows through parts of the image.

As an example, here's part of the HTML source for our Web-Developers site at **http://www.rapid.wrox.com**. It uses both a graphic 'button' and a text description to provide links to one of the resources provided for this book:

```
<A HREF="/html4db/" TARGET="_top"><IMG HSPACE=5 BORDER=0
    SRC="wd_images/HtmlDB.gif" WIDTH=136 HEIGHT=20
    ALT="The Ultimate HTML Database"></A>
<BR>
<FONT FACE="Arial" SIZE=2><B>Check out the Wrox
<BR>
<A HREF="/html4db/" TARGET="_top">Ultimate HTML Reference</A>
<BR>database now!</B>
</FONT>
```

This is the result it produces. You can see that the image we've chosen does look as if it's 'clickable'—and the pointer changes to a hand when over it. To make sure people know what it is, even if their browser can't display the graphic, we've used the **ALT** attribute of the **<IMG>** tag to provide a pop-up tooltip:

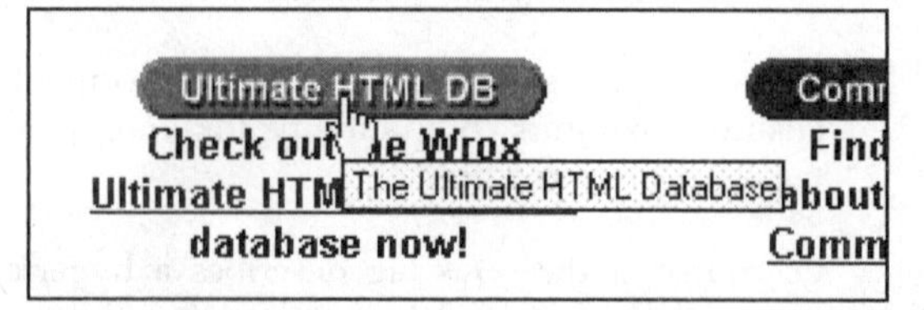

Hyperlink Image Borders

Below is another common use of image hyperlinks, to create a navigation bar or menu for a site. This example uses frames to divide the window up, a subject we'll be covering in chapter 7. In the meantime, look at the code for part of the navigation bar on our site:

```
...
<IMG BORDER=0 SRC="/navimages/webdevsm.gif"
 WIDTH=82 HEIGHT=76 ALT="web-dev.wrox">
<P>
<A HREF="/webdev/WhatsNew.asp" TARGET="mainframe"><IMG BORDER=0
 SRC="/navimages/home_dn.gif" WIDTH="81" HEIGHT="25" VSPACE="5"
 ALT="Web-Developer Home Page"></A>
<BR>
<A HREF="/webdev/BookList.asp" TARGET="mainframe"><IMG BORDER=0
 SRC="/navimages/samp_up.gif" WIDTH="81" HEIGHT="25" VSPACE="5"
 ALT="Books and Samples Page"></A>
<BR>
...
```

The first **<IMG>** element is simply the WEB-DEV logo at the top left. It is followed by a series of **<IMG>** elements that create the individual buttons. Each one of these is enclosed in an **<A>** element to turn it into a hyperlink, and the **TARGET** attribute is used to target the page to the other frame in the window. Here's the result:

By choosing an image that looks like a depressed button, we also indicate to the user which section of the site they're currently visiting. The page that creates this navigation bar is changed using **scripting** code automatically as visitors travel round the site—so that the correct button looks depressed. We examine some examples of scripting in Chapter 10.

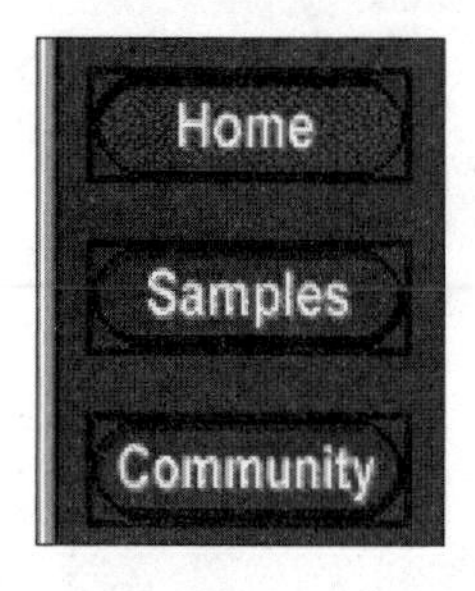

More important here is how we've used the **BORDER** attribute in the **<IMG>** element to prevent a border appearing. By default, images don't display a border. However, using one as the content of an **<A>** element causes the border to appear. This can often look untidy, especially with transparent GIF images. Setting **BORDER=0** prevents the border appearing.

Providing Alternate Text Links

In our first example in this section of the chapter, all the extra work we did making sure viewers realize that an image is 'clickable' wasn't really required, because there is a text link below the button as well. In other situations you may not provide a text link (as in our second example) so you should consider providing a full set of text links at the bottom of each page, as well as the graphical ones, within the main body of it. Our main *Wrox* sites do this in what is now the traditionally accepted way:

[HOME][HELP][CONTACT][SEARCH][DOWNLOAD][ORDER]
[Find By Subject] [Browse by Language] [Browse by Application]

The code that produces this is shown below. Notice that it references pages that are not normal HTML (**.html**) documents, but various kinds of server-side dynamic scripts:

```
<CENTER>
<FONT SIZE=2>
[ <A HREF="/scripts/Home.idc">H O M E</A> ]
[ <A HREF="/Help.stm">H E L P</A> ]
[ <A HREF="/Contact.stm">C O N T A C T</A> ]
[ <A HREF="/scripts/subjsearch.idc">S E A R C H</A> ]
[ <A HREF="/scripts/download.idc">D O W N L O A D</A> ]
[ <A HREF="/orders.stm">O R D E R</A> ]<BR>
[ <A HREF="/scripts/AllSubjects.idc">Find By Subject</A> ]
[ <A HREF="/languages.stm">Browse by Language</A> ]
[ <A HREF="/applications.stm">Browse by Application</A> ]
</FONT>
</CENTER>
```

Creating Image Maps

Image maps allow users to access different documents by clicking different *areas* in one image, rather than using several images. This is useful if the image is of a more 'artistic' nature than the simple button images we used in the earlier sections of this chapter. Image maps allows the author to provide links to various pages using different and complex shapes within a single image.

You can implement image maps in two ways: by storing image map information on the server; known as a **server-side image map**, or by including image map information in your document as a **client-side image map**. HTML 4.0 recommends that you use client-side image maps wherever possible.

Client-side Image Maps

Client-side image maps are defined within the HTML document. They can:

- be used offline
- reduce network traffic and server loading
- load more quickly
- show the destination for an area in the browser

Creating a Client-side Image Map

HTML 4.0 introduces the syntax of using an `<OBJECT>` element to display images and other objects (see Chapter 9). This element can display the image, and use the `<MAP>` and `<AREA>` elements to handle the resulting user interaction with it. However, in most current browsers there is little support for this use of `<OBJECT>`, and none at all in Netscape browsers up to and including version 4. We'll cover the more traditional techniques that use the `<IMG>` element here.

Until the new standards are more fully supported, you will generally use an `<IMG>` element to include a client-side image map in your document, along with the `<MAP>` and `<AREA>` elements. Together, these create the map definition, and define the links. The final step is to point the browser at the map using the **USEMAP** attribute of the `<IMG>` element that holds the image. The following code displays the image **map1.gif**, which uses the map section named **map1**:

```
<IMG BORDER=0 SRC="map1.gif" USEMAP="#map1">
...
<MAP NAME="map1">
  <AREA SHAPE="RECT" COORDS="0,0,16,16" HREF="Sample1.htm"
        ALT="View sample 1">
  <AREA SHAPE="RECT" COORDS="16,0,16,16" NOHREF>
  <AREA SHAPE="RECT" COORDS="0,16,16,16" HREF="Sample2.htm"
        ALT="View sample 2">
  <AREA SHAPE="RECT" COORDS="16,16,16,16"
        HREF="http://www.othersite.com/otherpage.htm"
        ALT="View another page on another site">
</MAP>
```

The `<MAP>` element encloses the `<AREA>` elements, and each of these defines one area within the image and connects it to the relevant document through a URL in the **HREF** attribute. Each `<AREA>` tag defines the shape of the 'active' area for that URL, and the alternative text for that link.

Using the <OBJECT> Element

To use the new HTML 4.0 syntax to create a client-side image map, we have two choices. The simplest is to replace the `<IMG>` element with an `<OBJECT>` element. This defines the image to display and uses the **USEMAP** attribute to point to the appropriate image map:

```
<OBJECT DATA="map1.gif" USEMAP="#map1"></OBJECT>
```

Alternatively, we can use the more 'correct' HTML 4.0 syntax. This replaces the **<AREA>** elements with normal **<A>** elements, therefore allowing us to use the extra attributes **SHAPE** and **COORDS** we met earlier in this chapter. Notice here that the alternative text is simply enclosed by the **<A>** and **</A>** tags:

```
<OBJECT DATA="map1.gif" SHAPES>
  <A HREF="Sample1.htm" SHAPE="RECT"
     COORDS="0,0,16,16">View sample 1</A>
  <A HREF="Sample2.htm" SHAPE="RECT"
     COORDS="0,16,16,16">View sample 2</A>
  <A HREF="http://www.othersite.com/otherpage.htm" SHAPE="RECT"
     COORDS="16,16,16,16>View another page on another site</A>
</OBJECT>
```

The <AREA> tag does not have a closing tag, so the alternative text in that case used the ALT attribute within the <AREA> tag.

Ways of using the **<OBJECT>** element to insert images into your documents is covered in depth in Chapter 9. Here, we'll look at the **<MAP>** and **<AREA>** elements next.

The <MAP> Element

The **<MAP>** element has the following attributes:

NAME

plus the usual HTML 4.0 attributes **ID**, **CLASS**, **TITLE** and **STYLE** as described in Chapter 1.

NAME

This attribute specifies the name of the map. The syntax is:

NAME="*name*"

where *name* is the name for the map, and is unique in this document. It is used together with the **USEMAP** attribute of the **<IMG>** tag to direct the browser to the correct map.

The <AREA> Element

The **<AREA>** element is used to define the different hot spots that the user can click on to load another document. This element has the following attributes:

ACCESSKEY ALT SHAPE COORDS HREF NOHREF TABINDEX TARGET

It also supports the universal attributes of **CLASS**, **ID**, **LANG**, **DIR**, **STYLE** and **TITLE**.

ACCESSKEY

This attribute specifies a keyboard character that can be pressed to activate the link, and load the resource it references. The syntax is:

ACCESSKEY="*key***"**

where *key* is the keyboard character, such as **"J"**, which is pressed in conjunction with the *Alt* or *Command* key (depending on the client system). The value *key* is case-insensitive. This attribute is defined in HTML 4.0, but only implemented by Internet Explorer 4 at present.

ALT

Specifies the text to display if the browser doesn't support graphics, or while the image is loading. The syntax is:

ALT="*text***"**

where *text* is the word or phrase to display.

SHAPE

Defines the shape of the active link. The syntax is:

SHAPE=*shape*

where *shape* is **RECT**, **CIRC** or **POLY**. The default is **RECT**.

In addition, you can use **SHAPE=DEFAULT** to provide a default target when a location outside any of your mapped shapes is selected. Some browsers also accept **RECTANGLE**, **CIRCLE** and **POLYGON** for this attribute.

COORDS

Defines the coordinates of the shape. The syntax is:

COORDS="*coordinate_list***"**

where *coordinate_list* is a string of *x* and *y* coordinates that define the shape within the image.

For **SHAPE=RECT** or **SHAPE=RECTANGLE** the syntax is:
COORDS="*left_x***,***top_y***,***right_x***,***bottom_y***"**

For **SHAPE=CIRC** or **SHAPE=CIRCLE** the syntax is:
COORDS="*center_x***,***center_y***,***radius***"**

For **SHAPE=POLY** or **SHAPE=POLYGON** the syntax is:
COORDS="*x1***,***y1***,***x2***,***y2***,***...etc***"** (i.e. a series of coordinate pairs that define the shape)

> **If the shapes you define overlap, the browser searches sequentially through the list of <AREA> elements in the map and uses the first one listed.**

HREF

Specifies the document or resource that will be loaded when the area of the image is clicked. The syntax is:

```
HREF="url"
```

where *url* is the URL or address of the document or resource.

NOHREF

Indicates that this area is not an active hyperlink. The syntax is simply:

```
NOHREF
```

When this area is clicked, no action is taken by the browser. It can be used to overlay inactive areas on top of other active ones (by defining it first in the list of areas), to provide finer control of the image map operation.

TABINDEX

Defines the position of each area within the tabbing order of the page. See the **<A>** element earlier in this chapter for more details.

TARGET

Defines the window or frame that the document defined by this area will be loaded into. See the **<A>** element earlier in this chapter for more details.

Extensions to the <AREA> Element

Internet Explorer supported the **NOTAB** attribute (which should always be avoided) in version 3.

In version 4, Navigator supports the **NAME** attribute for the **<AREA>** element as well as the HTML 4.0 attributes.

Server-side Image Maps

Even the oldest browsers support server-side image maps. However, they do have disadvantages when compared to the newer client-side image maps. The user must have access to the server where the information is stored in order to be able to activate the map. If they're working offline, the map won't work. On top of that, you have to make sure that the security settings give them the correct permissions to access the map and the server-based application that uses it.

Each time the map is clicked, the browser requests information from the server. This increases the time taken to process the mouse click as well as using bandwidth. Also, with client-side maps you get to see the URL your mouse pointer is hovering over, whereas with server-side maps you just see an x-y coordinate.

A server side image map requires three files:

- The image itself
- A file on the server containing the coordinates for the map
- A server script to process the request

> **Note that you should always supply text-based hyperlinks that correspond to the URLs defined by the image map for use by text-based browsers. You should also use the `ALT` attribute with the `<IMG>` element to inform text-based browsers that the image is in fact an image map.**

ImageMap HTML Code

To specify an image map in your HTML document, you use the following syntax:

```
<A HREF="http://mysite.com/mapdirectory/example.map">
  <IMG SRC="imagemap.gif" ISMAP ALT="Select a page to view">
</A>
```

Note the inclusion of the **`ISMAP`** attribute of the **`<IMG>`** tag. This is required to inform the browser that the image is a server-side image map. Also, the **`HREF`** attribute of the **`<A>`** tag points to the map file on the server, rather than to a URL as in the case of a normal hypertext link.

> **This is the only way to define a server-side image map in HTML 4.0, although it does suggest extensions to the `<A>` element (by providing the `ISMAP` attribute) that would allow it to be used inside an `<OBJECT>` element. This should be avoided and, wherever possible, you should aim to use client-side image maps instead.**

ImageMap Files

The **map** file is a plain text file which defines the different regions of your image, and is stored on the server with the script or application that handles it. There are two common formats for image maps: CERN and NCSA. CERN in Switzerland, and NCSA in America, both produced early versions of browsers which is where these formats originated. The CERN server can now be found on the W3C server at this address:

`http://www.w3.org/`

In addition, the popular Apache server uses a slightly different (but easier to use) format. Which one you use will depend upon your service provider. Both types allow you to define four kinds of region:

Circles Rectangles Polygons Points

To load a page when any area of the image that is not covered by one of the regions is clicked, you can use the keyword **default**. The syntax for the two types is different, as shown here:

NCSA Syntax:

default *url*
circle *url center-x,center-y radius*
rect *url left-x,top-y right-x,bottom-y*
poly *url x1,y1 x2,y2 x3,y3* **...** *xn,yn*
point *url x,y*

CERN Syntax:

default *url*
circle (*center-x*, *center-y*) *radius url*
rectangle (*left-x*, *top-y*) (*right-x*, *bottom-y*) *url*
polygon (*x1*, *y1*) (*x2*, *y2*) (*x3*, *y3*) ... (*xn*, *yn*) *url*
point (*x*, *y*) *url*

As you can see, the main difference is that the CERN map has parentheses around each pair of coordinates and the URL is at the end of each line. An example NCSA map might look like this:

```
default http://www.myserver.org/test/index.html
rect http://www.myserver.org/test/help.html 50,25 100,50
rect http://www.myserver.org/test/news.html 101,151 51,76
```

This would define two rectangular areas on the image, one referencing **help.html** the other **news.html**. If the user clicks on an area of the image that is not covered by the two rectangles, the default URL **index.html** will be referenced.

For more information, you should consult your service provider, or visit these addresses:

- **http://www.w3.org/hypertext/WWW/Daemon/Status.html** - the CERN server
- **http://hoohoo.ncsa.uiuc.edu/** - the NCSA server
- **http://www.apache.org/** - the Apache server.

Creating the Map Definition

Irrespective of whether you use client-side or server-side image maps, you still need to be able to create the definitions for each area within your image. You can do this with a normal graphics package, such as Windows Paint or an equivalent. PaintShop Pro is a popular tool, which we mentioned in the chapter on creating graphics.

There are also several good utility programs available that can do most of the work for you when it comes to generating the map file. They will display the image, and let you draw the 'active' areas on it. The program then generates the map definition for you, in the format you request. All you have to do is copy it to your page, or upload it to the server.

MapThis! is a good freeware program for this purpose; it can be found at **`http://www.vmi.edu/mpths131.exe`**.

Microsoft also provide a series of utilities within their FrontPage Web development package, including the GIF Animator, and tools to help with creating image maps. Visit their Web site at **`http://www.microsoft.com/frontpage/`**

Summary

This chapter has shown you how to add hypertext links to your documents. We introduced URLs (Uniform Resource Locators), which are the addresses used to uniquely identify the location of a document. We looked at how they are referenced within a browser using the **`<A>`** tag, which can refer to both the source and destination of a link. In particular, we saw how the **`NAME`** attribute can be used to jump to a specific location within a document. We also examined ways that images are used instead of text to create more attractive links between documents. Lastly, we looked at how image maps work, and how they can be used as hypertext links—both server-side and on the client.

Chapter 6

Tables

HTML Tables have been supported by Netscape Navigator and Internet Explorer since their respective version 2 browsers, and were included in the W3C HTML 3.2 standard. The original simple table elements are also compatible with Netscape Navigator 1.1. However, HTML 4.0 and the two new version 4 browsers add new capabilities to tables. The draft W3C standards go beyond the support currently provided by Navigator, while Internet Explorer supports almost all the new elements and attributes.

One topic that is currently under discussion for inclusion in HTML 4.0 is the dynamic linking of tables to client-side cached data supplied from the server, so that the data can be presented automatically in tabular format. This was originally proposed by Microsoft, and is supported in Internet Explorer 4.0. The technique is called data binding, and we explore it briefly in Chapter 12.

The HTML 4.0 draft standards also introduce the concept of a real 'behind-the-scenes' structure for a table, as well as the visible appearance that is created by the HTML elements. This provides opportunities for identifying cells by their row and column, and creating intelligent tables where the header and footer are fixed on the page and the body contents can be scrolled.

Creating Tables

You can use tables for many different purposes. The obvious use is for structuring information, such as a timetable, numerical results, technical data etc. The individual cells can contain almost any other HTML elements, meaning that they can also be used to improve the layout of your document—for example, you can use tables to place text in columns like a newspaper, or to align images.

The Structure of a Table

All tables are contained within the **<TABLE>** and **</TABLE>** element tags. Within this element, you use other tags to create individual row and cell elements, specifying how many columns and rows there are, and what kind of cell each one is, as well as the data that each cell contains.

The complete outline structure of a table is shown below. You don't have to include all the elements, however this shows the order that they must appear in if present:

```
<TABLE>
  <CAPTION>
    ... table caption goes here ...
  </CAPTION>
  <COLGROUP>
    <COL>
  </COLGROUP>
  <THEAD>
    <TR>
      <TH>
        ... content for heading cell goes here ...
      </TH>
    </TR>
  </THEAD>
  <TFOOT>
    <TR>
      <TD>
        ... content for footer cell goes here ...
      </TD>
    </TR>
  </TFOOT>
  <TBODY>
    <TR>
      <TD>
        ... content for table body cell goes here ...
      </TD>
    </TR>
  </TBODY>
</TABLE>
```

The actual contents you want to display are placed only in the **<TH>** and **<TD>** elements. Many of the closing element tags are optional, as shown by the unshaded lines in the listing above. However, some browsers can become confused if you omit the final closing tag of each type (such as the last **</TD>** or **</TR>** tag), so it is good practice to include all the closing tags.

> **The closing </CAPTION> tag is *always* required when the <CAPTION> element is present. Also note that Netscape Navigator does not support the <THEAD>, <TFOOT> and <TBODY> elements in the versions up to and including version 4.**

A Basic Table Example

Tables consist of a number of rows and columns, and you define these with the **<TR>** (table row) and **<TD>** (table data) tags. The **<TR>** tag indicates the start of a new row, and doesn't require an end tag because the next **<TR>** tag automatically implies that the previous row has ended. The **<TD>** tag starts a new cell within a row, and again, doesn't require an end tag. However, in our first example, we're using them all to make sure the table displays correctly in all browsers. Have a look at the following code:

```
<HTML>
<HEAD>
  <TITLE>A basic table</TITLE>
```

```
  </HEAD>
  <BODY>
    <TABLE>
      <CAPTION>
        Some of the things we write about:
      </CAPTION>
      <TR>
        <TD>
          Dynamic HTML
        </TD>
        <TD>
          The best way to create interactive Web pages
        </TD>
      </TR>
      <TR>
        <TD>
          Active Server Pages
        </TD>
        <TD>
          An easy way to program Web pages on the server
        </TD>
      </TR>
    </TABLE>
  </BODY>
  </HTML>
```

This uses only the basic elements for creating a table, and produces this result:

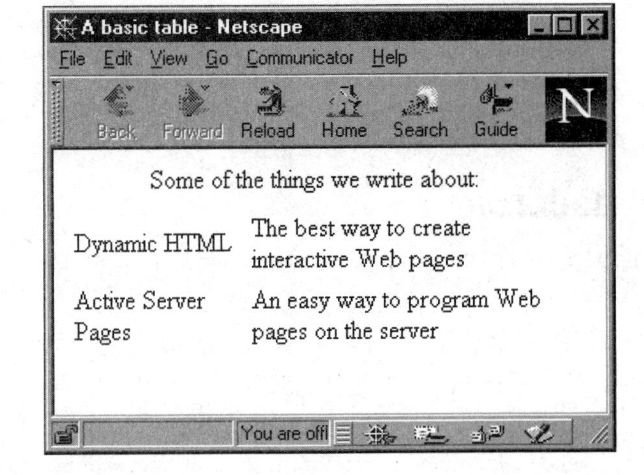

Note that, by default, the table and the contents are all left-aligned, while the caption is placed above and centered on the table. Also notice that the contents wrap around within the cell if they are too long to fit on one line. The contents are also centered vertically within the cells if they don't actually fill them, as you can see in the cell at the top left of the table.

Later in this chapter we'll look at some more complex examples of tables, and see how we format them to make them more attractive.

The HTML Table Elements

To create more sophisticated tables, you need to be aware of the full set of attributes that you can use with the table elements. We'll look at these now.

The <TABLE> Element

You can specify the following attributes for the **<TABLE>** element. These affect the entire table:

ALIGN	BGCOLOR	BORDER	CELLPADDING	CELLSPACING
FRAME	RULES	SUMMARY	WIDTH	

plus the standard HTML 4.0 attributes **ID**, **STYLE**, **CLASS**, **TITLE**, **DIR** and **LANG**. The **<TABLE>** element also provides several events that can be used in scripting. (See Chapter 10 for information about scripting). HTML 4 also proposes the **SUMMARY** attribute to provide a summary of the table's purpose and structure for user applications that are rendering the table to non-visual media, such as speech and Braille.

ALIGN

Defines the alignment of the complete table itself, relative to the page that contains it. The syntax is:

ALIGN=*type*

where type is either **LEFT**, **RIGHT** or **CENTER**. The default is **LEFT**. If you use **ALIGN=LEFT** or **ALIGN=right**, text will flow round the table. To avoid this use **<BR CLEAR=value>** after the **</TABLE>** tag, where value is left or right. This attribute is deprecated in HTML 4.0—you should now use style sheets to position elements on the page.

BGCOLOR

Specifies the background color for the table. The syntax is:

BGCOLOR=*color*

where *color* is the color, expressed either as a standard color name such as **"aliceblue"**; or as a numeric value in the form **"#***rrggbb***"** where the hexadecimal values for the red, green and blue components of each color are provided. Browsers offer varying levels of support for other numeric formats and color names, but for maximum compatibility use the **"#***rrggbb***"** format. It is deprecated in HTML 4.0—style sheets should now be used.

BORDER

Draws a border round both the table itself, and all the individual cells in it. The syntax is:

BORDER=*n*

where *n* is the width of the border in pixels. Setting **BORDER=0**, or omitting the attribute, results in no visible border. Using **BORDER** on its own, with no value, gives a border width of 1 pixel. This attribute is deprecated in HTML 4.0 and only supported for backward compatibility—style sheets should now be used instead.

CELLPADDING

Specifies the amount of space between all four edges of a cell and its contents. The syntax is:

CELLPADDING=*n*

where *n* is the amount of space in pixels. For a percentage value append the **%** percent sign. This is useful if you use colored backgrounds, otherwise the text content of the cell starts at the very edge of the colored area.

CELLSPACING

Specifies the amount of space between the individual cell boundaries in the table. The syntax is:

CELLSPACING=*n*

where *n* is the amount of space in pixels. For a percentage value append the **%** percent sign.

FRAME

Specifies which outer borders of the table are displayed, and allows more precise control than the **BORDER** attribute. The syntax is:

FRAME=*type*

where *type* can be one of the following:

VOID	No outer borders are displayed.
ABOVE	Displays the top border.
BELOW	Displays the bottom border.
HSIDES	Displays the top and bottom borders.
LHS	Displays the left border.
RHS	Displays the right border.
VSIDES	Displays the left and right borders.
BOX	Displays a border on all sides of the table frame.
BORDER	Displays a border on all sides of the table frame.

The default is **VOID**. The **FRAME** attribute defines only the outer border around the table. If both the **FRAME** and **BORDER** attributes are used, **FRAME** takes precedence. Using the **BORDER** attribute with no value has the same effect as **FRAME=BORDER**, while, **BORDER=0** has the same effect as **FRAME=VOID**. Note that this attribute is deprecated in HTML 4.0 and only supported for backward compatibility—style sheets now should be used instead.

RULES

Specifies which inner borders of the table are displayed. The syntax is:

RULES=*type*

where *type* is one of the following:

NONE	*Default*. No inner borders are displayed.
GROUPS	Displays inner borders between all table groups. Groups are specified by the **<THEAD>**, **<TBODY>**, **<TFOOT>** and **<COLGROUP>** elements.
ROWS	Displays horizontal borders between all table rows.
COLS	Displays vertical borders between all table columns.
ALL	Displays a border for all rows and columns.

The default is **NONE**. The **RULES** attribute defines only the inner borders of the table. This attribute is deprecated in HTML 4.0 and only supported for backward compatibility—style sheets should now be used.

SUMMARY

Provides a summary of the table's purpose and structure for browsers rendering non-visual media such as either speech or Braille. This isn't present in either IE4 or Navigator 4 yet.

SUMMARY=*text*

WIDTH

Sets the width of the table. The syntax is:

WIDTH=*n*

where *n* is the width in pixels or as a percentage of the window. To set a percentage you must append a **%** sign to the end of the value. This attribute is deprecated in HTML 4.0 and only supported for backward compatibility—style sheets should now be used.

Navigator <TABLE> Extensions

Navigator supports two other attributes for the **<TABLE>** tag:

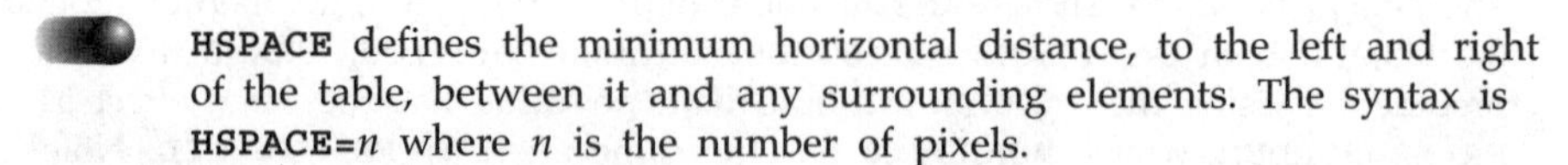

HSPACE defines the minimum horizontal distance, to the left and right of the table, between it and any surrounding elements. The syntax is **HSPACE=***n* where *n* is the number of pixels.

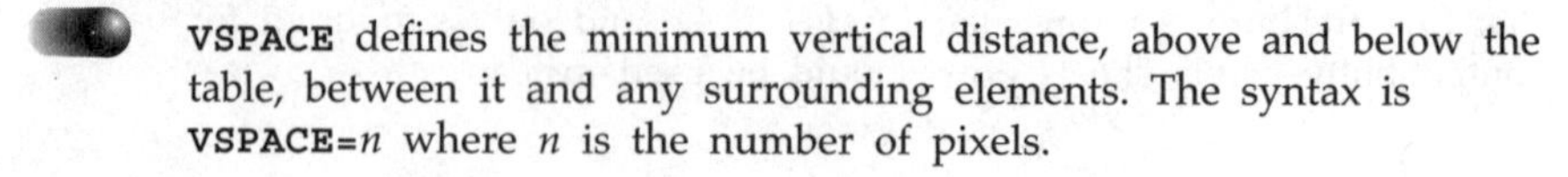

VSPACE defines the minimum vertical distance, above and below the table, between it and any surrounding elements. The syntax is **VSPACE=***n* where *n* is the number of pixels.

Internet Explorer <TABLE> Extensions

Internet Explorer supports six other attributes for the **<TABLE>** tag:

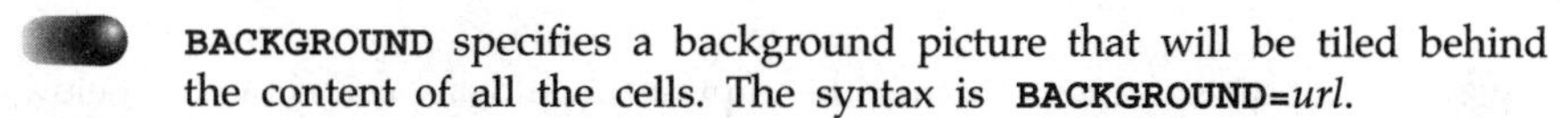

- **BACKGROUND** specifies a background picture that will be tiled behind the content of all the cells. The syntax is **BACKGROUND=***url*.
- **BORDERCOLOR** specifies the color of the table border. The syntax is **BORDERCOLOR=***color* where *color* can be a pre-defined color name or a set of hexadecimal values in the format **"#***rrggbb***"**.
- **BORDERCOLORDARK** and **BORDERCOLORLIGHT** allow you to specify the colors used when a table is rendered with 3-D borders in Internet Explorer. By swapping the usual colors over, you can provide an etched appearance rather than the usual raised border. See the examples later in this chapter.
- **DATAPAGESIZE** and **DATASRC** are used when the table is connected to cached client-side data in data binding. See Chapter 12 for a brief description of this technique.

The <CAPTION> Element

This element is used to describe the contents of the table, and provides a caption that is displayed next to, or above or below, the table. The element is optional, but if included must come directly after the opening **<TABLE>** tag.

The **<CAPTION>** element accepts the single attribute: **ALIGN**

plus the standard HTML 4.0 attributes **ID**, **STYLE**, **CLASS**, **TITLE**, **DIR** and **LANG**. The **<CAPTION>** element also provides several events that can be used in scripting. (See Chapter 10 for information about scripting).

ALIGN

Specifies the position of the caption in relation to the whole table. The syntax is:

ALIGN=*type*

where *type* can be one of:

TOP	Places the caption above the table.
BOTTOM	Places the caption below the table.
LEFT	Places the caption to the left of the table.
RIGHT	Places the caption to the right of the table.

Note that current browsers often use the **<CAPTION>** element in different ways from the HTML 4.0 proposals.

Extensions to the <CAPTION> Element

Current browsers generally use an extra attribute to the **<CAPTION>** element, and implement the **ALIGN** attribute in a different way:

VALIGN specifies whether the caption should appear above or below the table. The syntax is **VALIGN=***vtype*, where *vtype* can be **TOP** (the default) or **BOTTOM**.

In this case, the **LEFT** and **RIGHT** values will only align the caption in relation to the width of the table, rather than placing it physically to the left or right of the whole table. The **VALIGN** attribute is then included to control whether the caption appears above or below the table. Often the extra value **CENTER** is added to the **ALIGN** attribute to center-align the caption above or below the table.

The <THEAD>, <TFOOT> and <TBODY> Elements

HTML 3.2 introduced the concept of dividing a table into three sections; the **head**, **body** and **foot**, and this has been developed in HTML 4.0. This division of the content of the table into sections allows the browser to lay out the table in special ways so that, for example, the body section can scroll while the header and footer rows are fixed (although current browsers do not yet support this).

It also allows the browser to add appropriate header and footer sections to each page while printing the content as hard copy, or perhaps when exporting it to other applications. Above all, it also provides internal structure, which allows non-visual user agents or automated page readers to get information about the content. Notice that the correct ordering of the elements in the HTML is to have the **<TFOOT>** section before the **<TBODY>** section. This helps the browser lay out the table more quickly.

The entire **<THEAD>**, **<TBODY>** and **<TFOOT>** elements can be omitted if required, and in this case the table is assumed to consist of a single **<TBODY>** element. Note that the optional end tag **</THEAD>** can only be omitted when the next tag is either **<TFOOT>** or **<TBODY>**. Likewise, the optional end tag **</TFOOT>** can only be omitted when the next tag is **<TBODY>**.

The **<THEAD>**, **<TBODY>** and **<TFOOT>** elements support the following attributes, which are inherited by all the cells in that section, unless over-ridden within the row or cell:

ALIGN **CHAR** **CHAROFF** **VALIGN**

plus the standard HTML 4.0 attributes—**ID**, **STYLE**, **CLASS**, **TITLE**, **DIR** and **LANG**. The **<THEAD>**, **<TBODY>** and **<TFOOT>** elements also provide several events that can be used in scripting. (See chapter 10 for information about scripting).

ALIGN

Defines the alignment of the content of all the cells in this section of the table. The syntax is:

ALIGN=*type*

where *type* is one of:

LEFT	Cell contents are left aligned.
RIGHT	Cell contents are right aligned.
CENTER	Contents are centered horizontally within the cell.
JUSTIFY	Text content is justified to fill the cell.
CHAR	Cell contents are aligned horizontally around a specified character.

The default is **LEFT** for body and footer cells, and (usually) **CENTER** for header cells. The value is inherited by the individual rows and cells within that section. When *type* is **CHAR**, the text contents are aligned so that the first instances of a specified character in each cell are placed vertically above each other. For more details see the **CHAR** and **CHAROFF** attributes below. Note that most current browsers do not support the values **JUSTIFY** and **CHAR** for **ALIGN**.

CHAR

Specifies the character that will be used to align the text contents of the cells in each column. The syntax is:

CHAR="*character*"

where *character* is the **axis** character that will be used for the alignment. Special values can be used, such as **CHAR="."** which will align the contents so that values line up on the decimal place, depending on the language specified for the page or element. **CHAR="***letter***"** will align the contents on the first instance of the character *letter* in the content (the comparison is case-sensitive). Note that most browsers do not support this attribute at present.

CHAROFF

Specifies the offset to the first occurrence of the character specifies by the **CHAR** attribute. The syntax is:

CHAROFF=*offset*

where offset is the number of characters to offset the axis character. If a percentage of the text length is required as the offset, a **%** percent sign must be appended to the value. If the **CHAR** attribute is present and this attribute is omitted, the contents are shifted so that the text before the axis character in all the columns is visible. Note that most browsers do not support this attribute at present.

VALIGN

Specifies the vertical alignment of the content within the cells in that section. The syntax is:

VALIGN=*type*

where *type* can be:

TOP	Places the content at the top of the cells.
MIDDLE	Centers the text vertically within the cells. Note that some browsers use **CENTER** instead of **MIDDLE** for this attribute value.
BOTTOM	Places the content at the bottom of the cells.
BASELINE	Aligns the content so that the first line of text in each cell starts on the same horizontal line.

Internet Explorer Attribute Extensions

Internet Explorer adds another attribute to the **<THEAD>**, **<TBODY>** and **<TFOOT>** elements:

BGCOLOR defines the color for the background of the cells in that section of the table. See the **<TABLE>** element for details. This attribute is deprecated in HTML 4.0.

The <TR> Element

The **<TR>** element defines the start of a table row, which can contain either **<TH>** or **<TD>** elements. A complete table, or a **<THEAD>**, **<TBODY>** or **<TFOOT>** section, consists of one or more **<TR>** elements. Anything between the first **<TR>** element and the next will be on the same row. The optional end tag **</TR>** can be omitted, although this may cause some browsers to display the table incorrectly.

The **<TR>** element supports five attributes that control the presentation of the content within the row, and which are inherited by all the cells in this row unless over-ridden in the individual **<TD>** or **<TH>** elements. The attributes for **<TR>** are:

ALIGN **BGCOLOR** **CHAR** **CHAROFF** **VALIGN**

plus the standard HTML 4.0 attributes **ID**, **STYLE**, **CLASS**, **TITLE**, **DIR** and **LANG**. The **<TR>** element also provides several events that can be used in scripting. (See Chapter 10 for information about scripting).

ALIGN

Defines the alignment of the content of all the cells in this section of the table. See the section on the **<THEAD>**, **<TBODY>** and **<TFOOT>** elements for details.

BGCOLOR

Specifies the background color for the table. See the section on the **<TABLE>** element for details. This attribute is deprecated in HTML 4.0 and you should use style sheets instead.

CHAR

Specifies the character that will be used to align the text contents of the cells in this column. See the section on the **<THEAD>**, **<TBODY>** and **<TFOOT>** elements for details.

CHAROFF

Specifies the offset to the first occurrence of the character set in the **CHAR** attribute. See the section on the **<THEAD>**, **<TBODY>** and **<TFOOT>** elements for details.

VALIGN

Specifies the vertical alignment of the content within the cells in this section. See the section on the **<THEAD>**, **<TBODY>** and **<TFOOT>** elements for details.

Internet Explorer <TR> Extensions

Internet Explorer adds three more attributes to the **<TR>** element:

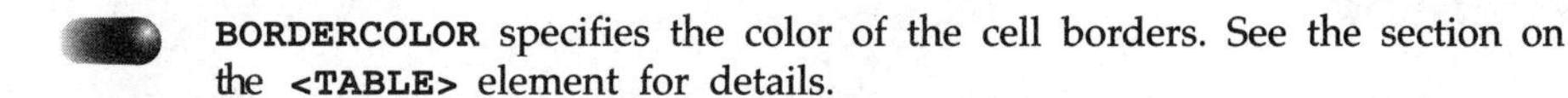

- **BORDERCOLOR** specifies the color of the cell borders. See the section on the **<TABLE>** element for details.

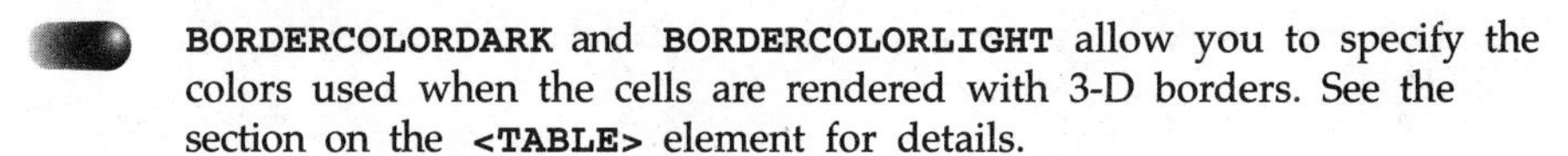

- **BORDERCOLORDARK** and **BORDERCOLORLIGHT** allow you to specify the colors used when the cells are rendered with 3-D borders. See the section on the **<TABLE>** element for details.

The <TH> and <TD> Elements

The **<TH>** and **<TD>** elements define an individual cell within a table row. **<TH>** elements are used for table headings, and the contents are usually displayed in a different way—generally in bold text and centered, whereas the default for a **<TD>** element is usually left-aligned.

Both have corresponding optional end tags **</TH>** and **</TD>** which can be omitted. Anything between one **<TH>** or **<TD>** tag and the next is displayed in that cell. Note, however, that this may cause some browsers to display the table incorrectly.

The **<TH>** and **<TD>** elements have a set of attributes that affect only that cell. These take precedence over the same attributes set by the enclosing **<TR>**, **<THEAD>**, **<TBODY>**, **<TFOOT>** and **<TABLE>** tags. The attributes supported by **<TH>** and **<TD>** are:

ABBR **ALIGN** **AXIS** **BGCOLOR** **CHAR** **CHAROFF**
COLSPAN **HEADERS** **NOWRAP** **ROWSPAN** **SCOPE** **VALIGN**

plus the standard HTML 4.0 attributes **ID**, **STYLE**, **CLASS**, **TITLE**, **DIR** and **LANG**. The **<TH>** and **<TD>** elements also provide several events that can be used in scripting. (See Chapter 10 for information about scripting).

ABBR

Provide an abbreviated version of the cell's content. This isn't supported in IE4 or Navigator 4.

ABBR=*text*

ALIGN

Defines the alignment of the content of the cell. See the section on the **<THEAD>**, **<TBODY>** and **<TFOOT>** elements for details.

AXIS

This attribute provides a way of assigning a name to a cell. The syntax is:

AXIS="*cellname*"

where *cellname* is a name for the cell. This can be used by a program that converts files to another format to identify the cell or column (if it is a **<TH>** cell). The most important use, however, is to allow the web page author to specify which column and row a cell's contents should be associated with. This makes it useful for programs that convert the page to speech. If omitted, the content of the cell is used as the **AXIS**.

BGCOLOR

Specifies the background color of the cell. See the section on the **<TABLE>** element for details. It is deprecated in HTML 4.0—style sheets should now be used.

CHAR

Specifies the character that will be used to align the text contents of the cell. See the section on the **<THEAD>**, **<TBODY>** and **<TFOOT>** elements for details.

CHAROFF

Specifies the offset to the first occurrence of the character specified in the **CHAR** attribute. See the section on the **<THEAD>**, **<TBODY>** and **<TFOOT>** elements for details.

COLSPAN

This attribute specifies the number of columns in the table that the cell will span. The syntax is:

COLSPAN=*n*

where *n* is the number of columns to span. **COLSPAN** allows you to join cells, just like you can in a spreadsheet program. It provides, for example, a way to place a heading or content across several columns to provide richer layout.

HEADERS

Specifies a list of header cells that provide header information for the current cell. The value of this attribute is a space-separated list of cell names and the cells must be named by setting their **ID** attribute. This attribute is not yet supported in IE4 or Navigator 4.

HEADERS=*idrefs*

ROWSPAN

This attribute specifies the number of rows in the table that the cell will span. The syntax is:

ROWSPAN=*n*

where *n* is the number of rows to span. Like **COLSPAN**, **ROWSPAN** allows you to join cells; but this time spanning over adjacent cells vertically rather than horizontally.

NOWRAP

The **NOWRAP** attribute stops the text from wrapping in the cell. The syntax is simply:

NOWRAP

This attribute is useful for laying out text content that would not make sense if allowed to wrap to the next line. It also provides some control over the way the available page width is distributed between the columns in the table. Use it with caution, however, because it can easily force the table to be wider that the available window width, therefore forcing the user to scroll the page sideways. Note that **NOWRAP** is deprecated in HTML 4.0, and supported for backward compatibility only—use style sheets now.

SCOPE

Specifies the set of data cells for which the current header cell provides header information. Can be used in place of the **HEADERS** attribute in simple tables. This isn't supported in IE4 or Navigator 4.

SCOPE=ROW | COL | ROWGROUP | COLGROUP

VALIGN

Specifies the vertical alignment of the content within the cell. See the section on the **<THEAD>**, **<TBODY>** and **<TFOOT>** elements for details.

Extensions to the <TH> and <TD> Elements

At various times in both the HTML specifications and the two browsers Netscape Navigator and Internet Explorer, two more attributes for **<TH>** and **<TD>** have appeared and then disappeared again. Neither are in the current HTML 4.0 proposals, and their use is not advisable if you intend to maximize the compatibility of your pages:

HEIGHT and **WIDTH** specify the size of an individual cell, either in pixels or as a percentage if the % percent sign is appended. Not supported in most browsers or HTML 4.0.

Internet Explorer <TH> and <TD> Extensions

Internet Explorer adds four more attributes to the **<TH>** and **<TD>** elements:

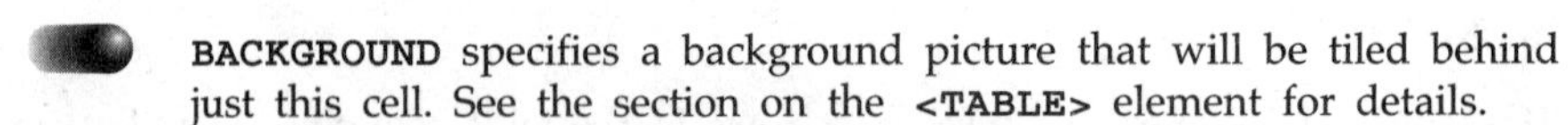

BACKGROUND specifies a background picture that will be tiled behind just this cell. See the section on the **<TABLE>** element for details.

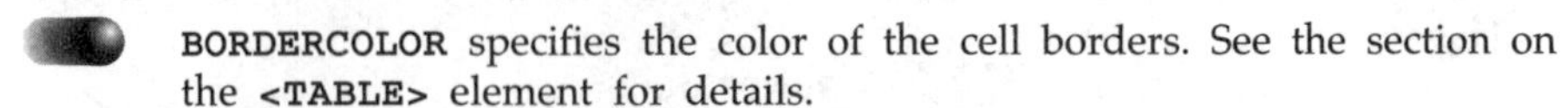

BORDERCOLOR specifies the color of the cell borders. See the section on the **<TABLE>** element for details.

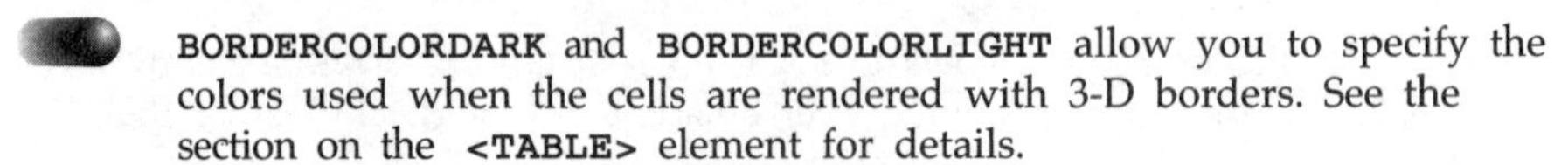

BORDERCOLORDARK and **BORDERCOLORLIGHT** allow you to specify the colors used when the cells are rendered with 3-D borders. See the section on the **<TABLE>** element for details.

Column Grouping Elements

The final two elements used in tables are **<COLGROUP>** and **<COL>**. They provide a way of grouping adjacent columns together, and applying formatting to them as a group rather than having to format each column separately. They are generally used in more complex tables, for example, where a set of adjacent columns contain similar kinds of information, while other groups of columns contain different types of information.

Using Column Grouping

As an example, if we were providing information about the location of printers in a company's offices we might use a table like this:

```
<HTML>
<HEAD>
<TITLE>Printer Locations</TITLE>
</HEAD>
<BODY>
<TABLE BORDER=1 CELLPADDING=5
       BORDERCOLORLIGHT="black" BORDERCOLORDARK="white">
  <CAPTION ALIGN=LEFT><B>Printer Locations</B></CAPTION>
  <TR ALIGN=CENTER>
    <TH><TH COLSPAN=3> Inkjet
    <TH COLSPAN=2> Laser
  <TR ALIGN=CENTER>
    <TH><TH>Original<TH>500<TH>600<TH>2ppm<TH>4ppm
  <TR ALIGN=CENTER>
    <TD><B>Software</B><TD>0<TD>2<TD>1<TD>0<TD>2
  <TR ALIGN=CENTER>
    <TD><B>Hardware</B><TD>1<TD>1<TD>0<TD>1<TD>0
  <TR ALIGN=CENTER>
    <TD><B>Sales</B><TD>0<TD>0<TD>0<TD>1<TD>1
  <TR ALIGN=CENTER>
    <TD><B>Admin<BR>Office</B><TD>0<TD>2<TD>0<TD>0<TD>0
</TABLE>
</BODY>
</HTML>
```

We've used **BORDER=1** to show all the borders, and **CELLPADDING=5** to prevent the content looking too cramped within the cells. Each row in the table uses **ALIGN=CENTER** so the text in every cell in that row is centered. Notice also how we've used the **BORDERCOLORLIGHT** and **BORDERCOLORDARK** attributes to create an etched table. This only works in Internet Explorer 4:

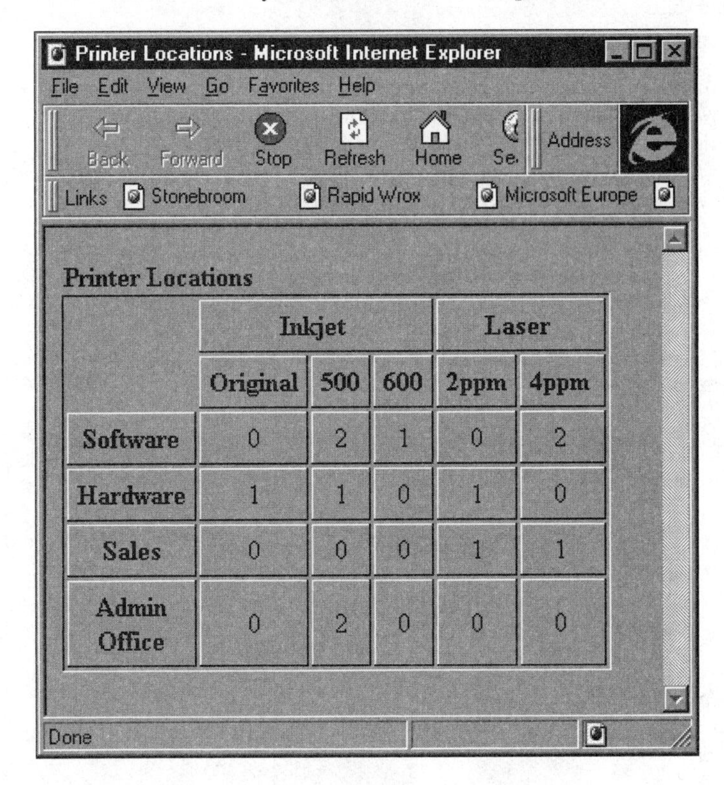

Applying the Groups

Rather than having borders around all the cells, we can include only borders that break the table into groups of columns. The following code still has the **BORDER=1** attribute; which makes all the borders inside and outside the table visible. However, we've added the **FRAME** and **RULES** attributes to control how the group borders will appear, this over-rides the **BORDER=1** (though it is still required):

```
...
<TABLE BORDER=1 FRAME="BOX" RULES="GROUPS" CELLPADDING=5
       BORDERCOLORLIGHT="black" BORDERCOLORDARK="white">
  <CAPTION ALIGN=LEFT><B>Printer Locations</B></CAPTION>
  <COLGROUP ALIGN=RIGHT>
  <COLGROUP SPAN=3 ALIGN=CENTER>
  <COLGROUP SPAN=2 ALIGN=LEFT>
  <TR>
    <TH><TH COLSPAN=3>Inkjet<TH COLSPAN=2>Laser
  <TR>
    <TH><TH>Original<TH>500<TH>600<TH>2ppm<TH>4ppm
  <TR>
    <TD><B>Software</B><TD>0<TD>2<TD>1<TD>0<TD>2
```

```
    <TR>
      <TD><B>Hardware</B><TD>1<TD>1<TD>0<TD>1<TD>0
    <TR>
      <TD><B>Sales</B><TD>0<TD>0<TD>0<TD>1<TD>1
    <TR>
      <TD><B>Admin<BR>Office</B><TD>0<TD>2<TD>0<TD>0<TD>0
  </TABLE>
  ...
```

We're using three **<COLGROUP>** elements to divide the table into sections. Notice how we span the first 'location' column, then the five printer type columns—splitting them into two groups. We've also specified a different alignment for each group so you can see the effect more clearly. Then, in the body of the table, we removed the **ALIGN** attributes from the **<TR>** tags. Here's the result:

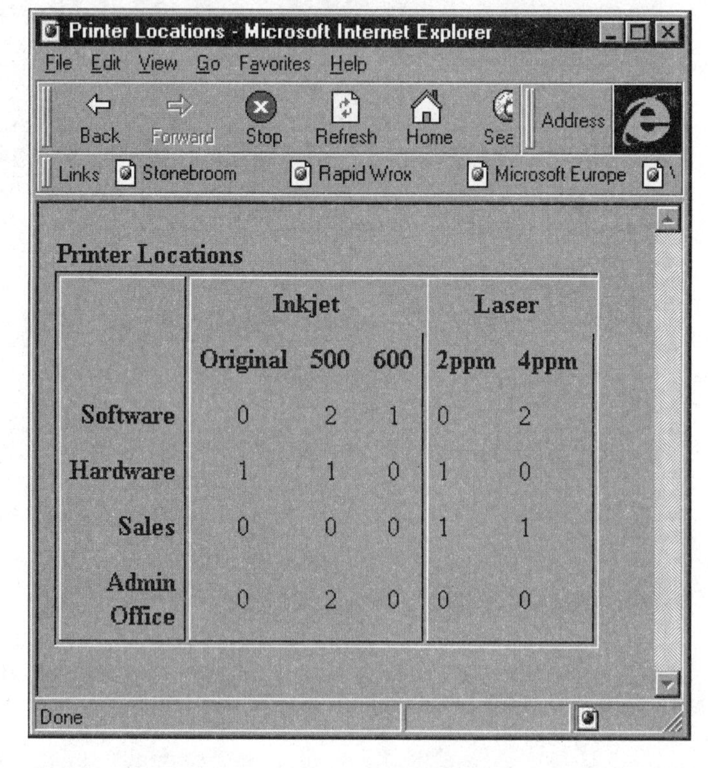

You can see from the screenshot that, in Internet Explorer 3, the rules get a little mixed up in the translation. The Inkjet and Laser cells have lost their right-hand internal border and, more to the point, they are both still centered, even though the third **<COLGROUP>** element specifies **LEFT** for the **ALIGN** attribute. However, the rest of the table has turned out reasonably as expected.

Column Group Compatibility

The biggest problem with using column groups is that they are poorly supported, except in Internet Explorer 4. In Internet Explorer 2 and 3 the results are (to say the least) unpredictable, and they aren't supported at all in Netscape Navigator. In general, they should be avoided until the standards are more fully implemented. However, we've described the standards, as proposed by W3C for HTML 4.0, in the next section, so that you are well prepared.

Note that the way we've applied styles and alignment in the previous example is not in line with the HTML 4.0 standards either. In reality, you would use cascading style sheets to apply all the formatting, and the table elements to create the content. This, again, is not well supported in current browsers and is probably best avoided for the present unless you have absolute control over which clients will visit your site.

The <COLGROUP> and <COL> Elements

You can specify that a number of columns belong to a group using the **<COLGROUP>** element. You can then specify any different individual attributes for a particular column within that group, by using the **<COL>** element. The **<COLGROUP>** and **<COL>** elements support the following attributes:

ALIGN CHAR CHAROFF SPAN WIDTH VALIGN

plus the standard HTML 4.0 attributes; **ID**, **STYLE**, **CLASS**, **TITLE** and **DIR**. In HTML 4.0, the **<COLGROUP>** and **<COL>** elements also provide several events that can be used in scripting. (See Chapter 10 for information about scripting).

ALIGN

Defines the alignment of the content of the cells within this group or for an individual column. See the section on the **<THEAD>**, **<TBODY>** and **<TFOOT>** elements for details.

CHAR

Specifies the character that will be used to align the text contents of the cells within this group or for an individual column. See the section on the **<THEAD>**, **<TBODY>** and **<TFOOT>** elements for details.

CHAROFF

Specifies the offset to the first occurrence of the character specified in the **CHAR** attribute. See the section on the **<THEAD>**, **<TBODY>** and **<TFOOT>** elements for details.

SPAN

This attribute specifies the number of columns in the table that this group will refer to. The syntax is:

```
SPAN=n
```

where *n* is the number of columns to span. This is useful when specifying an attribute for more than one column.

If **SPAN=0**, the next **<COL>** element applies to the remaining columns of the table. The **SPAN** attribute is ignored if there are any **<COL>** elements within the current group.

WIDTH

Specifies the width of each column within the group or for an individual column. The syntax is:

WIDTH=*n*

where *n* is the width in pixels. To specify a percentage of the available window width the **%** percent sign must be appended to the value. The special value **"0*"** means that columns will be the minimum width required to display all the contents.

VALIGN

Specifies the vertical alignment of the content within the cell in this group or for an individual column. See the section on the **<THEAD>**, **<TBODY>** and **<TFOOT>** elements for details.

A More Complex Table Example

You can include any other element you like inside a table cell. In other words, headers, paragraphs, lists, images, hypertext links, and even other tables (known as **nesting**). This practice is now becoming very popular among experienced authors as it affords a relatively simple way to lay out a complex document. Here's an example showing how to incorporate some of these effects:

```
<HTML>
<HEAD>
<TITLE>An example of tables</TITLE>
</HEAD>
<BODY BGCOLOR=white>

<TABLE BGCOLOR=white CELLPADDING=10 BORDER=0 WIDTH=100%>
  <TR ALIGN=RIGHT VALIGN=CENTER>
    <!-- the toolbar menu items -->
    <TD><IMG SRC="home.gif">
    <TD><IMG SRC="help.gif">
    <TD><IMG SRC="info.gif">
    <TD><IMG SRC="order.gif">
  <TR BGCOLOR=aqua VALIGN=TOP>
    <TD BGCOLOR=white><IMG SRC="coffee.gif" ALT="Coffee cup">
    <TD VALIGN=CENTER>Guess what? You can now order
        our range of coffee beans online!
    <TD ALIGN=RIGHT VALIGN=CENTER><B>For a limited period,
        we are giving away a free coffee cup with every
        purchase made</B>
    <TD BGCOLOR=aqua>
      <!-- beginning of nested table -->
      <TABLE BGCOLOR=white CELLPADDING=3 BORDER=0
             WIDTH=95% ALIGN=RIGHT>
        <TR ALIGN=CENTER >
          <TD>Why not check out our online tips for
              making better coffee?
          <TD BGCOLOR=pink>Better still, leave us your
              own hints and tips!
```

```
        </TABLE>
        <!-- end of nested table -->
    <TR>
      <TD COLSPAN=2 VALIGN=TOP WIDTH=50%>Welcome to our
          very special web site. From here you can find out
          everything you ever wanted to know about coffee,
          including how to make it, where the beans come
          from, what varieties are available and much,
          much more.
      <TD COLSPAN=2 VALIGN=TOP BGCOLOR=silver>
        <FONT COLOR=white><B>Ever wondered what goes on in
           a coffee making factory, then check this out. Our
           indispensible guide to coffee making shows you
           everything from harvesting to packaging.</B></FONT>
  </TABLE>
  </BODY>
  </HTML>
```

This code, viewed in Internet Explorer, is rendered as:

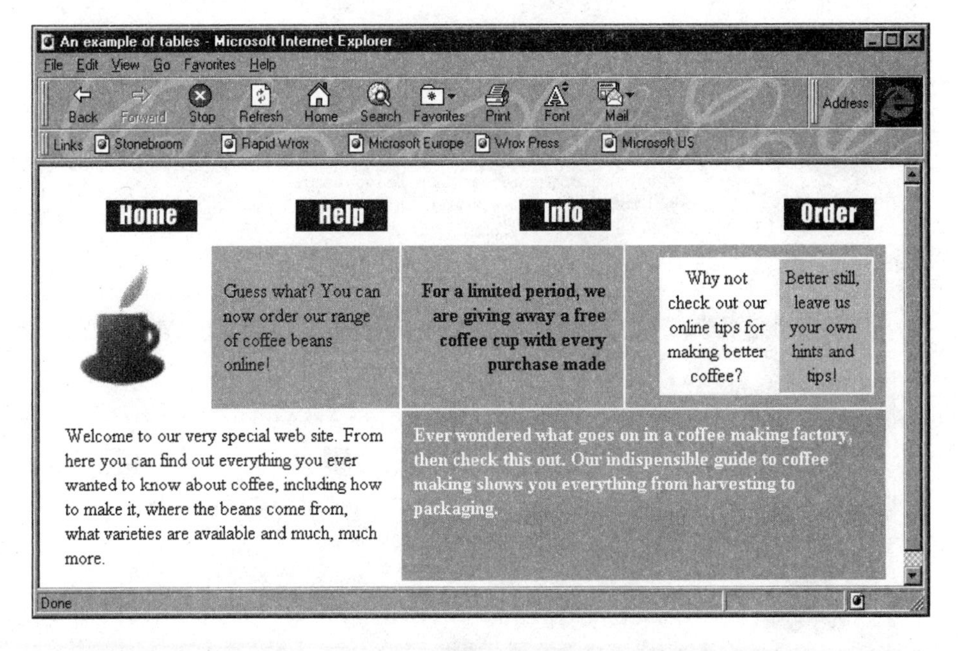

Missing Closing Tag Problems

However, load the same page into Navigator (this is version 4), and we lose a bit. The right-hand middle table cell only has one nested cell, not two:

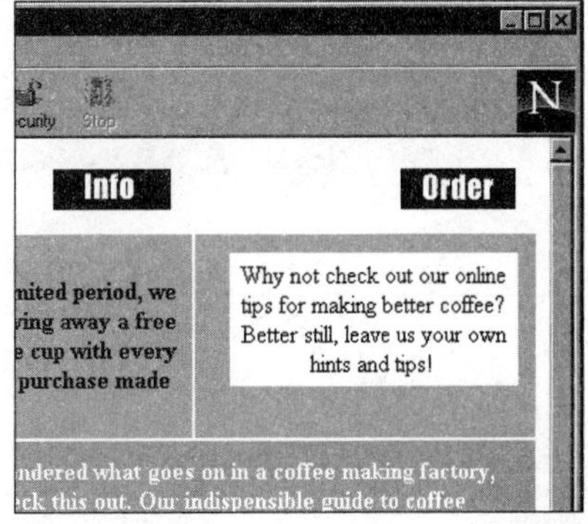

The reason is that Navigator is a lot stricter about the way it parses the HTML source to build the page. We took advantage of the freedom in HTML 3.2 and 4.0 to omit closing `</TD>` and `</TR>` tags, but Navigator isn't happy about this.

```
<!-- beginning of nested table -->
<TABLE BGCOLOR=white CELLPADDING=3 BORDER=0
      WIDTH=95% ALIGN=RIGHT>
  <TR ALIGN=CENTER >
    <TD>Why not check out our online tips for
        making better coffee?
    <TD BGCOLOR=pink>Better still, leave us your
        own hints and tips!
</TABLE>
<!-- end of nested table -->
```

Adding the missing tags does the trick. This is what the section of code should look like:

```
<!-- beginning of nested table -->
<TABLE BGCOLOR=white CELLPADDING=5 BORDER=0
      WIDTH=95% ALIGN=RIGHT>
  <TR ALIGN=CENTER>
    <TD>Why not check out our online tips for
        making better coffee?</TD>
    <TD BGCOLOR=pink>Better still, leave us your
        own hints and tips!</TD>
  </TR>
</TABLE>
<!-- end of nested table -->
```

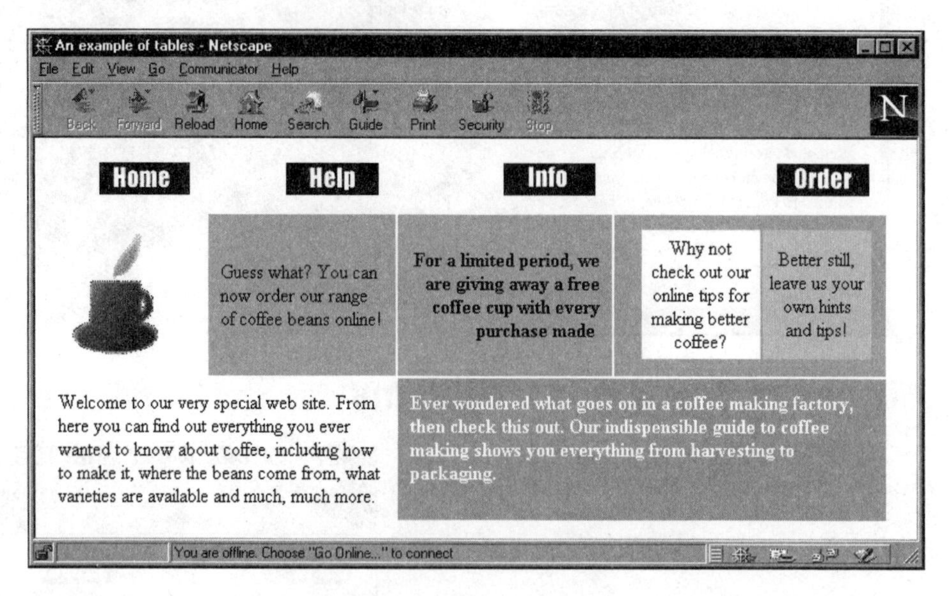

As you can see, omitting closing tags in tables (and in fact in other elements) is risky, because it's hard to know when a particular browser might complain. Make a point of always including all closing tags unless you are sure you have tested your page on all the browsers it will be viewed on.

Summary

In this chapter, we've looked at all aspects of creating HTML tables. We started with an example of the most basic table, before considering all of the attributes available for the HTML elements that are used in tables. We looked at how the formatting of individual cells can be affected, and how you can format an entire table and then override that format for specific cells. We also looked at the **COLGROUP** tag and how this can be used to simplify your code. Finally, we looked at how nested tables can be used to format whole pages of graphics and text.

Bear in mind that tables may not always be formatted on someone else's system in the same way as they are on yours. There are several extensions to the table model put forward by W3C, and there have been changes to the way attributes work throughout the life of the two main browsers, Internet Explorer and Netscape Navigator. Using these extensions is likely to limit the number of people that can view your pages correctly. It is even a good idea to provide alternative pages formatted without tables for those browsers incapable of utilizing them.

Frames

Frames give the web page author a way of organizing how information is displayed. They allow you to divide up the main browser window into independent sections (like panes in a 'real' window), and then display different documents in each section. For example, you could display a list of contents in one frame and the actual items in another. Other uses for frames include displaying logos, copyright notices, navigation buttons etc. Using frames in this way means that you can provide a consistent look and feel to your web site—you could have, for instance, a narrow frame at the bottom of the window that is displayed constantly, and a second frame in which important new information is shown.

Once you start using frames, it's very easy to get carried away and use them for everything: logo at the top, navigation aids down the side, adverts at the bottom, etc. Be sparing with your use of frames, and remember that not everyone will be viewing your site at the same resolution as you—leave enough room for the main frame, where the bulk of your information will appear. Also bear in mind the extra time and bandwidth required to download all the separate documents that they require.

Although the two mainline browsers have supported frames for some time (Netscape Navigator since version 2 and Internet Explorer since version 3) they have never been part of the W3C standards until HTML 4.0.

Creating Frames

To use frames, you need to create a document that uses the **<FRAMESET>** and **<FRAME>** elements to divide the main window into rectangular frames. It's important not to confuse their functions:

 **<FRAMESET>** is the container element, and defines how all your frames will behave.

 **<FRAME>** is the element that defines each individual frame, and how that particular frame will behave.

For each frame, you specify an HTML document that contains the content (text, images, etc) to fill the frame. A page made up of a series of frames is usually referred to as a **frameset**.

Frameset Structure

The basic structure of a frameset is:

```
<HTML>
<HEAD>
...
</HEAD>

<! the frameset definition must be first after HEAD >
<FRAMESET>
  <FRAME>
  <FRAME>
</FRAMESET>

<! an optional NOFRAMES section, if BODY is omitted >
<NOFRAMES>
...
</NOFRAMES>

<! an optional BODY section, if NOFRAMES is omitted >
<BODY>
...
</BODY>

</HTML>
```

Note that the **<FRAMESET>** must be the first element after the **<HEAD>** section, and that either a **<NOFRAMES>** or a **<BODY>** section can be placed after the **<FRAMESET>**. If any visible elements appear before the **<FRAMESET>**, the browser may fail to display the frames. This is the syntax as proposed by HTML 4.

However, some existing browsers complain about the presence of a **<BODY>** section in a frameset page, and in fact prefer the **<NOFRAMES>** section to be within the **<FRAMESET>**, like this. This is the preferred syntax for older browsers:

```
...
<FRAMESET>
  <FRAME>
  <FRAME>
  <NOFRAMES>
  ...
  </NOFRAMES>
</FRAMESET>
...
```

Either the <NOFRAMES> or the <BODY> section can be used to display content that will only be visible in browsers that don't support frames. You should not include both of these sections in a frameset document.

The Frameset Elements

We'll examine the three frameset elements, **<FRAMESET>**, **<FRAME>** and **<NOFRAMES>** in turn.

The <FRAMESET> Element

The **<FRAMESET>** element is used to enclose multiple **<FRAME>** elements, in order to create the frameset layout within the page. It supports the following attributes:

COLS **ROWS**

plus the usual HTML 4.0 attributes **ID**, **CLASS**, **STYLE** and **TITLE**. It also provides two events that can be used in scripting, **onload** and **onunload** (see chapter 10 for information on scripting).

COLS

Defines the number and size of columns that will be used when dividing the window up amongst the frames. The syntax is:

COLS=*column_list*

where *column_list* is a string containing the widths of each individual column, specified either as an absolute value in pixels, or a ratio or percentage of the browser window width. For example:

```
COLS="20%,*,*"
```

defines three columns: the first is 20% of the width of the browser window and the second and third take up the rest. The last two are equal in width—in other words, each of these take up 40% of the browser window.

```
COLS="100,*,50"
```

again defines three columns: this time the first is 100 pixels wide, the third is 50 pixels wide, and the middle one takes up the remaining width of the browser window.

```
COLS="1*,3*,2*"
```

also defines three columns: but this time using ratios rather than percentages. The first is one sixth of the width of the browser window, the second takes up half (three sixths), and the third the remaining third (two sixths) of the width of the browser window.

```
COLS="60,25%,2*,1*"
```

defines four columns using a mixture of values: this time the first column is 60 pixels wide. The other three take up the remaining width of the browser window in the ratios of a quarter, a half, and a quarter respectively. This is because the 25% wide column would leave 75% of the available width to the other two columns, which share it in the ratio of 2 to 1. It's not a good idea to mix the value types like this, however, as it makes it hard to tell what the result will be.

If you provide percentages that do not add up to 100%, or absolute values that do not add up to the size of the browser window, the browser will adjust each column width in proportion to fill the window.

ROWS

Defines the number and height of the individual rows that will produce frames. The syntax is:

ROWS=*row_list*

where *row_list* is a string made up of individual row details that are specified in the same way as in the **COLS** attribute above. By always providing a **ROWS** attribute, the frameset will appear more quickly because the browser can lay them out before reading the list of frames to see how many there are. Note that you can use just one or the other of these attributes, or both together. For example, this code:

```
<FRAMESET ROWS="30%,*,15%" COLS="1*,3*,2*" >
  <FRAME SRC="frame1.html">
  <FRAME SRC="frame2.html">
  <FRAME SRC="frame3.html">
  <FRAME SRC="frame4.html">
  <FRAME SRC="frame5.html">
  <FRAME SRC="frame6.html">
  <FRAME SRC="frame7.html">
  <FRAME SRC="frame8.html">
  <FRAME SRC="frame9.html">
</FRAMESET>
```

produces nine frames, laid out in rows and columns as specified in the **<FRAMESET>** element:

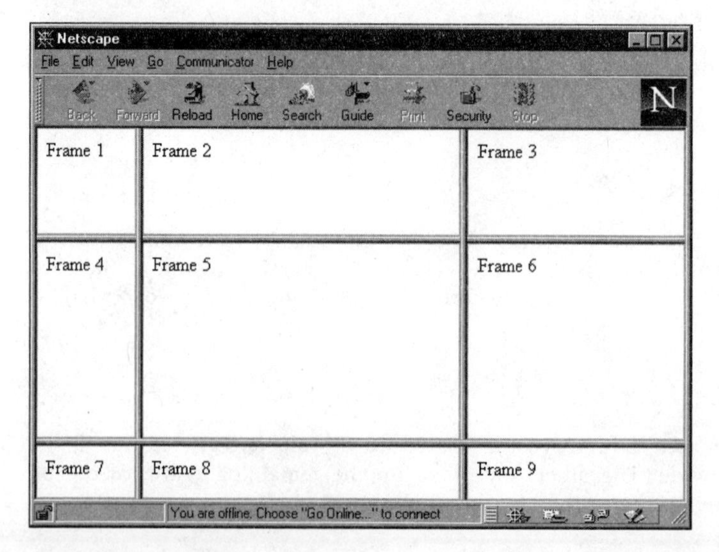

Nested Framesets

Alternatively, this code could have been written using several nested **<FRAMESET>** elements:

```
<FRAMESET COLS="1*,3*,2*" >
  <FRAMESET ROWS="30%,*,15%"
    <FRAME SRC="frame1.html">
    <FRAME SRC="frame2.html">
    <FRAME SRC="frame3.html">
  </FRAMESET>
  <FRAMESET ROWS="30%,*,15%"
    <FRAME SRC="frame4.html">
    <FRAME SRC="frame5.html">
    <FRAME SRC="frame6.html">
  </FRAMESET>
  <FRAMESET ROWS="30%,*,15%"
    <FRAME SRC="frame7.html">
    <FRAME SRC="frame8.html">
    <FRAME SRC="frame9.html">
  </FRAMESET>
</FRAMESET>
```

This creates the same effect as we saw earlier, but we can use this technique to create more off-beat frame layouts instead. For example, this code:

```
<FRAMESET COLS="50%,*">
  <FRAMESET ROWS="50%,*">
    <FRAME SRC="frame1.html">
    <FRAME SRC="frame2.html">
  </FRAMESET>
  <FRAMESET ROWS="33%,33%,*">
    <FRAME SRC="frame3.html">
    <FRAME SRC="frame4.html">
    <FRAME SRC="frame5.html">
  </FRAMESET>
</FRAMESET>
```

produces two columns, then divides each one into different frame layouts:

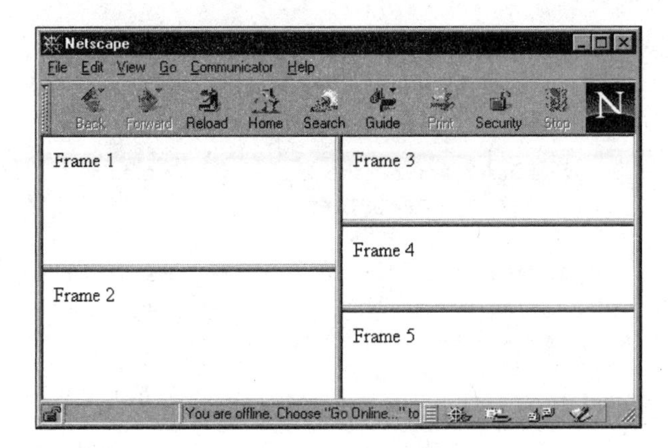

Extensions to the <FRAMESET> Element

Netscape Navigator and Internet Explorer implement extra attributes for the **<FRAMESET>** element:

FRAMEBORDER

This is supported by both browsers in versions 3 and 4, and specifies whether the frame will be shown with a 3-D border. The syntax is:

FRAMEBORDER=*value*

where *value* is either **1** (yes) or **0** (no) The default, if omitted, is yes, as you can see from the previous screen shots. You can use **YES** or **NO** instead of the values **1** and **0**.

FRAMESPACING

This is supported only by Internet Explorer 3 and 4, and is used to add extra space between frames. The syntax is:

FRAMESPACING=*spacing*

where *spacing* is the amount of space in pixels.

While you are experimenting with frames, you may notice problems using the 'reload' option on your browser. Some browsers only reload the current frame. Whilst this is often appropriate when viewing a document across a slow modem link, it may not be what you want if you are experimenting with frame layouts. Look instead for an option to re-open the entire document.

The <FRAME> Element

The **<FRAME>** element provides the following attributes:

FRAMEBORDER	**MARGINHEIGHT**	**MARGINWIDTH**	**NAME**
NORESIZE	**SCROLLING**	**SRC**	**LONGDESC**

plus the usual HTML 4.0 attributes **ID**, **CLASS**, **STYLE** and **TITLE**.

FRAMEBORDER

Renders a 3-D edge border around the frame. The syntax is:

FRAMEBORDER=*value*

where *value* is **0**, **1**, **NO** or **YES**. The default is **1** (**YES**) which inserts a border, while **0** (**NO**) displays no border. This will over-ride any **FRAMEBORDER** attribute set using the **<FRAMESET>** element.

MARGINHEIGHT

Defines the amount of space between the top and bottom edges of a frame and its contents. The syntax is:

MARGINHEIGHT=*height*

where *height* is the amount of space in pixels. This value cannot be less than one (i.e. when the contents touch the frame border).

MARGINWIDTH

Defines the amount of space between the left and right edges of a frame and its contents. The syntax is:

MARGINWIDTH=*width*

where *width* is the amount of space in pixels. As with **MARGINHEIGHT**, the value must be 1 or greater. You should generally use **MARGINHEIGHT** and **MARGINWIDTH** as a pair, as specifying one without the other can lead to some unexpected effects.

NAME

Allows you to specify a name for the frame. The syntax is:

NAME=*name*

This allows you to attach a name to a particular frame, so that pages can be targeted at it in hypertext links from another frame. We'll look at an example later in this chapter.

NORESIZE

Prevents the user from resizing the frame. The syntax is simply:

NORESIZE

By default, users can resize frames by dragging the borders. Including **NORESIZE** prevents this, but should be used only when necessary as the user may be viewing your documents at a lower resolution, and may prefer to resize the frame rather than scroll up and down or left and right.

SCROLLING

Creates a frame with or without scrollbars. The syntax is:

SCROLLING=*value*

where *value* can be **YES** (scrollbars are always displayed, even if the page content fits within the frame), **NO** (scrollbars are not displayed, even if the page content is too large for the frame) or **AUTO** (scrollbars are only displayed when the content is larger than the frame). Again, you need to use this only when absolutely necessary. Setting **SCROLLING=NO** and **NORESIZE** could render your site very difficult to use for someone with a low resolution screen, and hence a small browser window.

SRC

Specifies the source file for the frame. The syntax is:

SRC=*url*

where *url* is the full or partial (relative) URL of the page to display in the frame. The **SRC** cannot specify an anchor (created with an **<A NAME="...">** element) if that page is already displayed in another frame.

LONGDESC

This is a new HTML 4.0 attribute that allows you to add a link to another document that describes the frame contents in more detail. The syntax is:

LONGDESC=*url*

where *url* is the address of the other document or resource. This is useful for providing extra information about parts of the page, which the user can see if they wish, without cluttering up the page. It is also designed for use in non-visual applications. It is not supported in current browsers, however.

> **In most browsers, FRAMEBORDER and FRAMESPACING inherit their attributes from their containing <FRAMESET> element if they are defined there. If you want all frames to have the same FRAMEBORDER and FRAMESPACING attributes, you need only set the attributes once in the containing <FRAMESET> element. This is not part of the HTML 4.0 standard, however, which suggests you use style sheets instead.**

Extensions to the <FRAME> Element

Some versions of Netscape Navigator and Internet Explorer implement some extra attributes to the **<FRAMESET>** element. See Appendix A for more details:

ALIGN - sets the alignment of the frame. Should be avoided, use **STYLE** properties instead.

BORDERCOLOR defines the color of the border to be drawn around the element, using standard color values or color names.

Internet Explorer <FRAME> Extensions

Internet Explorer implements two other attributes for the **<FRAME>** element:

DATAFLD and **DATASRC** are used when the frame is connected to a client-side or server-side database during data-binding. This is briefly described in chapter 12.

The <NOFRAMES> Element

This element encloses HTML that is specifically aimed at browsers that do not support frames:

```
<NOFRAMES>
  Sorry, our site contains frames that your browser cannot
  display. You can view our frame-free area by clicking
  <A HREF="indexnf.html">HERE</A>.
</NOFRAMES>
```

Frame-compliant browsers will use this tag as an instruction to ignore the content, whereas those that don't support frames will ignore the **<NOFRAMES>** and **</NOFRAMES>** tags and display the alternative text 'hidden' between them.

You may also wish to provide a link to a non-frame version of your pages from within the normal pages. Many users, especially those with lower screen resolutions, may prefer versions that do not utilize frames.

Targets for Hyperlinks

When Netscape introduced frames, they also introduced the new **TARGET** attribute for some of the existing elements—**<A>**, **<AREA>**, **<BASE>**, and **<FORM>**. HTML 4.0 also adds the **TARGET** attribute to the **<LINK>** element.

By default, a hyperlink loads the page or resource it points to into the same frame as the hyperlink. Each frame acts like an independent window in this respect. To get around this problem, browsers that support frames allow each frame to be given a name, in the same way that separate browser windows can. Then, the hyperlink can target a page or resource to that frame instead of loading it in its own frame.

For example if we create a frameset like this:

```
<!-- Define the frames for display -->
<FRAMESET COLS=25%,*>
  <FRAME SRC="target.html">
  <FRAME SRC="intro.html" NAME="main_view">
</FRAMESET>
```

we can place a link in the left-hand frame (**target.html**) which loads a new page **moreinfo.html** into the right-hand frame which we've named **main_view**:

```
<A HREF="moreinfo.html" TARGET="main_view">More Info</A>
```

If the left-hand page contained a **<FORM>**, we could target the results of submitting the form to the right-hand window using the **TARGET** attribute:

```
<FORM TARGET="main_view" ...>
  ...
</FORM>
```

And if we want to target all returned pages to a particular frame, for all the hyperlinks on a page, we use the **<BASE>** tag in the **<HEAD>** section of the page that contains the hyperlinks:

```
<HEAD>
  <BASE TARGET="main_view">
  ...
</HEAD>
<BODY>
...
```

See Chapter 5 for more details about targeting pages that are loaded by **<A>** *tags and other links.*

Special Values for Target

The **TARGET** attribute works exactly the same way in a frame as it does in a normal **<A>** or **<FORM>** element. If the target value provided is the name of an existing frame or separate browser window, the page is loaded there. If a value for **TARGET** is supplied, but it isn't the name of an existing frame or window, a new browser window is created and the page is loaded there.

There are also four special values for **TARGET**:

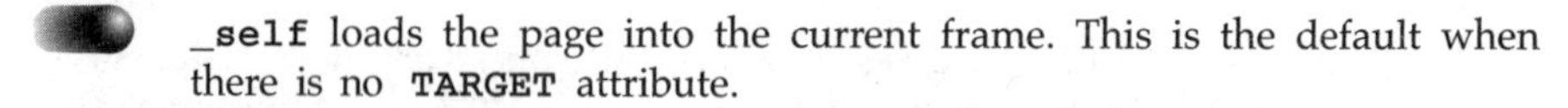

- **_self** loads the page into the current frame. This is the default when there is no **TARGET** attribute.

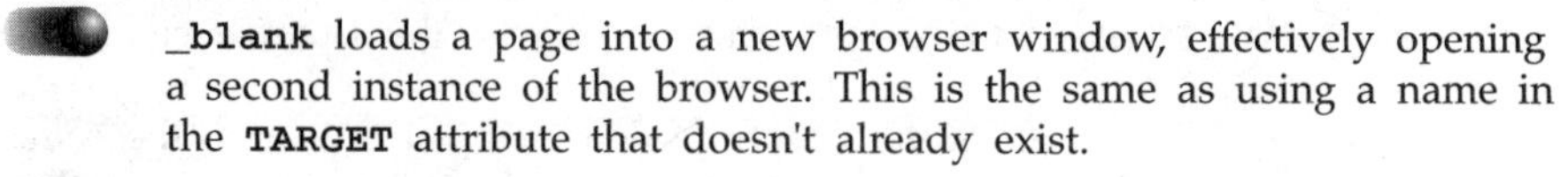

- **_blank** loads a page into a new browser window, effectively opening a second instance of the browser. This is the same as using a name in the **TARGET** attribute that doesn't already exist.

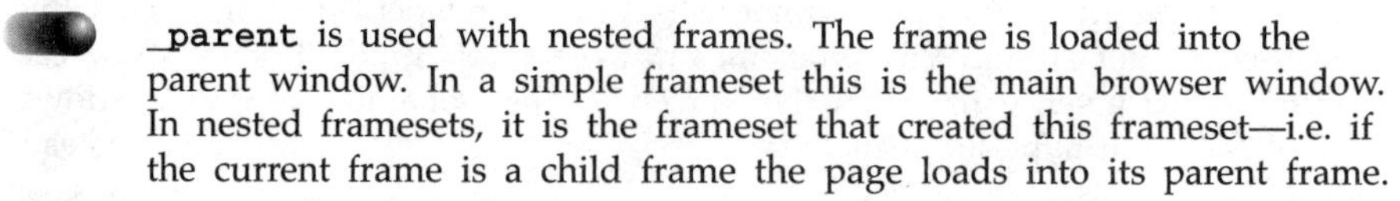

- **_parent** is used with nested frames. The frame is loaded into the parent window. In a simple frameset this is the main browser window. In nested framesets, it is the frameset that created this frameset—i.e. if the current frame is a child frame the page loads into its parent frame.
- **_top** loads the new page into the main browser window directly, replacing any frames that are there at present.

If you use frames on your page, remember that all external links should have the **TARGET** set to **top**—otherwise the external document may be unintentionally loaded into a frame of the current document. This can produce some strange, and very undesirable, screen layouts!

Inline or Floating Frames

HTML 4.0 also adds a second type of frame for displaying separate documents, the **floating frame** or inline frame. Floating frames, defined by the **<IFRAME>** tag, have been supported in the past by Internet Explorer. Currently, Navigator does not support the **<IFRAME>** element, though similar (and more powerful) effects can be obtained by using its proprietary **<LAYER>** and **<ILAYER>** tags—see chapter 11 for more details.

*It's also possible to create similar effects in HTML 4.0 and Internet Explorer 4 using the **<OBJECT>** tag, see chapter 9 for more details.*

Floating or inline frames are not part of the normal **<FRAMESET>** container, but are simply included in an HTML document in the same way as any other element—this is why they are often termed inline frames. Have a look at the following example:

```
<HTML>
<HEAD><TITLE>Floating frames</TITLE></HEAD>

<BODY>
  <IFRAME ALIGN=RIGHT SRC="float.html">
```

```
      You'll see this text if your browser doesn't
      support floating frames.
    </IFRAME>
    This text is part of a normal HTML document,
    and the code that creates the floating frame is in
    this document.
  </BODY>
  </HTML>
```

This code creates a page that looks like this:

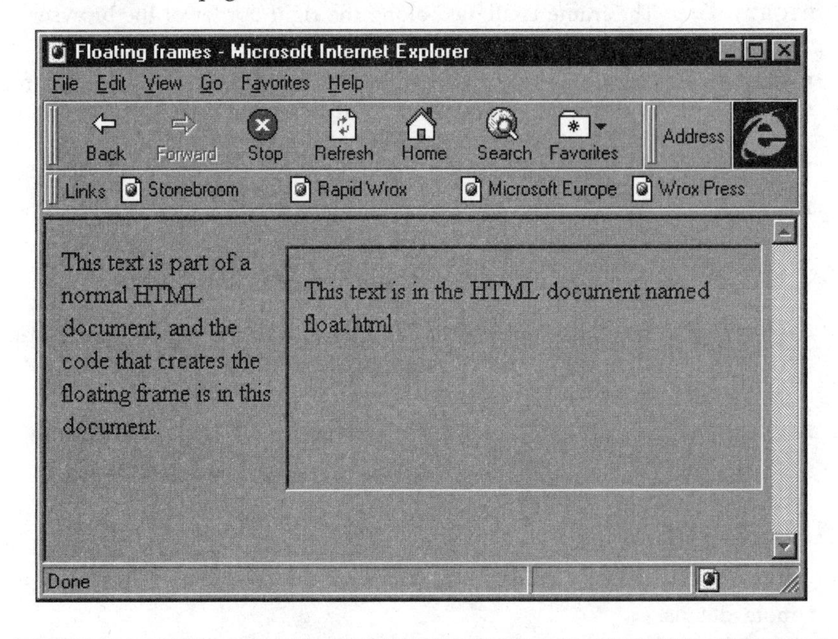

> **Notice how we can include text that will only be displayed if the browser doesn't support floating frames, by placing it between the `<IFRAME>` and `</IFRAME>` tags. Even if there is no text here, the closing `<IFRAME>` tag should always be included; otherwise any HTML following it in the page will not be displayed.**

The <IFRAME> Element

The **`<IFRAME>`** element has the following attributes::

ALIGN	**FRAMEBORDER**	**HEIGHT**	**MARGINHEIGHT**	**MARGINWIDTH**
NAME	**SCROLLING**	**SRC**	**WIDTH**	**LONGDESC**

plus the usual HTML 4.0 attributes **`ID`**, **`CLASS`**, **`STYLE`** and **`TITLE`**.

ALIGN

Defines the alignment of the frame with respect to the surrounding text, and is deprecated in HTML 4.0. The syntax is:

`ALIGN=`*alignment*

where *alignment* is one of the following values:

TOP	Text outside the frame is aligned with the top of the frame.
MIDDLE	Text outside the frame is aligned with the middle of the frame.
BOTTOM	Text outside the frame is aligned with the bottom of the frame.
LEFT	The frame is aligned along the left border of the browser window, and text flows around it to the right.
RIGHT	The frame is aligned along the right border of the browser window, and text flows around it to the left.
ABSBOTTOM	The frame is aligned so that the bottom of the element is in line with the absolute bottom of the surrounding text. The absolute bottom is the baseline of the text minus the height of the largest character descender.
TEXTTOP	The frame is aligned so that the top of the element is in line with the absolute top of the surrounding text. The absolute top is the baseline of the text plus the height of the largest character ascender.
ABSMIDDLE	Text outside the frame is aligned with the middle of the frame, using the midpoint between the **ABSBOTTOM** and **TEXTTOP** of the surrounding text.
BASELINE	The bottom of the frame is aligned with the baseline of the surrounding text.

FRAMEBORDER

Places a 3-D border around the frame. See the section on the **<FRAME>** element for more details.

HEIGHT and WIDTH

These attributes control the size of the floating frame. The syntax is:

HEIGHT=*n*
WIDTH=*n*

where *n* is the height or width in pixels. Either, both or neither can be included in the element tag. If not specified, a default value is used based on the size of the main browser window.

MARGINHEIGHT and MARGINWIDTH

Define the amount of space between the top and bottom edges, and the left and right edges, of the frame and its contents. See the section on the **<FRAME>** element for more details.

NAME

Provides a target name for the frame. See the section on the **<FRAME>** element for more details.

SCROLLING

Controls whether scroll bars will be displayed for the floating frame. See the section on the **<FRAME>** element for more details.

SRC

Specifies the source file for the frame. See the section on the **<FRAME>** element for more details.

LONGDESC

Specifies the URL of another page containing more information about the frame contents. See the section on the **<FRAME>** element for more details.

Internet Explorer <IFRAME> Extensions

Internet Explorer had already implemented several other attributes for the **<IFRAME>** element before it became part of HTML 4.0, and these are maintained for backward compatibility:

- **BORDER** defines the thickness of the border to be placed around the frame as a number. The default is zero.
- **BORDERCOLOR** defines the color of the border to be drawn around the element, using standard color values or color names.
- **DATAFLD** and **DATASRC** are used when the frame is connected to a client-side or server-side database during data-binding. This is briefly described in chapter 12.
- **FRAMESPACING** defines the distance in pixels between frames in the page.
- **HSPACE** and **VSPACE** define the minimum distance in pixels that other elements will appear either above and below, or to the left and right, of the frame.
- **NORESIZE**, if present, specifies that the frame cannot be resized by the user. Note that the HTML 4.0 standard does not permit floating frames to be resized.

In Internet Explorer, **<IFRAME>** also supports the standard **LANG** attribute, as discussed in chapter 1.

Some Frame Example Pages

While it's good to create really complex frame layouts, there are good reasons to stay with a fairly simple structure to make using your site easier, while not restricting the visible area for the real content. The generally accepted use of frames is to either create a 'navigation bar', so that users can select which part of the site to visit, or where a 'control panel' of some type is required.

Using a Navigation Frame

The first example, the 'welcome' page from our Web-developer community site at **http://rapid.wrox.com**, uses a two-column layout:

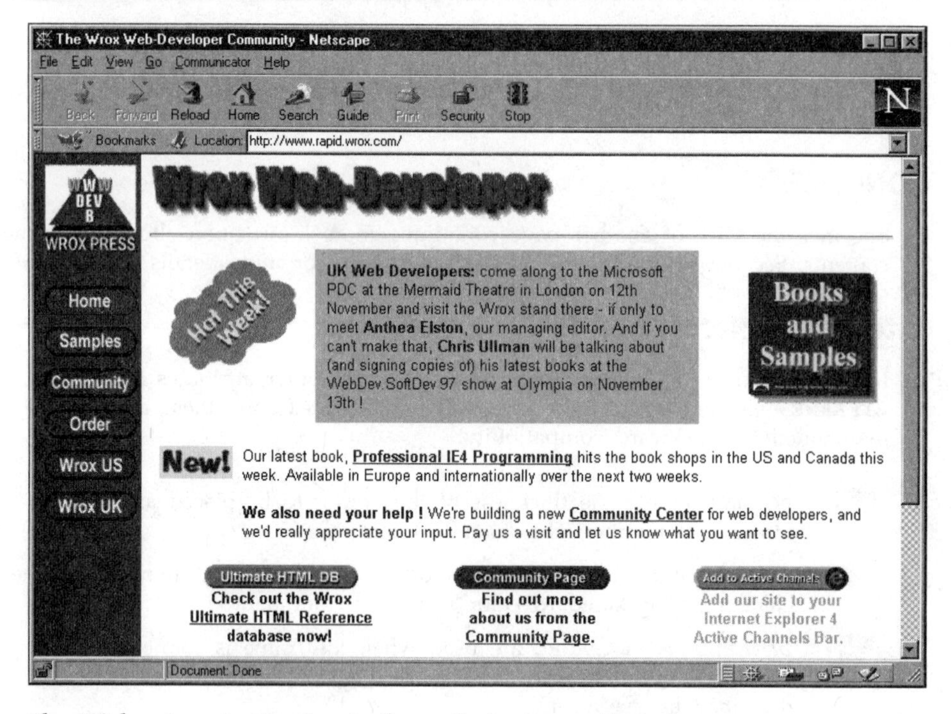

The left-hand navigation bar is there all the time, although we use some scripting code to change the button images so that each one appears depressed after you click it. We cover scripting in chapter 10.

The code for the frameset is simple enough. The left-hand frame has **SCROLLING** set to **NO**, but we do allow users to resize it if they wish, in order to make more width available for the content. They can always navigate around the site using the links in the pages instead of the navigation frame:

```
<FRAMESET cols="100,*" FRAMEBORDER="NO" BORDER="NO">
   <FRAME src="/navigate.htm" SCROLLING="NO">
   <FRAME src="/webdev/WhatsNew.htm" NAME="mainframe">
</FRAMESET>
```

Using a Control Panel Frame

The second example is the Wrox Ultimate HTML Database, which is based on this book. It uses a top non-scrolling frame for the title bar, and a bottom non-scrolling frame for the 'control panel'. You can see that the middle frame has a scroll bar, because it doesn't all fit in the available space:

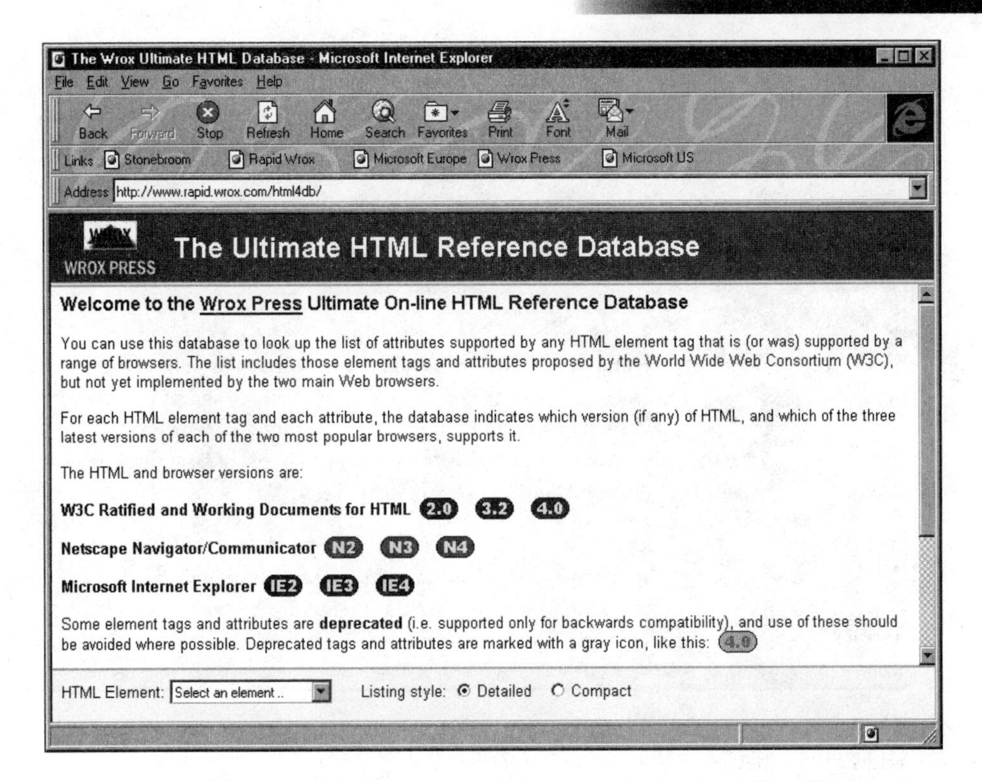

This time we prevent users from resizing the control panel, so that they can't 'lose it' and thus lose the ability to select elements or the display format. However, they can resize the title bar frame to get more vertical screen area if required:

```
<FRAMESET ROWS="60,*,45">
 <FRAME SCROLLING=NO SRC="title.htm">
 <FRAME FRAMEBORDER=0 SRC="intro.htm" NAME="winResult">
 <FRAME SCROLLING=NO FRAMEBORDER=0 NORESIZE SRC="select.asp">
</FRAMESET>
```

Using Non-Visible Frame Borders

Finally, here's an example that uses the **FRAMESPACING** and **FRAMEBORDER** attributes to create a newspaper-style layout. We've used a different color for the two frame backgrounds, and hidden the borders of the frames.

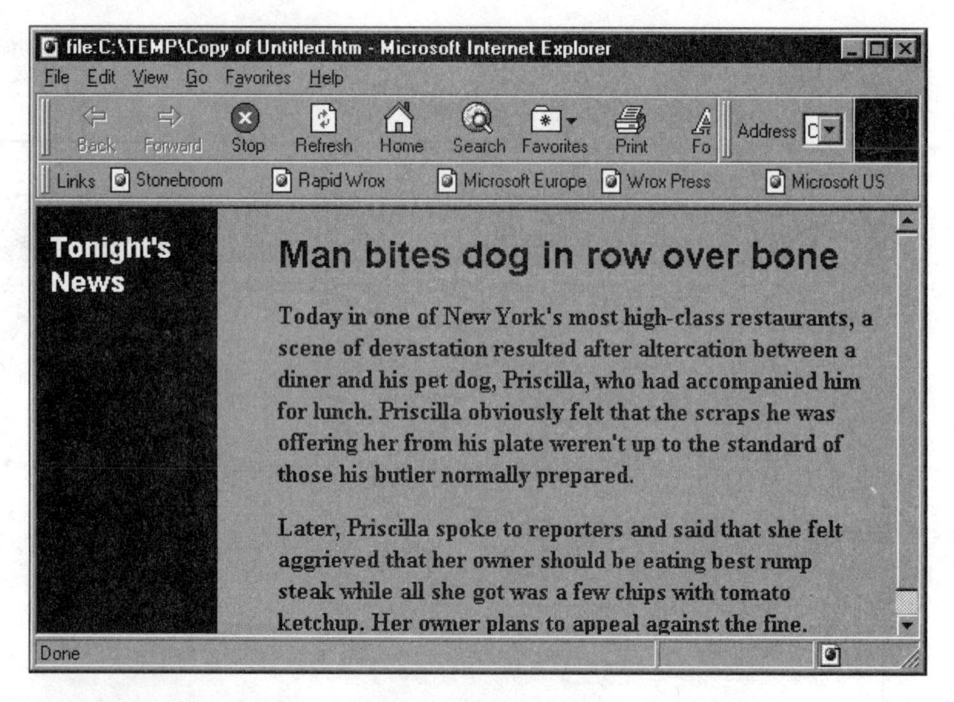

This is the frameset code. Notice how the **FRAMESPACING** attribute creates a wide gutter between the frame contents:

```
<FRAMESET COLS="120,*" FRAMESPACING=30 >
  <FRAME SRC="frame1.html"  FRAMEBORDER=0>
  <FRAME SRC="frame2.html"  FRAMEBORDER=0>
</FRAMESET>
```

Summary

In this chapter we have looked at how the browser window can be divided up into individual frames—each of which can display a different document. Frames were originally introduced by Netscape, and are already widely supported even though they only became part of the W3C standards with HTML 4.0.

We have seen how to create a frameset document that divides the screen into different areas, which can be useful for providing additional navigation features, and how to load the individual frames with the documents they should display. We've also seen how to target pages to specific frames when hyperlinks inside a frame are clicked. We also saw how to allow for browsers that do not support frames. Finally, we looked at the new HTML 4.0 floating frames proposals, and how they are supported in the two mainline browsers.

Forms and HTML Controls

One of the advantages that web sites have over traditional media, such as magazines and television, is that the web allows for the immediate processing of feedback and interaction from the 'audience'.

Forms provide a way to prompt the user for information, and then carry out actions based on that input. For example, they are commonly used to specify the criteria for a query when using a search engine. From a programming perspective, all HTML forms are broken into two parts: the client-side and the server-side code. The client-side is the form itself—that part of the document that accepts user input and submits it to the server. Once the data is submitted, it is up to the server to process it correctly—the browser simply assumes that the server will know what to do. If no script or other service exists to process the data, the browser should return an error.

> *This is not always true, however, if the form is being submitted with a* **`mailto:`** *action. In this case, the browser wraps the values up in an email message and sends it using its own email software direct to the specified recipient. It only works if the browser has suitable email software installed, though most modern ones do.*

The Structure of a Form

To create a form, you use the **<FORM>** element to enclose one or more HTML controls and other elements. The **<FORM>** element specifies the action to take when the user has provided the information. The HTML control elements define the type and function of the input controls in the form.

```
<FORM>
  ... form contents go here
</FORM>
```

Forms can be placed anywhere inside the body of an HTML document. You may also have multiple forms in one document, so long as one form ends before another begins (i.e. they can't overlap or nest). Normal body text, images and other visible elements can be included inside the **<FORM>** and **</FORM>** tags. This is useful for labeling user input fields, providing instructions and formatting. Even embedded objects such as Java Applets and ActiveX controls, and invisible elements, can be included—for example a table is often used to lay the control elements out neatly.

In HTML 4.0, new elements are introduced to make the forms appear more like traditional applications, by allowing grouping of elements, and captions that have a 'hot-key' or short-cut key to allow easier navigation. These are covered later in the chapter.

The <FORM> Element

The **<FORM>** element accepts the following attributes:

ACTION **ENCTYPE** **METHOD** **TARGET** **ACCEPT-CHARSET**
ACCEPT

plus the usual HTML 4.0 attributes **ID**, **CLASS**, **LANG**, **DIR**, **STYLE** and **TITLE** as described in chapter 1.

ACTION

This attribute is used to specify the URL that will receive the data when the form is submitted. The syntax is simply:

ACTION=*url*

The URL does not have to be on the same machine as the one that hosts the HTML document, although it generally is. An incorrect address generally means that the browser will return an error, since it won't be able to submit the form data.

You may also specify that the form data be emailed to a particular address, rather than passing it to a server script. This is easily accomplished, by using **mailto:sombody@somewhere.com** as your **ACTION**. This might be useful in automatically subscribing someone to a listserver or similar. Since listservers already take subscriptions by email request, you may be able to properly format your form data so that the server will automatically process the request without requiring any interfacing script etc.

ENCTYPE

This optional attribute is used to indicate the MIME-type (or Internet Media type) to be used when encoding the form data for submission when the **METHOD** is **"POST"**. Unless otherwise specified, it defaults to **"application/x-www-form-urlencoded"**. For documents that includes files to be submitted, as well as form data, the type should be **"multipart/form-data"**. At the moment, this isn't commonly used, but has been defined since HTML 3.2.

METHOD

This attribute defines the method used to send the data to the server. The syntax is:

METHOD=*method*

where *method* is **POST** or **GET**. If not specified, the default is **GET**

POST is the preferred method, and should be used in all cases—unless you have a compelling reason for not doing so. This method sends the data to the server as an actual data stream, and therefore avoids placing the severe limit on the maximum submission length that is imposed by **GET**.

Note that it is possible for a firewall to be configured to intercept and destroy this data stream, causing the form to be interpreted as empty.

GET is an older method, and should normally be avoided. It is deprecated in HTML 4.0, and only supported for backward compatibility. With this method, the data is appended to the URL itself after a question mark separator:

```
http://foobar.edu/cgi/query?Name=Smith
```

The **GET** method does have the advantage of allowing the form results to be bookmarked (useful in the case of searches), but has the disadvantage that the length of the data string is limited, since it is assigned to an environment variable on the server. In addition, the form data (within the URL) is often stored in the server logs for anyone to find.

TARGET

If the data submission results in another page being sent back to the client (the usual situation) the return page is loaded into the same frame or window as the page containing the **<FORM>** tag by default. To have the returned page loaded into a different frame or window, you can use the optional **TARGET** attribute to specify the frame or window name, just as you would for an **<A>** element.

ACCEPT-CHARSET

Specifies the character set used for the data from the form, and that the server must support. This attribute is optional, and was added in HTML 4.0. Most browsers do not support it at present.

ACCEPT

Specifies the MIME-type(s) that the server must support for the data submitted from the form. It can be a comma-delimited list if more than one type is required. This attribute is optional, and was added in HTML 4.0. Most browsers do not support it at present.

HTML Controls

The **<FORM>** tag, used to declare the opening and closing of a form, says nothing about what data it will collect. This is left to the 'data entry' elements within the form: **<INPUT>**, **<TEXTAREA>**, **<SELECT>**, **<OPTGROUP>**, **<BUTTON>**, **<LABEL>**, **<FIELDSET>** and **<LEGEND>**. The last five of these are new in HTML 4.0.

> **HTML 4.0 states that HTML controls should also be useable without being enclosed in a <FORM> element. This is useful where they are only present to allow scripting code to be executed on demand by the user, such as when creating interactive documents. Currently, Navigator does not display any HTML controls unless they are enclosed in the <FORM> and </FORM> tags. To overcome this, it is advisable to always use <FORM> tags, and omit all the attributes or just include ACTION="".**

The <INPUT> Element

The attributes supported by the `<INPUT>` element are:

TYPE	NAME	ALIGN	CHECKED	MAXLENGTH	SIZE
SRC	VALUE	DISABLED*	READONLY*	ALT*	USEMAP*
TABINDEX*		ACCEPT*	ACCESSKEY*		

plus the usual HTML 4.0 attributes **ID**, **CLASS**, **LANG**, **DIR**, **STYLE** and **TITLE** as described in Chapter 1.

Those marked with an asterisk are new in HTML 4.0, and are generally not supported in older browsers. The `<INPUT>` element can be used to create several different types of element, and the combination of attributes and events supported for each type is different.

TYPE

Specifies what type of control to use. The syntax is:

TYPE=*type*

where *type* is one of the following:

TEXT This is the default if **TYPE** is not specified. It produces a single line text field for user input. Used in conjunction with **MAXLENGTH** and **SIZE**. This type of `<INPUT>` control should be used in place of the `<ISINDEX>` element, which is deprecated in HTML 4.0.

PASSWORD This produces a similar control to the **TEXT** type, except that text is not displayed as you enter it. The text is displayed as asterisks, so that people looking over your shoulder cannot read it. Note that it doesn't automatically encrypt the transmission of a password—this can only be done using secure HTTP transmission protocols.

HIDDEN The user will see no field, but the value of the field (set by the **VALUE** attribute) will be submitted with the form as text. This is useful for sending information to the server that you don't want the user to see, and can be used in a variety of inventive ways, depending on the application.

CHECKBOX Creates a checkbox control. A selected (checked) checkbox will generate the value **"on"** when submitted. Used to provide a 'Yes' or 'No' type of control.

RADIO	Creates an option (or 'radio') button control. Usually used to provide a selection of alternatives from which only one can be chosen, by giving each button in the group the same value for the **NAME** attribute. The **VALUE** attribute of the selected radio button is the only one to generate a name/value pair when the form is submitted.
RESET	Creates a button that resets all the fields to their initial default values. Setting the **VALUE** attribute will alter the caption on the button itself, the default is Reset. If a value for the **NAME** attribute is provided, the button will generate a name/value pair that is sent to the server with the other form data.
SUBMIT	Creates a button that submits the form to the server. Setting the **VALUE** attribute will alter the caption on the button, the default is Submit or Submit Query (depending on the browser). If a value for the **NAME** attribute is provided, the button will generate a name/value pair that is sent to the server with the other form data. If not it will simply submit the form.
IMAGE	Creates an image map that the user can click to submit the form. The coordinates of the selected point on the image are sent to the server along with the data from the form. This is basically a complicated way of making a fancy Submit button, although it can be used for other purposes.
BUTTON	Creates a button that can be linked to a script, rather than directly submitting or resetting a form like the **SUBMIT** and **RESET** buttons.
FILE	New in HTML 4.0, although has been supported by Navigator in the past. This creates a control that looks like a text box, but is used to submit a file to the server. When the form is submitted, the file specified in the control is sent to the server as well.

NAME

Specifies the name of the control. The syntax is:

NAME=*name*

The *name* specified is sent to the server in a name/value pair, and used to identify the control. Except in the case of a **RADIO**-type control, you should use names that are unique for that form, and that your processing script will expect. For example, if your database is expecting a 'FirstName' entry, and you name the control '1stname' in the form, you will get errors since the server-side program won't know what it is supposed to do with the value you've sent it.

ALIGN

Use this attribute to define how the text will be aligned within or in relation to the element. The syntax is:

ALIGN=*alignment*

where *alignment* is **TOP**, **MIDDLE**, or **BOTTOM**. These values have the same effect as with inline images.

CHECKED

Forces a checkbox or radio button to be selected (i.e. 'on') when the form loads. The syntax is simply:

```
CHECKED
```

This is useful for 'presetting' certain values, in order to make them the default choice.

MAXLENGTH

Sets how many characters the user can enter into a text box. It does not set the actual size of the control. The syntax is:

MAXLENGTH=*n*

where *n* is the number of characters. Be careful when setting this value, as you never know how much space a user will need for the data. Only use **MAXLENGTH** if you have a good reason to do so—for example, if your processing script has strict limits on the number of characters it can accept for that field.

SIZE

Specifies the size of the control. The syntax is:

SIZE=*n*

where *n* is the size as a number of characters. Note that this is not the same as setting **MAXLENGTH**. If the **SIZE** attribute is set to a smaller value than **MAXLENGTH**, the characters will scroll. The actual on-screen dimension of the control depends on the client system's default font size, so will appear at different sizes on different machines even with the same value of **SIZE**.

SRC

Used when **TYPE=IMAGE** to specify the image to be used.

SRC=*url*

This attribute behaves in exactly the same way as for inline images.

VALUE

Specifies the default value of text or numeric controls. The syntax is:

VALUE=*value*

This value will be shown in the control when the form is first displayed, and so will be passed to the server when the form is submitted unless it's changed by the user. For Boolean controls (i.e. checkboxes and radio buttons), this specifies the value to be returned when the control is selected. Use this attribute with a **HIDDEN** control to set a value that you want to send to the server, and which can't be viewed or changed by the user.

DISABLED

Added in HTML 4.0, and supported in Internet Explorer 4. This attribute forces the control to be disabled, i.e. it is grayed out and the user cannot change the value in it. The syntax is simply:

```
DISABLED
```

This is normally used in conjunction with scripting code, which can change the setting of the attribute to enable the control at appropriate times.

READONLY

Added in HTML 4.0, and supported in Internet Explorer 4. This attribute forces the control to be read only, i.e. displayed normally, but the user cannot change the value in it. The syntax is simply:

```
READONLY
```

This attribute can be used to display a value that will be submitted, but that the user can't change. It can also be used in conjunction with scripting code, which can change the setting of the attribute to allow the value in the control to be edited by the user only at appropriate times.

ALT

Added in HTML 4.0, and supported in Internet Explorer 4. This attribute specifies the text that will be displayed for an **<INPUT TYPE=IMAGE>** control if the browser can't display the image itself. The syntax is:

ALT=*text*

USEMAP

Under consideration for inclusion in the final HTML 4.0 standard, and not supported in browsers at present. This attribute would specify that the image in an **<INPUT TYPE=IMAGE>** control was a client-side image map, whose **AREA**s define the value to be passed to the server. The syntax is:

USEMAP=*map_name*

TABINDEX

Added in HTML 4.0, and supported in Internet Explorer 4. This attribute allows the HTML author to set the order that the focus moves between controls when the *Tab* key is pressed. The default is the order of the controls in the HTML source. The syntax is:

TABINDEX=*n*

where *n* is the position in the tabbing order. A negative value means that the control will not receive the focus when tabbing.

ACCEPT

Optional and added in HTML 4.0, but not currently supported in most browsers. Specifies the MIME-type(s) that the server must support for the data submitted from the form. It can be a comma-delimited list if more than one type is required.

ACCESSKEY

Added in HTML 4.0 and supported in IE4, **ACCESSKEY** is used to define a keyboard character that can be pressed, usually in conjunction with the *Alt* or command key, to switch the focus directly to the control. It acts as a 'hot-key' or short-cut key allowing easier navigation. The syntax is:

ACCESSKEY=*character*

Extensions to <INPUT> in Internet Explorer

Internet Explorer adds extra attributes to the **<INPUT>** tag:

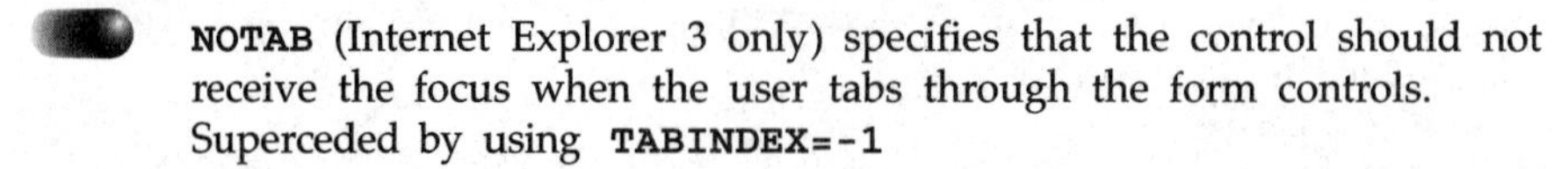

- **NOTAB** (Internet Explorer 3 only) specifies that the control should not receive the focus when the user tabs through the form controls. Superceded by using **TABINDEX=-1**
- **DATAFLD**, **DATASRC** and **DATAFORMATAS** are used in Internet Explorer 4 to achieve data binding of the controls to a data source on the server or client. This is briefly discussed in chapter 12.

The <TEXTAREA> Element

This element produces a multi-line text box area for user input. When the form is submitted, each line of text is sent to the server separated by a carriage return and line feed (**%0D%0A**). For the sake of simplicity, you should avoid using a **<TEXTAREA>** control if you need to parse the value after submission. Generally, such kinds of information can be handled more elegantly with checkboxes, **<SELECT>** lists, and **<INPUT>** controls.

The attributes of **<TEXTAREA>** are:

ACCESSKEY NAME COLS ROWS DISABLED* READONLY* TABINDEX*

plus the usual HTML 4.0 attributes **ID**, **CLASS**, **LANG**, **DIR**, **STYLE** and **TITLE** as described in chapter 1. The attributes marked with an asterisk are new in HTML 4.0, and are generally not supported in older browsers.

> **The end tag </TEXTAREA> is required. Text that is placed between the start and end-tags sets the control's initial value. A RESET button on the form may or may not reset the contents of a <TEXTAREA> in the same way as it does with the <INPUT> element, depending on the browser.**

ACCESSKEY

ACCESSKEY is used to define a keyboard character that can be pressed, usually in conjunction with the *Alt* or command key, to switch the focus directly to the control. It acts as a 'hot-key' or short-cut key allowing easier navigation.

NAME

Gives the text area a unique name. See the **<INPUT>** element for details.

COLS

Sets the width of the text area. The syntax is:

COLS=*n*

where *n* is the width in characters. The actual on-screen dimension of the control depends on the client system's default font size, so will appear at different sizes on different machines even with the same value of **COLS**.

ROWS

Sets the height of the text area. The syntax is:

ROWS=*n*

where *n* is the height in characters. The actual on-screen dimension of the control depends on the client system's default font size, so will appear at different sizes on different machines even with the same value of **ROWS**.

DISABLED

Forces the control to be disabled, i.e. it is grayed out and the user cannot change the value in it. See the **<INPUT>** element for details.

READONLY

Forces the control to be read only, i.e. displayed normally, but the user cannot change the value in it. See the **<INPUT>** element for details.

TABINDEX

This attribute allows the HTML author to set the order that the focus moves between controls when the *Tab* key is pressed. See the **<INPUT>** element for details.

Extensions to the <TEXTAREA> Element

Both Netscape Navigator and Internet Explorer support an extra attribute to the **<TEXTAREA>** tag:

WRAP defines how the text within the element is wrapped if the line is longer than will fit in the width of the control. It can be **OFF** (text is not wrapped in the control), **PHYSICAL** (text is wrapped in the control, and carriage returns are inserted at the end of each line when the value is sent to the server) or **VIRTUAL** (the default, text is wrapped in the control, but sent to the server as a single string with no extra carriage returns inserted).

Internet Explorer-Specific Extensions

Internet Explorer adds three other attributes to the **<TEXTAREA>** tag:

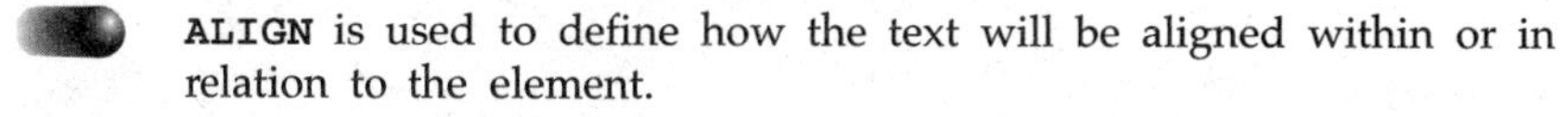

- **ALIGN** is used to define how the text will be aligned within or in relation to the element.
- **DATAFLD** and **DATASRC** are used in Internet Explorer 4 to achieve data binding of the controls to a data source on the server or client. This is briefly discussed in chapter 12.

The <SELECT> Element

The **<SELECT>** element is used to produce a list box or a drop-down combo-box from which one or more selections can be made. This tag can be extremely useful, if employed carefully. The closing **</SELECT>** tag is required in all cases.

The attributes it supports are:

MULTIPLE	NAME	SIZE	DISABLED*	TABINDEX*

plus the usual HTML 4.0 attributes **ID**, **CLASS**, **LANG**, **DIR**, **STYLE** and **TITLE** as described in Chapter 1. The attributes marked with an asterisk are new in HTML 4.0, and are generally not supported in older browsers.

MULTIPLE

Indicates that multiple items can be selected. If **MULTIPLE** is not specified, only one option can be chosen. Depending on your operating system, you would hold down the *Ctrl*, *Alt*, or command keys to click multiple selections. The syntax is simply:

```
MULTIPLE
```

NAME

Defines a unique name for the element. See the **<INPUT>** element for details.

SIZE

Specifies the height of the list control, and therefore how many options are visible at one time. The syntax is:

SIZE=*n*

where *n* is the number of options that will be shown at once. If **SIZE=1**, the control appears as a drop-down combo-box with only one option visible. When the drop-down button at the right-hand end of the control is clicked it opens to display a list of options. If **SIZE** is set to a value greater than one, it creates a scrollable list control with more than one entry visible at one time.

> **Note that SIZE does not set the width of the control, but the height of the list it displays. The only way to specify the width of the control is to use the STYLE attribute, and set the width property.**

DISABLED

Forces the control to be disabled, i.e. it is grayed out and the user cannot change the value in it. See the **<INPUT>** element for details.

TABINDEX

This attribute allows the HTML author to set the order that the focus moves between controls when the *Tab* key is pressed. See the **<INPUT>** element for details.

Extensions to <SELECT> in Internet Explorer

Internet Explorer adds four other attributes to the **<TEXTAREA>** tag:

- **ACCESSKEY** is used to define a keyboard character that can be pressed, usually in conjunction with the *Alt* or command key, to switch the focus directly to the control. It acts as a 'hot-key' or short-cut key allowing easier navigation.
- **ALIGN** is used to define how the text will be aligned within or in relation to the element.
- **DATAFLD** and **DATASRC** are used in Internet Explorer 4 to achieve data binding of the controls to a data source on the server or client. This is briefly discussed in chapter 12.

The <OPTION> Element

The **<OPTION>** element is used to specify the individual entries that appear in a **<SELECT>** list, and is only used in this context. A set of **<OPTION>** elements are enclosed by the **<SELECT>** and **</SELECT>** tags, and the text of the option appears after the **<OPTION>** tag. There is no closing tag for **<OPTION>**:

```
<SELECT NAME=MyList SIZE=1>
  <OPTION VALUE=0.5>Half an inch
  <OPTION VALUE=0.75>Three quarters of an inch
  <OPTION VALUE=2.5>Two and a half inches
</SELECT>
```

The attributes supported by the **<OPTION>** element are:

SELECTED　　**VALUE**　　**DISABLED***

plus the usual HTML 4.0 attributes **ID**, **CLASS**, **LANG**, **DIR**, **STYLE** and **TITLE** as described in chapter 1. The **DISABLED** attribute is new in HTML 4.0, and is generally not supported in older browsers.

SELECTED

Specifies if this option will be selected when the form is first displayed. The syntax is simply:

```
SELECTED
```

In a drop-down combo list, where **SIZE=1**, this sets the option that will be shown by default.

VALUE

Specifies the value that will be sent to the server if that option is selected. If more than one is selected (when the **<SELECT>** element include the **MULTIPLE** attribute), the values are sent as a comma-delimited list. The syntax is:

VALUE=*value*

If omitted, the text that follows the **<OPTION>** element (and is displayed in the list) is sent instead.

DISABLED

Forces the control to be disabled, i.e. it is grayed out and the user cannot change the value in it. See the **<INPUT>** element for details.

A Simple Form Example

Here is a simple example form that uses only the HTML controls that we've covered so far. These controls are supported by almost all browsers:

```
<!DOCTYPE HTML PUBLIC "-//W3C//DTD HTML 4.0 Draft//EN">
<HTML>
<HEAD>
<TITLE>Test Form</TITLE>
</HEAD>
<BODY>
<FORM METHOD="POST"
  ACTION="http://hoohoo.ncsa.uiuc.edu/cgi-bin/post-query">
Name:
<INPUT TYPE=TEXT NAME=YourName SIZE=40><P>
Favorite Color:
<INPUT TYPE=RADIO NAME=Color VALUE="B"> Blue
<INPUT TYPE=RADIO NAME=Color VALUE="G"> Green
<INPUT TYPE=RADIO NAME=Color VALUE="O"> Other<P>
Your pet is:
<SELECT NAME=PetName SIZE=1>
  <OPTION>Rover
  <OPTION>Smokey
  <OPTION>Dylan
  <OPTION>Alfred
</SELECT><P>
<INPUT TYPE=SUBMIT>
</FORM>
</BODY>
</HTML>
```

In Netscape Navigator it looks like this:

Testing Your Forms

Notice the **METHOD** and **ACTION** attributes in the **<FORM>** tag:

```
<FORM METHOD="POST"
  ACTION="http://hoohoo.ncsa.uiuc.edu/cgi-bin/post-query">
```

We're submitting our form to **http://hoohoo.ncsa.uiuc.edu/cgi-bin/post-query**. Why? Well, when creating your own forms for use on someone else's system (for example if you rent Web space from a service provider rather than hosting the site on your own server), it's often useful to test them before you actually try to use them. There is a special test server running at the National Center for Supercomputing Applications (NCSA) which makes it easy to do this. NCSA has created a server-side program that will take the data from any form, and return it as an HTML page that shows what data the form sent:

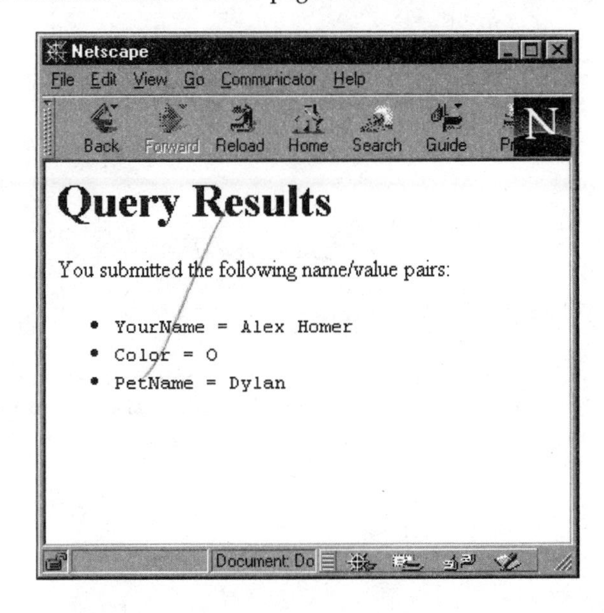

There are two versions of the program, one for each **METHOD** available for forms. We used the **POST** method above, for the **GET** method use:

```
<FORM METHOD=GET
ACTION="http://hoohoo.ncsa.uiuc.edu/cgi-bin/query">
```

Notice also that the color selection we made returned "O", the **VALUE** of the **RADIO**-type control that was selected when the form was submitted:

```
<INPUT TYPE=RADIO NAME=color VALUE="O"> Other
```

The New HTML 4.0 Controls

HTML 4.0 introduces five new HTML controls for use both on forms when submitting information to a server, and for integration with client-side scripting without using a form section in the page. They are **<OPTGROUP>**, **<BUTTON>**, **<LABEL>**, **<FIELDSET>** and **<LEGEND>**. Together with the existing controls and combined with scripting, they provide the opportunity to create **enhanced forms**.

The <OPTGROUP> Element

The **<OPTGROUP>** element allows authors to group choices into a hierarchy. It creates a hierarchical and collapsible list of options, which the user can browse and select from. It's intended to help with grouping options in non-visual renderings (flat lists of options tend to be hard to remember) and also will probably be of use in creating lists in drop down menus. It isn't supported in any browsers yet, as it was a very late addition to the HTML 4.0 recommendation.

The attributes supported by the **<OPTGROUP>** element are:

LABEL **DISABLED***

plus the usual HTML 4.0 attributes **ID**, **CLASS**, **LANG**, **DIR**, **STYLE** and **TITLE** as described in chapter 1.

LABEL

Specifies the label for the option group.

LABEL=*text*

The <BUTTON> Element

This element is new in HTML 4.0, and is supported in Internet Explorer 4 but not yet in Netscape Navigator. Internet Explorer 3 also supported the **<BUTTON>** tag, but in a limited way (see Appendix A for details).

The **<BUTTON>** tag is an alternative way of creating command buttons to the **<INPUT>** element with **TYPE=BUTTON**, and is more flexible. It requires the closing tag **</BUTTON>**, and the contents of the tag are rendered on the button face:

```
<BUTTON>
  <IMG SRC="stop.gif"><BR>Stop
</BUTTON>
```

This means that images, even animated GIFs, can be displayed on the button face—as well as or instead of text. Using the **STYLE** attribute, the size of the button can be controlled in browsers that support absolute positioning via Cascading Style Sheets.

The button can also be used as the default **SUBMIT** or **RESET** button for a form by setting an appropriate value for the **TYPE** attribute. This gives a similar effect to the **<INPUT TYPE=IMAGE>** control.

> **Unlike the <INPUT TYPE=IMAGE> button, the image used on the face of a <BUTTON> element *cannot* be an image map. If you use just an image on the button face, you should always include the ALT attribute in the <IMG> element for use in browsers that don't support images.**

The attributes supported by the **<BUTTON>** element are:

NAME	VALUE	TYPE	DISABLED	TABINDEX

plus the usual HTML 4.0 attributes **ID**, **CLASS**, **LANG**, **DIR**, **STYLE** and **TITLE** as described in chapter 1.

NAME

Defines a unique name for the element. See the **<INPUT>** element for details.

VALUE

Assigns a value to the button. This attribute is defined in draft proposals for HTML 4.0 but not supported in most browsers at present.

TYPE

Specifies the type of button to create. The syntax is:

TYPE=*button_type*

where *button_type* can be **BUTTON**, **RESET** or **SUBMIT**. This does not affect the appearance of the control, and the caption will be the text included between the **<BUTTON>** and **</BUTTON>** tags. However, if button is **RESET** or **SUBMIT** it will have the same effect as the equivalent **<INPUT>** type when clicked. The default is **BUTTON**.

DISABLED

Forces the control to be disabled, i.e. it is grayed out and the user cannot change the value in it. See the **<INPUT>** element for details.

TABINDEX

This attribute allows the HTML author to set the order that the focus moves between controls when the *Tab* key is pressed. See the **<INPUT>** element for details.

ACCESSKEY

Added in HTML 4.0 and supported in IE4, **ACCESSKEY** is used to define a keyboard character that can be pressed, usually in conjunction with the *Alt* or command key, to switch the focus directly to the control. It acts as a 'hot-key' or short-cut key allowing easier navigation. The syntax is:

ACCESSKEY=*character*

Extensions to <BUTTON> in Internet Explorer

Internet Explorer adds three other attributes to the **<BUTTON>** tag:

DATAFLD, **DATAFORMATAS** and **DATASRC** are used in Internet Explorer 4 to achieve data binding of the controls to a data source on the server or client. This is briefly discussed in chapter 12.

The <LABEL> Element

This element is new in HTML 4.0. It is partly supported in Internet Explorer 4, but not yet in Navigator. It provides a way to link a caption or label for an HTML control to that control. By specifying a 'hot-key' or short-cut key combination, the appropriate key will be indicated in the label—generally by underlining or highlighting that letter. When the user presses that key combination, the input focus moves to the control to which the label is linked.

To explicitly link a **<LABEL>** with another control, the **FOR** attribute is used, however if you just want to implicitly link this element with another control, then just add the chosen control between the opening and closing **<LABEL>** tags.

The **<LABEL>** element supports the following attributes:

ACCESSKEY	**ALIGN**	**FOR**	**TABINDEX**

plus the usual HTML 4.0 attributes **ID**, **CLASS**, **LANG**, **DIR**, **STYLE** and **TITLE** as described in chapter 1.

ACCESSKEY

This attribute is used to define a keyboard character that can be pressed, usually in conjunction with the *Alt* or command key, to switch the focus directly to the control linked to the label. The syntax is:

ACCESSKEY=*character*

where *character* is the keyboard character to be pressed.

ALIGN

Use this attribute to define how the text will be aligned within the label. The syntax is:

ALIGN=*alignment*

where *alignment* is **LEFT**, **RIGHT** or **CENTER**. These values have the same effect as with inline images.

FOR

The attribute provides the link between the label and the control. The syntax is:

FOR=*control_name*

where *control_name* is the **ID** (not the **NAME** unless it is the same as the **ID**) of the control to link to. This can be any HTML control type.

TABINDEX

This attribute allows the HTML author to set the order that the focus moves between controls when the *Tab* key is pressed. See the **<INPUT>** element for details.

Using <LABEL> in Internet Explorer 4

Internet Explorer 4 adds three other attributes to the **<TEXTAREA>** tag:

DATAFLD, **DATAFORMATAS** and **DATASRC** are used in Internet Explorer 4 to achieve data binding of the controls to a data source on the server or client. This is briefly discussed in chapter 12.

Internet Explorer does *not* currently render the text of the **<LABEL>** element to highlight or underline the short-cut key. To get round this, use either the **<U>** tags or the **text-decoration** style property to indicate the letter in Windows:

```
<LABEL FOR=txtName ACCESSKEY="N">
  <U>N</U>ame
</LABEL>
```

Currently, IE4 does not position the label in relation to the control automatically (in the same way as a **<CAPTION>** is positioned with relation to a **<TABLE>** element). Positioning the labels can be done using the **STYLE** attribute in the normal way instead.

The <FIELDSET> Element

This element is new in HTML 4.0. It is partly supported in Internet Explorer 4, but not yet in Navigator. It creates a 'box' (or visible frame) around controls, and should act as a container for them.

The HTML 4.0 documentation suggests that this container should not only provide grouping information and allow absolute positioning within the container, but should also act as a 'value container' for Boolean controls so that it reflects the value of the selected one. In Internet Explorer, the **<FIELDSET>** element acts as a positioning container, but not as a value container.

The **<FIELDSET>** control supports just the usual HTML 4.0 attributes **ID**, **CLASS**, **LANG**, **DIR**, **STYLE** and **TITLE** as described in chapter 1.

The <LEGEND> Element

This element is new in HTML 4.0. It is partly supported in Internet Explorer 4, but not yet in Navigator. It is used in conjunction with a **<FIELDSET>** element, and provides a caption for the frame created by **<FIELDSET>**. By specifying a 'hot-key' or short-cut key combination, the appropriate key will be indicated in the label—generally by underlining or highlighting that letter. When the user presses that key combination, the input focus moves to the first control within the **<FIELDSET>**.

The **<LEGEND>** element supports the following attributes:

ACCESSKEY **ALIGN**

plus the usual HTML 4.0 attributes **ID**, **CLASS**, **LANG**, **DIR**, **STYLE** and **TITLE** as described in chapter 1.

ACCESSKEY

This attribute is used to define a keyboard character that can be pressed, usually in conjunction with the *Alt* or command key, to switch the focus directly to the control linked to the label. The syntax is:

ACCESSKEY=*character*

where *character* is the keyboard character to be pressed.

ALIGN

Use this attribute to define how the legend will be aligned with respect to the fieldset. The syntax is:

ALIGN=*alignment*

where *alignment* is **TOP**, **BOTTOM**, **LEFT** or **RIGHT**. These values have the same effect as when placing a caption with a table, and can place the legend at various places around the fieldset frame.

An Enhanced Form Example

The combination of existing HTML controls (as supported by almost all browsers) and the new HTML 4.0 controls can be used to create Web pages that appear to be 'real' applications. The following screenshot shows some of the possibilities. This page was created for Internet Explorer 4, which can display pages in a dialog-style window:

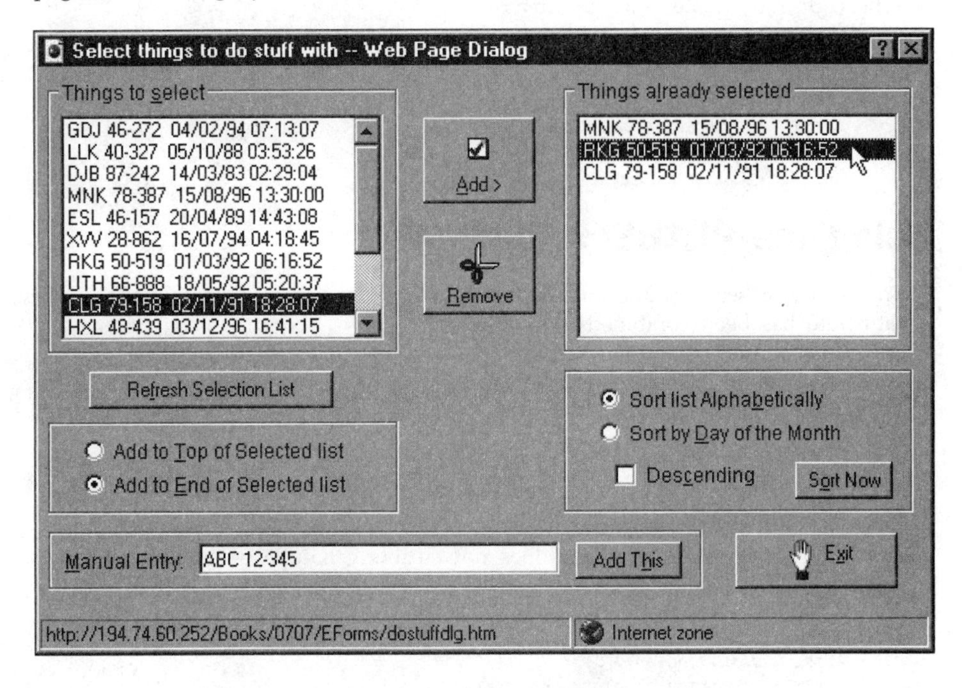

Using <FIELDSET> and <LEGEND>

The page we've just seen creates a **<FIELDSET>** with a **<LEGEND>**, and places a **<SELECT>** list within it. We've used absolute positioning to place the frame and the list in the correct positions:

```
<! The left-hand 'select from' list >
<FIELDSET ID=fldFrom
 STYLE="position:absolute;width:215;
        height:165;top:5;left:5">
 <LEGEND>Things to <U>S</U>elect</LEGEND>
 <SELECT ID=lstFrom ACCESSKEY="S" TABINDEX=1 SIZE=10
   TITLE="Select a thing to do stuff with"
   STYLE="position:absolute;width:200;
          top:20;left:5;font-size:9pt">
 </SELECT>
</FIELDSET>
```

Using the TITLE Attribute

The **TITLE** attribute of a control provides a pop-up 'tooltip' when the mouse pointer pauses over a control:

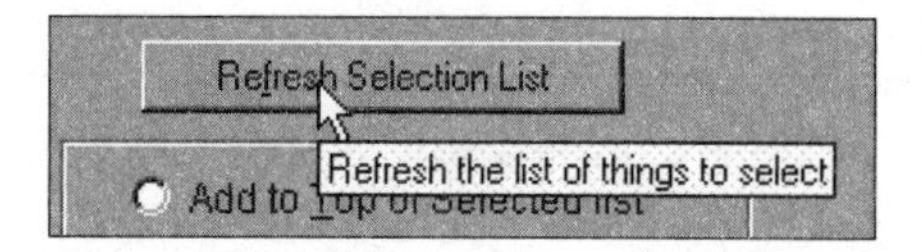

The code that creates this button is:

```
<BUTTON ID=btnRefresh ACCESSKEY="F" TABINDEX=2 DISABLED
  TITLE="refresh the list of things to select"
  STYLE="position:absolute;width=100;top=30;
         left=235;font-size:9pt">
  Re<U>f</U>resh Selection List
</BUTTON>
```

Using the <LABEL> Element

You can also see how the **ACCESSKEY** attribute has been combined with the use of **<U>** and **</U>** tags to create short-cuts to the button in the previous example. The same is done with the option buttons:

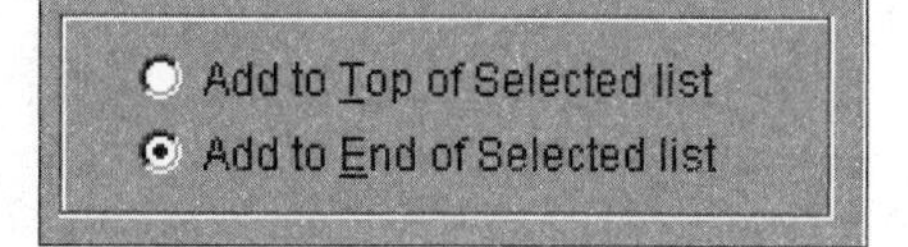

In this case, we've used **<LABEL>** elements to create the labels for the option buttons. We've put them inside **<DIV>** elements to be able to position them absolutely, as Internet Explorer does not currently handle positioning of labels correctly.

```
<! The 'Add to top or end' option buttons >
<FIELDSET ID=fldOrder
  STYLE="position:absolute;width:215;
         height:55; top:210; left:5">
  <INPUT TYPE=RADIO ID=optAtTop NAME=optOrder TABINDEX=6
    TITLE="Add this entry to the top of the Selected list"
    STYLE="position:absolute;top:5;left:15;
           background-color:silver">
  <INPUT TYPE=RADIO ID=optAtEnd NAME=optOrder TABINDEX=7
    CHECKED
    TITLE="Add this entry to the end of the Selected list"
    STYLE="position:absolute;top:25;left:15;
           background-color:silver">
</FIELDSET>

<DIV STYLE="position:absolute;width:150;height:20;
           top:220;left:45">
  <LABEL ID=lblAtTop ACCESSKEY="T" FOR="optAtTop">
    Add to <U>T</U>op of Selected list
  </LABEL>
</DIV>

<DIV STYLE="position:absolute;width:150;height:20;
           top:240;left:45">
  <LABEL ID=lblAtEnd ACCESSKEY="E" FOR="optAtEnd">
    Add to <U>E</U>nd of Selected list
  </LABEL>
</DIV>
```

You can try this page yourself from our Web site at **`http://www.rapid.wrox.com/books/0707`**. *This site contains several examples of different techniques for building interactive Web pages in both Netscape Navigator 4 and Internet Explorer 4. Open the main page at* **`http://www.rapid.wrox.com`** *and follow the* Books and Samples *link to see them all.*

Processing Forms

While this book is mainly concerned with client-side HTML issues, remember that forms are a two-part equation. Once you've designed your form and got the client-side working, you need a program on the server to process the form's data. When you come to programming a form, remember that there's a good chance that someone else has already designed a program that does most of the things you want; you'll just need to modify it to meet your particular requirements.

Have a look around the web and you'll find several sites with programs that you can use specifically for this purpose. They are often freeware programs that just require an acknowledgment to the original author. Most web site hosting companies and service providers also offer generic programs, available on their server, that you can use. Often these require you to include **`HIDDEN`** controls on your form with preset values that specify how you want the values to be processed and where you want the results to be sent to.

Name/Value Pairs

All form elements that provide data to be sent to the server use the **`NAME`** and **`VALUE`** attributes. The names are specified in the **`NAME`** attributes of form input elements. The values can initially be blank or set in the HTML using the **`VALUE`** attribute, and can usually be edited by the user of the form.

Data is sent to the server as name/value pairs by the browser when the form is submitted. Each name/value pair is of the format *name=value*, and the pairs are separated from each other by ampersands (`&`). Each name/value pair is URL encoded before being transmitted, i.e. spaces are changed into plus signs and some characters (plus signs, ampersands, accented letters, etc.) are encoded into hexadecimal preceded by a percent (`%`) sign.

At the server, the basic processing procedure is to split the data up at the ampersand characters, and then—for each name/value pair—URL decode the name and value to get the original input. The results can then be used by other server-based programs as required.

When a form is submitted, the browser should not submit the values of any controls that don't have a valid `NAME` attribute, any controls that are `DISABLED`, or the `value` property of any `<OBJECT>` elements that either have the `DECLARE` attribute present or the `NAME` attribute missing. Most browsers currently do submit controls that don't have a `NAME` attribute, and this can cause errors when the form is processed.

The Common Gateway Interface

The Common Gateway Interface, or CGI, is the recognized method of communication between the HTTP server and gateway programs. Any data sent to the server from the client has to be processed by a gateway program, the CGI handles the transmission of the data between the Internet server and any other program that will use it.

Gateway programs can be of several types. They can be compiled programs, written in any language (C++, Visual Basic and Delphi are commonly used), or executable scripts written in special scripting languages like Perl. Writing CGI programs can be fairly involved, depending on what you want to do, so we recommend checking out the following sources of information:

```
http://hoohoo.ncsa.uiuc.edu/cgi/
http://www.lpage.com/cgi/
http://snowwhite.it.brighton.ac.uk/~mas/mas/courses/html/html3.html
```

Other Server-Side Technologies

While the Common Gateway Interface is standard amongst most types of Internet Server software, each manufacturer often implements their own server-side processing languages as well.

Microsoft offer (amongst other technologies) a system called **Active Server Pages** (ASP), which uses a combination of HTML pages with embedded script that is executed on the server. This is one of the easiest ways to start server-side programming if you run Microsoft Internet Information Server. There is also a search and query engine called **Index Server** built into Windows NT, which can use standard HTML forms as the client-side interface. For more details look out for Professional Active Server Pages Programming, ISBN 1-861000-72-3, or visit: `http://www.microsoft.com/iis/UsingIIS/Developing/Samples/`

Netscape offer their own Web server software, under the umbrella of the **Open Network Environment** (ONE). This is based around the technology called **JavaBeans**, a way of creating components that can be executed either on the client (the browser) or the server. Many existing components are available for working with user-supplied information from a form, for providing access to databases on the server or another network, and many other tasks. For more details see: `http://developer.netscape.com/library/wpapers/crossware/`

Summary

This chapter has shown you how to create forms that can be used to interact with users and collect information. We discussed the `<FORM>` element and its associated HTML control tags: `<INPUT>`, `<TEXTAREA>`, and `<SELECT>` and `<OPTION>`. We then went on to look at the new HTML 4.0 elements, `<OPTGROUP>`, `<BUTTON>`, `<LABEL>`, `<FIELDSET>` and `<LEGEND>`, and saw how they can be used to make forms more like 'real' applications.

We also looked at how data is passed to the server as name/value pairs, and indicated ways that they can be processed. Obviously, you have to check that your form works, so we have also provided pointers as to how this can be achieved.

Remember that the layout of a form is important—your user must be able to navigate their way through the form easily. This can be achieved by placing the controls into HTML tables, or by using the absolute positioning properties of the **STYLE** attribute.

Objects, ActiveX Controls and Applets

The real power in web pages comes when you start to insert objects into them. With HTML 2.0, you could only insert images, videos, sounds and text. This improved with HTML 3.2, but if you wanted to add anything more, such as simple animated messages, spreadsheets, word documents or even full 3-D renderings of landscapes, then you needed to insert them as objects. HTML 4.0 allows for this by making the **<OBJECT>** tag the standard way of doing this.

There are two different methods of adding objects to your pages. These are ActiveX controls and Java applets, which were created by two rival companies (Microsoft and Sun Microsystems) as competing standards. IE4 is able to execute both Microsoft's own ActiveX technology and Sun Microsystem's Java, while currently Navigator 4 can execute Java only. Navigator needs third party plug-ins to allow it to deal with ActiveX technology. We'll give a brief overview of both the technologies now, and then we'll take a look at how they can be used within your pages.

Java

Java originated from Sun Microsystems **http://java.sun.com/**. Sun were working on a language that would be cross platform capable and, at the same time, help them to propel their products in the market. They recognized its suitability as a language for embedding executable objects within an HTML page for processing by a Java enabled Web Browser. These embeddable objects were termed **applets** as they were mini-applications that needed to be controlled from within the browser environment. The **<APPLET>** tag was introduced in HTML 3.2 as the primary method for incorporating applets into your web pages, but has since been overtaken by developments.

While the term Java encompasses a number of Sun owned technologies, it is frequently used to refer to the Java programming language. This is distinct from JavaScript (formerly developed by Netscape as LiveScript) which is very loosely based on Java and C++, and is used in scripting.

JavaScript should not be confused with Java. JavaScript has recently been standardized by ECMA (European Computer Manufacturers Association) after joint submissions from Microsoft and Netscape, and is now called ECMAScript.

ActiveX

ActiveX has to be one of the most misunderstood and ambiguously used expressions in the Internet technology arena. When Microsoft released their first set of Internet tools in March 1996, they called it **ActiveX** technology—which in all truth was just a new marketing name for their existing **OLE** technology. ActiveX (or 3rd generation OLE technology) is a framework that allows software components to cooperate even if they have been written by different vendors, at different times, using different tools and different languages, and if the objects are located in the same process, same machine or distributed over multiple machines. The way to insert ActiveX controls into web documents is with the `<OBJECT>` tag.

The <OBJECT> Element

Originally, the HTML 2.0 Proposed Standard provided only one method for incorporating media into HTML documents: the `<IMG>` tag. This element has certainly proved worthwhile, but it is, of course, restricted to image media—which means that its usefulness is limited as richer media finds its way onto the Web.

The `<OBJECT>` tag was introduced by Microsoft Corporation for the inclusion of Microsoft **Component Object Model** or **COM** objects (e.g. ActiveX Controls and a wide variety of different media types and plug-ins). Internet Explorer introduced this tag with support for ActiveX controls, and Microsoft has continued to develop around it. Netscape doesn't support the `<OBJECT>` tag even in version 4 of Navigator, but have announced that they will implement it when the final HTML 4.0 standard appears.

It is proposed in HTML 4.0 to make the `<OBJECT>` tag a generic tag for inserting all kinds of content into a web page, including Java applets and images. Indeed, the `<OBJECT>` element is cited to supercede the `<APPLET>`, `<EMBED>` and `<IMG>` elements, and Microsoft's existing `<BGSOUND>` element and `DYNASRC` attribute (covered in Chapter 4). This will provide a single way to embed a whole range of objects into Web documents, and offer more universal, cross-platform support for HTML pages.

While currently, Internet Explorer 3.0 and 4.0 are the only browsers that natively support the `<OBJECT>` tag, Netscape Navigator does support usage of the `<OBJECT>` tag through a plug-in from NCompass Labs. While Navigator users miss out on this bit of (perhaps) important functionality, they don't have to worry what happens when Navigator, without the plug-in, crosses the `<OBJECT>` tag, as it simply ignores it and keeps on moving.

For more information on NCompass Labs plug-in for ActiveX objects and scripting, please visit: `http://www.ncompasslabs.com`

Now, let's take a look at the `<OBJECT>` tag's attributes, and see how you can use an object in your web page.

<OBJECT> Attributes

The `<OBJECT>` element supports the following attributes:

ALIGN	ARCHIVE	BORDER	CLASSID
CODEBASE	CODETYPEDATA	DECLARE	HEIGHT
WIDTH	HSPACEVSPACE	NAME	STANDBY
TABINDEX	TYPE	USEMAP	

plus the usual HTML 4.0 attributes **ID**, **CLASS**, **STYLE**, **DIR**, **LANG** and **TITLE**. The `<OBJECT>` element also supports a range of events that can be used in **scripting**. We look briefly at this topic in Chapters 10 and 12.

ALIGN

Use this attribute to align the object within the page and the surrounding elements. The syntax is:

```
ALIGN=TOP | MIDDLE | BOTTOM | LEFT | RIGHT |
ABSBOTTOM* | TEXTTOP* |ABSMIDDLE* | BASELINE*
```

For explanations of the values, please refer back to Chapter 4. This attribute is deprecated in HTML 4.0.

ARCHIVE

Specifies a list of URLs which have information relevant to the resource specified in **CLASSID** and **DATA** attributes. This is new to the HTML 4.0 recommendation and consequently isn't supported in IE4 or Navigator 4 yet.

ARCHIVE=*urllist*

BORDER

Specifies the width of the border to be drawn around the object.

BORDER=*n*

where *n* is an integer. For **BORDER=0**, no border is drawn.

CLASSID

Specifies a class identifier in the Windows Registry for an object.

CLASSID=*class_identifier*

The class identifier is the information used to create an object on your web page. The class identifier tells your browser to draw an object of a specified type. The **CLASSID** attribute is the key to the whole element. This is a value that is unique for every version of the object, and this is how the browser knows which object to load into the page. Here's an example of the **CLASSID** for the ActiveMovie ActiveX control.

```
<OBJECT ID="ActiveMovie" CLASSID="CLSID:05589FA1-C356-11CE-BF01-00AA0055595A"
...
```

CODEBASE

Allows you to specify the URL location and version of the object to be used.

CODEBASE=*url*

Many ActiveX controls need to be installed on your system before you can use them in your web pages. The **CODEBASE** attribute points to a location where the object can be downloaded and installed on your system for use. It also identifies the version of the file that should be downloaded. If an object isn't available already on your local machine then your system will have to go to the *url* specified. Of course if the site specified in the **CODEBASE** is busy or out of action, then unfortunately your page won't download correctly. An example **CODEBASE** for the timer control looks like this:

```
CODEBASE="http://activex.microsoft.com/controls/iexplorer/
timer.ocx#version=4,70,0,1161"
```

CODETYPE

Specifies the Internet Media Type of the referenced **CLASSID** attribute, before the object is actually downloaded.

CODETYPE=*media_type*

Browsers may use the value of the **CODETYPE** attribute to skip over unsupported media types, without the need to download unnecessary objects. See **TYPE** for more details on media types.

DECLARE

Declares the object without instantiating it.

DECLARE

Use this when you are creating cross-references to objects that occur later in the document, or when you are using the object as a parameter within another object.

DATA

Defines the URL, or the data itself, that is the source for the object. The syntax is:

DATA=*source*

where *source* can be a URL from which the data can be downloaded, or the data itself as a string of hexadecimal values. We'll look at an example of this later in the chapter.

HEIGHT and WIDTH

Specifies the height and width that an object is to be displayed at. The syntax is:

WIDTH=*n* **HEIGHT=***n*

where *n* is the width and height in pixels. When using the **<OBJECT>** element to display images, you'll find that **WIDTH** and **HEIGHT** are scaleable. That is, you can use them to specify the size of box that you want the image to fit into, and the browser will scale the image to suit. Using **WIDTH** and **HEIGHT** with the **<OBJECT>** element helps the page to load faster, because the browser can lay out the rest of the page as it knows the dimensions of the object before loading it.

HSPACE and VSPACE

These attributes are used to control the white space around an object. The syntax is:

HSPACE=*n* **VSPACE=***n*

where *n* is a numerical value in pixels. Other elements next to, or above and below, the image will be moved away the specified number of pixels.

NAME

Provides a name to refer to the object by. The syntax is:

NAME=*name*

where *name* is a unique name within the page. In HTML 4.0, this is equivalent to the **ID** attribute.

STANDBY

This attribute specifies a text string that will be used while the object data is loading. The syntax is:

STANDBY=*text*

where *text* is a word, phrase or sentence that describes the object, or is meaningful when displayed while it loads.

TABINDEX

The tab index for the object's container. The syntax is:

TABINDEX=*n*

where *n* is the position within the tabbing order of the page. By default, all elements in the page that can receive the input focus are part of the tabbing order, in the order they are defined in the HTML source. Each receives the focus in turn as the *Tab* key is pressed. By setting the value of **TABINDEX** to **-1**, the element is removed from the tabbing order.

TYPE

Defines the Mime type for the object, as defined in the registry. The syntax is:

TYPE=*mime-type*

where *mime-type* is a unique text string of a standard format, which tells the browser what kind of information the file contains, and which application to use to read or execute it—as appropriate. The Mime-types for popular image formats are "**image/gif**", "**image/jpeg**" and "**image/png**".

USEMAP

Indicates that the object is an image map containing defined areas that are individual hyperlinks. The **USEMAP** attribute indicates the map file to use with this object.

Internet Explorer <OBJECT> Extensions

Internet Explorer adds other attributes to the **<OBJECT>** element:

- **ACCESSKEY** defines the 'hot-key' that can be used to activate the element, or switch the input focus to it. This is often used where the image forms a hyperlink. For details of using an image as a hyperlink see Chapter 5. For more about the uses of the **ACCESSKEY** attribute see Chapter 8.
- **CODE** defines the class name of a Java applet, if this is the object source instead of an image or ActiveX control.
- **DATAFLD** and **DATASRC** are used to connect the **<IMG>** element to a client-side cached data source in Internet Explorer 4, in a technique called **data binding**. We will look briefly at this in Chapter 12.
- **NOTAB** was present very briefly in Internet Explorer 3, although dropped by version 4. It was used to exclude an element from the tabbing order, but now this can be achieved by setting the **TABINDEX** attribute to –1.

Tags <OBJECT> Can Enclose

The **<OBJECT>** element operates in conjunction with the **<PARAM>** element, which is used to specify the different parameters that each object can take. These parameters are values that the object will require at run time. They must be placed at the beginning of the content of the **<OBJECT>** element.

The <PARAM> element

The **PARAM** element can take the following attributes:

ID	NAME	TYPE	VALUE	VALUETYPE

ID is universal.

NAME

Specifies the name or property of the parameter.

NAME=*string*

VALUE

Specifies the value to set for the parameter.

VALUE=*string*

TYPE

The MIME type that is retrieved if **VALUETYPE** is set to **REF**.

TYPE=*string*

VALUETYPE

Specifies how the parameter value will be obtained.

VALUETYPE=DATA | REF | OBJECT

REF is via a **URL**, while **DATA** is the default, an implicit value.

Using the <OBJECT> Element

The **<OBJECT>** element is a general purpose element, designed to insert many different types of content into an HTML document. In order to cope with this diversity, the **CODETYPE** and **TYPE** attributes are used to indicate the type of data that the object comprises. Of interest to us when working with images is the **TYPE** attribute, which is a string description of the content—such as **"image/gif"** for a GIF image, or perhaps **"application/avi"** for an AVI video clip. In general terms, the application that is required to display the data is defined by **"application/***<document_type>***"**. In the case of the generic image types, like GIF and JPEG, the browser itself handles the display of the image.

In Windows, a list of all the Mime types supported by your machine can be found in registry under:
HKEY_CLASSES_ROOT\MIME\Database\ContentType\

Specifying the Data

The **DATA** attribute provides the data for the object, either as a URL from where it can be downloaded, or in-line as a string of values. As an example, this code will display an AVI file named **MyVideo.avi**. If the browser doesn't support the **<OBJECT>** element, it will display the text My Video:

```
<OBJECT DATA="http://mysite.com/video/MyVideo.avi"
        TYPE="application/avi">
  My Video
</OBJECT>
```

This is a general example of how we can take advantage of the **<OBJECT>** element as a container.

The **TYPE** attribute is, however, optional. But if it's not present, the only way that the browser can be sure of knowing whether it can handle the object is by downloading it first—not all files can be uniquely identified from, say, a file extension, and not all systems use file extensions anyway. For ActiveX controls the **TYPE** is **'x-oleobject'**. By including the **TYPE** (or **CODETYPE**) attribute, we can tell the browser exactly what type of file it is. Then, if it can't handle it, it won't waste time and bandwidth downloading it.

Fall Back in Browsers That Don't Support an Object

If the browser recognizes the **<OBJECT>** element, it doesn't display the content between the opening and closing tags. However, if it doesn't recognize the **<OBJECT>** element, or can't handle the data that forms the source of the object, it should display this content instead.

So, we can include text and other elements that are only visible on browsers that either don't recognize the **<OBJECT>** element, or that can't handle the content type of the data it specifies. This is done by placing the text or other elements between the opening and closing **<OBJECT>** tags, and outside any parameter tags. Here's another example:

```
<OBJECT DATA="http://mysite.com/video/MyVideo.avi"
        TYPE="application/avi">
    <IMG SRC="http://mysite.com/stills/MyPicture.gif"
        ALT="This is a picture of my dog">
</OBJECT>
```

Here, the viewer will see an ordinary image defined by the **<IMG>** element if their browser either doesn't support the **<OBJECT>** element; or can't display AVI files. And if it doesn't recognize the **<IMG>** element, or can't display the content of it for any reason, the alternative text in the **<IMG>** element's **ALT** attribute will be used.

Inline Data Definitions for Objects

If the data content of the object is reasonably small, it can be defined by including the data itself in the **<OBJECT>** tag. This is called an **in-line** definition:

```
<OBJECT DATA="data:application/x-oleobject;3300,FF00,E3A0, .. etc">
</OBJECT>
```

Inserting Images with an <OBJECT> Tag

One of the most intriguing proposals in HTML 4.0, as we've seen, is the use of the **<OBJECT>** tag to embed ordinary graphics files, such as GIF and JPEG files. This is also likely to extend the kinds of graphic files that are supported, possibly to include platform-specific files such as Windows WMF or other graphics metafiles. In its most basic form the use is simple:

```
<OBJECT DATA="MyPicture.gif">
</OBJECT>
```

The **DATA** attribute works just like the **SRC** attribute in an **<IMG>** tag, but can also accept in-line data where the image is small. This can speed up the time to view of a page, by reducing the number of server connections required.

```
<OBJECT TYPE="image/jpeg"
  DATA="data:image/jpeg;3300,FF00,2756,E5A0,E3A0,22F6, ... etc">
</OBJECT>
```

And finally, by adding the usual **WIDTH** and **HEIGHT** attributes, we have a system that can emulate all the usual **<IMG>** attributes:

```
<OBJECT DATA="MyDog.gif" WIDTH=120 HEIGHT=100>
   A picture of my dog
</OBJECT>
```

Displaying a GIF File

Here's a simple example of the **<OBJECT>** element being used to insert a standard GIF image. We specify the Mime type in the **TYPE** attribute, and the filename in the **DATA** attribute. In the current release of Internet Explorer 4, we also have to specify the **HEIGHT** and **WIDTH** attributes. Unlike the **<IMG>** element, the **<OBJECT>** element doesn't (at the moment) use the default size of the file to size the container:

```
<OBJECT TYPE="image/gif" DATA="wroxlogo.gif" WIDTH=250 HEIGHT=70>
  This is our Wrox Logo
</OBJECT>
```

Looking at the result, you can see what's meant by the **container** in an **<OBJECT>** element. The **HEIGHT** and **WIDTH** we've specified are used to size the **<OBJECT>** element itself (the container), but not the image. Because it's larger than the available space, the browser automatically adds scroll bars:

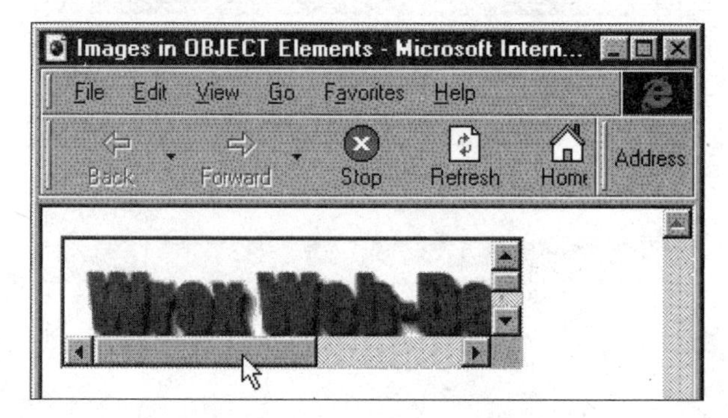

Of course, the 'proper' way to size an element in HTML 4.0 is to use the **STYLE** attribute to specify the CSS1 styles, as you saw in the previous chapter. This code produces the same page as you see above:

```
<OBJECT TYPE="image/gif" DATA="wroxlogo.gif"
        STYLE="width:250; height:70">
  This is our Wrox Logo
</OBJECT>
```

Hidden Image Elements

We can also specify other style properties, for example this code:

```
<OBJECT TYPE="image/gif" DATA="wroxlogo.gif"
        STYLE="visibility:hidden">
  This is our Wrox Logo
</OBJECT>
```

loads the image into the **<OBJECT>** element on the page, but makes it invisible. While it may seem a little pointless, it is a good way to get the browser to cache images that you want to make available quickly. When the image needs to be displayed, it doesn't need to be downloaded—just lifted from the local system's cache.

The Alternative Content

Finally, what happens if the browser doesn't know how to handle the object specified by the **TYPE** and **DATA** attributes? Here, we've used an unknown value for **TYPE**:

```
<OBJECT TYPE="havent/aclue" DATA="wroxlogo.gif"
        STYLE="width:250; height:70">
  This is our Wrox Logo
</OBJECT>
```

The result is that, after a few moments indecision, Internet Explorer 4 reports that it can't handle the file and displays the alternative text content of the **<OBJECT>** element:

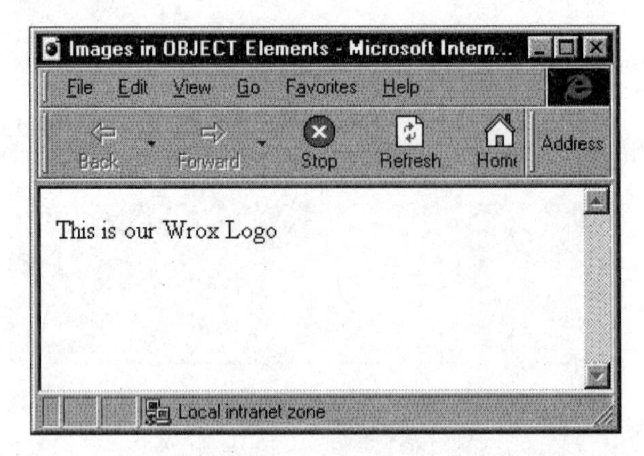

An Introduction to ActiveX Controls

ActiveX controls are objects that can be inserted into web pages or other applications. If you are a Visual Basic developer, you will be very familiar with ActiveX controls, as they were formerly known as OLE controls or OCXs.

There are several ActiveX controls that are included with Internet Explorer 4.0, which give you the ability to make your own web pages come alive by providing special formatting features, animation, video, and much more.

Currently, there are more than 1,000 ActiveX controls available, with functionality ranging from a simple label control to a control that gives you the ability to see another desktop across the Internet. If you can think of a particular control that you need for some specialized purpose, chances are that someone has probably created it.

You can add ActiveX controls to your Web pages using the **`<OBJECT>`** tag. The **`<OBJECT>`** tag includes a set of parameters that you use to specify which data a particular control should use. These parameters allow you to control the appearance and behavior of that control.

> *For more information on ActiveX Controls and Technology, please visit:*
> ***`http://www.microsoft.com/workshop/default.asp`***

Showing an ActiveX Movie

ActiveMovie or AM is Microsoft's Audio and Video technology and comes with the full version of Internet Explorer 4.0. ActiveMovie allows you to play back popular media formats on the web, including progressive playback of MPEG Audio and Video, AVI files, QuickTime MOVies, AU, WAV Files, MIDI, and AIFF.

We are going to show you one more way of putting in-line video into your web page, by giving you an example of how to implement the ActiveMovie ActiveX Control, also known as an object, into your web page.

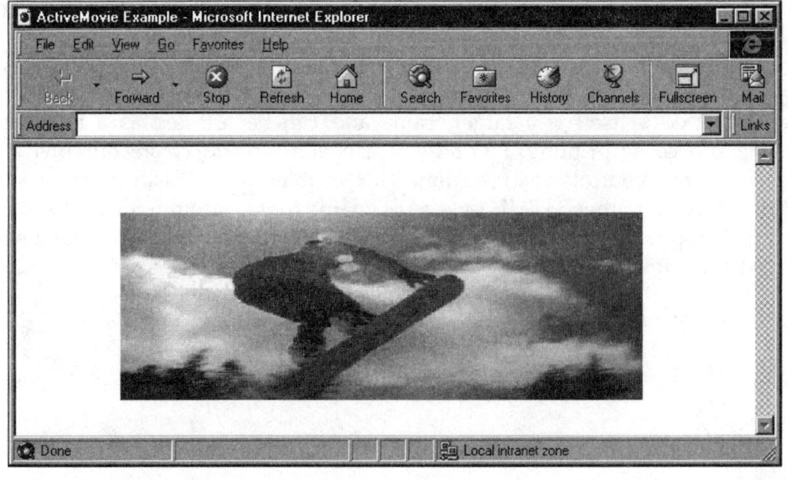

Take a look at the following code:

```
<HTML>
<HEAD>
<TITLE>ActiveMovie Example</TITLE>
</HEAD>
<BODY>

<OBJECT ID="ActiveMovie" CLASSID="CLSID:05589FA1-C356-11CE-BF01-00AA0055595A"
style="WIDTH:445;HEIGHT:155;position:absolute;top:55;left:90">
 <PARAM NAME="ShowDisplay" VALUE="0">
 <PARAM NAME="ShowControls" VALUE="0">
 <PARAM NAME="MovieWindowWidth" VALUE="445">
 <PARAM NAME="MovieWindowHeight" VALUE="162">
 <PARAM NAME="AutoStart" VALUE="1">
 <PARAM NAME="AutoRewind" VALUE="-1">
 <PARAM NAME="Volume" value="-5000">
 <PARAM NAME="FileName"
 VALUE="http://rapid.wrox.co.uk/books/1568/chapter9/RockClmb.avi">
</OBJECT>

</BODY>
</HTML>
```

As you can see, there are a number of **<PARAM>** tags included within the **<OBJECT>** tag itself: these are all specific parameters for the ActiveMovie object. If you wanted to embed a different object in your page, the properties for that object would be different, and you would need to enter those different parameters. We are not actually going to spend any time explaining each of the properties, but rather, give you a pointer to where you can get more information on ActiveMovie:

http://www.microsoft.com/directx/pavilion/default.asp

You will see that the **FileName** property of the ActiveMovie control is set to an AVI Video (**.avi**) on our own web server. You will also notice that there is no **CODEBASE** for the ActiveMovie object, because it is shipped as part of the full version of Internet Explorer 4.0. Try the code, and check out the video!

Including HTML in another HTML document

The HTML 4.0 proposals for the **<OBJECT>** element also allow you to "insert HTML documents into your web pages." This might seem like a pointless pastime inserting web pages into web pages, but there are two reasons why it might be very useful. First it acts as an alternative to the **<IFRAME>** element, when **<IFRAME>** itself is a target frame and can be selected as a focus for viewing source or printing. Secondly it can allow us to create our own small, simple ActiveX controls for insertion. This enables us to easily reuse a single section of code (either HTML or script) many times throughout a site, without having to reproduce the code in its entirety. You can embed a document using the **DATA** attribute as follows:

```
<OBJECT data="embedded_document.htm">
Couldn't include document specified.
</OBJECT>
```

Microsoft have termed the ability to embed script code within HTML document using the **<OBJECT>** element as **Scriptlets**. Scriptlets are platform independent (with the upcoming release of IE4 for the UNIX and Macintosh platforms) components that can be deployed on the Web. Netscape are developing their own version of this technology by allowing HTML and JavaScript code to be wrapped up as Java components (known as Java Beans) and used on the client side in a similar manner. This is very much a technology for the future and beyond the scope of this book.

> *To find out more about Scriptlets, look at the sample chapter from* Professional IE4 Programming *on our site at* **http://www.wrox.com** *and watch out for our forthcoming book on Scriptlets. To find out about Netscape's alternative proposals for an "Open Network Environment", go to their site* **http://home.netscape.com**

Applets and Java

First things first: Java is currently supported by Microsoft Internet Explorer 3.0 and 4.0, Netscape Navigator 3.0 and 4.0, and Sun Microsystems's HotJava browser. When Java was introduced, the **<APPLET>** tag was proposed as the way that Java applets were to be added into HTML.

The <APPLET> Element

The **<APPLET>** element was incorporated into the HTML 3.2 specification from the World Wide Web Consortium, but has already been deprecated in the HTML 4.0 proposed recommendation, in favor of **<OBJECT>**. However, it's still a very easy way to add Java functionality to your web pages.

Since the focus of this chapter is how to add objects, we are going to discuss how you can use Java to add an object. **<APPLET>**, like **<OBJECT>**, can also enclose the **<PARAM>** element. Also, we're not going to address how to build Java applets here, instead, we'll insert an applet that has already been developed. Creating a Java applet is another book in itself.

Attributes of the <APPLET> Element

Java Applets are inserted into a web page using the **<APPLET>** tag. The **<APPLET>** tag has several attributes associated with it, which are as follows:

ALIGN	**ALT**	**CODE**	**CODEBASE**	**HEIGHT**
WIDTH	**NAME**	**HSPACE**	**VSPACE**	

The **<APPLET>** tag also supports the universal attributes; **CLASS**, **ID**, **STYLE** and **TITLE**.

ALIGN

Determines where to place the applet on the web page.

ALIGN=*value*

where *value* is **TEXTTOP, MIDDLE, ABSMIDDLE, BASELINE, ABSBOTTOM, LEFT, CENTER,** or **RIGHT**.

ALT

Defines the alternative text to be displayed if the applet cannot be loaded.

ALT=*text*

CODE

Specifies the name of the Java class to be executed.

CODE=*"java.class"*

An example is **CODE="Animator.class"**

One important note to remember is that names of Java class files are case-sensitive. So be sure that whatever you place in your HTML is case correct.

CODEBASE

Specifies the location of the Java class file. This parameter is optional, but is always needed if the Java class is not in the same directory as the referencing HTML document. The syntax is:

CODEBASE=*"path | url"*

where *path* is equivalent to a relative path and *url* is the uniform resource locator for a class. This allows for the inclusion of applets in your web pages from remote systems. An example is:

CODEBASE="http://java.sun.com/applets/Animator/"

HEIGHT and WIDTH

Specifies the height and width of the applet.

HEIGHT=*n*
WIDTH=*n*

where *n* is the height and width in pixels.

NAME

Specifies the name of the applet.

NAME=*name*

VSPACE and HSPACE

Defines how many pixels of space are reserved above and below the applet, and to either side of it.

VSPACE=*n*
HSPACE=*n*

Navigator 4 Only Attributes

There are a couple of attributes that are only supported on Navigator 4, that are of interest.

ARCHIVE **MAYSCRIPT**

ARCHIVE

Archive holding the *url* of the file with the digital signature of the applet.

ARCHIVE=*url*

MAYSCRIPT

Indicates if an applet is capable of accepting instructions from script code.

MAYSCRIPT= Yes | No

IE4 Only Attributes

These IE4 only attributes are all described in conjunction with the **<OBJECT>** tag, earlier in this chapter.

DATAFLD **DATASRC** **SRC**

Incorporating the <APPLET> Tag into HTML

Here is an example of how to incorporate the **<APPLET>** tag in your web pages:

```
<APPLET CODEBASE="JAVA" CODE="YOURJAVA.CLASS" WIDTH=200 HEIGHT=200>
```

Java applets have the ability to accept parameters from your HTML web pages. These parameters are passed to the applet using the **<PARAM>** tag. They allow information to be passed into a Java applet; a simple example would be passing a color into an applet to change the color of text.

Using the Animator Applet

The Animator applet is a general purpose animation tool that was produced by a developer at Sun Microsystems. This applet is available on the web at:

http://java.sun.com/applets/Animator/index.html

We encourage you to try this applet so that you can get an understanding of how Java handles animation. You can also get information about Animator by pressing the *Shift* key while clicking the mouse in an animation.

Here is the necessary HTML code to use the Animator applet in your web pages. As long as your browser supports Java, this example will work with a connection to the Internet. Note that all the attributes in the previous section are used within this example.

```
<HTML>
<HEAD>
<TITLE>Java Applet Example</TITLE><BODY>
</HEAD>
<APPLET CODEBASE="HTTP://java.sun.com/applets/Animator/1.0.2/"
CODE="Animator.class" WIDTH=460 HEIGHT=160>
<PARAM NAME=IMAGESOURCE VALUE="HTTP://java.sun.com/applets/Animator/1.0.2/
images/Beans">
<PARAM NAME=ENDIMAGE VALUE=10>
<PARAM NAME=BACKGROUNDCOLOR VALUE="0X00FF00">
<PARAM NAME=SOUNDSOURCE VALUE="HTTP://java.sun.com/applets/Animator/1.0.2/
audio">
<PARAM NAME=SOUNDTRACK VALUE="spacemusic.au">
<PARAM NAME=SOUNDS VALUE="1.au|2.au|3.au|4.au|5.au|6.au|7.au|8.au|9.au|0.au">
<PARAM NAME=PAUSE VALUE=200>
<PARAM NAME=STARTUP VALUE="HTTP://java.sun.com/applets/Animator/1.0.2/images/
loading-msg.gif">
</APPLET>
</BODY>
</HTML>
```

This is how it looks running inside IE4:

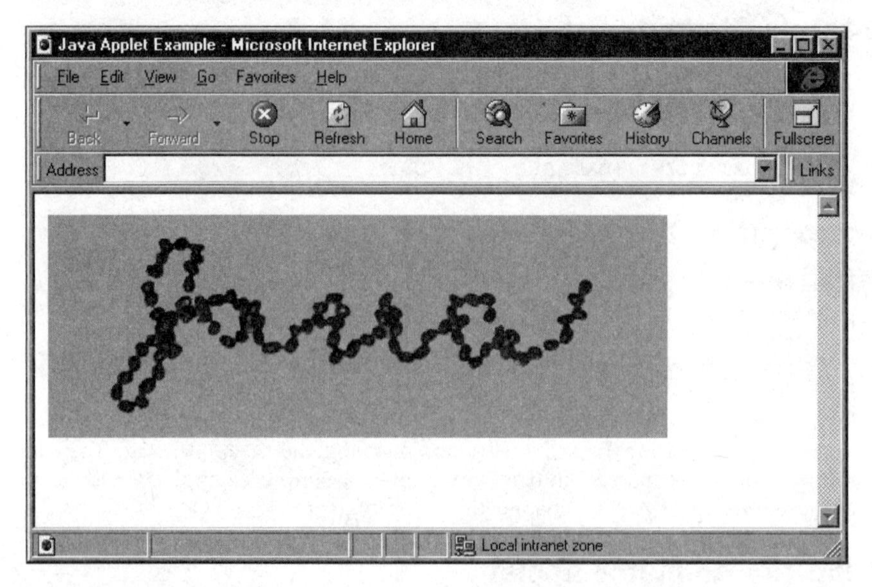

Using this Animator applet, you can create your own images and sounds by replacing the actual ones referenced within it. You're on your way to creating your very own Java animation.

Vendor-specific Tags for Other Media

<OBJECT> and **<APPLET>** aren't the only methods that can be used to embed executable content into web pages. Before **<OBJECT>**, browser developers used their own tags to reference other media from the web, to cope with the shortcomings of **<IMG>**. For example, Netscape used the **<EMBED>** tag to embed different objects into an HTML document. Although this is rapidly becoming obsolete, it's still possible to use it in both major browsers, so we'll look briefly at how to use it.

<EMBED>

The **<EMBED>** tag originated from Netscape and allows different media, of varying data types, to be embedded into an HTML document. The types of media that are supported under the current version of Netscape Navigator (without having to download any plug-ins) are:

- QuickTime **MOV**ies (via a shipping plug-in)
- LiveAudio (**MIDI**, **AIF**, **AU**, **WAV**)
- LiveVideo (**A**udio **V**ideo **I**nterleave)

Now that you can see the different multimedia types that are supported, let's discuss how you can take advantage of them using the **EMBED** tag.

<EMBED> Tag Attributes

The **<EMBED>** tag has the following attributes:

ALIGN WIDTH HEIGHT HSPACE VSPACE UNITS SRC NAME

The **<EMBED>** tag also supports the universal **CLASS**, **ID** and **STYLE** attributes.

ALIGN

Use this attribute to align the object within the page and the surrounding elements. The syntax is:

```
ALIGN=TOP | MIDDLE | BOTTOM | LEFT | RIGHT |
ABSBOTTOM* | TEXTTOP* |ABSMIDDLE* | BASELINE*
```

For explanations of the values, please refer back to Chapter 4.

SRC

The *url* of the source document

SRC=*url*

WIDTH and HEIGHT

Specifies the width and height of the embedded document.

```
WIDTH=n
HEIGHT=n
```

where *n* is the number of pixels.

HSPACE and VSPACE

Specifies the horizontal and vertical spacing or margins between elements or objects.

```
HSPACE=n
VSPACE=n
```

where *n* is the number of pixels.

NAME

The name used by other objects or elements to refer to this object.

```
NAME=identifier
```

UNITS

Defines how the size units of the contents should be used within the document.

```
UNIT=EN | EMS | PIXELS
```

Navigator 4 only Attributes

As the **<EMBED>** tag was never made part of the HTML standard (and the **<OBJECT>** tag renders it virtually redundant) there were a lot of proprietary attributes that either Navigator or Explorer supported. We'll start with the Navigator 4 ones.

BORDER	HIDDEN	PALETTE	PLUGINSPACE	TYPE

BORDER

Specifies the width of the border to be drawn around the object.

```
BORDER=n
```

where *n* is an integer. For **BORDER=0**, no border is drawn.

HIDDEN

Forces the **<EMBED>**ded object to be invisible.

```
HIDDEN=Yes | No
```

PALETTE

Sets the color palette to the foreground or background color. This was also supported in IE3, but is not in IE4.

```
PALETTE=foreground|background
```

PLUGINSPAGE

Defines the plugin to be used with the document.

PLUGINSPAGE=*string*

TYPE

Defines the Mime type for the object. The syntax is:

TYPE=*mime-type*

where *mime-type* is a unique text string of a standard format, which tells the browser what kind of information the file contains, and which application to use to read or execute it—as appropriate.

IE4 only Attributes

IE4 supports the **CODE** and **CODEBASE** attributes already seen in the **<OBJECT>** tag. Refer back to the **<OBJECT>** tag section for descriptions of what they do. IE4 also supports these attributes:

ALT   **TITLE**

TITLE is universal.

ALT

Specifies the text to be displayed if the object cannot be displayed with the environment.

ALT=*text*

Summary

In this chapter, we've introduced and explained how to add objects to your web pages whether they are animation, embedded documents, ActiveX Controls or Java applets.

We gave a very brief overview of the two competing standards, ActiveX and Java. We introduced the **<OBJECT>** tag and showed you how it could be used to add images to your HTML documents and also objects such as videos. This is the method that is recommended by the HTML 4.0 standard, however as Navigator 4 doesn't yet support the **<OBJECT>** tag you will need to continue to use the **<IMG>** element at present. We also showed you a couple of the older HTML tags that are no longer in the HTML standard and showed how they work, and, more importantly, how you can use them in your web pages.

Scripting

While HTML offers a wide array of facilities for the display of text, graphics, and other objects, it doesn't actually do much more than display a static web page. Visitors to the page can't alter the information in the page, or perform even simple calculations by just clicking on the visible HTML elements. If you're going to achieve anything more interactive, you actually need another programming language to run on the browser—the process called **scripting**.

A **scripting language** can be used to make your pages interactive. It is a programming language that provides control in a host environment. They frequently lack some of the more advanced programming capabilities, however, such as file handling and graphics. Programs built by scripting languages can't be run as stand-alone applications, they can only be run within a browser that supports them. The programs created are known as **scripts**, and are included within the code of the HTML document. They are recognized by the browser as being separate from the HTML, and are interpreted and executed, rather than just being displayed (as in case of the HTML).

Reasons for Using Scripting

Scripting can achieve many different effects in the page, limited only by the capabilities of the scripting language and the objects and elements exposed by the browser to the script. The most common uses are:

- Displaying dialog boxes and messages in the browser's status bar
- Writing content dynamically while the page is loaded, or after it has finished loading
- Changing the contents of the page, such as the `SRC` of an image or the contents of HTML controls on the page, and reacting to their events
- Validating user input, and controlling submission of a form or navigation to other pages
- Working with embedded objects such as Applets and ActiveX controls.

In Internet Explorer and (to some extent) Netscape Navigator, scripting is the primary way to make documents dynamic—by changing the HTML content while the page is loaded and interacting with the viewer. These topics are briefly covered in Chapters 11 and 12.

There are two main scripting language families available in current browsers, JavaScript and VBScript. JavaScript was originally introduced in Netscape Navigator, and a functionally similar language called JScript is available in Internet Explorer. The other common language, VBScript, is native to Internet Explorer. We'll look at how you can run both JavaScript and VBScript, and the reasons you might use one instead of the other. First though, we'll look at how you include a script within your HTML code.

The <SCRIPT> Element

Scripts are enclosed by the **<SCRIPT>** and **</SCRIPT>** tags, which tells the browser to begin parsing program information (i.e. that it isn't text for display but program code that will be executed). The simplest syntax is:

```
<SCRIPT LANGUAGE="script_language">
   script goes here...
</SCRIPT>
```

where *script_language* is usually one of:

JavaScript	Recognized by Navigator, Internet Explorer and other browsers
JScript	Microsoft's implementation of JavaScript in Internet Explorer
VBScript or **VBS**	Microsoft's implementation of VBScript in Internet Explorer

** Note that capitalization is not important when specifying the script language. Where the script language name does not contain spaces the quotation marks can be omitted.*

Other browsers can implement scripting, either directly or with a plug-in interpreter, and may offer different languages as well. For example, a VBScript plug-in is available for Netscape Navigator from *NCompass Labs* at: **http://www.ncompasslabs.com**

When the **<SCRIPT>** element is encountered, the interpreter is called. Usually, the code is executed in the order in which it appears in the document. Therefore, any reference to an object or element must appear in the script *after* the part of the page where that object or element has been defined.

As the introduction of the two main scripting languages has been a relatively recent innovation, many older browsers won't be able to run scripts. Since most browsers will simply ignore elements that they don't understand, visitors using an old browser will see your script as text in the page, right alongside the rest of the content. This is unsightly, and is why you can 'hide' your **<SCRIPT>** element inside the HTML comment tags. In JavaScript or JScript:

```
<SCRIPT LANGUAGE="JavaScript">
  <!-- hide from older browsers
  ...
  script goes here
  ...
  // end hiding -->
</SCRIPT>
```

In VBScript:

```
<SCRIPT LANGUAGE="VBScript">
  <!-- hide from older browsers
  ...
  script goes here
  ...
  ' end hiding -->
</SCRIPT>
```

Browsers that understand `<SCRIPT>` will see the tag and run the script, while older browsers will simply ignore everything within the script section.

> **The code comment markers `//` and `'` are not required in all browsers, which treat the closing HTML comment `-->` as a script comment marker as well. However, they should be included for completeness.**

Attributes of the <SCRIPT> Element

The `<SCRIPT>` tag has the following attributes in HTML 4.0:

TYPE	LANGUAGE	SRC	CHARSET	DEFER

TYPE

Specifies the Internet Content Type of the script, such as `"text/javascript"`, `"text/vbscript"` or `"text/tcl"`. This attribute is new and not yet supported in most browsers, so you will probably still need to use the `LANGUAGE` attribute for the time being.

LANGUAGE

Specifies the scripting language to be used, and is deprecated in HTML 4.0. The syntax is:

LANGUAGE="*script_language*"

If the scripting language is not recognized by the browser, the code inside the `<SCRIPT>` tags will be ignored. This attribute is not required in browsers that recognize the `TYPE` attribute. In Netscape Navigator and Internet Explorer, the default if no other language is specified is JavaScript and JScript respectively.

SRC

Specifies a URL for a script, stored in a separate file, to be included as part of the current page. The syntax is:

SRC="*url*"

This is particularly useful when several web pages all use the same script, as it saves copying and pasting the script into each page's code. In this form, the script can be any relative or absolute URL. JavaScript files in Navigator usually have the **.js** file extension. This property wasn't supported in IE3.

CHARSET

Specifies the ISO character encoding of the data pointed to by the link. This isn't supported in IE4 or Navigator 4.

CHARSET=*string*

DEFER

Indicates that the script doesn't change any parts of the page during loading, so that the browser can continue parsing and rendering the rest of the page while interpreting the script. This isn't supported in IE4 or Navigator 4.

DEFER

Setting the Default Scripting Language

It's possible to declare a default language for a page in HTML 4.0 using a **<META>** tag in the **<HEAD>** section of the page, for example:

```
<META http-equiv="Content-Script-Type" Content="text/vbscript">
```

This avoids each script section from requiring a **TYPE** attribute. Individual script sections in the page can still use different languages by declaring the local script type in the **TYPE** tag:

```
<SCRIPT TYPE="text/javascript">
...
</SCRIPT>
```

The <NOSCRIPT> Element

Because some browsers don't recognize script, we have to consider the effect this has on the usability of the page. If the script is hidden inside comment tags, as we saw earlier, the non-script capable browser won't show anything, but the code won't work as intended either. To get round this we use the **<NOSCRIPT>** element:

```
...
<SCRIPT TYPE="text/javascript">
<!-- start hiding
  ... script code here
// end hiding -->
</SCRIPT>
<NOSCRIPT TYPE="text/javascript">
  Your browser doesn't support scripts, so this page will not
  work correctly. Instead, you can use pages that don't require
  script capabilities by
  <A HREF="noscriptpage.html">clicking here</A>.
</NOSCRIPT>
...
```

Netscape Extensions for <SCRIPT>

Netscape Navigator 4 implements the new attributes **ARCHIVE** and **ID** for the **<SCRIPT>** tag. The universal attributes **CLASS**, **STYLE** and **TITLE** also apply to **<SCRIPT>**.

ARCHIVE

If the script is in a separate file, and has been digitally signed for security purposes, the **ARCHIVE** attribute denotes the signature file for the script, and creates a place-holder for the script in the document:

```
<SCRIPT ARCHIVE="MyJarFile.jar" SRC="MyScript.js">
</SCRIPT>
```

ID

Assigns a name or identifier to the **<SCRIPT>** tag so it can be referred to in other script code:

```
<SCRIPT ID="Script1" TYPE="text/javascript">
```

IE Extensions for <SCRIPT>

Internet Explorer introduced two extensions to the **<SCRIPT>** tag, **FOR** and **EVENT**, and it also supports the **ID**, **CLASS**, **STYLE** and **TITLE** attributes (as in Navigator) in version 4.

FOR

Associates the script within the **<SCRIPT>** tags with a particular object or control within the HTML document. The syntax is:

FOR="*object_name***"**

Using this method, each object in the document can have its own independent script, which is executed when the object associated with it is activated by an event—see the **EVENT** attribute for more details.

EVENT

Specifies the event that causes a certain script to be executed. It can be used in conjunction with **FOR** to indicate the event of a specific control. The syntax is:

EVENT="*event_name***"**

To create code that runs when a button named **Button1** is clicked, we could use the following:

```
<SCRIPT LANGUAGE="VBScript" FOR="Button1" EVENT="onclick">
```

Browser Event Names

Events are a subject in their own right, and an **event handler** is the script that runs as a result of either a user or a system event. For instance, if you click on a button with the mouse, this generates an event. If you have a script associated with that event, that script is executed by the browser.
Here are the events defined in HTML 4.0. Not all browsers support all events for all elements. Version 3 or earlier browsers generally only react to those marked with an asterisk:

Event Name	Description
`onblur*`	occurs when an element loses focus, either by clicking with the mouse or through the *Tab* key.
`onchange*`	occurs when the value in a control has been changed and it loses the focus, such as when clicking in a **`SELECT`** list.
`onclick*`	occurs when the mouse is clicked over an element or the document.
`ondblclick`	occurs when the mouse is double-clicked over an element or the document.
`onfocus*`	occurs when an element receives focus, either by clicking with the mouse or through the *Tab* key.
`onkeydown`	occurs when a key is first pressed and is in the down position.
`onkeypress`	occurs when a key is pressed and released.
`onkeyup`	occurs when a key is released after being pressed.
`onload*`	occurs when the browser finishes loading the page in a window or, if the window is divided into frames, when the contents of all the frames have loaded.
`onmousedown`	occurs when the mouse button is pressed down.
`onmousemove`	occurs repeatedly while the mouse is moving over an element or the document.
`onmouseout`	occurs once just as the mouse moves off an element.
`onmouseover`	occurs when the mouse first moves onto an element.
`onmouseup`	occurs when the mouse button is released.
`onreset*`	occurs when a form is reset.
`onselect*`	occurs when a user selects some text with in a **`TEXT`**-type or **`TEXTAREA`** control.
`onsubmit*`	occurs when a form is submitted.
`onunload*`	occurs when the browser unloads a document, either when moving to another page or when closing the browser altogether.

There are other browser-specific events as well, for example Internet Explorer 4 supports events like `ondatasetcomplete`, `onhelp` and `onerror`

Functions and Subroutines in Scripts

The script code in a simple **`<SCRIPT>`** section is parsed (or interpreted) as the page loads, as part of the incoming HTML stream. To prevent this happening, we can create sections of code that run only on demand, either when an event occurs or when we want to run it from another place in the code. To achieve this we place the code in a **function** or **subroutine**.

JavaScript only supports functions:

```
<SCRIPT LANGUAGE="JavaScript" TYPE="text/javascript">

code here runs as the page loads

function someFunction()
{
  code here only runs when the function is called
}

</SCRIPT>
```

In VBScript, we can use a function or a subroutine. The difference is that a function can be used to return values to the code that called it, while a subroutine cannot:

```
<SCRIPT LANGUAGE="VBScript" TYPE="text/vbscript">

code here runs as the page loads

Function SomeFunction()
  code here only runs when the function is called
End Function

Sub SomeSubroutine()
  code here only runs when the subroutine is called
End Sub

</SCRIPT>
```

Closing a Script Section

Script section are closed with the **</SCRIPT>** tag. However, the rules of HTML suggest that any occurrence of the character string **</** followed by an alphabetic character should close the script section. This means that a command that uses these characters in it's arguments, such as **document.write**, must avoid placing these characters into the HTML stream it creates. For example, the following is not legal code:

```
document.write("<P>Some Text</P>");  // illegal code
```

In JavaScript, JScript or most other languages, use:

```
document.write("<P>Some Text<\/P>");
```

In VBScript, use:

```
document.write("<P>Some Text<" & Chr(47) & "P>");
```

Working with JavaScript

JavaScript was introduced by Netscape in order to extend and supplement HTML. The name is often confused with Java, which is an entire programming language in its own right. JavaScript owes some of its syntax and structures to Java, but is quite different. It can be used to manipulate Java Applets and ActiveX controls, but the basic aim of JavaScript was to provide programmers with a way to enhance the interactivity and capabilities of web pages without requiring server-side programming—this was a real innovation when it was first introduced.

JavaScript Versions

JavaScript from Netscape is available in three versions; 1.0, 1.1 and 1.2. Each of the newer versions are backwards compatible with earlier ones, but add extra language features. If the version is specified in the `<SCRIPT>` tag, Netscape will only execute it if it has the correct interpreter available:

```
<SCRIPT LANGUAGE="JavaScript1.2">

code here will be executed by:
* Navigator 4.0
* Internet Explorer 4.0

</SCRIPT>
```

```
<SCRIPT LANGUAGE="JavaScript1.1">

code here will be executed by:
* Navigator 3.x and Navigator 4.0
* Internet Explorer 4.0

</SCRIPT>
```

```
<SCRIPT LANGUAGE="JavaScript1.0">

code here will be executed by:
* Navigator 2.x, Navigator 3.x and Navigator 4.0
* Internet Explorer 4.0

</SCRIPT>
```

Notice that Internet Explorer 4 will attempt to execute all the versions of JavaScript. Its script interpreter is broadly JavaScript 1.2 compatible, but not completely. Details of the latest extensions in JavaScript version 1.2 are included in Appendix F.

A New Standard - ECMAScript

To get round the problems of script version compatibility, HTML 4.0 recommends a new standardized version of JavaScript named **ECMAScript**. Recently, Netscape released the language definition for JavaScript to the public, and subsequently agreed to create a vendor-neutral standard. **ECMA**, a standards body in Switzerland, produced the standard in July 1997—calling the language ECMAScript. This standard is roughly equivalent to JavaScript 1.1, minus any support for HTML.

Meanwhile, Netscape released JavaScript 1.2 in Navigator 4.0, and Microsoft released JScript 2.0 for Internet Explorer 3.0. Neither complies 100% with the ECMAScript standard. Microsoft has also made JScript available as a DLL, which is a programming format that allows the interpreter to be included in non-browser programs. The latest version 3.0 of JScript is claimed to be ECMA-script compatible, and both of the major browser vendors have said they will continue to move towards complete ECMAScript conformity in new products.

Connecting JavaScript to an Event

In JavaScript or JScript there are three ways of connecting events to our code that work in both the mainline browsers, and are defined in HTML 4.0. There is another method supported by both browsers, and others which are supported only in Internet Explorer. Two things to watch out for are that JavaScript only supports functions, and the language interpreter is case-sensitive in all browsers.

The commonest way of making the connection between the function and the element is by defining the name of the function (including the parentheses even if it doesn't require any arguments) in the element tag itself:

```
<H2 ONCLICK="myClickCode()">Some Text</H2>
...
<SCRIPT LANGUAGE="JavaScript" TYPE="text/javascript">
function myClickCode()
{
  alert("You clicked me!");
}
</SCRIPT>
```

This is fine for connecting script to specific elements in the page, but what about when we want to connect event handlers to the document itself? In this case, we simply put them all in the **<BODY>** tag:

```
<BODY ONMOUSEMOVE="myMouseMoveCode()" ONCLICK="myClickCode()">
```

The second method is to use inline code, within the element tag. This time, we're using the **LANGUAGE** description of **JScript**:

```
<H2 LANGUAGE="JScript" ONCLICK="alert('You clicked me!');">Some Text</H2>
```

And because JavaScript is the default language in the browser (unless we use a **<META>** tag to change it), we can omit the **LANGUAGE** attribute if we want to, making our code more compact:

```
<H2 ONCLICK="alert('You clicked me!');">Some Text</H2>
```

The third method is to attach the event handler to the element using script code within the document. This requires a knowledge of the object model of the document to use it on individual elements within the page. Here, we're using it to set the double-click event handler for the document itself:

```
<SCRIPT LANGUAGE="JavaScript" TYPE="text/javascript">
function myNewEventCode()
{
  code for mouse double-clicks on the document goes here
}

document.ondblclick = myNewEventCode;
</SCRIPT>
```

All elements that provide events are represented internally as JavaScript objects, and the event handler function is just a property of that object. Hence, our code actually sets the **ondblclick** *property of the* **document** *object.*

JavaScript URLs

We can create **javascript:** pseudo functions that can be placed in a link, such as an **<A>** (anchor) tag. The code is executed when the link is clicked. These are often referred to as JavaScript URLs. This technique is not supported in the HTML standards:

```
<A HREF="javascript:alert('You clicked me!');">Click Me</A>
```

Internet Explorer Specific Event Handling

The technique we saw earlier of using the **FOR** and **EVENT** attributes of the **<SCRIPT>** tag works with JavaScript and JScript, as well as VBScript, in Internet Explorer. We create the separate **<SCRIPT>** sections for each event, making sure that the name of the event is all lower-case:

```
<H2 ID=MyHeading>Some Text</H2>
...
<SCRIPT LANGUAGE="JScript" FOR=MyHeading EVENT=onclick>
  alert("You clicked me!");
</ SCRIPT>
```

We've seen how we can place event handler declarations, such as **onmousemove**, in the **<BODY>** tag of the document to cause them to occur at **document** level. The other situation is how we handle events at **window** level. In Internet Explorer 4, we can place the event handler declarations on the opening **<HTML>** tag:

```
<HTML ONMOUSEMOVE="myMouseMoveCode()" ONCLICK="myClickCode()">
...
</HTML>
```

Alternatively, we can name event handlers using a combination of the **ID,** or name of the element, and the event name (in lower case) separated by a period (full stop). For example, the following are both supported in Internet Explorer 4—but bear in mind that this is not the generally accepted method for connecting events and their code. (It works because the functions are themselves actually stored as properties of the element object).

```
<H2 ID=MyHeading>Some Text</H2>
...
<SCRIPT LANGUAGE="JavaScript" TYPE="text/javascript">
function MyHeading.onclick()
{
  alert("You clicked me!");
}
</SCRIPT>
```

This also works for the main browser objects, such as the **document** and **window**:

```
<SCRIPT LANGUAGE="JavaScript" TYPE="text/javascript">
function window.onload()
{
  alert("I've just loaded!");
}
</SCRIPT>
```

Creating Strings for Event Handlers

When defining inline code within the event-name attribute, we have to supply it as a string. HTML suggests that this string should be surrounded with double quotes, but single quotes are OK in most browsers. Both of these are acceptable:

```
<H2 ONCLICK="myClickCode;">Some Text</H2>
<H2 ONCLICK='myClickCode;'>Some Text</H2>
```

If the string has to contain another string, we can use the opposite type of quotation mark to create one string within another. Again, both of these are acceptable:

```
<H2 ONCLICK="alert('You clicked me!');">Some Text</H2>
<H2 ONCLICK='alert("You clicked me!");'>Some Text</H2>
```

However, HTML 4.0 suggests using the appropriate **named entities** instead:

```
<H2 ONCLICK="alert(&quot;You clicked me!&quot;);">Some Text</H2>
```

or

```
<H2 ONCLICK="alert(&#34;You clicked me!&#34t;);">Some Text</H2>
```

`"` and `"` both produce a double quote (`"`). Any '`&`' characters must be replaced by `&` or `&`

Using JavaScript in your Pages

Here are some simple examples of the kinds of tasks we can perform in our pages using JavaScript.

Displaying Dialogs and Messages

JavaScript provides built-in dialogs that we can display using `alert`, `prompt` and `confirm` methods:

```
alert("You'll have to choose where to go next.");
strLocation = prompt("Enter your preferred location", "Birmingham");
blnResult = confirm("Are you ready to load this page ?");
```

The following example uses these dialogs to open a new page:

```
<SCRIPT LANGUAGE="JavaScript" TYPE="text/javascript">
alert("You'll have to choose where to go next.");
strLocation = prompt("Enter your preferred location", "Birmingham");
if (strLocation != "" && strLocation != null)
{
  if (strLocation == "Birmingham")
  {
    strAddress = "http://www.wrox.co.uk"
  }
  else
  {
    strAddress = "http://www.wrox.com"
  };
  window.status = "New location will be " + strAddress;
```

```
    if (confirm("Are you ready to load this page ?"))
    {
      location.href = strAddress
    }
  }
  </SCRIPT>
```

The code in this page runs when it is loaded. The first line displays an **alert** dialog with a simple message:

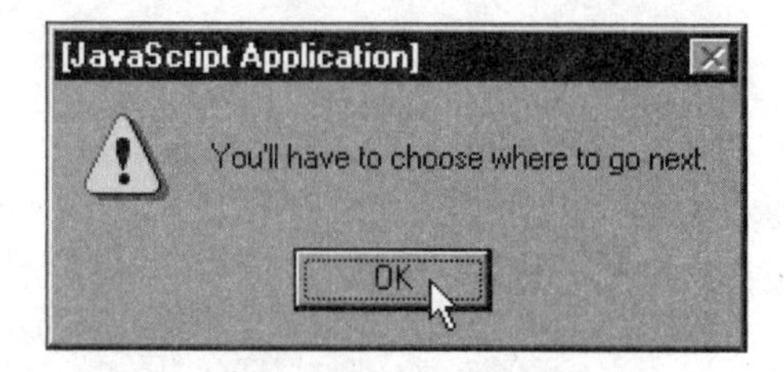

The second line uses the **prompt** method to display a dialog where the user can enter some information. The first argument is the prompt itself, and the second is the default value for the text box in the dialog:

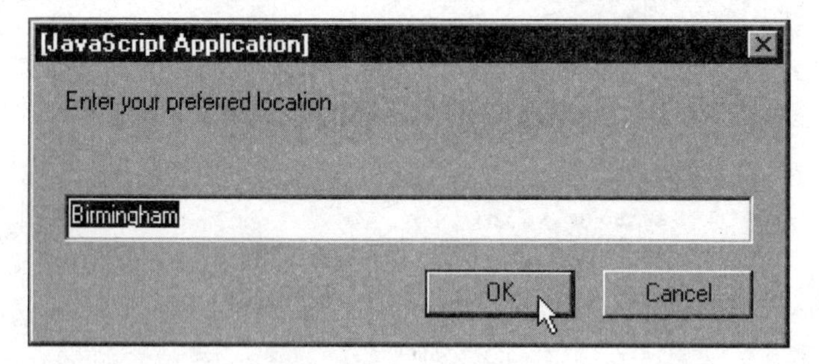

The value in the text box is returned to our code when the user clicks the OK button, and we assign it to a variable named **strLocation**. If the user clicked the Cancel button in the dialog, or deleted all the text and didn't enter anything, we'll get either an empty string or a **null** value back from the **prompt** method (depending on the browser version). We test for this first by comparing **strLocation** to an empty string (**""**) and to **null**, and only execute the following code if it isn't either of these values:

```
  ...
  if (strLocation != "" && strLocation != null)
  ...
```

If the value is still Birmingham, the default, we set the value of another variable, **strAddress**, to the address of our UK web site. If not, we'll use the main US site address:

```
    ...
    if (strLocation == "Birmingham")
    {
      strAddress = "http://www.wrox.co.uk"
    }
    else
    {
      strAddress = "http://www.wrox.com"
    };
    ...
```

> **The double equals sign is used to test for equality, i.e. is the value of `strLocation` equal to "Birmingham"? However, we use a single equals sign to assign a value to a variable, i.e. `strAddress = "http://www.wrox.com"`**

By now, we know we've got an address to go to, so we can display a message in the browser's status bar, by setting the **`window`** object's **`status`** property. We use some text and add the address string from the variable **`strAddress`** to the end of it like this:

```
...
window.status = "New location will be " + strAddress;
...
```

Now we can perform a final check to see if they really want to do it. We use the **`window`** object's **`confirm`** method to display the OK or Cancel dialog. The string argument is the message displayed, and it returns **`true`** or **`false`** depending on which button the user clicks. Once they've clicked a button, we can check the result, and load the new page if it is **`true`**.

```
...
if (confirm("Are you ready to load this page ?"))
...
```

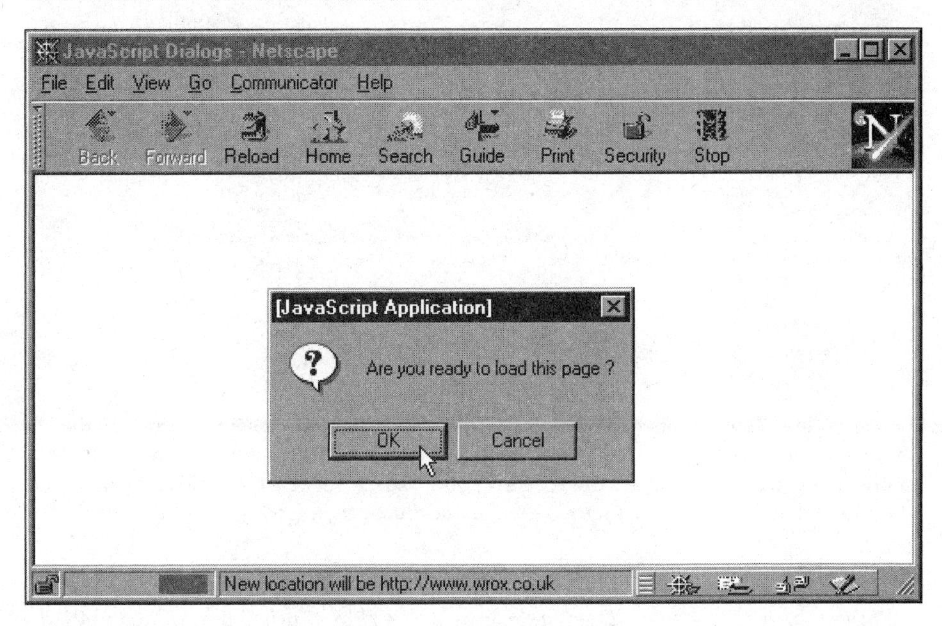

Notice the status bar displaying our message as well. Finally, the last line of code loads the new page by setting the **`href`** property of the **`location`** object to the new address in the string variable **`strAddress`** we set earlier:

```
location.href = strAddress
```

The Browser Objects

From this example, you'll see that we depend on the objects that the browser provides, such as the `location` object which holds details of the address of the page currently being displayed. The main object in the browser is the `window` object, and the dialogs we've used are **methods** of that object, while `status` is a **property** of it. We used the `window.status` property to display a message in the status bar. In general, we refer to the methods and properties of objects by placing a 'period' (full stop) between the object and the property/method name.

The provision of a set of objects in a pre-defined hierarchy within the browser, with which the script can interact, is known as the **Document Object Model** (DOM), or sometimes the **browser object model**. The HTML 4.0 working documents aim to define a standard DOM, so that pages will work in any browser that supports this. At present, the two mainline browsers, Navigator and Internet Explorer, support a very similar DOM.

You'll see a little more of this in a while, and we look at compatibility issues in general in Chapters 11 and 12. However, we don't have the space to cover all the objects and their properties, methods and events in this book. The reference section at the end of this chapter gives details of where you can find out more.

Writing Content Dynamically

One way of creating documents that are different each time they are opened is to use the `write` method of the `document` object (the object that represents the page currently displayed in the browser). This inserts text and HTML code into the document at the point it occurs, which effectively replaces the script section:

```
<HTML>
<HEAD><TITLE>What's The Time?</TITLE></HEAD>
<BODY>
The local date and time according to your computer's clock is:
<SCRIPT LANGUAGE="JavaScript" TYPE="text/javascript">
  datToday = new Date();
  document.write(datToday.toLocaleString());
</SCRIPT>
</BODY>
</HTML>
```

The code creates a new JavaScript `Date` object, which has the value of the current time and date unless we specify otherwise. We then use the `toLocaleString()` method to convert it into a local time, and pass it as an argument to the `write` method of the `document` object.

Opening New Browser Windows

We can also create a new, separate browser window, using the `open` method of the `window` object, and then write to it. This time we have to open the document, write the text, and then close it afterwards:

```
...
<SCRIPT LANGUAGE="JavaScript" TYPE="text/javascript">
  datToday = new Date();
  document.write(datToday.toLocaleString());
```

```
    myWindow = window.open();
    myWindow.document.open();
    myWindow.document.write("The date and time in London, England, is: ");
    myWindow.document.write(datToday.toGMTString());
    myWindow.document.close();
</SCRIPT>
...
```

This final code produces a page containing the current local time (using our **datToday** object), opens a new browser window, and writes the time as Greenwich Mean Time into it. The **open** method returns a reference to the window that we store in a variable named **myWindow**, and we can then call the window's methods using this reference. The page is not updated to show the new content until the **close** method is executed. Here's the result:

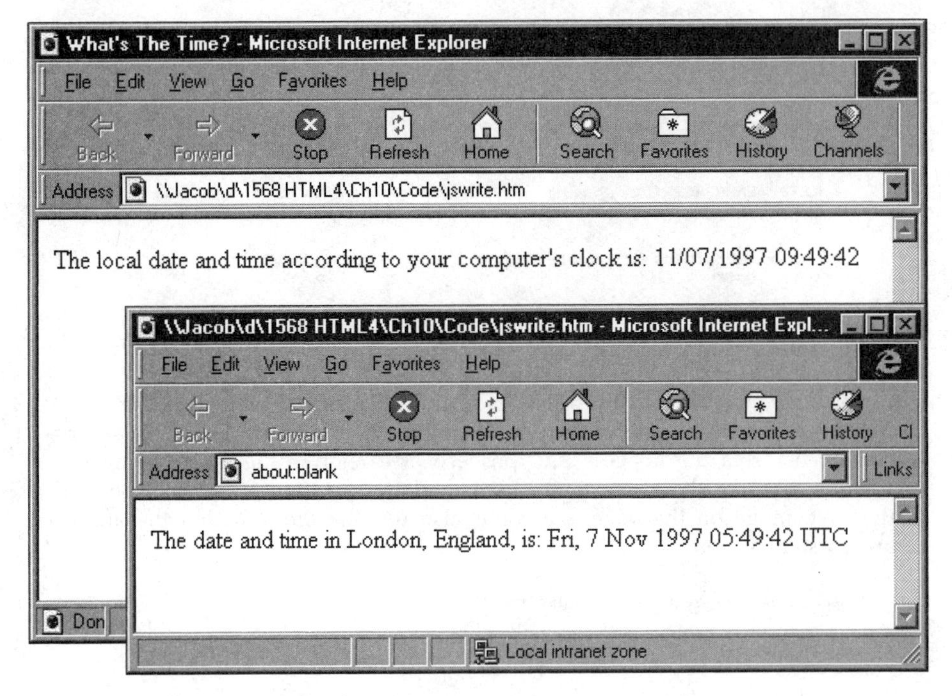

In our example code, we've used the **open()** method of the window object to open a new window, without providing any parameters. However, we can add parameters to it to get more control over how the new window is presented. The full syntax is:

window.open(*source_URL*, *window_name*, *features***)**

where *features* can be a string of instructions concerning the position, size and type of window, and whether it should contain scrollbars, a toolbar, etc. In Internet Explorer up to version 3, we actually *have* to supply the first two of these arguments to make the code work. We can provide an empty string for the *source_URL*, and any name we like for the *window_name*:

```
...
myWindow = window.open("", "new_win");
...
```

Working With Images and HTML Controls

Scripting languages can access some of the contents of a page, and change the way it looks. The range of elements that are available depends on the browser. In version 3 browsers and earlier, only the built-in HTML controls and images were commonly accessible, though in Netscape browsers you could embed other documents as well.

Here's how we can change the source of an image, just as if we had changed the **SRC** attribute. However, bear in mind that this won't work in Internet Explorer except in version 4—earlier versions don't allow you to change the source of an image element:

```
<HTML>
<HEAD><TITLE>Changing an Image Source</TITLE></HEAD>
<BODY>
<IMG SRC="picture1.gif" NAME="MyPicture">
<FORM>
<INPUT TYPE="BUTTON" NAME="btnChange" VALUE="Change Source"
       ONCLICK="changeSource()">
</FORM>
<SCRIPT LANGUAGE="JavaScript" TYPE="text/javascript">
  function changeSource()
  {
    document.images["MyPicture"].src = "picture2.gif"
  }
</SCRIPT>
</BODY>
</HTML>
```

In this case, we have a button created with an **<INPUT>** tag, and we've connected it with a function named **changeSource()** that simply assigns a new filename to the image's **SRC** property. We refer to the image using the **images** array of the **document** object, and by specifying its name. Because it is the first image on the page, we could also use the index within the array—all arrays start at zero:

```
document.images[0].src = "picture2.gif"
```

Here's the result:

Canceling an Event Action in JavaScript

Some events, such as **onsubmit**, allow us to provide a return value that controls how the browser behaves. To return a value from a function we use the **return** keyword within the function. The code in the **checkAddress()** function simply makes sure there is an **@** character in the email address entered into the text box. If not, it instructs the browser not to submit the form—in other words it cancels the browser's default action:

```
...
<FORM NAME=MyForm ONSUBMIT="return checkAddress()"
      ACTION="http://www.somesite.com/scripts/doit.asp">
  <INPUT TYPE=TEXT NAME=Email>
  <INPUT TYPE=SUBMIT>
</FORM>

<SCRIPT LANGUAGE="JavaScript" TYPE="text/javascript">
function checkAddress()
{
  strAddress = document.forms[0].elements["Email"].value;
  if (strAddress.indexOf("@") != -1)   // contains @ somewhere
    return true
  else
  {
    alert("You must supply a valid email address.");
    return false
  }
}
</SCRIPT>
...
```

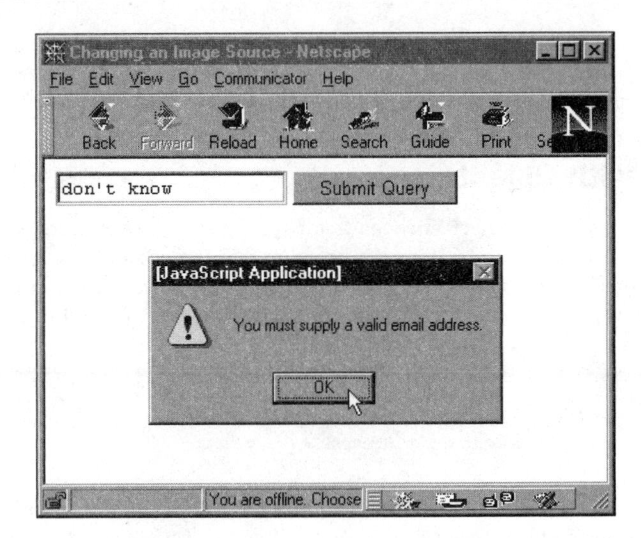

The script gets the value from the **EMail** text box, which is on the form named **MyForm**, and places it into the variable named **strAddress**. The **document** object has an array of **forms**, and we specify the one we want using its index within the page. Each form has an **elements** array that contains all the elements on that form, so we have to specify our **Email** text box within that array—this time we're using its name. Finally, we want to get its **value** property:

```
strAddress = document.forms[0].elements["Email"].value;
```

The reason that we specified the index for the form, rather than the name, is that earlier versions of Internet Explorer don't recognize form names. In Navigator and other browsers, we could have used the name instead:

```
strAddress = document.forms["MyForm"].elements["Email"].value;
```

Alternatively, we could have used indexes for the form and the **`EMail`** text box:

```
strAddress = document.forms[0].elements[0].value;
```

Finally, we can also use a short-cut method by specifying just the names of the objects:

```
strAddress = document.MyForm.Email.value;
```

Once we've got the address, we can use the **`indexOf()`** method of the string (which is itself a JavaScript object) to see if there is an **`@`** character in it. The **`indexOf()`** method returns the index of the character starting from zero if it's the first character in the string. If it's not in the string, it returns **`-1`**.

An important point to note in this example is that we have to use the **`return`** keyword in the **`ONSUBMIT`** attribute of the **`<FORM>`** tag as well, to return the value of the function back to the browser's internal mechanism:

```
<FORM ID=MyForm ONSUBMIT="return checkAddress()"
```

*In Internet Explorer 4, instead of returning a value from the function directly, we can cancel the default action for an event by setting the **`returnValue`** property of the **`event`** object. This technique is shown in Chapter 12.*

Working with Objects

When we insert an object such as a Java Applet or an ActiveX control into our page, we can manipulate it using broadly the same methods as we would any other element. We can change its properties, call its methods, and react to its events. If we have an object with the **`ID`** or **`NAME`** of **`MyObject`**, then we might use:

```
MyObject.color = "sicklyGreen"                // set a property
intWidth = MyObject.width                     // read a property
strStatus = MyObject.calculateResult(x, y, z) // call a method
```

*In general, either the **`NAME`** or the **`ID`** attribute can be used to set the name of an element in the HTML source, as long as they are both the same. HTML 4.0 suggests that they should both return the same value even if they are different, and that the **`NAME`** attribute should take preference. This may cause problems with grouped controls like option (**`RADIO`**) buttons, where the name is the same for several controls, but the **`IDs`** are different.*

Working with VBScript

VBScript was introduced by Microsoft as a competitor to JavaScript. It is broadly derived from VBA (Visual Basic for Applications) and, like VBA, is a cut-down version of Visual Basic. It includes many of the statements from Visual Basic; such as most of the string, date, and number manipulation functions and the common control structures, but little else. No graphics or file handling functions are available, so you are limited in what you can achieve. The main reason for this is that once you've opened an HTML page in your browser, the code is loaded into memory and can be executed at any time. Many of the omitted functions could have been used to damage your system.

VBScript is not natively supported by Netscape Navigator. The main attraction of VBScript is that it's a lot simpler to learn than JavaScript, but offers a similar level of speed and power. However, given that **ECMAScript**, which may well be accepted by W3C as one of the standard languages for scripting in browsers, is very close to Microsoft's JScript it is unlikely that support for VBScript will grow.

Connecting VBScript to an Event

In VBScript, we have four ways of connecting our code to an event. The easiest way is to create a subroutine or function whose name is a combination of the *element* name and the *event* name. To react to a click on some heading text, we can use:

```
<H2 ID=MyHeading>Some Text</H2>
...
<SCRIPT LANGUAGE="VBScript" TYPE="text/vbscript">
  Sub MyHeading_onClick()
    MsgBox "You clicked me!"
  End Sub
</SCRIPT>
```

The code above uses a **subroutine**, but we can just as easily use a **function** instead:

```
<H2 ID=MyHeading>Some Text</H2>
...
<SCRIPT LANGUAGE="VBScript" TYPE="text/vbscript">
  Function MyHeading_onClick()
    MsgBox "You clicked me!"
  End Function
</SCRIPT>
```

The second method is to create a routine with almost any name, and link it to the event and the element by declaring the name of the routine in the element tag. And we don't need an `ID` in the HTML element tag in this case:

```
<H2 LANGUAGE="VBScript" ONCLICK="MyClickCode">Some Text</H2>
...
<SCRIPT LANGUAGE="VBScript" TYPE="text/vbscript">
  Sub MyClickCode()
    MsgBox "You clicked me!"
  End Sub
</SCRIPT>
```

The third way is to use 'inline' script code, which removes the need for a separate code routine. We simply write the code inside the tag as the value of the event name attribute. Notice how we have to use single quotes inside the **ONCLICK** attribute, because this itself is a string:

```
<H2 LANGUAGE="VBScript" TYPE="text/vbscript"
ONCLICK="MsgBox 'You clicked me!'">Some Text</H2>
```

The fourth method is to use a different script section for each event. This is done by identifying the element and the event in the **<SCRIPT>** tag:

```
<H2 ID=MyHeading>Some Text</H2>
...
<SCRIPT LANGUAGE="VBScript" FOR=MyHeading EVENT=onclick>
  MsgBox "You clicked me!"
</SCRIPT>
```

Using VBScript in your Pages

Almost anything that we can do using JavaScript can equally be achieved with VBScript. However, the techniques and syntax can be very different. Some simple examples follow. We're using only Internet Explorer because Navigator does not support VBScript directly.

One thing that makes VBScript less error-prone is that it doesn't require braces to identify and separate individual statements, like JavaScript and JScript do, because it relies on each line ending with a carriage return. The other point in its favor is that it is NOT case sensitive. Errors involving case sensitivity in JavaScript and JScript can be very difficult to find.

> **If you want to split a long line in VBScript over several lines in the page, you can use the underscore as a line-continuation character:**
>
> ```
> This is a long line in VBScript, so we use an underscore _
> to break it over two lines.
> ```

Displaying Dialogs and Messages

We can use the built-in **alert**, **prompt**, and **confirm** dialog methods in VBScript, because they are methods of the **window** object and, therefore, are created by the *browser* and *not* the scripting language. However, VBScript provides its own more flexible dialogs and message boxes that we can use instead. Everything is done with either a **MsgBox** or **InputBox**:

```
MsgBox "You'll have to choose where to go next."
strLocation = InputBox("Enter your preferred location", "Birmingham")
blnResult = MsgBox("Are you ready to load this page ?")
```

Here's the example we used earlier, but this time in VBScript, and using these dialogs plus several of their arguments. In VBScript, if we want a line of code to continue onto the next line, we end the first part of the line with an underscore and a carriage return. Other than that, you should be able to see how the code follows the same structure as the earlier JavaScript example:

```
<SCRIPT LANGUAGE="VBScript" TYPE="text/vbscript">
MsgBox "You'll have to choose where to go next.", _
       vbOKOnly + vbExclamation, "Warning..."
strLocation = InputBox("Enter your preferred location", _
                       "Go where?", "Birmingham")
If strLocation <> "" Then
  If strLocation = "Birmingham" Then
    strAddress = "http://www.wrox.co.uk"
  Else
    strAddress = "http://www.wrox.com"
  End If
  window.status = "New location will be " & strAddress
  If MsgBox("Are you ready to load this page ?", _
            vbYesNo + vbQuestion, "Your Choice...") = vbYes Then
    location.href = strAddress
  End If
End If
</SCRIPT>
```

The **MsgBox** statement takes several arguments, but we're only using the first three. The first is the message, the second is the sum of a set of predefined constant values that define which buttons and icons appear (and which button is the default and how the message box behaves in relation to other windows). The third argument is the title for the message box's title bar:

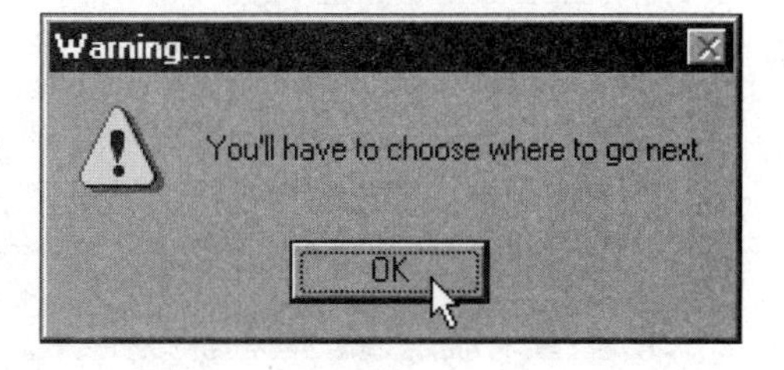

The VBScript **InputBox** is very similar to the **window** object's **prompt** method. However, we supply the title as the second argument and the default text as the third one. In some browsers, it's also possible to specify the x and y position as the fourth and fifth arguments:

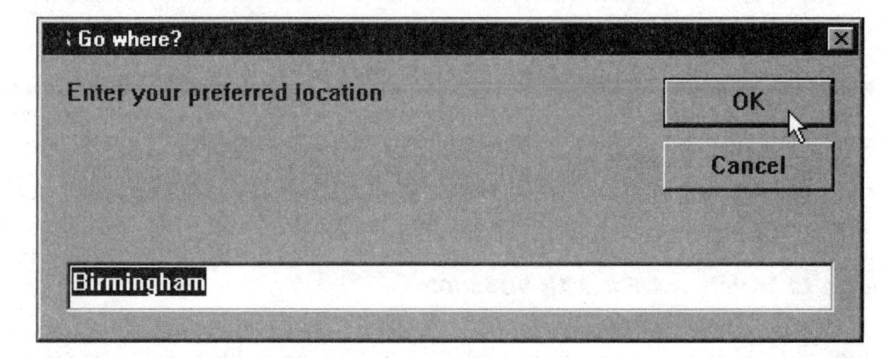

Again, we check to see what the user entered, and make a decision on where to go. We display a message in the browser's status bar, and perform a final check to see if they really want to do it. This time, we're using the function form of **MsgBox** so that it can return a value, and we've specified Yes and No buttons, and the question mark icon:

```
If MsgBox("Are you ready to load this page ?" _
          vbYesNo + vbQuestion, "Your Choice...") = vbYes Then
```

Notice that we can test the returned value using the intrinsic constants as well. In the example, the code in the `If` section will only run if 'Yes' is clicked.

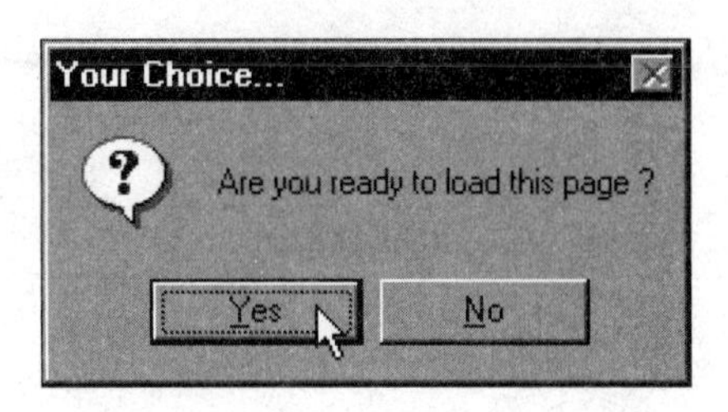

The intrinsic constants are listed and defined in the VBScript appendix at the end of this book. However, bear in mind that some old browsers may not support the constant names, and you may wish to use the actual numeric values shown there instead.

Writing Content Dynamically

We write content to a page using the same methods of the same object model as we did in JavaScript—the same **`window`** object has the same **`open`** method, and the same **`document`** object has the same **`write`** method, it's just the language we use to access it that is different:

```
<HTML>
<HEAD><TITLE>What's The Time?</TITLE></HEAD>
<BODY>
The local date and time according to your computer's clock is:
<SCRIPT LANGUAGE="VBScript" TYPE="text/vbscript">
  document.write Now
</SCRIPT>
</BODY>
</HTML>
```

However, as you see from the code, the way we create and use the value for the current date and time is different. VBScript provides the **`Now()`** function, which returns the current time and date. In JavaScript, we had to create a **`Date`** object, and use its methods instead.

The other important point is that we have to omit the parentheses (brackets) around the arguments in two cases when using VBScript. The **`write`** method of the **`document`** object acts like a **subroutine** rather than a **function**, and does not return a result. Therefore, we omit the parentheses round its arguments. Secondly, the **`Now`** function (which does return a result) doesn't take any arguments and therefore we can omit the parentheses from it if we wish.

Things to Watch Out For with VBScript

In VBScript, we can also use the **`open`** and **`close`** methods of a browser's **`window`** object, just as we did in JavaScript. The main difference is in the way we save a reference to the window. In JavaScript, all variables are in fact objects, so we can assign a **`window`** object to an 'ordinary' variable. In VBScript, we have to use the **`Set`** keyword to indicate that we want to create an **object variable** to store a reference to the object.

This is in fact a simplistic explanation of what's going on behind the scenes, but serves to act as an indication of when it's required, and why it's important.

The only other problem we have is how we convert the current local time into a GMT time. VBScript doesn't provide a **toGMTString()** method or its equivalent, so we have a problem. One way round to is use a separate JavaScript or JScript function which performs the action we need.

However, passing values between scripts written in the two languages is difficult in some browsers, especially Internet Explorer 3. To make sure our page is compatible, we have used a JavaScript function that doesn't require a parameter to be passed to it:

```
...
<SCRIPT LANGUAGE="JavaScript" TYPE="text/javascript">
  function showLondonTime()
  {
    datThisDate = new Date();
    myWindow = window.open("", "new_win");
    myWindow.document.open();
    myWindow.document.write("The date and time in London, England, is: ");
    myWindow.document.write(datThisDate.toGMTString());
    myWindow.document.close();
  }
</SCRIPT>

The local date and time according to your computer's clock is:
<SCRIPT LANGUAGE="VBScript" TYPE="text/vbscript">
  document.write Now
  dummy = javascript:showLondonTime
</SCRIPT>
...
```

This is an example of how we can mix scripting languages in the same page, and demonstrates some of the difficulties. In IE3, the scripting language must be JavaScript (not JScript), and we have to use the strange syntax:

```
dummy = javascript:showLondonTime
```

to force the VBScript code to execute the JavaScript function. Because we can't pass any values to it (such as the local time or the window reference), we also need to do a lot of the processing within the JavaScript code section.

In Internet Explorer 4, none of this is necessary. Functions can be executed, and values passed to them, seamlessly. However, it's often not worth the effort of creating a page with more that one scripting language unless you are willing to sacrifice browser compatibility.

Working With Images and HTML controls

In VBScript, we generally use very similar techniques and syntax to manipulate the elements and other contents of a page to those we used in JavaScript earlier. However, as we saw earlier, we can't change the source of an image element in Internet Explorer except in version 4—earlier versions didn't support this. Here's the code for IE4:

```
<HTML>
<HEAD>Changing a Image Source</HEAD>
<BODY>
<IMG SRC="picture1.gif" NAME="MyPicture"
<FORM>
<INPUT TYPE="BUTTON" NAME="btnChange" VALUE="Change Source"
       ONCLICK="ChangeSource">
</FORM>
<SCRIPT LANGUAGE="VBScript" TYPE="text/vbscript">
Sub ChangeSource()
  document.images("MyPicture").src = "picture2.gif"
End Function
</SCRIPT>
</BODY>
</HTML>
```

The major changes are that we can use a subroutine, because we don't need to return a value. There's no reason why we can't use a function, it's just good practice to only use functions when we want to return values to the calling code. Again, we refer to the image using the **images** array of the **document** object, and specify its name. Notice that in VBScript the arrays are accessed using parentheses rather than square brackets. And, again, we can use the index of the object in the array, instead of the name:

```
document.images(0).src = "picture2.gif"
```

The result is the same as we saw earlier with Navigator.

Canceling an Event Action in VBScript

When we come to cancel events in VBScript, we use the same technique as in JavaScript. We can cancel the **onsubmit** event by returning the value **False**. After all, it's the browser that defines the events, not the scripting language, so the same events are available to whichever language we choose to use (and which the browser supports).

This is the VBScript implementation of the code we saw used earlier in the chapter to cancel the submission of a form. Remember, to be able to return a value in VBScript we have to use a **function** rather than a **subroutine**:

```
<FORM NAME=MyForm ACTION="http://www.mysite.com/scripts/doit.asp">
  <INPUT TYPE=TEXT NAME=Email>
  <INPUT TYPE=SUBMIT>
</FORM>
<SCRIPT LANGUAGE="VBScript" TYPE="text/vbscript">
Function MyForm_onsubmit()
  strAddress = document.MyForm.Email.value
  If InStr(strAddress, "@") > 0 Then   'contains @ somewhere
    MyForm_onsubmit = True
  Else
    MsgBox "You must supply a valid email address.", 64, "Whoops!"
    MyForm_onsubmit = False
  End If
End Function
</SCRIPT>
```

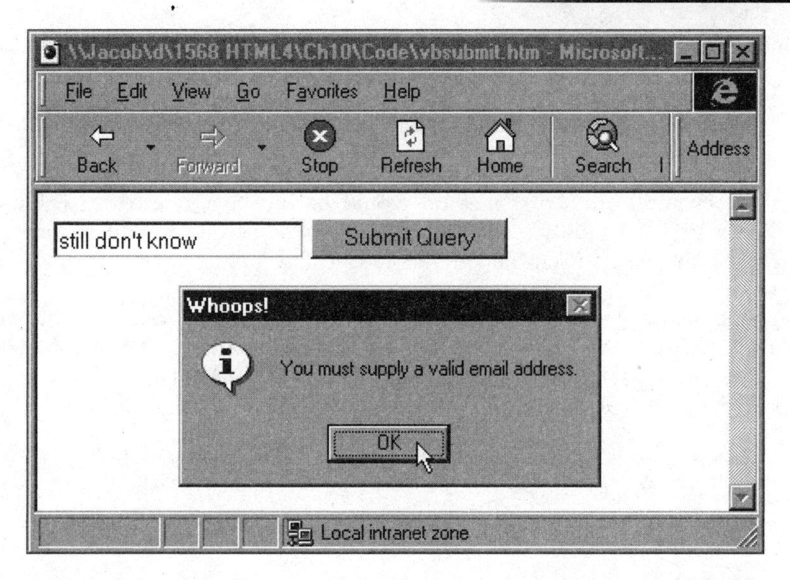

This code uses the **`InStr()`** function to find the position of the first **`@`** character in the string the user enters into a textbox named **`Email`** on the form. Unlike the JavaScript equivalent **`indexOf()`**, however, **`InStr()`** returns **`0`** if there isn't a **`@`** character in the string, and **`1`** if it's the first character (**`indexOf()`** returns **`-1`** if it's not found, and **`0`** if it's the first character).

The actual connection of the event to the script function is made by defining the function with the name **`MyForm_onsubmit()`**, which means we don't need to use the element's **`ONSUBMIT`** attribute to define the function name. To cancel the submission we just return **`False`** by assigning it to the function name within the function body.

You can also see how we have used the browser's object model to get at the text in the text box in this case. The string we want is again the **`value`** property of the element object named **`Email`** in the **`elements`** collection of the form named **`MyForm`**, which is stored in the **`forms`** collection of the **`document`** object. And, as in JavaScript, we can use the short-cut syntax:

```
strAddress = document.MyForm.Email.value
```

*We could have started with **`window.document`**, but it's not actually required because the **`window`** object is the default anyway.*

Working with Objects

When using VBScript, we work with objects and other elements in the page in an almost identical way as when using JavaScript. We can retrieve and change property values, call methods and react to events. For an object with the **`ID`** or **`NAME`** of **`MyObject`** we might use:

```
MyObject.color = "sicklyGreen"                  'set a property
intWidth = MyObject.width                       'read a property
strStatus = MyObject.calculateResult(x, y, z)   'call a method
```

The main difference is that when we call a method that doesn't return a result, we omit the parentheses around the arguments:

```
intResult = MyObject.countStuff(x, y, z)  'returns the result
MyObject.displayCountOfStuff x, y, z      'doesn't return a result
```

In these examples, the first method would be one that returned a result, which is then assigned to the variable **`intResult`**. The second would be one that just displayed the result itself, and didn't return a value.

VBScript is also useful with non-intrinsic objects, such as Java Applets and ActiveX controls. As long as we have provided a **`NAME`** or **`ID`** in the appropriate attribute when we create the element, we can write event handlers that will be executed when that object fires an event:

```
Sub MyObject_onsomethinghappened()
  'some code to react to the event
End Sub
```

Security

As with any Internet technology, scripting has introduced a number of security concerns. To address these worries, JavaScript and VBScript omit any commands that can access the local file system, or other crucial system resources. This should prevent them from executing hostile instructions, but it also limits their power—and still doesn't entirely prevent 'unfriendly' programming (for example, spawning endless windows until the browser crashes).

Scripting languages are also basically un-secure in that the viewer can see the script within the page when they view the source, and save the page to their own local system. This means that they can tamper with the script, and then use it themselves or pass it on to others. Therefore, scripting should never be used to check passwords directly, or accomplish any tasks such as those that use a 'secret formula'. This kind of processing should always be done on the server. However, they are useful for many tasks, as you've seen in this chapter. Netscape's latest browser, Navigator 4, can use **signed scripts**, which guarantee that the script has not been tampered with since it was originally written. See Chapter 11 for more information.

Additional Sources of Information

We recommend that you have a look at the following resources:

JavaScript: *Instant JavaScript*, Wrox Press, (ISBN 1-861001-27-4)

`www.netscape.com`

`www.gamelan.com`

`www.inquiry.com/techtips/js_pro/`

VBScript: *Instant VBScript* by Wrox Press. (ISBN 1-861000-44-8)

www.microsoft.com

www.inquiry.com/thevbpro/vbscentral/gallery.html

ECMAScript: **www.ecma.ch/stand/ecma-262.htm**

Summary

In this chapter, we have considered what a scripting language actually is, and why you'd want to use one. We looked at how the browser differentiates the script from the HTML with the use of the **<SCRIPT>** tag, and at how JavaScript works—including some basic examples. We then examined VBScript, and again included some simple examples. Finally, we looked at one concern which affect both scripting languages—security.

Dynamic HTML in Navigator/Communicator 4

In this chapter, we become browser-specific and look at the new version of Navigator from Netscape. At present the two mainstream browser manufacturers, Netscape and Microsoft, have version 4 browsers available. Both of these implement a new concept, which they both call **Dynamic HTML**—but unfortunately the capabilities and implementation are quite different between the two versions.

We'll briefly cover what Dynamic HTML actually is, and where it comes from, then move on to look at how it's implemented in Netscape's **Navigator 4** and **Communicator** products. In the next chapter, we cover the implementation of Dynamic HTML in Microsoft's Internet Explorer 4 browser.

What is Dynamic HTML?

Web pages created using the tags and attributes from HTML 3.2 or earlier, combined with scripting, can produce some very attractive and usable pages. However, the bulk of the content of a Web page has always been essentially static, and impossible to access from a scripting language. While we can change the source of an image (in Netscape 3 and 4 and IE4), change the color of the page background (and the foreground as well in Internet Explorer) with script code, any other dynamic effects depend on embedded objects of various kinds, such as Java applets, ActiveX controls .

In contrast, Dynamic HTML aims to provide an environment within the page where *all* the content, including the basic body text and formatting elements, is available to scripting code. On top of this, a browser should be able to dynamically redraw the visible parts of a page if the content is changed within a script running in the page.

A New Browser Structure

This is a fundamentally different concept from the way pages have behaved before, and requires many changes within the workings of the browser. In particular, the entire page contents need to be arranged into some type of hierarchical structure so that each part (i.e. each element) is accessible. This is generally termed the **Document Object Model** (DOM). On top of that, there must be a way of specifying the visible appearance and internal properties of all these elements.

The two mainstream browsers provide an environment for Web pages that allows the contents to be accessed as individual items. Of the two, however, only Internet Explorer currently offers the full package. In Navigator, more of the content is accessible to scripting than ever before, but still not all of it. No doubt we will see updated versions of both, however, as new standards are ratified.

A new version of HTML, HTML 4.0, is also appearing as a proposed recommendation from W3C. This has evolved from a long-term examination of the direction that HTML should take for the future, as well as how it can be enhanced to provide better accessibility for all users (such as support for foreign languages and people with disabilities). A series of drafts originally titled **Project Cougar** have been available for some time, and at the time of writing these have partially metamorphosed into a proposed recommendation for HTML 4.0. It includes many of the concepts that the two browser manufacturers have already christened Dynamic HTML.

The reference section of this book covers the current recommendations for HTML 4.0, as well as earlier versions of HTML and the two mainstream browsers. In this section of the chapter, we'll briefly look at the overall aims and requirements of the HTML 4.0 proposed recommendation.

A Better HTML - Version 4.0 Proposals

The main proposals of HTML 4.0 are to create a language that supports:

- Interactive documents and rich forms
- Dynamic pages driven by script code
- More flexible frames and subsidiary windows
- Better multimedia object handling
- Improved access for people with disabilities
- Support for different fonts and internationalization issues
- Security in scripts through digital signatures
- An improved mechanism for providing information about the page to both web search engines and 'viewing control programs' that monitor the page for the type of content.

We've already seen in earlier chapters the way HTML 4.0 provides support for styles and style sheets, and how these can be used to change the appearance of the contents of the page dynamically. We've also seen some of the ways that it provides enhanced abilities when using HTML forms and the browser's built-in HTML controls. In the previous chapter, we also looked at how script code can be used to access more parts of the page.

In fact, we've already covered much of Dynamic HTML and HTML 4.0 in earlier chapters of this book. What we'll look at in this and the next chapter is how closely the individual browsers match the requirements of HTML 4.0, and how to achieve some of the new effects they provide. Bear in mind, however, that HTML 4.0 is *not* actually 'Dynamic HTML', and even the versions of Dynamic HTML supported by the two mainstream browsers are very different. In fact, 'Dynamic HTML' is really just a buzzword that refers very broadly to the new capabilities of the version 4 browsers.

What's New in Navigator 4?

Navigator 4 is part of the new Communicator suite from Netscape, which incorporates several other related products such as messaging, authoring, and group-ware applications. It is also available in browser only configuration. The main new feature groups are:

- A new document object model
- Style support and absolute positioning of elements
- The new `<LAYER>` and `<ILAYER>` tags
- New events and event handling techniques
- Changes to JavaScript and the `<SCRIPT>` tag
- Netscape Dynamic Fonts

Dynamic Fonts are not really related to DHTML, but Netscape classify them as part of their Dynamic HTML implementation, so we will cover them and the other new features in turn.

The New Document Object Model

To manage the new objects and document structure, Navigator has some new additions to its object model. These include:

- The new `Event` object, for handling events that occur in the document.
- The new `Screen` object, which provides information about the user's browser display capabilities.
- The new `Layer` object, and a corresponding array of these objects within the document.

Three new arrays for managing styles and identifying elements in the document. These are the **classes**, **ids**, and **tags** arrays, and we'll examine them in the next section.

The complete browser and document object model looks like this:

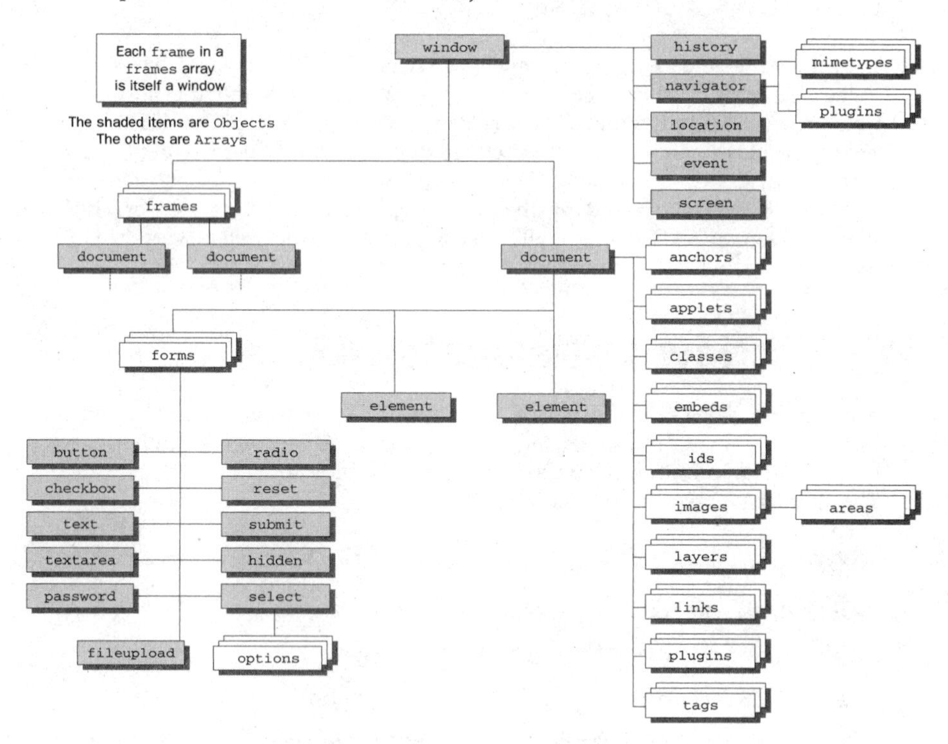

Styles and Absolute Positioning

In general, Navigator 4 now supports the CSS1 and HTML 4.0 style recommendations of the W3C, although some are not fully functional. For example, it does not handle imported style sheets using the **@import** instruction, or the full set of positional style properties.

The <SPAN> Tag

Netscape Navigator 4 now supports the **<SPAN>** tag, which is part of the proposals for HTML 4.0. It was not supported in earlier versions of Navigator. It is used to apply a style to a section of 'inline' text or other elements. This is different to **<DIV>**, which is a 'block' element:

```
<HTML>
 <STYLE TYPE="text/css">
  .onestyle {color:red; font-weight:bold; font-style:italic}
  .andanother {color:blue; font-weight:normal; text-decoration:underline}
 </STYLE>
 <BODY>
  <DIV CLASS="onestyle">Some text in a division.</DIV>
  <DIV CLASS="andanother">Some text in another division.</DIV>
```

```
  <P>
  <SPAN CLASS="onestyle">Some text in a span.</SPAN>
  <SPAN CLASS="andanother">Some text in another span.</SPAN>
 </BODY>
</HTML>
```

In this example, the two **<DIV>** elements are displayed on consecutive lines, while the two **<SPAN>** elements are displayed on the same line:

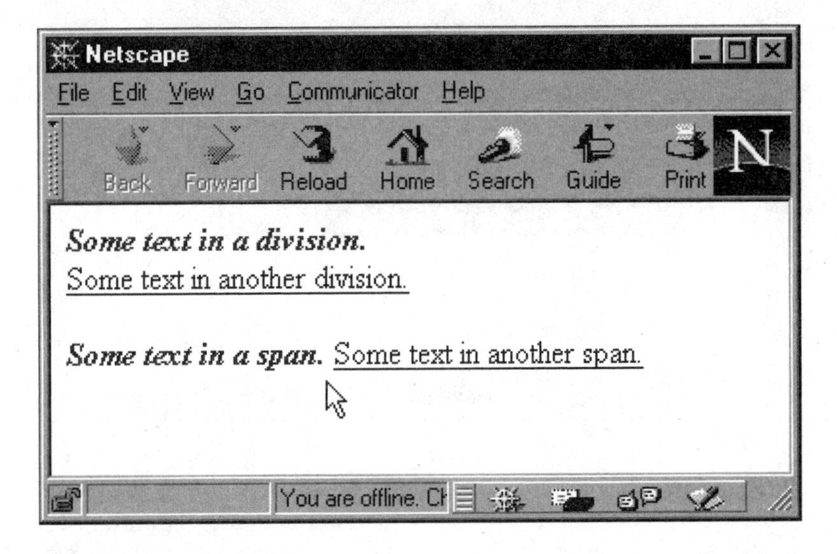

CSS1 Positioning Support

Navigator 4 now supports absolute positioning of document content via the document division **<DIV>** element. This is in line with the W3C proposals for HTML 4.0, for example:

```
<DIV STYLE="position:absolute; top:20; left:20; width:100; height:50">
  This is some text inside a positioned document division.
</DIV>
```

The position can also be specified as 'inflow', or **relative**, as defined in Chapter 3:

```
<DIV STYLE="position:relative; top:20; left:20; width:100; height:50">
  This is some text inside a positioned document division.
</DIV>
```

The style itself can also be defined in a separate **<STYLE>** section. This example places white text on a blue background inside a relatively positioned division:

```
...
<STYLE TYPE="text/css">
  DIV {position:relative; top:20; left:20; width:200;
       font-weight:bold; color:white;
       background-color:blue}
</STYLE>
...
<BODY>
```

```
<DIV>
  This is some text inside a positioned document division.
</DIV>
...
```

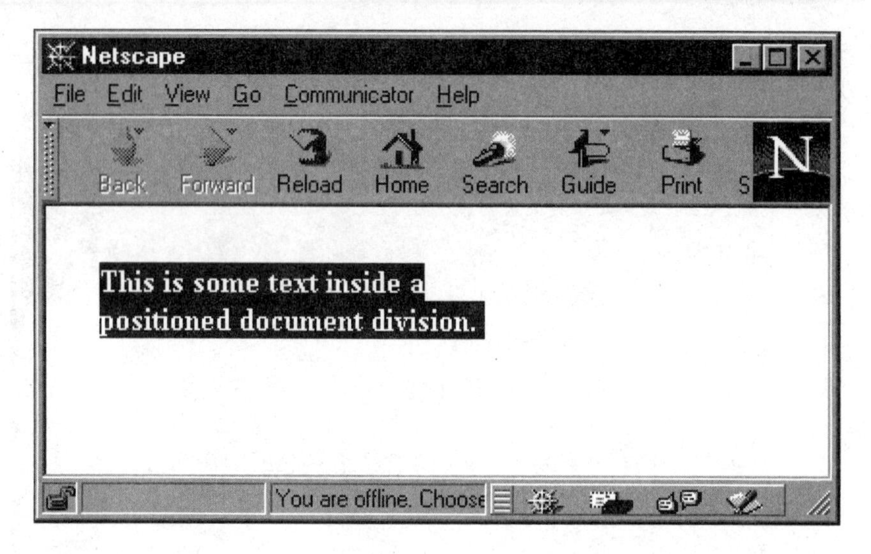

While the <DIV> element can be positioned either absolutely or relatively within the document, it does not offer opportunities for making pages dynamic. The position or appearance of a <DIV> element cannot be changed once the page has been downloaded and rendered. Instead, in Navigator, we have to use the new <LAYER> and <ILAYER> elements.

JavaScript Style Sheets

Navigator also adds a new type of style sheet called **JavaScript Style Sheets** (JSS). These are defined in a broadly similar way to CSS, using a **<STYLE>** tag, but with the **TYPE** attribute set to **"text/javascript"**. The individual style definitions are quite different, however. This code produces the same effect as the CSS example at the end of the previous section:

```
<HTML>
<STYLE TYPE="text/javascript">
  tags.DIV.position="relative";
  tags.DIV.top=20;
  tags.DIV.left=20;
  tags.DIV.width=200;
  tags.DIV.fontWeight="bold";
  tags.DIV.color="white";
  tags.DIV.backgroundColor="blue";
</STYLE>
<BODY>
<DIV>
  This is some text inside a positioned document division.
</DIV>
</BODY>
</HTML>
```

Any individual CSS style properties that contain a hyphen are replaced with a JSS-specific name (JavaScript does not allow hyphens in variable or property names). Neither are all the CSS properties supported, see Appendix G for details.

JavaScript style properties can also be applied to **classes** of elements, rather than using the tag name, or to individual elements via their `ID`:

```
<STYLE TYPE="text/javascript">
  classes.greentext.SPAN.color="green";
</STYLE>
...
<SPAN CLASS="greentext"> This is some green text.</SPAN>
```

or

```
<STYLE TYPE="text/javascript">
  ids.myspantag.color="green";
</STYLE>
...
<SPAN ID="myspantag"> This is some green text.</SPAN>
```

Accessing JavaScript Styles

The JavaScript styles applied to elements in the page are made available to scripts as properties. These will be in the `document` object's `tags` array if they were assigned as styles using the `tags` method:

```
document.tags.H1.color          // returns the font color for the element
document.tags.H1.fontFamily     // returns the font family for the element
document.tags.H1.fontSize       // returns the font size for the element
```

If the styles were applied using classes or the individual element's `ID`, the values are obtainable from the `classes` or `ids` arrays:

```
document.classes.greentext.SPAN.color
document.ids.myspantag.color
```

The `tags`, `classes` and `ids` arrays are not true JavaScript arrays. They have no length property, and cannot be iterated through in code like other arrays.

The New <LAYER> and <ILAYER> Tags

One of the most exciting of the new features in Netscape's implementation of Dynamic HTML is the concept of **layers**. We can use the `<LAYER>` and `<ILAYER>` tags to create either absolute-positioned or in-line layers within a page, just like a `<DIV>` tag. However, with layers, each acts like a separate window, and holds a document and arrays of that document's contents. They are like frames in that respect, but do not need to be created using a separate `<FRAMESET>` page.

Dynamic Pages with Layers

Unlike the **<DIV>** tag in Navigator, however, layers are dynamic. We can change the position and appearance of a layer while the page is loaded using script, and the changes are displayed in the browser. We can also change the source of a layer, using its **SRC** property, and have the new content loaded from the server and displayed without the whole document being reloaded. Again, this is similar to the way frames work.

It's even possible to open a layer's document and write to it using script. This way, we can replace the entire content with new HTML, without any download from the server. We've provided an example page that uses several of these techniques to demonstrate layers in action, in the final example of this chapter.

The <LAYER> And <ILAYER> Attributes

The **<LAYER>** and **<ILAYER>** tags accept the same set of attributes, and both create **Layer** element objects within the page. The major difference is that the **<ILAYER>** tag creates an inflow (or inline) layer, while the **<LAYER>** tag creates a normal independent layer. Only **Layer** elements created with **<LAYER>** can be written to once created.

Attribute	Description
ABOVE	Indicates the layer that should be immediately above this layer in the z-order of the page.
BACKGROUND	URL of an image to display behind the elements in the layer.
BELOW	Indicates the layer that should be immediately below this layer in the z-order of the page.
BGCOLOR	Specifies the background color to be used for the layer.
CLASS	The name of a previously defined style class to apply to the layer.
CLIP	The co-ordinates of the clipping rectangle for the layer.
HEIGHT	Height of the layer in pixels.
ID	Specifies the ID to use to refer to the layer. Same as **NAME**.
LEFT	Horizontal position of the layer in relation to its containing layer or the document.
NAME	Specifies the name to use to refer to the layer. Same as **ID**.
PAGEX	Horizontal position of the layer with respect to the document's window.
PAGEY	Vertical position of the layer with respect to the document's window.
SRC	An external file that contains the source data for the layer.
TOP	Vertical position of the layer in relation to its containing layer or the document.
VISIBILITY	Specifies whether the layer should be displayed or hidden on the page.

Attribute	Description
WIDTH	Width of the layer in pixels.
Z-INDEX	Position in the z-order or stacking order of the page, i.e. the z co-ordinate.

For example, this code creates three layers holding text, which overlap each other. One is made invisible, by setting its **VISIBILITY** attribute to **HIDDEN**. However, we could make it visible later in script code by changing the visibility property to **SHOW**:

```
<HTML>
<STYLE TYPE="text/css">
  .abovetext {color:black; font-size:26pt}
  .belowtext {color:white; font-style:italic; font-weight:bold}
</STYLE>
<BODY>

 <LAYER NAME=AboveLayer BGCOLOR="lightgreen"
        TOP=60 LEFT=30 WIDTH=250 HEIGHT=50>
  <SPAN CLASS="abovetext">The Above Layer</SPAN>
 </LAYER>

 <LAYER NAME=BelowLayer ABOVE="AboveLayer" BGCOLOR="blue"
        TOP=20 LEFT=170 WIDTH=70 HEIGHT=120>
  <SPAN CLASS="belowtext">The Below Layer</SPAN>
 </LAYER>

 <LAYER NAME=HiddenLayer
        TOP=50 LEFT=120 WIDTH=60 HEIGHT=80
        VISIBILITY=HIDDEN>
  Can't see this layer
 </LAYER>

</BODY>
</HTML>
```

Notice that the second layer uses the **ABOVE** attribute to place itself underneath the previous layer. Normally, layers appear stacked in the order of the HTML source. Here's the result:

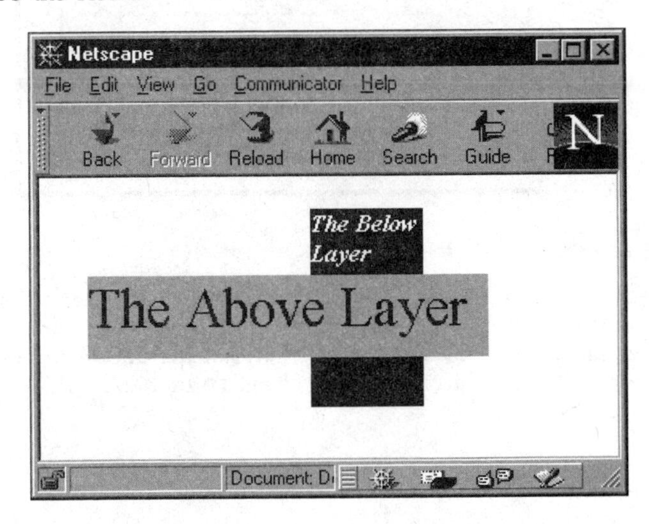

The Document's Layers Array

To keep track of the layers in a document, the object model provides a **layers** array. It holds a reference to each **Layer** object in that page. A layer holds a document that can itself contain other layers, in other words each layer's **document** object can contain an array of its 'child' layers. In the following code, we create a single layer in the document, with the **ID** of **MainLayer**, and then, within its document, two layers **InnerLayer1** and **InnerLayer2**:

```
<BODY BGCOLOR=FFFFFF>
  The actual HTML document
  <LAYER ID="MainLayer">
    A single layer contained within the document.
    <LAYER ID="InnerLayer1">
      A layer contained within the main layer.
    </LAYER>
    <LAYER ID="InnerLayer2">
      Another layer contained within the main layer.
    </LAYER>
  </LAYER>
</BODY>
```

We can think of this as forming a hierarchy of layers, as illustrated by the next diagram:

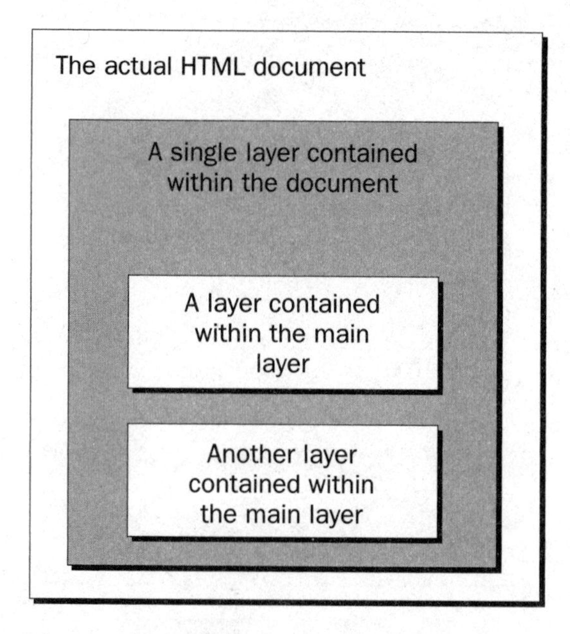

Accessing Layers and their Contents

To access a layer, we use the **layers** array of the **document** object and—in the case of contained layers—the **layers** array of each layer's **document** object. The layers are indexed by their position within the document, and within each layer. They can also be accessed using their **ID** or **NAME**, which are interchangeable:

```
// the top property of the main layer in the document
document.layers[0].top;
document.layers["MainLayer"].top;

// the top property of the second layer within the main layer
document.layers[0].document.layers[1].top;
document.layers["MainLayer"].document.layers["InnerLayer2"].top;
```

Notice how, in the last two examples, we have to refer to the **`document`** object within the layer to get at *its* **`layers`** array.

Layer Properties, Methods and Events

Layers give an enormous boost to the capabilities of the browser for client-side scripting with JavaScript or other languages. They have many properties, methods and events to make this possible.

The Properties of the Layer Object

Layers have many properties, some of which reflect the values we set in the attributes in the **`<LAYER>`** tag. We've grouped them into three sections—**position** properties, **clipping** properties, and **content** properties.

The **position** properties allow us to access information about the physical position of the layer in relation to the page (**`pageX`** and **`pageY`**), or a layer and document that contains it (**`top`** and **`left`**). We can also get information about the z-order of the layer, using the **`above`**, **`below`**, and **`zIndex`** properties. Finally, we have properties that provide references to other layers that are parents or children of the current layer:

Position Properties	Description
`left`	Position in pixels of the left-hand side of the layer in relation to its containing layer or the document.
`top`	Position of the top of the layer in relation to its containing layer or the document.
`pageX`	Horizontal position of the layer in relation to the document window.
`pageY`	Vertical position of the layer in relation to the document window.
`above`	Indicates that the layer should be above another element in the z-order of the page, or returns the element above it.
`below`	Indicates that the layer should be below another element in the z-order of the page, or returns the element below it.
`zIndex`	Position in the z-order or stacking order of the page, i.e. the z co-ordinate.
`parentLayer`	Reference to the layer that contains the current layer.
`siblingAbove`	Reference to the layer above the current layer if they share the same parent layer.
`siblingBelow`	Reference to the layer below the current layer if they share the same parent layer.

Each layer has a clipping rectangle, beyond which the contents are not visible. It's possible to control the size of this rectangle by setting the clipping properties:

Clipping Properties	Description
`clip.bottom`	Y co-ordinate of the bottom of the clipping rectangle for the layer.
`clip.top`	Y co-ordinate of the top of the clipping rectangle for the layer.
`clip.left`	X co-ordinate of the left of the clipping rectangle for the layer.
`clip.right`	X co-ordinate of the right of the clipping rectangle for the layer.
`clip.height`	Height of the clipping rectangle for the layer.
`clip.width`	Width of the clipping rectangle for the layer.

Finally, the remaining properties provide us with a way of accessing the background image and color of the layer (if these are set to `null`—the default—the layer is transparent). We can also access the **NAME** or **ID**, as provided in the **<LAYER>** tag, the URL of a separate page that provides the contents for the layer if available, and the visibility of the layer:

Content Properties	Description
`background`	URL of an image to display behind the elements in the layer.
`bgColor`	Specifies the background color to be used for the layer.
`name`	Specifies the name to use to refer to the layer.
`src`	An external file that contains the source data for the layer.
`visibility`	Defines whether the layer should be displayed on the page.

The Methods of the Layer Object

We've divided the methods of the `Layer` object into three groups. The first group is concerned with moving and resizing the layer. We can move a layer in script by relative amounts, or to an absolute position in relation to the containing layer or the main document itself (if the layer is contained within another document, for example).

We can also move a layer in the z-plane, so that it lies below or on top of other layers. This can provide the 2.5-D effect in pages, by overlapping different layers.

Move and Size Methods	Description
`moveAbove`	Changes the z-order so that the layer is rendered above (overlaps) another element.
`moveBelow`	Changes the z-order so that the layer is rendered below (overlapped by) another element.
`moveBy`	Moves the layer horizontally and vertically by a specified number of pixels.
`moveTo`	Moves the layer so that the top left is at a position x, y (in pixels) within its container.
`moveToAbsolute`	Moves the layer to a position specified in x and y in relation to the page and not the container.
`resizeBy`	Resizes the layer horizontally and vertically by a specified number of pixels.
`resizeTo`	Resizes the layer to a size specified by x and y (in pixels).

A layer contains a document, and this document is the HTML that creates the content of the layer. To make our pages dynamic, we can change this content while the layer is displayed. We can write to it by using the **`write`** and **`writeln`** methods of the **`document`** object within the layer, or load a whole new document using the **`Layer`** object's **`load`** method:

Load Method	Description
`load`	Loads an HTML page into the layer, and can change the width of the layer.

The third group of methods are those that we use when working with events that occur in the layer. We'll be looking at these in the next section, when we examine the whole concept of event handling in more detail.

Event Handling Methods	Description
`captureEvents`	Instructs the layer to capture events of a particular type.
`handleEvent`	Invokes the appropriate event handling code of the object for this event.
`releaseEvents`	Instructs the layer to stop capturing events of a particular type.
`routeEvent`	Passes an event that has been captured back up through the normal event hierarchy.

The Events of the Layer Object

Layers, like windows and frames, have several events available for scripting:

Events	Description
`onBlur`	Occurs when the layer loses the focus.
`onFocus`	Occurs when the layer receives the focus.
`onLoad`	Occurs immediately after the layer's contents have been loaded.
`onMouseOut`	Occurs when the mouse pointer leaves the layer.
`onMouseOver`	Occurs when the mouse pointer first enters the layer.

Of course, layers cannot be resized or moved by the user directly—only script in the page can do this. Therefore they don't have the **`OnMove`** and **`OnResize`** events that are available for the browser window itself. Notice, though, that there is an **`onLoad`** event that we can use to trigger a script once the layer has completed loading. Because we can change the contents of a layer to a different URL once the page is loaded (and even write new content into it directly while it is loading) this event allows us to manage the process and detect when it is properly complete before we manipulate these new contents.

New Events and Event Handling Techniques

Several of the elements in the document support new events in Navigator 4, allowing the DHTML author more control over how the page behaves. These are:

Event	Now applies as well to:
`onAbort`	`Image`
`onError`	`Image, Window`
`onClick`	`Document`
`onDblClick`	`Area, Document, Link`
`onDragDrop`	`Window`
`onKeyDown`	`Document, Input, Image, Link, TextArea`
`onKeyPress`	`Document, Input, Image, Link, TextArea`
`onKeyUp`	`Document, Input, Image, Link, TextArea`
`onLoad`	`Image, Layer`
`onMouseDown`	`Document, Input, Link`
`onMouseMove`	`Document, Window`
`onMouseOut`	`Area, Layer, Link`
`onMouseOver`	`Area, Layer, Link`
`onMouseUp`	`Document, Input, Link`

Event	Now applies as well to:
onMove	Frame, Window
onResize	Frame, Window

This means, for example, that we can react to key presses, mouse clicks, or movements of the mouse over various elements, or to changes in the size or position of the main browser window and its frames.

Event Handling in Layers

This code reacts to the **onMouseOver** and **onMouseOut** events of a layer, and changes the background color when the mouse pointer is over the layer. Notice how we can include a **<SCRIPT>** section within the layer. Recall that its content is just like a separate page, and the script here is entirely independent from script in other parts of the page:

```
...
<STYLE>
  P {color:blue; fontfamily:"Impact", "sans-serif"; fontsize:96}
</STYLE>
<BODY>
 <LAYER NAME=MyLayer BGCOLOR="white" TOP=50 LEFT=50
  ONMOUSEOVER="colorlayer('red')" ONMOUSEOUT="colorlayer('white')" >
  <P>Wrox Press</P>
  <SCRIPT LANGUAGE=JavaScript1.2>
   function colorlayer(changeto)
   { bgColor=changeto }
  </SCRIPT>
 </LAYER>
</BODY>
```

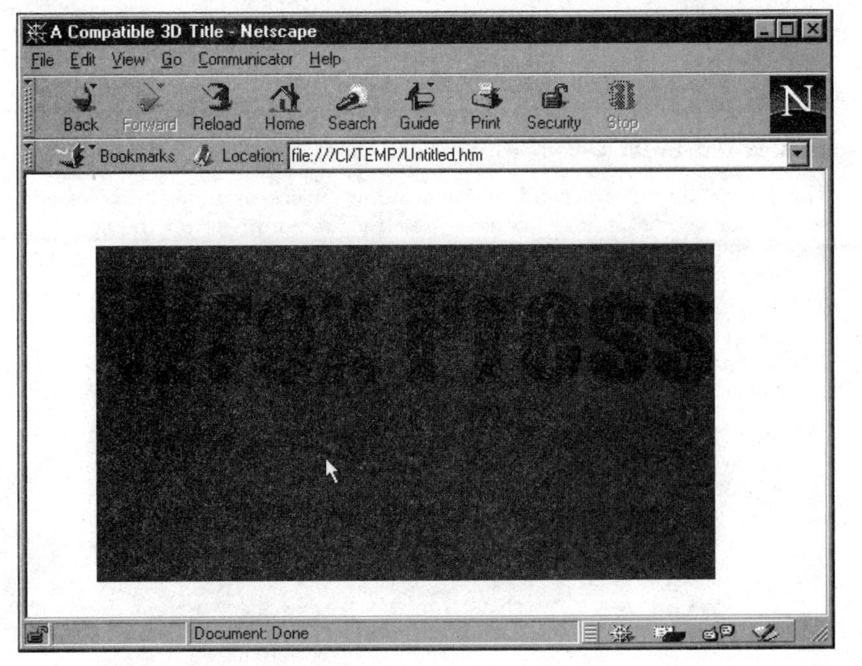

The new Event Object

To be able to handle events that occur in the page, Navigator implements a new **Event** object. This provides a set of properties which are updated each time an event occurs. They can be used to get more information about the event, and the browser environment at the point the event occurred. The **Event** object properties are:

Properties	Description
`type`	The type of event, as a string.
`target`	The name of the object where the event was originally sent.
`screenX`	Horizontal position in pixels of the mouse pointer on the screen for an event.
`screenY`	Vertical position in pixels of the mouse pointer on the screen for an event.
`pageX`	Horizontal position in pixels of the mouse pointer in relation to the document's window.
`pageY`	Vertical position in pixels of the mouse pointer in relation to the document's window.
`layerX`	Horizontal position of the mouse pointer in pixels in relation to the containing layer.
`layerY`	Vertical position of the mouse pointer in pixels in relation to the containing layer.
`which`	ASCII value of a key that was pressed, or indicates which mouse button was clicked.
`modifiers`	Details of the keys held down for a key-press or mouse event.
`data`	The URLs of the objects dropped onto the Navigator window, as an array of strings.

Accessing the Event Object Properties

The **Event** object is a child of the window object, and can be accessed with script code. For example, this code gets the *x*-coordinate on the screen from the **Event** object:

```
HorizScreenOffset = window.Event.screenX
```

The **Event** object is also passed to JavaScript event handler functions as a parameter, and the properties are usually accessed within that event handler:

```
<SCRIPT LANGUAGE="JavaScript1.2">

function MyMouseEventCode(e)
{
  strMesg = "You clicked the "
  if (e.which == 1) strMesg += "left ";
  if (e.which == 3) strMesg += "right ";
  strMesg += "mouse button, at position x = " + e.pageX;
  strMesg += ", y = " + e.pageY + String.fromCharCode(10);
```

```
    strMesg += "The keyboard modifiers value is " + e.modifiers;
    alert(strMesg);
  }

  // now connect the event to our event handler
  document.onmouseup = MyMouseEventCode;
  </SCRIPT>
```

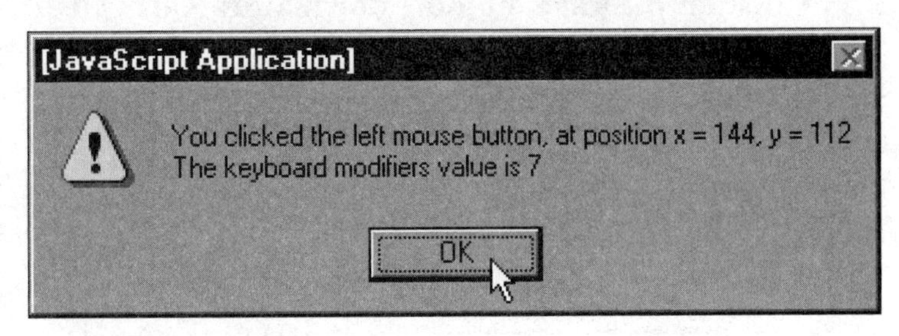

Using the modifiers Property

The value of the **modifiers** property is not terribly useful as it is. What does **7** mean anyway? In the case of the message shown above, we were holding down the *Ctrl, Shift* and *Alt* keys at the time. In fact, the value is a combination of special **Event** object constant values, each one defining a particular key. These constants are:

Constant	Key	Value
Event.ALT_MASK	*Alt* key	1
Event.CONTROL_MASK	*Ctrl* key	2
Event.SHIFT_MASK	*Shift* key	4
Event.META_MASK	*Meta* or *Command* key	8

To decide which keys were being held down we can use the logical operator **AND** on the values together with the value of the **modifiers** property:

```
function MyMouseEventCode(e)
{
  strMesg = "You clicked the "
  if (e.which == 1) strMesg += "left ";
  if (e.which == 3) strMesg += "right ";
  strMesg += "mouse button, at position x = " + e.pageX;
  strMesg += ", y = " + e.pageY + String.fromCharCode(10);
  if (e.modifiers > 0)
  {
    strMesg += "while holding down the ";
    if (e.modifiers & Event.SHIFT_MASK) strMesg = strMesg + "Shift key ";
    if (e.modifiers & Event.CONTROL_MASK) strMesg = strMesg + "Ctrl key ";
    if (e.modifiers & Event.ALT_MASK) strMesg = strMesg + "Alt key ";
    if (e.modifiers & Event.META_MASK) strMesg = strMesg + "Meta key ";
  }
  alert(strMesg);
}
```

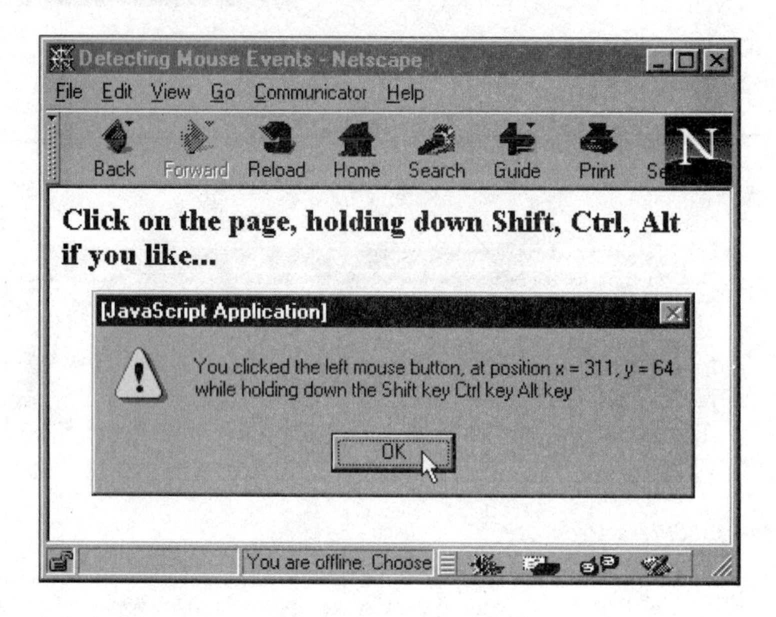

Capturing and Routing Events

One major topic that makes Dynamic HTML different from scripting in earlier versions, either with JavaScript or any other language, is the way that the browser manages the events that are occurring in the page. We've already seen this to some extent when we looked at the **`Event`** object earlier.

However, there is another innovation that plays a major role in the way we create script routines in Dynamic HTML. The **`Event`** object comes into play again here by providing two properties, **`target`** and **`type`**.

The Itinerary of an Event

When an event occurs in a page, the object that gets first look at it is the element that was current at the time. For example, this could be the object under the mouse pointer for a mouse event, a **`<TEXTAREA>`** control on a form for a key-press event, or a layer within the page:

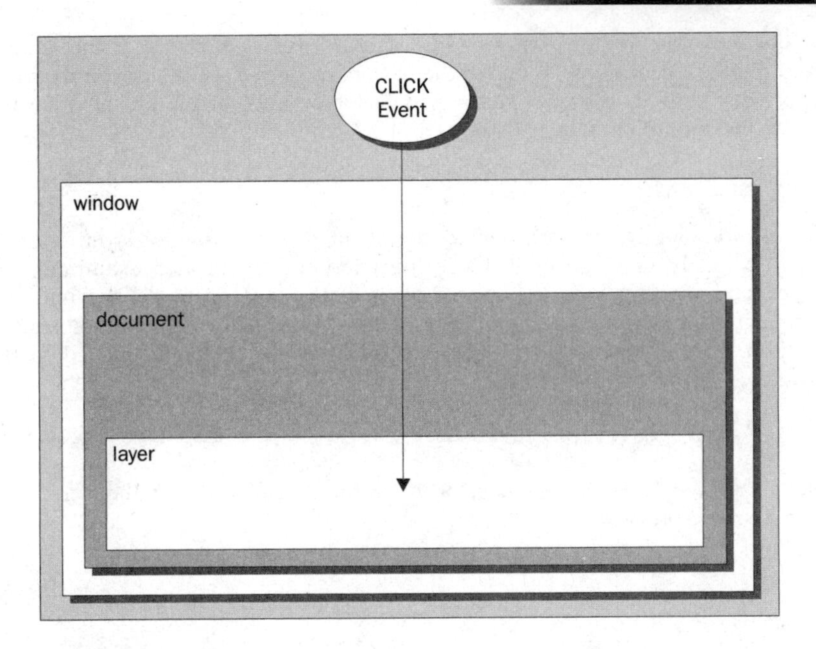

Capturing an Event

This chain of events is the case by default, if we don't do anything to change it. However, as the name suggests, the new **event capturing** feature of Dynamic HTML means that we can allow other objects to see the event before it gets to its originally-intended target. This is done using the **`captureEvents`** method. If we execute the code:

```
window.captureEvents(Event.CLICK)
```

the browser will divert all the **`onClick`** events occurring in the window to the **`window`** object first, rather than sending them to the intended objects—in our example the layer on the page. It's as if the window just sticks out its hand as the event goes past and grabs it. The layer doesn't get to see it at all:

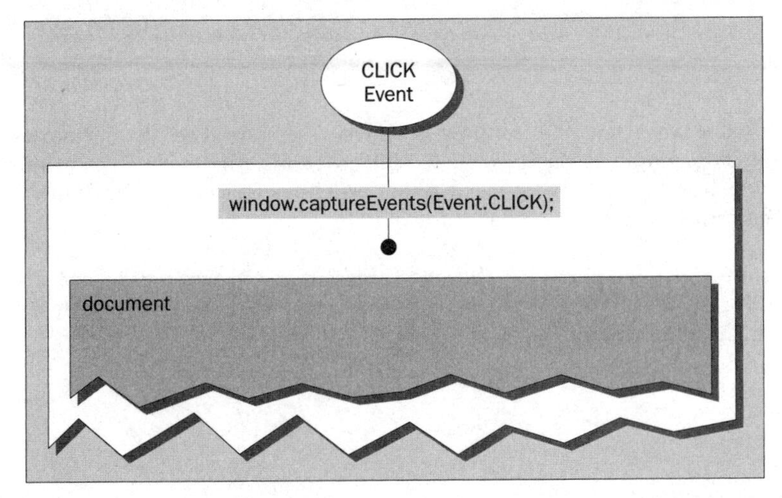

In this example, we're capturing only **`CLICK`** events. Notice that the code requires the event name without the '**on**' part, and it must also be in wholly upper-case letters. These events are in fact properties of the global **`Event`** object, hence the syntax of **`Event.`***eventname*.

Routing an Event

The **`window`** object has intercepted the event destined for the layer, and the layer is totally unaware of it. Once the window has finished examining the event, and reacting to it if it wants to, it can pass it on to the original intended recipient as if nothing had happened. This is done with the **`routeEvent`** method. The argument is the reference to the event originally passed to the window's event handling function:

```
window.routeEvent(event_reference)
```

Now, the layer gets the event as well—without realizing that the window has had a sneak preview:

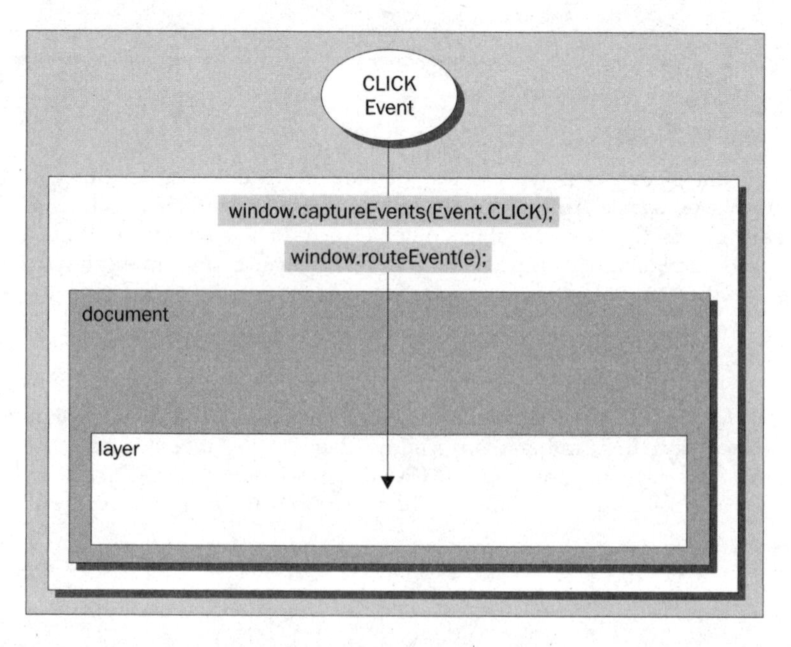

By routing an event, the window effectively hands it back to the browser. The event then continues on its way. It will go to the intended target element, as if nothing had happened. Notice that the window doesn't need to know which element this is when it routes the event.

Of course, the window isn't the only object that can capture an event like this. The document and any layers it contains can also capture and route events using the same technique.

Capturing Events in Other Windows

So, the **`window`** object can capture events within its own window, followed by the document and then any layers. But event capturing can also be established in windows other than the one that is running our script. This requires a signed script to be used, even if the other window is just a separate frame within the same frameset.

> ***Signed scripts*** *are a security feature provided in Navigator 4 to replace the* ***tainting*** *methods used in previous versions. More information about signed scripts can be obtained from:*
> ***`http://developer.netscape.com/library/documentation/`***

To capture the events occurring in all the frames in a window, for example, we would first request security privilege, then turn on **external event capturing**. Finally, we call the **`captureEvents`** method as usual:

```
// request security privilege to use external event capturing
netscape.security.PrivilegeManager.enablePrivilege("UniversalBrowserWrite");
enableExternalCapture();
captureEvents(Event.CLICK);
```

External event capturing only works for the **`window`** object.

Capturing Different Events

In our example, we've only been capturing **`CLICK`** events. Other events are passed directly on to the target element, as usual. However, we can capture several different kinds of events by specifying them all in the call to the **`captureEvents`** method, separating each one with vertical bar (**`|`**) character, which acts as the mathematical **`OR`** between the event identifiers:

```
captureEvents(Event.KEYPRESS | Event.MOUSEDOWN | Event.MOUSEUP);
```

Remember, one of the properties of the **`Event`** object is **`type`**. When an event occurs, we can read the type of event from this property, as you'll see in the next example.

Directing an Event

When we route an event using the **`routeEvent`** method, we don't have any control over where it goes. The destination will be the original target element, unless another object (such as the document or a layer) has enabled event capturing as well.

Instead, we can call the **`handleEvent`** method of a different element instead. Every element or object that can support events (i.e. to which an event handler function can be attached) has the **`handleEvent`** method. Providing we have written a function and connected it to that particular event, we can send an event to that object or element directly. It no longer passes to the original target.

For example, if we have 20 checkbox elements on a page, we might create one function to handle them all. To connect this function with the **onMouseDown** events for all the checkboxes, we might decide to capture the event at document level:

```
document.captureEvents(Event.MOUSEDOWN);
document.onMouseDown = MyMouseCode;
...
```

Now, the function **MyMouseCode()** will run every time an **onMouseDown** event occurs in the entire document. By examining the **target** property of the **Event** object, we can tell which element the event was aimed at. If we decide to send it to a different element, we can simply use **handleEvent**:

```
function MyMouseCode(e)
{
  strTarget = " " + e.target    // convert target property into a string
  if (strTarget.indexOf("MyCheck1") != -1)
    document.forms["MyForm"].elements["MyCheckMaster"].handleEvent(e);
  ...
}
```

This code checks to see if the original target for the event was the checkbox named **MyCheck1**, by examining the target property of the **Event** object. This property contains the complete element tag, and we are implicitly converting it to a string by concatenating it with a space character. If it contains the name **MyCheck1**, we send the event to the element named **MyCheckMaster** instead.

Event Return Values

Events can return either a **true** or **false** value to attempt to change the outcome of that event. For example, returning **false** from a **SUBMIT** button's event handler will cancel submission of that form. Several events can be cancelled this way, including **onClick** for links, **onKeyDown**, **onKeyPress**, **onMouseDown**, **onMouseUp**, **onReset**, **onSubmit**, and **onDragDrop**.

When we have enabled event capturing, these effects still apply. If the user clicked on a link, the link will not be followed. However, many events are not cancelable. In this case, returning **false** from a routine that has captured that event will end event handling for that event.

Releasing Event Capture

We can turn on event capturing at any time in code, it doesn't have to be set when the page is first loaded. Event capturing becomes effective as soon as the **captureEvents** method has been called. If we then decide to stop capturing events, we just need to call the equivalent method, **releaseEvents**. Again, we specify which event or events we wish to release, and we don't have to release all the ones we're currently capturing:

```
// release just CLICK events, or release several events in one go
releaseEvents(Event.CLICK);
releaseEvents(Event.KEYPRESS | Event.MOUSEDOWN | Event.MOUSEUP);
```

If we have previously enabled external event capturing, we can turn this off using the **disableExternalCapture** method. Of course, we still need to switch off event capturing for the **window** object itself first:

```
releaseEvents(Event.CLICK);
disableExternalCapture();
```

The Screen Object

The new **Screen** object provides the scripting language with information about the client's screen resolution and rendering abilities. Its properties are:

Properties	Description
availHeight	Height of the available screen space in pixels (excluding screen furniture).
availWidth	Width of the available screen space in pixels (excluding screen furniture).
colorDepth	Maximum number of colors that are supported by the user's display system.
height	Overall height of the user's screen in pixels.
pixelDepth	Returns the number of bits used per pixel by the system display hardware.
width	Overall width of the user's screen in pixels.

For example, we could use the **screen** object to examine the user's screen size settings, and then decide what size images to include in our page:

```
...
if (window.screen.width > 640)
  document.images[0].src = "bigpic.jpg"
else
  document.images[0].src = "smallpic.jpg";
...
```

Changes to JavaScript and the <SCRIPT> Tag

Navigator 2 used version 1.0 of JavaScript, and this is the default for script sections if we just use **LANGUAGE=JAVASCRIPT** (or omit the **LANGUAGE** attribute altogether). Navigator 3 introduced an updated version of JavaScript called version 1.1. Navigator 4 brings with it another new version, 1.2. Each version is backward compatible with earlier ones.

To use the features added in the newer versions, we specify the minimum version that the browser must support. To tell the browser it must support the latest version, we just use **LANGUAGE=JAVASCRIPT1.2** in the **<SCRIPT>** tag. Likewise, we can use **LANGUAGE=JAVASCRIPT1.1** to specify the Navigator 3 version of the language. If the browser can't support the minimum version we specify, it should ignore the script altogether.

When we use a specific version tag, the way that some JavaScript features work changes. In other words, the version specified in the **LANGUAGE** attribute actually makes the language interpreter behave differently. In Navigator 4, for example, some aspects of the interpreter (such as the **split** and **substring** methods) will still work like they did in earlier versions. Only if we use **LANGUAGE=JAVASCRIPT1.2** will the new behavior and features become available to our script code. We cover the changes to JavaScript in Navigator 4 in the Reference section of this book.

> **Note that version 4 of Microsoft Internet Explorer has a JavaScript interpreter that is compatible with JavaScript version 1.1. However it will also execute any script in a <SCRIPT> section that has the LANGUAGE attribute set to JavaScript1.2. See Chapter 12 for a work-around.**

Netscape Dynamic Fonts

When a font is specified in a **<FONT>** tag, the browser looks for that font on the user's system. If it isn't installed, the next font in the list specified by the tag is used. If none are found, a default font is used instead. This means that the fonts you specify must be already installed on the client, or your page will not look like it was designed to appear.

However, now Navigator can import a font using a special **Portable Font Resources** (PFR) format file. This requires a **<LINK>** tag with the **REL** attribute set to **fontdef**:

```
<LINK REL=fontdef SRC="http://netscape.com/examplefont.pfr">
```

Once the font is downloaded it is cached locally on the client for use as specified by the font creator. For example, you can't use the downloaded font in other pages. It can only be used with pages from the original site. To be able to specify Dynamic Fonts in your own pages, you have to have the PFR file, and these are not freely available at the time of writing. For more information, visit:

http://home.netscape.com/comprod/products/communicator/fonts/

To use the new font, we specify the name in the usual **<FONT>** tag. Navigator supports the **POINT-SIZE** and **WEIGHT** (with values from 100 to 900) attributes:

```
<FONT FACE="MyNewFont" POINT-SIZE=28 WEIGHT=600>
```

The **SIZE** attribute of the **<FONT>** tag can now also accept increment values that specify the size in relation to the base font size:

```
<FONT FACE="MyNewFont" SIZE=+2>
<FONT FACE="MyNewFont" SIZE=-1>
```

An Example Page

On our samples site at **`http://rapid.wrox.co.uk/books/1568`** we have supplied a page that can be used to preview what different colors look like in the browser. It changes the foreground and background colors of a sample of text dynamically—while the page is being displayed.

While changing the background color is easy—we just need to assign the new color to the **`bgColor`** property of the document object—it's not so easy with the foreground color. Some browsers, like Internet Explorer, reflect changes in the page. Unfortunately, Netscape's browser doesn't in its Communicator 4 incarnation. Instead, we have to find a different method.

Of course, layers provide the solution. In our example, the text at the bottom of the page, which changes color as you select from the lists, is contained within a **`<LAYER>`** in the main body of the page. Here's how the page looks when you are using it:

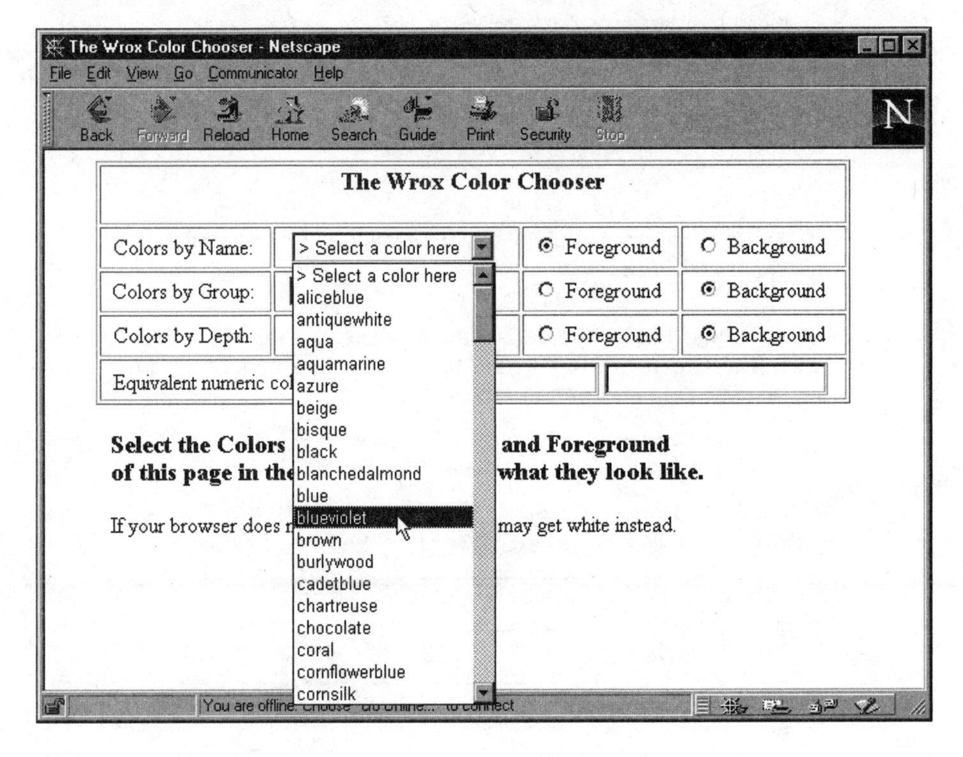

The HTML Part of the Color Chooser Page

The HTML that creates the page is pretty huge, because it contains the 100+ color names for each list box. However, the important part as far as we're concerned here is the section that creates two layers—one absolute-positioned and one in-line. In the first layer, we place the text you see on the page. The second layer simply has the background color set to the default white. It's also invisible, because we've set the **`VISIBILITY`** attribute to **`HIDDEN`** in the **`<LAYER>`** tag:

```
...
<!-- The layer that holds the text that will change color -->
<!-- Note: you can't write to an ILAYER, you must use a LAYER -->
<LAYER ID="textlayer" LEFT=50>
  <H3>Select the Colors for the Background and Foreground<BR>
  of this page in the Lists above, to see what they look like.</H3>
  If your browser does not support the color, you may get white instead.
</LAYER>

<!-- Hidden layer that is used to convert the color name to a value -->
<!-- There is no content, because we're just changing its bgColor -->
<ILAYER NAME="convertlayer" VISIBILITY="HIDDEN">
  <BODY BGCOLOR=FFFFFF>
  </BODY>
</ILAYER>
...
```

*You can see how close layers are to frames and windows here. We can use a **`<BODY>`** tag to set their appearance just as we would with a document displayed in a **`window`** object.*

The reason for that hidden frame is shown when you select a color for the foreground. The two text boxes in the table show the numerical equivalent of the colors as RGB triplets (**`#RRGGBB`**):

The Wrox Color Chooser			
Colors by Name:	blueviolet	◉ Foreground	○ Background
Colors by Group:	> Select a color here	○ Foreground	◉ Background
Colors by Depth:	> Select a color here	○ Foreground	◉ Background
Equivalent numeric color values:	Foreground: #8A2BE2	Background: #FFFFFF	

To convert the color name selected in the list into a numerical value is easily done by assigning it to the color property of an object like the background of the page (**`bgColor`**), then reading it back. It's returned as the RGB triplet value we want. However, we can't do this in Communicator with the foreground color, because it's read-only once the page has been rendered. Instead, we assign the color to the background of our hidden in-line layer, then read it back from there.

The Script in the Color Chooser Page

Here's the code of the first of two functions in the page that perform all this magic. It creates a whole new page for the visible fixed layer, with the correct foreground color. Because layers are transparent, if we don't apply a background color we will see the background color of the main page through it:

```
function ChangeTextLayer(fgcol)
  {
    // create a string containing the new layer content
    newcontent = '<BODY TEXT="' + fgcol + '"><H3>Select the Colors for the ';
    newcontent += 'Background and Foreground<BR> of this page in the Lists ';
    newcontent += 'above, to see what they look like.</H3> If your browser ';
    newcontent += 'does not support the color you may get white instead.</
BODY>';

    // write it to the layer's document and close it to update the display
    document.layers["textlayer"].document.write(newcontent);
    document.layers["textlayer"].document.close();

    // change the background of the hidden layer to the new foreground color
    // so we can read back the converted RRGGBB value from it for the textbox
    document.layers["convertlayer"].document.bgColor = fgcol;
  }
```

Once we've created the string, we write it to the layer using the **`write`** method of that **`Layer`** object and then **`close`** it—just as we would with a **`document`** object. Notice how we refer to the methods of the document in the layer, using:

```
    document.layers["textlayer"].document.write(newcontent);
    document.layers["textlayer"].document.close();
```

The final line then changes the background color of the other (hidden) layer. Again, we refer to the layer by name, though we could just as easily have used **`document.layers[1]`** because it is the second layer in the document:

```
document.layers["convertlayer"].document.bgColor = fgcol;
```

The other function does the work of extracting the values from the list boxes and radio buttons when a selection is made. In particular, we refer to the Foreground radio button using its index, which is one more than the associated list box element:

```
thisform.elements[listnumber + 1].checked
```

The rest of the function is concerned with retrieving the RGB color triplet values from the **`bgColor`** property of the main page, and the background of the hidden layer:

```
  function ChangeColor(listnumber)
  {
    // get a reference to the form, and then to the color selector list
    thisform = document.forms[0];
    thislist = thisform.elements[listnumber];

    // find out which entry is selected, and get the text for it
    thisindex = thislist.selectedIndex;
    thiscolor = thislist.options[thisindex].text;
```

```
      // change appropriate setting and update two text boxes with new values
      // but only if a color is selected, not an entry starting with '>'
      if (thiscolor.indexOf('>') == -1)
        { if (thisform.elements[listnumber + 1].checked)
            ChangeTextLayer(thiscolor)
            else document.bgColor = thiscolor;

          // to get foreground color query background color of hidden layer
          thisform.elements['txtFG'].value = 'Foreground: ' +
            document.layers["convertlayer"].document.bgColor.toUpperCase();
          thisform.elements['txtBG'].value = 'Background: ' +
            document.bgColor.toUpperCase()
        }
    }
```

Summary

Netscape Navigator version 4 adds a range of new features that make it easy for programmers to create more dynamic and interactive pages, without resorting to using Java applets or plugins. In the broadest terms, these new features include:

- More of the elements in the page (tags, images, layers, text, etc) are now accessible to script written in the page.
- An extension to the implementation of styles and style sheets provides more hooks to the page elements from JavaScript
- Absolute positioning of the elements in the page, including control of the z-order, allows a desk-top publishing style of authoring, and '2.5D' appearance.
- Dynamic redrawing of any or all parts of the page allows changes to a loaded page to be made visible. Pages no longer need to be reloaded from the server to show the latest version.
- New event handling techniques are supported, including capturing of events that occur in the page and routing them back up the document hierarchy.

To learn more about the capabilities of Netscape Navigator/Communicator 4, visit the Netscape web site at **http://www.netscape.com/comprod/products/communicator/index.html**. You can also learn more about programming Navigator 4 from our sister book Instant Netscape Dynamic HTML Programmer's Reference from Wrox Press, ISBN 1-861001-19-3.

Dynamic HTML in Internet Explorer 4

This chapter gives an overview of new features in Microsoft's latest browser, Internet Explorer 4, followed by some suggestions on how to make your pages cross browser compatible. As this is an HTML reference book, we won't be covering all the other new features in Internet Explorer 4 (IE4), as many of these have more to do with the changes to the interface than with the operating system—especially in Windows 95 and Windows 98. That's not to say that they *can't* be programmed, just that it is not the subject of this book. To learn more about how to program all aspects of Internet Explorer 4 look out for **Professional IE4 Programming** from Wrox Press, ISBN 1-861000-70-7.

Internet Explorer 4 follows the W3C working drafts for HTML 4.0 quite closely in its current version, and implements many of the extensions to HTML proposed by Microsoft and other manufacturers as well. For example, it supports most of the current proposals for 'enhanced forms', as we saw back in Chapter 8. We can't hope to cover all the new features in detail, but we will offer pointers to the kinds of things that are possible.

What's New in Internet Explorer 4?

In order to support the broad aims of Dynamic HTML, Internet Explorer 4 supports many new features that are similar to those in Netscape Navigator 4. However, they are implemented in most cases in an entirely different way, and authoring pages for the two browsers requires very different techniques. The new areas we'll be looking at in this chapter are:

- changes to the Document Object Model
- dynamic element styles
- static and dynamic element positioning
- changing the contents of the page while it is displayed
- new event-handling techniques
- data binding

We'll end with a brief look at how we can create sites and pages that are compatible with the two very different version 4 browsers, IE4 and Navigator 4.

New Extended Browser and Document Object Model

Internet Explorer 4 has an extended browser and document object model, which achieves two purposes. By adding the **`applets`**, **`embeds`** and **`plugins`** collections, it provides better compatibility with Netscape Navigator 3. Secondly, there are new objects and collections that are provided to support the new abilities of the browser, including Dynamic HTML.

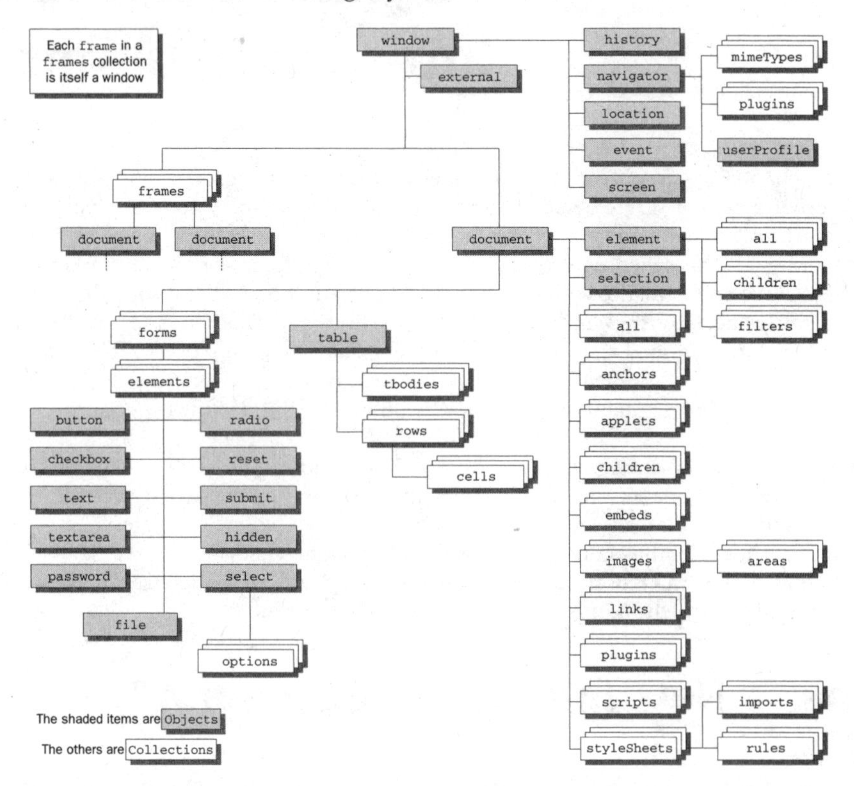

The main additions are:

- The **`all`** collection, which is a collection of all the elements in the page
- The **`event`** object, which provides information about events that occur in the browser
- The **`filters`** collections, for all the visible elements within the document
- The **`selection`** object, which provides information about the current selection in the loaded pages
- The collection of **`styleSheets`**, which store details of each imported style sheet

Using the all Collection

You'll recall that all elements in HTML and the version 4 browsers have an **ID** attribute. The **all** collection provides a neat way to access any element, given its **ID**. It can also be used to access elements in the order they appear in the source HTML, using this as an index to the collection:

```
document.all["MyTextBox"]   // the element with an ID of MyTextBox
document.all[3]             // the fourth element on the page
```

Remember that collections, like JavaScript and VBScript arrays, have the first item indexed zero—so the fourth item has the index 3. The examples above use the JavaScript syntax of enclosing the array element in square brackets. In VBScript, we use ordinary brackets, i.e. parentheses.

We can easily use the **all** collection to get a reference to an individual element in the page, without having to worry about which form or document division it is contained within. Then, we can use this reference to get at the various properties of the element:

```
// in JavaScript or JScript:
var objTextBox = document.all["MyTextBox"];
alert(objTextBox.value);

'and in VBScript:
Set objTextBox = document.all("MyTextBox")
alert objTextBox.value

'or using a VBScript message box:
Set objTextBox = document.all("MyTextBox")
MsgBox objTextBox.value
```

Using the styleSheets Collection

When we include one or more style sheets in a document, either with a **<LINK>** tag or a **STYLE** element, IE4 adds them to the **styleSheets** collection. We can retrieve information about the style sheets, such as the title, by referencing the collection:

```
document.styleSheets[0].title;
```

When a style sheet is imported using the CSS **@import** instruction, it is included in the **imports** collection (which is a collection of all the imported style sheets), within the appropriate **styleSheets** object. To get information about it, such as its **href** property, we might use:

```
document.styleSheets[0].imports[0].href;
```

Dynamic Element Styles

Internet Explorer 4 supports almost the entire range of CSS1 style properties, including the importing of style sheets through the **@import** instruction. We can use styles to set the appearance of elements, in line with the proposals of HTML 4.0. And, because IE4 redraws the page when any of the style properties change, we can change things like the color and appearance of elements dynamically, by changing the values of their style properties.

In Internet Explorer, each visible element has its own **style** object, which holds the styles that have been applied to it. We can access these like any other object:

```
<P ID=MyHeading STYLE="font-family:Arial; font-size:18px; color:red;"
ONCLICK="changeStyle();"> Some Text </P>

<SCRIPT LANGUAGE=JAVASCRIPT>
function changeStyle()
{
  theStyle = document.all["MyHeading"].style;
  theStyle.fontFamily = "Tahoma";
  theStyle.fontSize = "24px";
  theStyle.color = "green";
}
</SCRIPT>
```

Notice how the **style** object's property names are not always the same as the CSS style property, for example we set the font size using the CSS **font-size** property, but access it in code through the **style** object's **fontSize** property.

Examining an Element's Properties

Rather than changing the **style** properties of elements, we can also change their 'direct' properties. Every element in a page has a set of properties, which are usually set by the attributes in the HTML tag. For example, this **<H2>** heading has an **align** property, which indicates how the text was aligned when the page was created in HTML:

```
<H2 ALIGN=CENTER> Some Text </H2>
```

The element's **align** property can be examined in code, either by specifying the element as part of the document's **all** collection, or with the **Me** or **this** keywords. In any event handler's code, these keywords provide a reference to the element that the event is bound to. In VBScript, we use **Me**:

```
<H2 ID=MyHeading ALIGN=CENTER> Some Text </H2>
<SCRIPT LANGUAGE=VBSCRIPT>
  Sub MyHeading_onclick()
    MsgBox Me.align
  End Sub
</SCRIPT>
```

In JavaScript or JScript, we use the keyword **this**:

```
<H2 ALIGN=CENTER ONCLICK="myClickEvent();"> Some Text </H2>
<SCRIPT LANGUAGE=JSCRIPT>
  function myClickEvent()
```

```
  {
    alert(this.align);
  }
</SCRIPT>
```

In these cases, the heading will have the value **`center`** for its **`align`** property. (Notice that the value is returned in lower case). We can then change the value in our code, just as we would for a style property.

> **One point you need to watch out for is that many elements return an empty string as the value of a property that has not been set explicitly. For example, the default alignment of a `<H2>` tag, if no `ALIGN` attribute is included, is `left`. However the `align` property in this case returns an empty string.**

Element Properties vs Style Properties

While manipulating the 'direct' properties of elements, bear in mind that the technique recommended by W3C in version 4.0 of the HTML standard is to use the style properties instead. Recall that we can align text headings using style properties, like this:

```
<H2 ID=MyHeading STYLE="text-align:center"> Some Text </H2>
```

To query or change the alignment in this case, we use the values in the element's **`style`** object—in this case the value of the **`textAlign`** property:

```
Sub MyHeading_onclick()
  MsgBox Me.style.textAlign
End Sub
```

Here's the equivalent in JavaScript:

```
<SCRIPT LANGUAGE=JAVASCRIPT>
function myClickEvent()
{
  alert(this.style.textAlign);
}
</SCRIPT>
```

Remember that when we align text using a style attribute, as in the earlier code, the 'direct' **`align`** property of the element returns an empty string unless it has *also* been set to a specific value.

Static and Dynamic Element Positioning

We can position elements within the page either absolutely or relatively by setting the appropriate style properties. The following code creates two document divisions. One has a blue background, and is absolutely positioned on the page. The other has a yellow background, and is relatively positioned and nested inside the blue one:

```
<BODY ID=MyBody>
  <DIV ID=OuterDiv STYLE="position:absolute; left:50; top:50; width:300;
                          height:100; background-color:blue">
```

```
      <DIV ID=InnerDiv STYLE="position:relative; left:50; top:25; width:200;
                              height:50; background-color:yellow">
      </DIV>
    </DIV>
  </BODY>
```

As in Netscape's Navigator browser, we can resize and move the elements around with script by changing the values of their properties. However, Navigator only allows us to do this with its proprietary **<LAYER>** elements, while in Internet Explorer we can move and resize *any* element that is absolutely positioned:

```
document.all["OuterDiv"].top = 100;    // move outer division down page
document.all["InnerDiv"].left = 100;   // move inner division across page
document.all["OuterDiv"].width = 200;  // make outer division narrower
```

The Event Object's Position Properties

Internet Explorer has a new **event** object, as we saw earlier. When an event occurs, this object provides four pairs of position properties: **offsetX** and **offsetY**, **clientX** and **clientY**, **screenX** and **screenY**, and plain **x** and **y**.

The **screenX** and **screenY** properties return the mouse pointer position in absolute terms, with respect to the screen. So the bottom right corner in vanilla VGA mode will be **screenX = 640** and **screenY = 480**. The other sets of properties return values that are based on the mouse pointer position with respect to the browser window and document.

If the element that receives the event is not inside another container element, such as a division, all the pairs of properties except for **screenX** and **screenY** return the same values. For example, the **offsetX** and **offsetY**, and **clientX** and **clientY** properties are all based on the document itself. However, once we add containers such as document divisions, all this changes.

- **clientX** and **clientY** return the position of the mouse pointer in relation to the 'client area' of the browser window. This is the part of the browser that displays the page itself, excluding the window frame, scrollbars, menus, etc.

- **offsetX** and **offsetY** return the position of the mouse pointer in relation to the top left corner of the element that actually received the event. In some cases, such as when the element is a container itself and the contents of the container are not all visible and have been scrolled within it, the values reflect the position of the top left corner of the content with respect to the top left corner of the container. Where there is no container, the values returned are with respect to the document itself.

- **x** and **y** return the position of the mouse pointer in relation to the top left corner of the first absolutely or relatively positioned container which holds the element that received the event. If none of the containers are positioned (i.e. do not have **position:relative** or **position:absolute** in their **STYLE** attribute) then the values returned are in relation to the main document, and are the same as the **clientX** and **clientY** properties.

An Event Position Property Example

Using the same HTML code as earlier to create a page containing two divisions, we can add code that returns the values of all the **event** object's position properties:

```
<BODY ID=MyBody>
  <DIV ID=OuterDiv STYLE="position:absolute; left:50; top:50; width:300;
                          height:100; background-color:blue">
    <DIV ID=InnerDiv STYLE="position:relative; left:50; top:25; width:200;
                            height:50; background-color:yellow">
    </DIV>
  </DIV>
</BODY>
<SCRIPT LANGUAGE=VBSCRIPT>
Sub document_onclick()
  Set e = window.event
  strMesg = "srcElement is " & e.srcElement.id & chr(10) _
          & "clientX = " & e.clientX _
          & ", clientY=" & e.clientY & chr(10) _
          & "offsetX = " & e.offsetX _
          & ", offsetY = " & e.offsetY & chr(10) _
          & "screenX = " & e.screenX _
          & ", screenY = " & e.screenY & chr(10) _
          & "x = " & e.x & ", y = " & e.y & chr(10)
  MsgBox strMesg
End Sub
</SCRIPT>
```

Clicking inside the inner division will produce different values for each set of properties. The **x** and **y** properties reflect the position with respect to the outer (parent) division, while the **offsetX** and **offsetY** properties reflect the position with respect to the inner division. The **clientX** and **clientY** properties show the position with respect to the document—i.e. the client area of the browser:

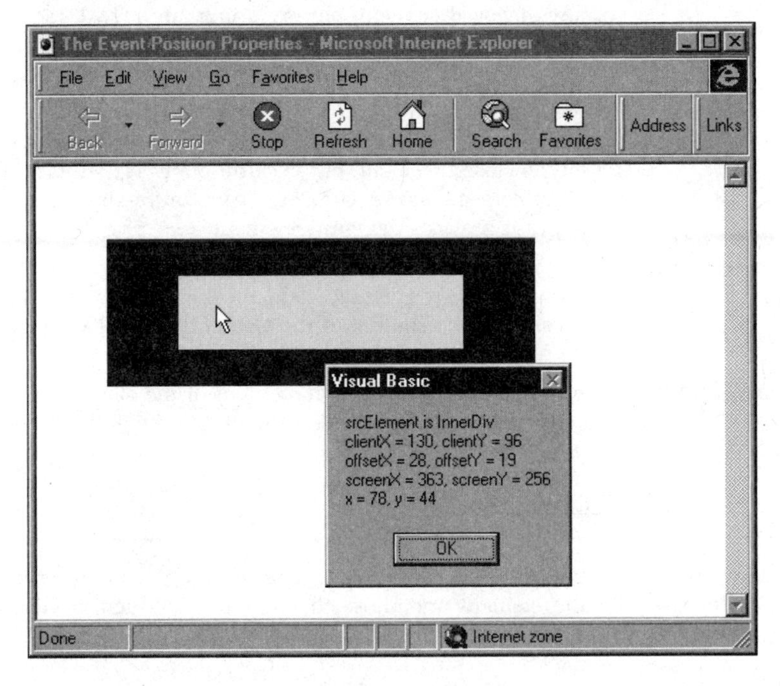

Changing the Contents of a Page

The previous sections of this chapter covered changing the position and appearance of elements. We can also change the actual element itself, just as though we had changed the HTML source that created it. We can also add elements to a page, and remove them, while it is displayed.

The easiest way to manipulate the contents of a page is to use the special properties that are supported by the majority of visible elements. They expose the contents of each part of the document, almost as it appears in the source code. By assigning new values to these properties, we can change the contents of the page that is displayed.

By **document**, we mean a stream of characters that represents the current page, consisting of both text and HTML. Don't confuse the document with the *actual* HTML source code though. This is why we said 'almost as it appears in the source code'. The browser translates the source code into its own representation of the page before displaying it. Changing the contents of an element on the page does not update the original HTML source—just the browser's internal representation of it.

The Element 'Content' Properties

There are four properties that are supported by most of the visual elements in the page:

Property	Description
`innerText`	The complete text content of the element, including the content of any enclosed element, but excluding any HTML tags. Assigning a new string to it replaces only the content of the element, and any new HTML tags are rendered as text, and not interpreted.
`outerText`	The complete text content of the element, including the content of any enclosed element, but excluding any HTML tags. It returns the same string as **`innerText`**, but assigning a new string to it replaces the entire element.
`innerHTML`	The complete text and HTML content of the element, including the content of any enclosed element. Assigning a new string to it replaces only the content of the element, and HTML tags within it are rendered correctly.
`outerHTML`	The complete text and HTML content of the element, including the start and end tags of the element and the entire text and HTML content of any enclosed element. Assigning a new string to it replaces the entire element, and the HTML content of the new string is rendered correctly.

You can see that there are two 'classes' of property, those that preserve the HTML tags within the element and those that ignore it. Which we use depends on the task we want to accomplish.

The innerText Property

If the element is a simple heading, such as:

```
<H3 ID=Heading1>This is my Heading</H3>
```

The **innerText** property can easily be used to change this to And this is my NEW Heading:

```
objHead1 = document.all["Heading1"];
objHead1.innerText = "And this is my NEW Heading";
```

This preserves the original **<H3>** tags, and only replaces their content. However, if we have some formatting within the heading to contend with, we need to consider using the **innerHTML** property instead. If this is the original HTML source:

```
<H3 ID=Heading1>This is <I>my</I> Heading</H3>
```

and we apply the same action to it:

```
objHead1.innerText = "And this is my NEW Heading";
```

we'll lose the formatting of **<I>** and **</I>** tags, because the **innerText** (and **outerText**) properties don't preserve it. Conceptually, the resulting HTML source will be:

```
<H3 ID=Heading1>And this is my NEW Heading</H3>
```

If we change the assignment to include the HTML tags we want, like this:

```
objHead1.innerText = "And this is <I>my</I> NEW Heading";
```

we still get the wrong result. In the page, the heading will be This is <I>my</I> NEW Heading—in other words the **<I>** and **</I>** tags will be visible as text, and the word my will not be italic. Remember that **innerText** and **outerText** do not interpret any HTML within the strings, it's just rendered as text.

The innerHTML Property

However, if we use the **innerHTML** property, we'll get the result we want:

```
objHead1.innerHTML = "And this is <I>my</I> NEW Heading";
```

This is because the 'HTML' content properties cause the browser to interpret any HTML within the strings correctly. They are even clever enough to force the new content to be structurally correct—although we might not get quite the result we want. For example if we only provide an opening **<I>** tag in our new content, the browser will add the closing **</I>** tag automatically to prevent the rest of the page being affected. Using:

```
objHead1.innerHTML = "And this is <I>my NEW Heading";
```

will actually produce the conceptual HTML source:

```
<H3 ID=Heading1>And this is <I>my NEW Heading</I></H3>
```

Of course, this time the words 'NEW' and 'Heading' will also be rendered as italic—probably not what we wanted to happen.

*Not every visible element supports all four 'content' properties. Some only support the 'text' properties, and others may only support a single property—for example the **`<TD>`** tag only provides the **`innerText`** property.*

The outerText and outerHTML Properties

The other two 'content' properties for most visible elements are **`outerText`** and **`outerHTML`**. These return the complete element, including the opening and closing tags that created it in the original source. Of course, the **`outerText`** property only returns actual text, not the HTML tags themselves, so will usually give the same result as the **`innerText`** property. The **`outerHTML`** property, however, returns all the HTML—so it will include the opening and closing tags as well. For example, if we have the HTML source:

```
<H3 ID=Heading1>This is <I>my</I> Heading</H3>
```

the **`outerText`** property will return the complete HTML source for the element, just as it appears in the original document. However, the **`outerText`** property returns just **`This is my Heading`**.

At first, these two properties don't seem very useful. It's when we *write* to them that they show their worth. We effectively replace the entire element in the page with the new value, removing the complete original element including the opening and closing tags. If we write to the **`outerHTML`** property, we can include the HTML tags to create a new replacement element. If we write to the **`outerText`** property, the text just becomes part of the document at that point, and not an element in itself. Using our previous heading element:

```
objHead1.outerHTML = "<H1 ID=NewHeading>This is a larger heading</H1>";
```

replaces the original **`<H3>`** heading with a new **`<H1>`** heading, while:

```
objHead1.outerText = "This isn't an element at all";
```

removes the original **`<H3>`** heading, leaving text which becomes part of any element that encloses the **`<H3>`** heading. Ultimately, this may just be the page's **`<BODY>`** element.

*If we assign an empty string to the **`outerText`** or **`outerHTML`** property of an element, we just remove the element from the page altogether.*

The Element InsertAdjacent Methods

As well as using the four properties to change an element's contents, we can use two methods that are supported by many of the visible elements:

Method	Description
insertAdjacentText	Inserts text into or adjacent to the element. Any HTML tags are ignored. Text can be inserted either side of the element's opening or closing tags.
insertAdjacentHTML	Inserts text and HTML into or adjacent to the element. HTML within the string is correctly rendered after insertion. Text and HTML can be inserted either side of the element's opening or closing tags.

You can immediately see that, in some respects, these two methods mirror the workings of the content properties we looked at in the previous section. The first disregards any HTML content (rendering it as plain text), while the second causes the browser to render it correctly. The syntax of the methods is:

insertAdjacentText(*where*, *text_to_insert***)**
insertAdjacentHTML(*where*, *HTML_and_text_to_insert***)**

The *where* argument controls where the new content is inserted; it's a string that can be one of

BeforeBegin	Immediately before the element's opening tag.
AfterBegin	Immediately after the element's opening tag.
BeforeEnd	Immediately before the element's closing tag.
AfterEnd	Immediately after the element's closing tag.

These methods will preserve the structure of the document, by adding a closing tag if it is omitted in the new string. However, again this may not behave exactly as you would expect. For example, if we use the **insertAdjacentHTML** method to insert a **<B>** tag before the beginning of an element, with the intention of inserting the **</B>** tag after the end, we don't actually get any formatting of the element's content:

```
objHead.insertAdjacentHTML("BeforeBegin", "<B>");
```

results in the conceptual HTML source of:

```
<B></B><H3 ID=Heading1>And this is <I>my NEW Heading</I>< /H3>
```

New Event Handling Techniques

Earlier, we briefly mentioned the **event** object, which is part of the new object model and a subsidiary object to the top-level **window** object. The **event** object is constantly being updated to include information about each event that occurs in our page—it is global to all events in this sense. When an event occurs we can query the **event** object's properties to learn more about the event.

The Properties of the Event Object

Property Name	Description
`altKey`	Returns the state of the *Alt* key when an event occurs.
`button`	The mouse button, if any, that was pressed to fire the event.
`cancelBubble`	Set to prevent the current event from bubbling up the hierarchy.
`clientX`	Returns the *x* coordinate of the element, excluding borders, margins, padding, scrollbars, etc.
`clientY`	Returns the *y* coordinate of the element, excluding borders, margins, padding, scrollbars, etc.
`ctrlKey`	Returns the state of the *Ctrl* key when an event occurs.
`fromElement`	Returns the element being moved from for an `onmouseover` or `onmouseout` event.
`keyCode`	ASCII code of the key being pressed. Changing it sends a different character to the object.
`offsetX`	Returns the *x* coordinate of the mouse pointer when an event occurs, relative to the containing element.
`offsetY`	Returns the *y* coordinate of the mouse pointer when an event occurs, relative to the containing element.
`reason`	Indicates whether data transfer to an element was successful, or why it failed.
`returnValue`	Allows a return value to be specified for the event or a dialog window.
`screenX`	Returns the *x* coordinate of the mouse pointer when an event occurs, in relation to the screen.
`screenY`	Returns the *y* coordinate of the mouse pointer when an event occurs, in relation to the screen.
`shiftKey`	Returns the state of the *Shift* key when an event occurs.
`srcElement`	Returns the element deepest in the object hierarchy that a specified event occurred over.
`srcFilter`	Returns the filter that caused the element to produce an `onfilterchange` event.
`toElement`	Returns the element being moved to for an `onmouseover` or `onmouseout` event.
`type`	Returns the name of the event as a string, without the 'on' prefix, such as 'click' instead of 'onclick'.
`x`	Returns the *x* coordinate of the mouse pointer relative to a positioned parent, or otherwise to the window.
`y`	Returns the *y* coordinate of the mouse pointer relative to a positioned parent, or otherwise to the window.

> **Netscape Navigator 4 also provides an `event` object, as we saw in the previous chapter, but the Internet Explorer 4 version is different—they have different properties, and so cannot be scripted with the same code.**

Mouse Information and the Event Object

In the previous chapter we used the **`event`** object in Navigator 4 to discover which mouse buttons were pressed, and the position of the mouse pointer, when an **`onmousedown`** event occurred. This was the function code for Navigator:

```
<SCRIPT LANGUAGE="JavaScript1.2">
function MyMouseEventCode(e)    // in Netscape Navigator 4
{
  strMesg = "You clicked the "
  if (e.which == 1) strMesg += "left ";
  if (e.which == 3) strMesg += "right ";
  strMesg += "mouse button, at position x = " + e.pageX;
  strMesg += ", y = " + e.pageY + String.fromCharCode(10);
  if (e.modifiers > 0)
  {
    strMesg += "while holding down the ";
    if (e.modifiers & Event.SHIFT_MASK) strMesg = strMesg + "Shift key ";
    if (e.modifiers & Event.CONTROL_MASK) strMesg = strMesg + "Ctrl key ";
    if (e.modifiers & Event.ALT_MASK) strMesg = strMesg + "Alt key ";
    if (e.modifiers & Event.META_MASK) strMesg = strMesg + "Meta key ";
  }
  alert(strMesg);
}
</SCRIPT>
```

In Explorer, we have a different set of properties. Functionally, they provide the same information—but the property names are different:

```
<SCRIPT LANGUAGE="JScript">
function MyMouseEventCode ()    // in Internet Explorer 4
{
  strMesg = "You clicked the "
  if (event.button == 1) strMesg += "left ";
  if (event.button == 2) strMesg += "right ";
  if (event.button == 4) strMesg += "middle ";
  strMesg += "mouse button, at position x = " + event.x;
  strMesg += ", y = " + event.y + String.fromCharCode(10);
  strMesg += "while holding down the ";
  if (event.shiftKey == true) strMesg = strMesg + "Shift key "
  if (event.ctrlKey == true) strMesg = strMesg + "Ctrl key "
  if (event.altKey == true) strMesg = strMesg + "Alt key "
  alert(strMesg);
}
</SCRIPT>
```

> **Notice that Internet Explorer doesn't require the `event` object to be specified as a parameter of the function, and we reference the global `event` object directly in the code. In Navigator, we pass the event object as a parameter, e, and reference it instead.**

The equivalent in VBScript looks like this:

```
<SCRIPT LANGUAGE="VBScript">
Sub MyHeading_onmousedown()
  strMesg = "You clicked the "
  If window.event.button = 1 Then strMesg = strMesg & "left "
  If window.event.button = 2 Then strMesg = strMesg & "right "
  If window.event.button = 4 Then strMesg = strMesg & "middle "
  strMesg = strMesg & "button, at position x = " & window.event.x _
          & ", y = " & window.event.y
  strMesg = strMesg & Chr(10) & "and you held down the "
  If window.event.shiftKey Then strMesg = strMesg & "Shift key "
  If window.event.ctrlKey Then strMesg = strMesg & "Ctrl key "
  If window.event.altKey Then strMesg = strMesg & "Alt key "
  MsgBox strMesg
End Sub
</SCRIPT>
```

Notice that in the VBScript example, we've preceded the `event` object with the default `window` object. This is not necessary in JavaScript or JScript, but must be done in VBScript to prevent a clash between the `event` object and the VBScript `event` keyword.

Finally, here's the result of our VBScript version, when the *Shift* and *Ctrl* keys are held down while clicking on the heading:

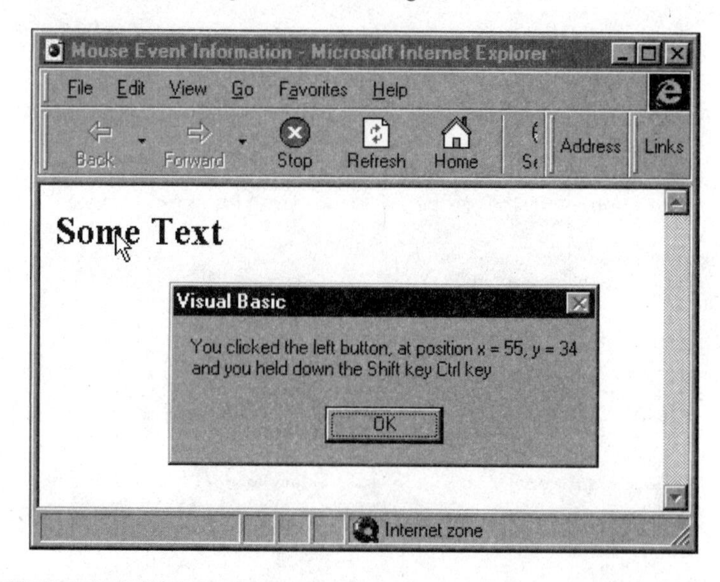

Because many *Alt* and *Ctrl* key combinations have special functions when combined with a mouse click in the browser, you won't actually get the dialog displayed in these cases—Internet Explorer will just carry out a special operation.

Key-press Information and the Event Object

If we query the **event** object for a key-press event, we can use the same techniques as we did for a mouse event to find out where the mouse pointer is, and use the **shiftKey**, **ctrlKey** and **altKey** properties. However, more than that, we can use the **keyCode** property to find out which key was pressed. For example, we can react to the **onkeypress** event of the **document**:

```
<SCRIPT LANGUAGE="VBScript">
Sub document_onkeypress()
  strMesg = "You pressed the " & Chr(window.event.keyCode) & " key, _
           which has an ASCII value of " & window.event.keyCode
  strMesg = strMesg & Chr(10) & "while holding down the "
  If window.event.shiftKey Then strMesg = strMesg & "Shift key "
  If window.event.ctrlKey Then strMesg = strMesg & "Ctrl key "
  If window.event.altKey Then strMesg = strMesg & "Alt key "
  strMesg = strMesg & Chr(10) & "The mouse pointer is at position _
           x = " & window.event.x & ", y = " & window.event.y
  MsgBox strMesg, vbInformation, "The Event object parameters"
End Sub
</SCRIPT>
```

Here's the result. Look where the mouse pointer is in the screenshot, and at the values of the mouse position retrieved from the **event** object. It still works if the pointer isn't over the page:

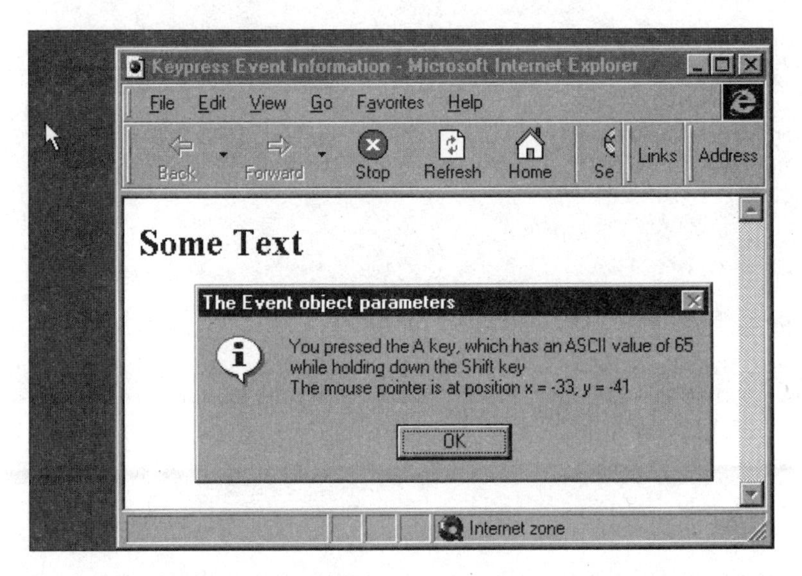

Because many *Alt* and *Ctrl* key combinations are used to execute menu commands (as shortcut keys) in the browser, you won't actually get the dialog displayed in these cases—Internet Explorer will just carry out the command.

Bubbling and Canceling Events

One major topic that makes Dynamic HTML different from scripting in earlier versions, either with VBScript, JavaScript, or any other language, is the way that the browser manages the events that are occurring in the page. We've already seen this to some extent in the previous chapter when we looked at Netscape Navigator, and when we looked at the IE4 **event** object earlier in this chapter.

However, the **event** object plays another major role in the way we create script routines in Dynamic HTML. It not only stores the values of the environment as each event comes along, it also plays a part in controlling how these events are propagated to our code. It does this through two properties, **cancelBubble** and **srcElement**.

The Event Object's Control System

When an event occurs in a page, the **event** object gets first look at it, and decides which element should receive it. For example, we may have a **<H3>** heading inside a **<DIV>** document division on the page like this:

```
<DIV ID=MyDiv STYLE="background-color=aqua">
<H3 ID=MyTitle> Click Here To Fire An Event </H3>
</DIV>
```

When the **event** object receives an **onclick** event, it looks to see which element the mouse pointer was over at the time. (If two elements are overlapped, it uses the one with the higher z-index). If it was the heading line (which has the **ID** of **MyTitle**), it looks for a routine connected to this event, and—if it finds one—executes it:

```
Sub MyTitle_onclick()
  ...
End Sub
```

Bubbling Events to the Container Element

Next, it looks to see which element is the **container** of the heading tag. In our case, it's the **<DIV>** tag named **MyDiv**, so it runs the **onclick** event code for this as well:

```
Sub MyDiv_onclick()
  ...
End Sub
```

This process continues while there are containers available. In our case, the only remaining one is the document itself, so it looks for the equivalent event code for this and executes it:

```
Sub document_onclick()
  ...
End Sub
```

This is very different from the way Navigator 4 handles the transfer of events between elements. Recall that it does not pass events to other elements unless we specifically set up **event capturing** for an element and event combination.

Internet Explorer 4 'bubbles' all events by default, passing them back up through each element in the hierarchy of the document.

Event bubbling, as this process is actually called, is very useful. For one thing, it helps to minimize the code we have to write, by letting one routine handle an event for several elements. Now that all the elements support events, this is particularly helpful.

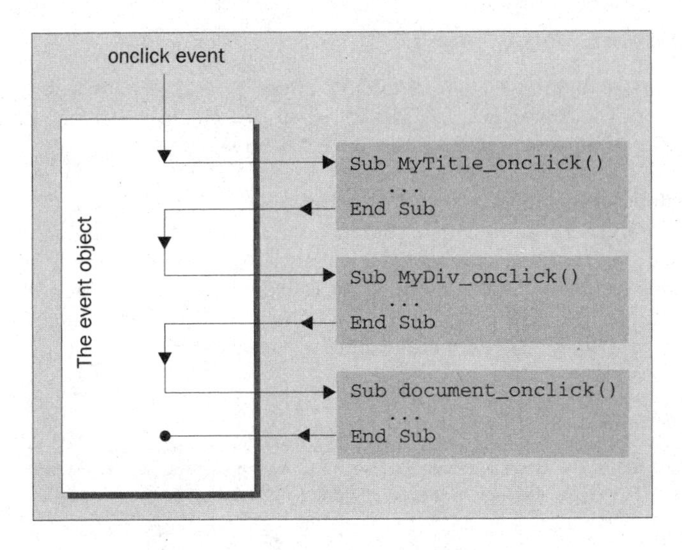

Using a Single Event Handler

Event bubbling can help to minimize the code we need to write. Think about what happens when we have a lot of similar elements on the page, such as this jigsaw page. There are 24 image elements holding the different pieces of the puzzle:

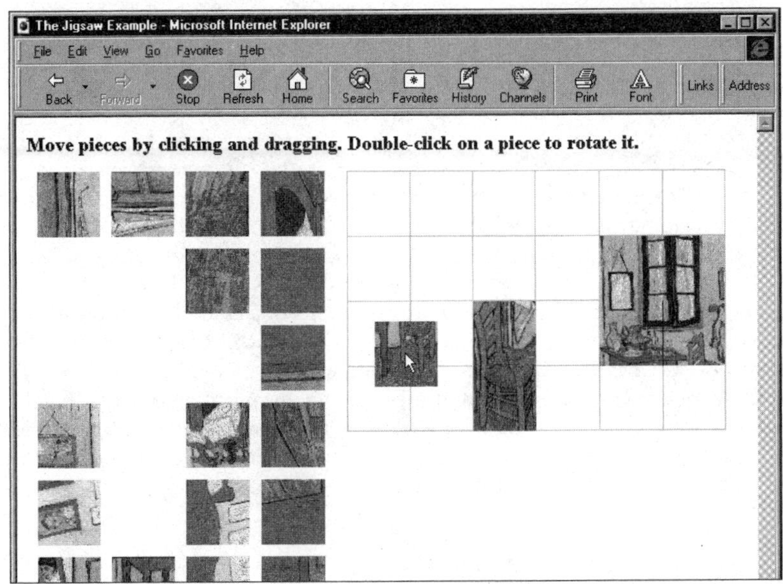

However, there is only one event handling routine that takes care of rotating all the pieces when the user double-clicks on one of them. It responds to the **ondblclick** event at document level, and stores the unique **ID** of the image that was clicked (you'll see how we can find the **ID** of the element that received the event shortly). Then it can apply the rotation code to that image only, using the **ID**. If we didn't have event bubbling, we would have to attach every one of the images to an event handler that rotated the piece separately.

Using Containers in Dynamic HTML

The second advantage event bubbling offers is that it allows us to work with the concept of **containers**. In HTML, when we create a list of items in the page, we group them together in **<UL>** or **<OL>** tags.

In the following HTML section of a page, we have a simple ordered list with an **ID** of **MyList**, and which contains four items. It acts as a container to the individual **<LI>** list elements. The page also has two different style class definitions **oldstyle** and **newstyle** (not shown here), which can be used to set the font, size and color of the list items. Notice that we've also given each item in the list an **ID** as well—you'll see why later:

```
...
<OL ID=MyList>
 <LI ID=Item1 STYLE="oldstyle">Change the font and size of text</LI>
 <LI ID=Item2 STYLE="oldstyle">Change the position of elements</LI>
 <LI ID=Item3 STYLE="oldstyle">Change the color and style of things</LI>
 <LI ID=Item4 STYLE="oldstyle">Make elements appear and disappear</LI>
</OL>
...
```

Now, if we want to react to the **onmouseover** event for all the items in the list, we can just create one single event handler for the list itself—the **container** of the list items:

```
Sub MyList_onmouseover
  ...
End Sub
```

Finding the Source Element

With event bubbling, we can choose to react to an event by using a handler that collects the event when it gets down to the **document**, or down as far as the element's container. However, we generally need to know where the event actually came from—i.e. which element actually received it first. This is where the **srcElement** property of the **event** object comes in.

Inside any event routine, we can retrieve the object that was 'topmost' and active when the user clicked the page, or when the event occurred, from the event object's **srcElement** property. For example, if they click on a heading tag inside a document division on the page, the topmost element is the heading tag. If they click on the division, but not the heading, the topmost element is the division. If they click on the blank page, there is no topmost element, and the event goes straight to the document.

By reacting to events for the list container, we can use the **srcElement** property to discover which individual element the mouse is over when the event occurs. We're reacting to two events, **onmouseover** which occurs when the mouse first moves onto an element, and **onmouseout** which occurs when it moves off it again. All we have to do is change the style by assigning a new value to the **classname** property:

```
Sub MyList_onmouseover
  window.event.srcElement.classname = "newstyle"
End Sub

Sub MyList_onmouseout
  window.event.srcElement.classname = "oldstyle"
End Sub
```

Here's an example of this technique in action:

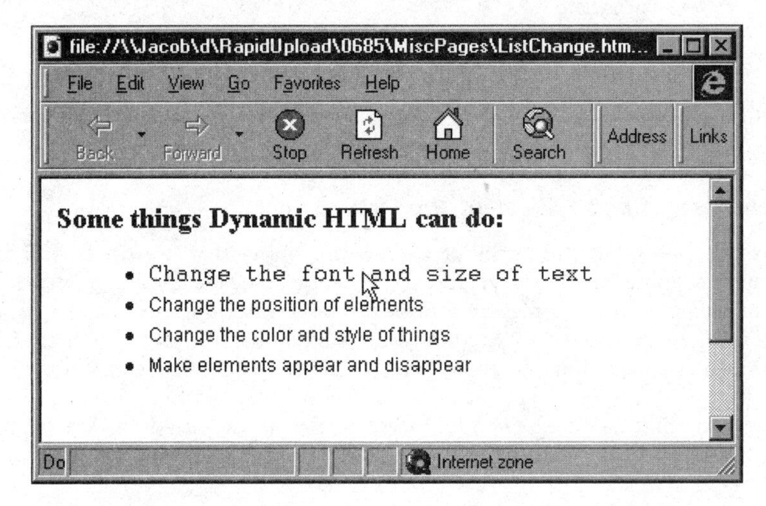

Using the cancelBubble Property

Sometimes we want to be a little more selective about the way we react to an event. For example, we may want most of the elements on a page to react to an event, but for one or two particular ones not to. Normally, once the code in this event handler has finished executing, the event will be bubbled up the object hierarchy to the next container, or to the top-level document object. To prevent this, all we have to do is set the **event** object's **cancelBubble** property to **True** in the event handler.

For example, if we wanted to do this for an element with the **ID** of **picture**, we just need to add the **cancelBubble** property assignment to the **onclick** event handler of that element:

```
Sub picture_onclick()
  'some code to react to the onclick event
  'now stop the event being bubbled to any other event handlers
  window.event.cancelBubble = True
End Sub
```

This breaks the chain of events, and the **document** object will not receive this **onclick** event. Of course, we can set the **cancelBubble** property in any of the events in the chain, and stop the processing at any point we choose. There's not much point in doing it in the **document** event handler, which is at end of the chain, and we can't stop the first event handler from running because this is our first chance to set the **cancelBubble** property.

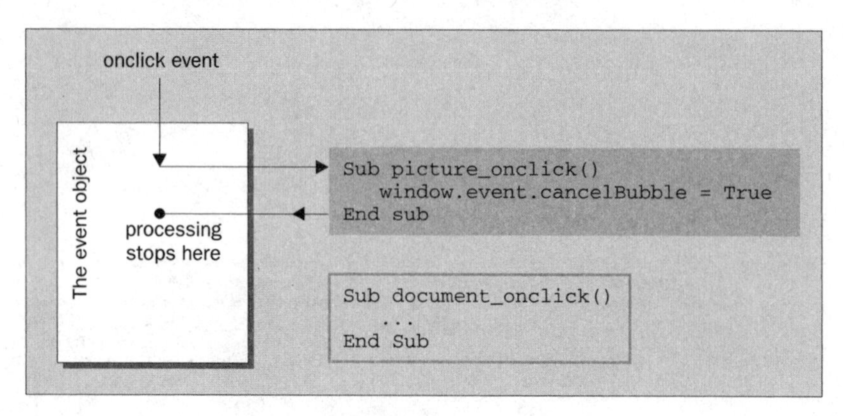

The fromElement and toElement Properties

There are two other properties of the **event** object that are useful for finding out what's going on in a Dynamic HTML page. As the mouse moves into and out of elements, it fires the **onmouseover** and **onmouseout** events, as we saw earlier. These are useful for updating the object that the event is fired for, but not much use in telling us about what's going on in other elements.

As an example, here's the HTML to create the list we used earlier:

```
...
<OL ID=MyList>
 <LI ID=Item1 STYLE="oldstyle">Change the font and size of text</LI>
 <LI ID=Item2 STYLE="oldstyle">Change the position of elements</LI>
 <LI ID=Item3 STYLE="oldstyle">Change the color and style of things</LI>
 <LI ID=Item4 STYLE="oldstyle">Make elements appear and disappear</LI>
</OL>
...
```

By adding a line to the **onmouseover** code in the **<SCRIPT>** section, we can display the value of the **event** object's **fromElement** or **toElement** property as an event is received. The useful one here is **fromElement**, which returns a reference to the element that the mouse was leaving when the event was fired:

```
Sub MyList_onmouseover
  window.event.srcElement.classname = "newstyle"
  window.status = window.event.fromElement.id
End Sub
```

Here, you can see that it was previously over the element with an **ID** of **Item3**—the last but one item in the list—and is now over **Item2**:

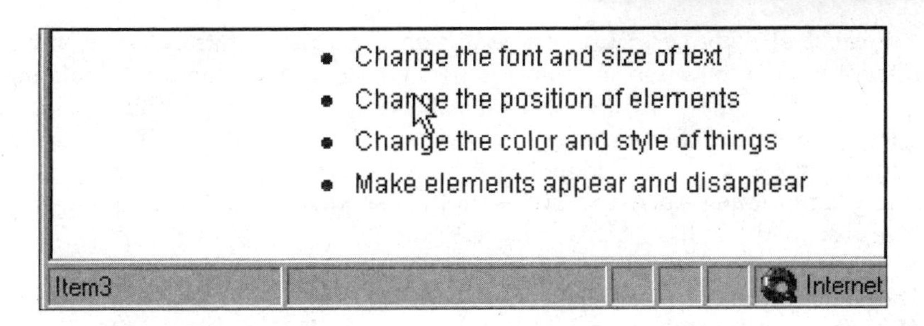

The returnValue Property

Earlier in the book, we saw how some events allow us to use a function to prevent the browser's default action from taking place, by setting the return value of the function to **false**. The **event** object in Dynamic HTML allows us to use another technique. All we have to do is set the **returnValue** property of the **event** object to **false**. This cancels the default action. For example, here's a page containing an **<A>** tag, which jumps to our home page when clicked:

```
...
<A ID=MyLink HREF="http://www.wrox.com">Wrox Press Limited</A>

<SCRIPT LANGUAGE=VBSCRIPT>
Sub MyLink_onclick()
  If MsgBox("Go to our site?", vbYesNo + vbQuestion, "Jump?") = vbNo Then
    window.event.returnValue = False
  End If
End Sub
</SCRIPT>
...
```

Clicking on the link in the page runs the **MyLink_onclick()** event handler code, which displays a message box asking the viewer to confirm their action. If they select No, we just have to set the **returnValue** property to **False**, and the browser ignores the jump, as though they hadn't clicked it in the first place.

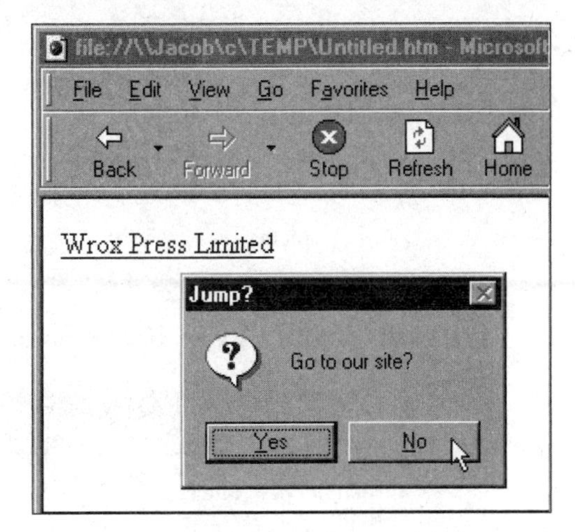

Data Binding in Internet Explorer 4

There is just one more subject that we intend to cover in any detail in this chapter. This technology has been proposed to the W3C for inclusion in HTML 4.0, and is under active consideration. It is implemented comprehensively in Internet Explorer 4, and for that reason deserves a little coverage here.

A great deal of browser use, especially on a corporate Intranet or web-based client/server application interface, is to do with viewing and manipulating the contents of databases. These will often be databases in the traditional sense, systems like Oracle, SQL Server, Access, or other specialist implementations. To achieve this task, the traditional route has been through some type of server-side programming—perhaps CGI, scripting languages like Perl, or more specialist methods like Active Server Pages.

This is an excellent solution in most situations, because the server executes the code at its end, and sends the client the final HTML-only page. However, when the user wants to interact with the database, perhaps updating information or just scrolling through the records, it involves repeated server-side processing and the regular transfer of data and instructions between the server and the browser. While this isn't usually a problem on a local network or intranet, unless the demands on the server are so high as to absorb all its processing capacity, out on the Web the repeated connections and data transfer demand a more elegant approach.

Caching Data Client-side

Internet Explorer 4 provides a method of caching the data at the client (browser), rather than only sending extracts each time, and allows the browser to extract what it wants and display it. This adds another advantage in that the user can update several rows of a data set (i.e. several records), then send back the complete package of changes in one go.

We're not going to be concerned with the internal workings of all this here, as you can appreciate it's a very involved subject. Instead, we'll use a simple example to show you how the proposed extensions to the Dynamic HTML language provide the 'hooks' that allow it to be implemented. The current specification, as implemented in IE 4.0, is still very much a draft and will change over time. But it is such an important concept that you should be aware of how it's developing.

Providing a Data Source

To achieve data binding in a Dynamic HTML page, there has to be a way of connecting the controls on the page with a data source. In our example, we're using a very simple source—a small text file containing nutritional information. The next screen shot shows our 'database':

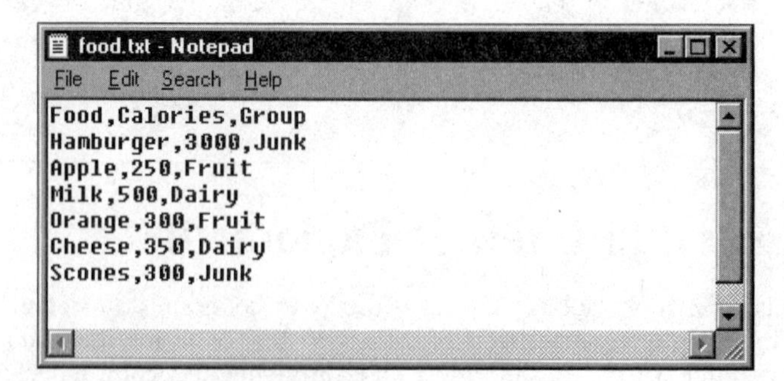

The first step is to connect this database to our page, so that the controls in the page can access the data. This requires a connector component that can read the data and access our page, and currently this means either the Microsoft **Remote Data Service** (RDS) control or the **Simple Tabular Data** (STD) control. The RDS control is designed to access ODBC-equipped data sources, and offers the ability to update the data from within the browser. These controls are ActiveX controls, supplied and installed with IE4. However, there is no reason why other browser manufacturers or software suppliers cannot offer their own versions, as the interface is defined and available to other companies.

Inserting the Simple Tabular Data Control

We insert the data connector control, in our case the Simple Tabular Data control, using a normal **<OBJECT>** tag. Here, we've given it an **ID** of **food**, specified our database **food.txt** (in the same directory as the page) for the **DataURL** property, and set the **FieldDelim** property to a comma—this is the field delimiter within our file's 'records'. The final **<PARAM>** tag sets the **UseHeader** property to **True**, because our database has the field names in the first record (or row):

```
<OBJECT ID="food" WIDTH=100 HEIGHT=51
  CLASSID="CLSID:333C7BC4-460F-11D0-BC04-0080C7055A83">
  <PARAM NAME="FieldDelim" VALUE=",">
  <PARAM NAME="DataURL" VALUE="food.txt">
  <PARAM NAME="UseHeader" VALUE=True>
</OBJECT>
```

Once the page is loaded, the browser will fetch the data from the **DataURL** and cache it on the client side (or in the case of RDS, create a connection to it and cache an appropriate set of records on the client). Once a connection is made to a data source, the browser has two options. It can either show individual values from this source in separate controls (called **single-value data binding**), or display lists of whole or partial records in a set of table controls (called **tabular data binding**).

Single-Value Data Binding

To connect the fields in the database with controls on our page, we use the new tag attributes **DATASRC**, **DATAFLD**, and **DATAFORMATAS**. For each control in single-value data binding, we have to provide two items of information: a reference to the connector object for that data source, and the name of a field within the data source for this control. For example, we can bind an **<INPUT>** tag to the **Calories** field in our **food** data source like this.

```
<INPUT TYPE="TEXT" DATASRC="#food" DATAFLD="Calories">
```

Notice that **food** is the **ID** of the STD control we inserted into our page, not the name of the database file. It is preceded by a hash sign (#) to indicate this. When the page is loaded, the control will display the value of that field for the first record in our database.

This method works for different kinds of controls, depending on the type of data the data source contains. We can display text or numeric data in **TEXT**-type **INPUT** controls, **SELECT** lists, **TEXTAREA** and **MARQUEE** controls, plus ordinary document **SPAN** and **DIV** controls. We can also use it as a **PARAM** to an object tag, if the control is an ActiveX control or Java applet. And if the text is the name of an image file, we can use it in an **IMG** tag as well. **True/False** values can be displayed in **CHECKBOX**- and **RADIO**-type **INPUT** controls, as well as in the **PARAM** tag of an object.

This page shows how we can display the contents of a record from our **food** database. It also contains buttons to move around the recordset created by the STD control:

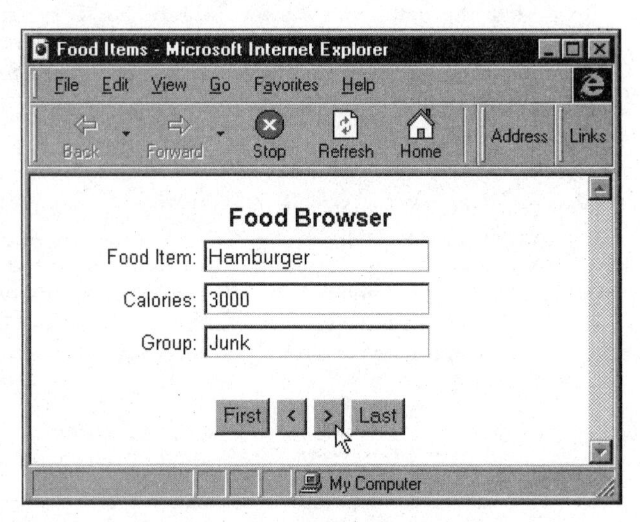

Here's an extract of the HTML source for the page. It uses two tables. The first holds the heading and the three text **<INPUT>** tags. The second holds the four navigation buttons:

```
<TABLE WIDTH=100%><TR><TH COLSPAN=2> Food Browser </TH></TR>
  <TR>
    <TD ALIGN=RIGHT> Food Item: </TD>
    <TD> <INPUT TYPE="TEXT" DATASRC="#food" DATAFLD="Food"> </TD>
  </TR>
  <TR>
    <TD ALIGN=RIGHT> Calories: </TD>
    <TD> <INPUT TYPE="TEXT" DATASRC="#food" DATAFLD="Calories"> </TD>
  </TR>
  <TR>
    <TD ALIGN=RIGHT> Group: </TD>
    <TD> <INPUT TYPE="TEXT" DATASRC="#food" DATAFLD="Group"> </TD>
  </TR>
</TABLE><P>
<TABLE WIDTH=100%>
  <TR >
    <TD ALIGN=CENTER>
      <INPUT NAME="cmdFirst" TYPE="BUTTON" VALUE=" First">
      <INPUT NAME="cmdPrevious" TYPE="BUTTON" VALUE=" < ">
      <INPUT NAME="cmdNext" TYPE="BUTTON" VALUE=" > ">
      <INPUT NAME="cmdLast" TYPE="BUTTON" VALUE="Last">
    </TD>
  </TR>
</TABLE>
```

Navigating the Recordset

To move through the records, we use objects and methods exposed by the STD control. These are similar to those provided by most Microsoft (and other) database technologies. The control provides a **recordset** object that represents our data, and this has methods that allow us to manipulate it:

```
Sub cmdPrevious_onclick()
  If Not food.recordset.bof Then food.recordset.movePrevious
End Sub

Sub cmdNext_onclick()
  If Not food.recordset.eof Then food.recordset.moveNext
End Sub

Sub cmdFirst_onclick()
  food.recordset.moveFirst
End Sub

Sub cmdLast_onclick()
  food.recordset.moveLast
End Sub
```

Notice here that we check the **bof** (beginning of file) and **eof** (end of file) properties before we move to the previous or next record. When we are at the first record in the recordset, we can still **movePrevious** without an error, and the controls display an 'empty' record. At this point the **bof** property becomes **True**, and any further attempt to **movePrevious** produces as error. The same kind of process works at the end of the file, with **eof**.

Tabular Data Binding

When we want to display the contents of several records, in a tabular view, we need to repeat certain parts of our page once for each record. This can be done in different ways. The most usual is to create a table with the special tags that define the heading and body sections of the table.

Here's an example. We use a **<DIV>** tag to denote an area of the page as a division, and inside it build a table. This time, we use the **DATASRC** attribute in the **<TABLE>** tag, to indicate that the whole table is bound to the data connector control we named **food**:

```
<DIV ALIGN=CENTER>
<TABLE ID=Data WIDTH=75% DATASRC=#food>
  <THEAD>
    <TH> Group </TH> <TH> Food </TH> <TH> Calories </TH>
  </THEAD>
  <TBODY>
    <TR>
      <TD ALIGN=CENTER> <SPAN DATAFLD="Group"> </SPAN> </TD>
      <TD ALIGN=CENTER> <SPAN DATAFLD="Food"> </SPAN> </TD>
      <TD ALIGN=CENTER> <SPAN DATAFLD="Calories"> </SPAN> </TD>
    </TR>
  </TBODY>
</TABLE>
</DIV>
```

Inside the table, we want to display the field names (the headings of the columns) then repeat the data from the records—one per table row. To indicate to the browser which section of the table is which, we use **<THEAD>** and **<TBODY>** tags. The **<THEAD>** section will only appear once, but the **<TBODY>** section will be repeated for each record in our recordset.

However, we can't provide the field value to the <TD> tag, like we did earlier with the <INPUT> tag—it doesn't accept 'values' as such. Instead, we just place a <SPAN> (or <DIV>) tag in the appropriate position and set *its* **DATAFLD** attribute to the field name.

Sorting and Filtering

Sometimes, we don't want to display all the records in the data source, or we may want to display them in a different order from the order they exist in the data source. In our earlier single-value data binding example, it would be easier to find a particular food if the records appeared in alphabetical order. If we are listing records in tabular format, it would be handy if we could just list records that matched certain criteria—calorie values below `250`, for example.

We can do both of these things, and more, by setting other properties of our data connector control. Here, we're filtering on the field (or column) named **Group**, and selecting only values where it is equal to **"Dairy"**. We're also sorting the resulting recordset by the value in the field named **Food**:

```
<OBJECT ID="food" WIDTH=100 HEIGHT=51
  CLASSID="CLSID:333C7BC4-460F-11D0-BC04-0080C7055A83">
  <PARAM NAME="FieldDelim" VALUE=",">
  <PARAM NAME="DataURL" VALUE="food.txt">
  <PARAM NAME="UseHeader" VALUE=True>
  <PARAM NAME="FilterColumn" VALUE="Group">
  <PARAM NAME="FilterCriterion" VALUE="=">
  <PARAM NAME="FilterValue" VALUE="Dairy">
  <PARAM NAME="SortColumn" VALUE="Food">
</OBJECT>
```

When combined with the earlier code to create a tabular format, this is what we get:

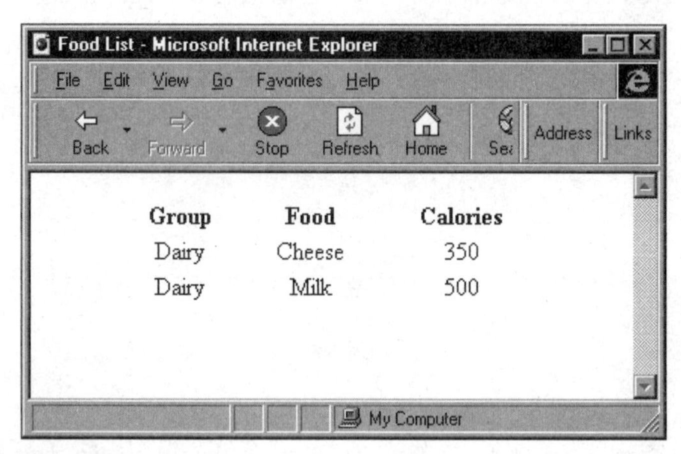

Remote Data Services

In these examples, we've used the Simple Tabular Data control, but the principle is exactly the same for other controls. The Advanced Data Control (ADC) is Microsoft's client-side object for working with Remote Data Services, and has a different set of properties. It also offers more features, and can download data in blocks, instead of as a complete recordset. With RDS, it's possible to arrange for the data source to be updated—the cached 'local' data is returned to the server.

Of course, this is only a taster of what data binding can achieve. To find out more about data binding, and client/server programming with data binding, look out for *Professional IE4 Programming* from Wrox Press. This book also covers all of the other new features in Internet Explorer 4, which we haven't looked at in detail. Two of these are Visual and Transaction Filters, and Scriptlets.

Visual and Transition Filters

Internet Explorer 4 provides a set of style-like properties for almost all visible elements that allow filters to be applied to them, to achieve the same kinds of effects as seen in presentation packages or slide shows. These are implemented through the `filters` collection. In fact, this isn't really a collection of the `document` object at all, it's more a collection of many of the elements that go to make up the `document` object. They are also available as properties within cascading style sheets. To find out more about filters and what they can do for your page, check out two more books from Wrox, *Instant IE4 Dynamic HTML Programmer's Reference ISBN 1-861000-68-5* and *Professional IE4 Programming, ISBN 1-861000-70-7.*

Reusable Code as Scriptlets

Until the release of IE4, the only way to create a custom ActiveX control was to use a 'real' programming language like C++. While this is still the case for large and complex controls, often we (as Web developers) would like to create smaller, simple controls that encapsulate code we reuse many times on our site. Since the development time to create real ActiveX controls is greater than the time it takes to copy and paste that reusable code onto every page, or into a linked client-side code file, we are often tempted to take the easy way out.

With the availability of Scriptlet technology, we have an easy way to encapsulate client-side code as an ActiveX control component. This allows us to quickly create platform independent (with the upcoming release of IE4 for the UNIX and Macintosh platforms) components that we can deploy onto the Web. To find out more, look at the sample chapter from *Professional IE4 Programming* on our site at `http://www.wrox.com` and watch out for our forthcoming book on Scriptlets.

Creating Compatible Sites and Pages

As you'll have gathered from our brief tour of Netscape Navigator 4 and Internet Explorer 4, we have some difficulties to face if we need to build a Web page, or a complete Web site, which performs properly for all our visitors. It's also pretty obvious that anything designed specifically for a browser that supports Dynamic HTML is not going to look good on an earlier browser unless we go to some lengths to make this happen—it's never going to be an automatic process. We'll generally need to either add extra code to pages so that they behave properly in both browsers, or create two or more separate copies of each page and have the correct one loaded as appropriate.

Cross-Browser Compatible Pages

It would be great if we could create pages that use the capabilities of Dynamic HTML, and will work in both the version 4 browsers. How easy this is depends on the complexity of the page, and the actual effects we are trying to achieve. We'll look at three general situations, static 2.5-D pages using style and font properties, pages that simply access the browser object model in script, and pages that use more complex mixtures of scripting and event handling techniques.

Compatible Style and Font Properties

One of the simplest ways of using Dynamic HTML is to take advantage of the new absolute positioning properties in Cascading Style Sheets, in conjunction with some font style properties. Most of the CSS properties are compatible with both browsers, and so this is not generally a problem.

Accessing the Browser Object Model

Much of the browser and document object model is the same as that in version 3 browsers, and so it's quite possible to create pages that use these objects, and their properties, methods and events. For example, the **`location`**, **`history`** and **`navigator`** objects are almost completely compatible. Where things go wrong is with the new additions. As we've seen, the **`event`** objects are different in both browsers; Navigator supports layers through a **`layers`** collection that is not supported in IE4; but IE4 does include an **`all`** collection that Navigator doesn't.

Managing More Complex Pages

When we have pages that are more complex than those you've generally seen in this book, we have to do a great deal more work to make them compatible with both Internet Explorer 4 and Netscape Communicator 4. In general, we can use a mixture of techniques to create a page where parts of the content are either ignored by one of the browsers or an appropriate section of HTML code is generated dynamically as the page loads.

Coping with <LAYER> and <DIV> Compatibility

Communicator supports the **`<LAYER>`** tag to create dynamic document divisions and adds the **`<NOLAYER>`** tag for use when browsers don't support layers. Internet Explorer uses the **`<DIV>`** tag to create dynamic document divisions and doesn't recognize the **`<LAYER>`** or **`<NOLAYER>`** tags. Communicator also recognizes the **`<DIV>`** tag, though it doesn't behave quite the same way when we use events in our page.

So, if we need to create an area in the page that responds to mouse events, we have to use a **<LAYER>** tag in Communicator, and a **<DIV>** tag in Internet Explorer. The trick is to get the browser to react correctly in both cases. By enclosing the **<DIV>** tags inside **<NOLAYER>** and **</NOLAYER>** tags, we prevent Communicator from seeing them, while Internet Explorer will—but it won't recognize the **<LAYER>** tags. We have to do this with the opening and closing **<DIV>** tags separately, however, so that the content of the layer/division is only included once.

```
<LAYER ... >          <- start of layer in NC4

  <NOLAYER>
    <DIV ... >        <- start of division in IE4
  </NOLAYER>

    Content           <- the contents of the layer or division

  <NOLAYER>
    </DIV>            <- end of division in IE4
  </NOLAYER>

</LAYER>              <- end of layer in NC4
```

Including Two Sections of Code

Another trick is to create two script sections in the page, only one of which is executed in either browser. All browsers that support scripting should make available one or more properties that contain the name and version of the browser. These will generally be properties of the **navigator** object:

Property	Description
appCodeName	The code name of the browser.
appName	The product name of the browser.
appVersion	The version of the browser.
userAgent	The user-agent (browser name) header sent as part of the HTTP protocol.

If we use the **appName** and **appVersion** properties, we can easily identify the manufacturer and the actual version number string. This code displays both in an **alert** dialog:

```
...
<SCRIPT LANGUAGE="JavaScript">
  alert(navigator.appName + ' : ' + navigator.appVersion)
</SCRIPT>
...
```

The results with Internet Explorer 3.01, Internet Explorer 4 and Communicator 4 are shown here:

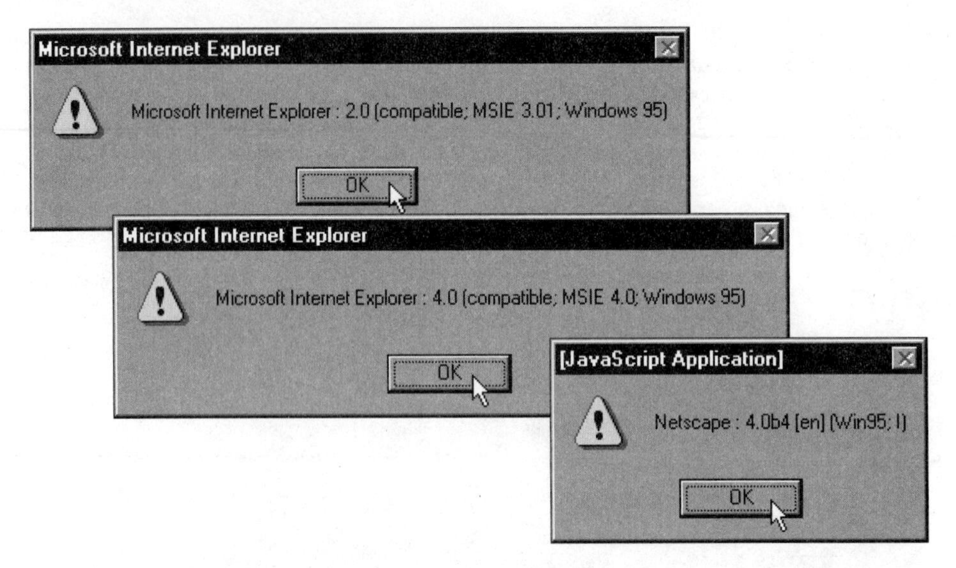

Our code can read these properties, and decide what to do next. Here's an example outline—it's written in 'generic' JavaScript, so that it will work on almost all script-enabled browsers:

```
<SCRIPT LANGUAGE="JavaScript">

  // Get the manufacturer and version information
  manufacturer=navigator.appName
  version=navigator.appVersion;

  // Look for Communicator 4
  if (manufacturer.indexOf('Netscape')>=0 && version.indexOf('4.0')>=0)
  {
    // code to run in Netscape Navigator 4 goes here
  };

  // Look for Internet Explorer 4
  if (manufacturer.indexOf('Microsoft')>=0 && version.indexOf('4.0')>=0)
  {
    // code to run in Internet Explorer 4 goes here
  };

  // Look for some version 3.0x browser
  if (version.indexOf('3.0')>=0)
  {
    // code to run in any version 3 browser goes here
  };

</SCRIPT>
```

Navigating by Browser Type

If we decide to offer different versions of our pages (or even separate parts of a complete site) depending on the browser version, it means that we must be able to differentiate between the browsers when they hit our index, or 'welcome' page.

Redirecting Visitors Automatically

The easiest way to automatically load a different page, depending on the browser that is accessing our site, is to create a **redirector page**. It is loaded as the default page for the whole site, and uses the different properties or capabilities of each browser to load another page. This second page will be the home page, or index, of the set of pages appropriate for that browser.

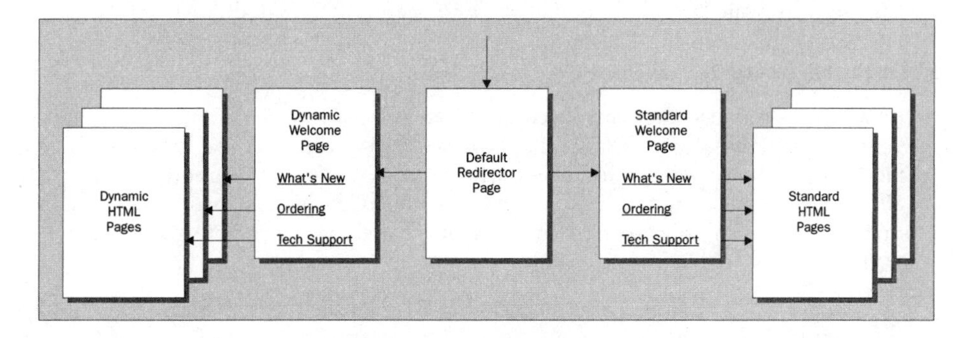

The default redirector page appears as a blank document, and the code in it loads the appropriate home page, a menu for a set of other pages or a single page that is browser specific. All the viewer sees is the browser window clearing, followed by the new page loading.

We could include a welcome message, and even a logo or graphic. However, this slows down loading of the page, and—depending on how we load the next page—may disappear again as soon as it's finished loading. Visitors might not get time to read it. Instead, we can give the redirector page a **<TITLE>** of Loading, please wait, which is displayed in the title bar while the next page loads.

Redirection with a META HTTP-EQUIV Tag

One of the most reliable ways to redirect the user is to include a **meta-refresh instruction** in the **<HEAD>** section of the page. This tells the browser to fetch a different page, and we can specify a delay before it does so:

```
<HTML>
<HEAD>
  <TITLE> Loading, please wait </TITLE>
  <META HTTP-EQUIV=REFRESH CONTENT="2;URL=http://mysite.com/std_menu.htm">
</HEAD>
<BODY>
</BODY>
</HTML>
```

This waits 2 seconds (the first part of the **CONTENT** attribute), then loads the URL specified. However, this will always load the *same* new page. We want to be able to load a different page if the browser can support it. This is done by adding some script that redirects the browser before the 2 second delay has expired:

```
...
<BODY>
<SCRIPT LANGUAGE=VBSCRIPT>
  location.href="http://www.mysite.com/vbs_menu.htm"
</SCRIPT>
</BODY>
...
```

Now, the browser will load the page **vbs_menu.htm** if the browser supports VBScript, or wait 2 seconds and load **std_menu.htm** if it doesn't.

Redirection Using the Browser's Properties

Instead, we can use the same technique we saw earlier of reading the browser version properties from the **navigator** object. We can also use a **<NOSCRIPT>** tag to provide a message for users whose browser doesn't support scripting at all. They can click on the link we place in the page in this case, and it means that the page can still be used in browsers that don't support the **META HTTP-EQUIV** method either:

```
<HTML>
<HEAD>
<TITLE> Loading, please wait </TITLE>
<META HTTP-EQUIV=REFRESH CONTENT="2;URL=http://mysite.com/std_menu.htm">
</HEAD>
<BODY>
<SCRIPT LANGUAGE="JavaScript">

  // Get the manufacturer and version information
  manufacturer=navigator.appName
  version=navigator.appVersion;

  // Look for Communicator 4
  if (manufacturer.indexOf('Netscape')>=0 && version.indexOf('4.0')>=0)
    location.href='http://mysite.com/nc4_menu.htm';

  // Look for Internet Explorer 4
  if (manufacturer.indexOf('Microsoft')>=0 && version.indexOf('4.0')>=0)
    location.href='http://mysite.com/ie4_menu.htm';

  // Look for some version 3.0x browser
  if (version.indexOf('3.0')>=0)
    location.href='http://mysite.com/v3_menu.htm';

</SCRIPT>

<NOSCRIPT>
  Your browser doesn't support scripting. However, we do
  have a special area of our site for you to visit.
  <A HREF="http://mysite.com/std_menu.htm"> Click here to continue </A>
</NOSCRIPT>

</BODY>
</HTML>
```

Doing It on the Server

Finally, we might decide to do all the work on the server instead. Technologies like server-side includes (SSI), Active Server Pages, or other CGI programming methods, can create pages dynamically. We simply need to read the user agent details from the HTTP header that the browser sends to the server when it requests a page, and dynamically create a fully compatible page to send back.

This topic is outside the scope of the book, but you can learn more about server-side programming techniques from other books in our range: Professional Active Server Pages 2.0, ISBN 1-861001-266 and Professional NT C++ ISAPI Programming, ISBN 1-8614416-66-4

Going Your Own Way

Of course, when it comes down to your own site, you don't *have* to do any of this. If you want to get the best out of your chosen browser, you might decide to program it all in one scripting language and use all of its new features—and not worry about backwards compatibility. After all, getting your page to display correctly in one browser is often enough of a task. In this case, you just put the 'Best viewed in Internet Explorer / Netscape Navigator' logo at the foot of your page. While your pages will look much better if you exploit all the latest features of your preferred browser, you'll be well on the way to admitting that the intense rivalry of the two market-leader browser vendors is destroying the heart of the Web as an inherently cross-platform medium.

The Color-Chooser Page in IE4

In the previous chapter, we looked at a page created for use in Netscape Communicator, which allows the viewer to see what the different colors for the foreground and background of a page look like. Changing the foreground color of a page in Navigator is difficult, because changing the foreground `COLOR` attribute value, via the `fgColor` property, has no effect while the page is loaded.

Internet Explorer does react to changes in this property, so creating the same page to run in IE4 is easy enough. The code just needs to update the `fgColor` and/or `bgColor` properties each time a selection is made, or a radio button clicked. This is the entire script section of the page:

```
<SCRIPT LANGUAGE=JAVASCRIPT>

  function ChangeColor(listnumber)
  {
    thisform = document.forms[0];
    thislist = thisform.elements[listnumber];
    thisindex = thislist.selectedIndex;
    thiscolor = thislist.options[thisindex].text;
    if (thiscolor.indexOf('>') == -1)
      { if (thisform.elements[listnumber + 1].checked)
          document.fgColor = thiscolor
        else document.bgColor = thiscolor;
        thisform.elements['txtFG'].value = 'Foreground: '
            + document.fgColor.toUpperCase();
        thisform.elements['txtBG'].value = 'Background: '
            + document.bgColor.toUpperCase();
      }
  }

</SCRIPT>
```

The Color-Chooser Redirector Page

Now we've got two different pages for two different browsers. To get round this, we've provided a redirector page that loads the appropriate version:

```
<HTML>
<HEAD>
<TITLE> Loading, please wait </TITLE>
</HEAD>
<BODY>
<SCRIPT LANGUAGE="JavaScript">

  // Get the manufacturer and version information
  manufacturer=navigator.appName
  version=navigator.appVersion;

  // Look for Communicator 4
  if (manufacturer.indexOf('Netscape')>=0 && version.indexOf('4.0')>=0)
    location.href='http://rapid.wrox.co.uk/books/miscpages/nc4_color.htm';

  // Look for Internet Explorer 4
  if (manufacturer.indexOf('Microsoft')>=0)
    location.href='http://rapid.wrox.co.uk/books/miscpages/ie4_color.htm';

</SCRIPT>

<NOSCRIPT>
  Sorry, your browser can't run our Color-Chooser page.<P>
  <A HREF="http://rapid.wrox/co.uk/">
    Click here to continue
  </A>
</NOSCRIPT>

</BODY>
</HTML>
```

Some Internet Explorer 4 Examples

If you want so see some more examples of what Dynamic HTML does in IE4, then our Web-developer samples site contains a wide range of IE4 samples pages that you can run directly, including most of those you've seen in the screenshots in this chapter. Point your browser to **`http://www.rapid.wrox.com`** or **`http://rapid.wrox.co.uk`**, and follow the links to the two books Professional IE4 Programming and Instant IE4 Dynamic HTML Programming.

Summary

Like Navigator 4, Microsoft's Internet Explorer version 4 adds plenty of new features that make it easy for programmers to create more dynamic and interactive pages. While you can still include new types of ActiveX controls, as well as using Java applets or plugins, many of the effects can now be achieved with just Dynamic HTML and scripting code.

In outline, some of the new features we've looked at in this chapter seem remarkably similar to that for Navigator 4 in the previous chapter. Remember, however, that the way they are achieved is often substantially different:

- All of the elements in the page (tags, images, text, etc.) are now accessible to script written in the page.
- An extension to the implementation of styles and style sheets provides more hooks to the page elements from JavaScript, JScript, VBScript, or other scripting languages that are supported by add-ins.
- Extensions to the browser object model are included, thus providing more programmability from any scripting language
- Absolute positioning of the elements in the page, including control of the z-order, allows a desk-top publishing style of authoring, and '2.5-D' appearance.
- Dynamic redrawing of any or all parts of the page allows changes to a loaded page to be made visible. Pages no longer need to be reloaded from the server to show the latest version.
- New event handling techniques are supported, including bubbling events that occur in the page back up through the document hierarchy.

To learn more about the capabilities of Internet Explorer 4, visit the Microsoft web site at `http://www.microsoft.com/ie/`. You can also learn more about programming Internet Explorer 4 from our two sister books, Instant IE4 Dynamic HTML Programmer's Reference (ISBN 1-861000-68-5) and Professional IE4 Programming (ISBN 1-861000-70-7)—both from Wrox Press, of course.

The Wrox Ultimate HTML Database Listing

This section lists all the HTML element tags in alphabetical order, showing which versions of HTML and which browsers support each one. For each element, we also list all the available attributes for use with it. Again, each one shows which versions of HTML and which browsers support each attribute.

!— —

Denotes a comment that is ignored by the HTML parser.

!DOCTYPE

Declares the type and content format of the document.

A

Defines a hypertext link. The **HREF** or the **NAME** attribute must be specified. ALL.

Attributes	2.0	3.2	4.0	N2	N3	N4	IE2	IE3	IE4
<event_name>=script_code	✗	✗	✓	✗	✗	✓	✗	✓	✓
ACCESSKEY=key_character	✗	✗	✓	✗	✗	✗	✗	✗	✓
CHARSET=*string*	✗	✗	✓	✗	✗	✗	✗	✗	✗
CLASS=*classname*	✗	✗	✗	✗	✗	✓	✗	✓	✓
COORDS=*string*	✗	✗	✓	✗	✗	✓	✗	✗	✗
DATAFLD=column_name	✗	✗	✗	✗	✗	✗	✗	✗	✓
DATASRC=id	✗	✗	✗	✗	✗	✗	✗	✗	✓
DIR=LTR|RTL	✗	✗	✓	✗	✗	✗	✗	✗	✗
HREF=url	✓	✓	✓	✓	✓	✓	✓	✓	✓
HREFLANG=langcode	✗	✗	✓	✗	✗	✗	✗	✗	✗
ID=*string*	✗	✗	✓	✗	✗	✓	✗	✓	✓
LANG=language_type	✗	✗	✓	✗	✗	✗	✗	✗	✓
LANGUAGE=JAVASCRIPT|JSCRIPT|VBSCRIPT|VBS	✗	✗	✗	✗	✗	✗	✗	✗	✓
METHODS=*string*	✓	✗	✗	✗	✗	✗	✗	✗	✓
NAME=*string*	✓	✓	✓	✓	✓	✓	✓	✓	✓
REL=SAME|NEXT|PARENT|PREVIOUS|*string*	✓	✓	✓	✗	✗	✗	✗	✓	✓
REV=*string*	✓	✓	✓	✗	✗	✗	✗	✓	✓
SHAPE=CIRC|CIRCLE|POLY|POLYGON|RECT|RECTANGLE	✗	✗	✓	✗	✗	✗	✗	✗	✗
STYLE=*string*	✗	✗	✓	✗	✗	✓	✗	✓	✓
TABINDEX=*number*	✗	✗	✓	✗	✗	✗	✗	✗	✓
TARGET=<window_name>|_parent|_blank|_top|_self	✗	✗	✓	✓	✓	✓	✗	✓	✓
TITLE=*string*	✓	✓	✓	✗	✗	✗	✗	✓	✓
TYPE=BUTTON|RESET|SUBMIT	✗	✗	✓	✗	✗	✗	✗	✗	✓
URN=*string*	✓	✗	✗	✗	✗	✗	✗	✗	✓

ABBR

Indicates a sequence of characters that compose an acronym (e.g., "WWW"). **HTML 4.0, IE4.**

Attributes	2.0	3.2	4.0	N2	N3	N4	IE2	IE3	IE4
`<event_name>=script_code`	×	×	✓	×	×	×	×	×	✓
`CLASS=classname`	×	×	✓	×	×	×	×	×	✓
`DIR=LTR|RTL`	×	×	✓	×	×	×	×	×	×
`ID=`*string*	×	×	✓	×	×	×	×	×	✓
`LANG=language_type`	×	×	✓	×	×	×	×	×	✓
`LANGUAGE=JAVASCRIPT|JSCRIPT|VBSCRIPT|VBS`	×	×	×	×	×	×	×	×	✓
`STYLE=`*string*	×	×	✓	×	×	×	×	×	✓
`TITLE=`*string*	×	×	✓	×	×	×	×	×	✓

ACRONYM

Indicates a sequence of characters that compose an acronym (e.g., "WWW"). **HTML 4.0.**

Attributes	2.0	3.2	4.0	N2	N3	N4	IE2	IE3	IE4
`<event_name>=script_code`	×	×	✓	×	×	×	×	×	×
`CLASS=classname`	×	×	✓	×	×	×	×	×	×
`DIR=LTR|RTL`	×	×	✓	×	×	×	×	×	×
`ID=`*string*	×	×	✓	×	×	×	×	×	×
`LANG=language_type`	×	×	✓	×	×	×	×	×	×
`LANGUAGE=JAVASCRIPT|JSCRIPT|VBSCRIPT|VBS`	×	×	×	×	×	×	×	×	×
`STYLE=`*string*	×	×	✓	×	×	×	×	×	×
`TITLE=`*string*	×	×	✓	×	×	×	×	×	×

ADDRESS

Specifies information such as address, signature and authorship. **ALL.**

Attributes	2.0	3.2	4.0	N2	N3	N4	IE2	IE3	IE4
`<event_name>=script_code`	×	×	✓	×	×	×	×	×	✓
`CLASS=classname`	×	×	✓	×	×	✓	×	×	✓
`DIR=LTR|RTL`	×	×	✓	×	×	×	×	×	×
`ID=`*string*	×	×	✓	×	×	✓	×	×	✓
`LANG=language_type`	×	×	✓	×	×	×	×	×	✓
`LANGUAGE=JAVASCRIPT|JSCRIPT|VBSCRIPT|VBS`	×	×	×	×	×	×	×	×	✓
`STYLE=STRING`	×	×	✓	×	×	✓	×	×	✓
`TITLE=STRING`	×	×	✓	×	×	×	×	×	✓

APPLET

Places a Java Applet or other executable content in the page. **HTML 3.2, N2, N3, N4, IE3, IE4, deprecated in HTML 4.0.**

Attributes	2.0	3.2	4.0	N2	N3	N4	IE2	IE3	IE4
`<event_name>=script_code`	×	×	D	×	×	×	×	×	×
`ALIGN=TOP|MIDDLE|BOTTOM|LEFT|RIGHT|ABSMIDDLE|BASELINE|ABSBOTTOM|TEXTTOP`	×	✓	D	✓	✓	✓	×	✓	✓
`ALT=text`	×	✓	D	✓	✓	✓	×	✓	✓
`ARCHIVE=url`	×	×	D	×	✓	✓	×	×	×
`BORDER=number`	×	×	D	×	×	×	×	×	×
`CLASS=classname`	×	×	D	×	×	✓	×	×	✓
`CODE=filename`	×	✓	D	✓	✓	✓	×	✓	✓
`CODEBASE=Path|url`	×	✓	D	✓	✓	✓	×	✓	✓
`DATAFLD=column_name`	×	×	×	×	×	×	×	×	✓
`DATASRC=id`	×	×	×	×	×	×	×	×	✓
`DOWNLOAD=number`	×	×	×	×	×	×	×	✓	×
`HEIGHT=number`	×	✓	D	✓	✓	✓	×	✓	×
`HSPACE=number`	×	✓	D	×	×	✓	×	✓	✓
`ID=`*string*	×	×	D	×	×	✓	×	×	✓
`MAYSCRIPT=YES|NO`	×	×	×	×	×	✓	×	×	×
`NAME=`*string*	×	✓	D	×	×	×	×	✓	✓
`OBJECT=`*string*	×	×	D	×	×	×	×	×	×
`SRC=url`	×	×	×	×	×	×	×	×	✓
`STYLE=`*string*	×	×	D	×	×	✓	×	×	✓
`TITLE=`*string*	×	×	D	×	×	×	×	✓	✓
`VSPACE=number`	×	✓	D	×	×	✓	×	✓	✓
`WIDTH=number`	×	✓	D	✓	✓	✓	×	✓	✓

AREA

Specifies the shape of a "hot spot" in a client-side image map. **ALL except HTML 2.0.**

<table>
<tr><th>Attributes</th><th>2.0</th><th>3.2</th><th>4.0</th><th>N2</th><th>N3</th><th>N4</th><th>IE2</th><th>IE3</th><th>IE4</th></tr>
<tr><td><event_name>=script_code</td><td>×</td><td>×</td><td>×</td><td>×</td><td>×</td><td>✓</td><td>×</td><td>×</td><td>✓</td></tr>
<tr><td>ALT=text</td><td>×</td><td>✓</td><td>✓</td><td>✓</td><td>✓</td><td>✓</td><td>×</td><td>✓</td><td>✓</td></tr>
<tr><td>CLASS=classname</td><td>×</td><td>×</td><td>D</td><td>×</td><td>×</td><td>✓</td><td>×</td><td>✓</td><td>✓</td></tr>
<tr><td>COORDS=string</td><td>×</td><td>✓</td><td>✓</td><td>✓</td><td>✓</td><td>✓</td><td>✓</td><td>✓</td><td>✓</td></tr>
<tr><td>DIR=LTR|RTL</td><td>×</td><td>×</td><td>✓</td><td>×</td><td>×</td><td>×</td><td>×</td><td>×</td><td>×</td></tr>
<tr><td>HREF=url</td><td>×</td><td>✓</td><td>✓</td><td>✓</td><td>✓</td><td>✓</td><td>✓</td><td>✓</td><td>✓</td></tr>
<tr><td>ID=string</td><td>×</td><td>×</td><td>D</td><td>×</td><td>×</td><td>✓</td><td>×</td><td>✓</td><td>✓</td></tr>
<tr><td>LANG=language_type</td><td>×</td><td>×</td><td>D</td><td>×</td><td>×</td><td>×</td><td>×</td><td>×</td><td>✓</td></tr>
<tr><td>LANGUAGE=JAVASCRIPT|JSCRIPT|
VBSCRIPT|VBS</td><td>×</td><td>×</td><td>×</td><td>×</td><td>×</td><td>×</td><td>×</td><td>×</td><td>✓</td></tr>
<tr><td>NAME=string</td><td>×</td><td>×</td><td>×</td><td>×</td><td>×</td><td>✓</td><td>×</td><td>×</td><td>×</td></tr>
<tr><td>NOHREF</td><td>×</td><td>✓</td><td>✓</td><td>✓</td><td>✓</td><td>✓</td><td>✓</td><td>✓</td><td>✓</td></tr>
<tr><td>NOTAB</td><td>×</td><td>×</td><td>×</td><td>×</td><td>×</td><td>×</td><td>×</td><td>✓</td><td>×</td></tr>
<tr><td>SHAPE=CIRC|CIRCLE|POLY|POLYGON|
RECT|RECTANGLE</td><td>×</td><td>✓</td><td>✓</td><td>✓</td><td>✓</td><td>✓</td><td>✓</td><td>✓</td><td>✓</td></tr>
<tr><td>STYLE=string</td><td>×</td><td>×</td><td>D</td><td>×</td><td>×</td><td>✓</td><td>×</td><td>×</td><td>✓</td></tr>
<tr><td>TABINDEX=number</td><td>×</td><td>×</td><td>✓</td><td>×</td><td>×</td><td>×</td><td>×</td><td>✓</td><td>✓</td></tr>
<tr><td>TARGET=<window_name>|_parent|
_blank|_top|_self</td><td>×</td><td>×</td><td>✓</td><td>✓</td><td>✓</td><td>✓</td><td>×</td><td>✓</td><td>✓</td></tr>
<tr><td>TITLE=string</td><td>×</td><td>×</td><td>D</td><td>×</td><td>×</td><td>×</td><td>×</td><td>✓</td><td>✓</td></tr>
</table>

B

Renders text in boldface where available. **ALL.**

<table>
<tr><th>Attributes</th><th>2.0</th><th>3.2</th><th>4.0</th><th>N2</th><th>N3</th><th>N4</th><th>IE2</th><th>IE3</th><th>IE4</th></tr>
<tr><td><event_name>=script_code</td><td>×</td><td>×</td><td>✓</td><td>×</td><td>×</td><td>×</td><td>×</td><td>×</td><td>✓</td></tr>
<tr><td>CLASS=classname</td><td>×</td><td>×</td><td>✓</td><td>×</td><td>×</td><td>✓</td><td>×</td><td>×</td><td>✓</td></tr>
<tr><td>DIR=LTR|RTL</td><td>×</td><td>×</td><td>✓</td><td>×</td><td>×</td><td>×</td><td>×</td><td>×</td><td>×</td></tr>
<tr><td>ID=string</td><td>×</td><td>×</td><td>✓</td><td>×</td><td>×</td><td>✓</td><td>×</td><td>×</td><td>✓</td></tr>
<tr><td>LANG=language_type</td><td>×</td><td>×</td><td>✓</td><td>×</td><td>×</td><td>×</td><td>×</td><td>×</td><td>✓</td></tr>
<tr><td>LANGUAGE=JAVASCRIPT|JSCRIPT|
VBSCRIPT|VBS</td><td>×</td><td>×</td><td>×</td><td>×</td><td>×</td><td>×</td><td>×</td><td>×</td><td>✓</td></tr>
<tr><td>STYLE=string</td><td>×</td><td>×</td><td>✓</td><td>×</td><td>×</td><td>✓</td><td>×</td><td>×</td><td>✓</td></tr>
<tr><td>TITLE=string</td><td>×</td><td>×</td><td>✓</td><td>×</td><td>×</td><td>×</td><td>×</td><td>×</td><td>✓</td></tr>
</table>

BASE

Specifies the document's base URL. **ALL.**

Attributes	2.0	3.2	4.0	N2	N3	N4	IE2	IE3	IE4
HREF=url	✓	✓	✓	✓	✓	✓	✓	✓	✓
TARGET=<window_name>|_parent|_blank|_top|_self	×	×	✓	✓	✓	✓	×	✓	✓

BASEFONT

Sets the base font values to be used as the default font when rendering text. **HTML 3.2, N2, N3, N4, IE2, IE3, IE4, deprecated in HTML 4.0.**

Attributes	2.0	3.2	4.0	N2	N3	N4	IE2	IE3	IE4
CLASS=classname	×	×	×	×	×	✓	×	×	✓
COLOR=color	×	×	D	×	×	×	×	✓	✓
FACE=font_family_name	×	×	D	×	×	×	×	✓	✓
ID=*string*	×	×	D	×	×	✓	×	×	✓
LANG=language_type	×	×	×	×	×	×	×	×	✓
LANGUAGE=JAVASCRIPT|JSCRIPT|VBSCRIPT|VBS	×	×	×	×	×	×	×	×	✓
SIZE=1|2|3|4|5|6|7	×	✓	D	✓	✓	✓	✓	✓	✓

BDO

Turns off the bi-directional rendering algorithm for selected fragments of text. **HTML 4.0.**

Attributes	2.0	3.2	4.0	N2	N3	N4	IE2	IE3	IE4
CLASS=classname	×	×	✓	×	×	×	×	×	×
DIR=LTR|RTL	×	×	✓	×	×	×	×	×	×
ID=*string*	×	×	✓	×	×	×	×	×	×
LANG=language_type	×	×	✓	×	×	×	×	×	×
STYLE=*string*	×	×	✓	×	×	×	×	×	×
TITLE=*string*	×	×	✓	×	×	×	×	×	×

BGSOUND

Specifies a background sound to be played while the page is loaded. **IE2, IE3, IE4.**

Attributes	2.0	3.2	4.0	N2	N3	N4	IE2	IE3	IE4
BALANCE=number	×	×	×	×	×	×	×	×	✓
CLASS=classname	×	×	×	×	×	×	×	×	✓
ID=*string*	×	×	×	×	×	×	×	×	✓
LANG=language_type	×	×	×	×	×	×	×	×	✓
LOOP=number	×	×	×	×	×	×	✓	✓	✓
SRC=url	×	×	×	×	×	×	✓	✓	✓
TITLE=*string*	×	×	×	×	×	×	×	×	✓
VOLUME=number	×	×	×	×	×	×	×	×	✓

BIG

Renders text in a relatively larger font than the current font. **HTML 3.2, 4.0, N2, N3, N4, IE3, IE4.**

Attributes	2.0	3.2	4.0	N2	N3	N4	IE2	IE3	IE4
<event_name>=script_code	×	×	✓	×	×	×	×	×	✓
CLASS=classname	×	×	✓	×	×	✓	×	×	✓
DIR=LTR|RTL	×	×	✓	×	×	×	×	×	×
ID=*string*	×	×	✓	×	×	✓	×	×	✓
LANG=language_type	×	×	✓	×	×	×	×	×	✓
LANGUAGE=JAVASCRIPT|JSCRIPT|VBSCRIPT|VBS	×	×	×	×	×	×	×	×	✓
STYLE=*string*	×	×	✓	×	×	✓	×	×	✓
TITLE=*string*	×	×	✓	×	×	×	×	×	✓

BLINK

Causes the text to flash on and off within the page. **N2, N3, N4.**

Attributes	2.0	3.2	4.0	N2	N3	N4	IE2	IE3	IE4
CLASS=classname	×	×	×	×	×	✓	×	×	×
ID=*string*	×	×	×	×	×	✓	×	×	×
STYLE=*string*	×	×	×	×	×	✓	×	×	×

BLOCKQUOTE

Denotes a quotation in text, usually a paragraph or more. **ALL**.

Attributes	2.0	3.2	4.0	N2	N3	N4	IE2	IE3	IE4
`<event_name>=script_code`	×	×	✓	×	×	×	×	×	✓
`CITE=url`	×	×	✓	×	×	×	×	×	×
`CLASS=classname`	×	×	✓	×	×	✓	×	×	✓
`DIR=LTR|RTL`	×	×	✓	×	×	×	×	×	×
`ID=`*string*	×	×	✓	×	×	✓	×	×	✓
`LANG=language_type`	×	×	✓	×	×	×	×	×	✓
`LANGUAGE=JAVASCRIPT|JSCRIPT|VBSCRIPT|VBS`	×	×	×	×	×	×	×	×	✓
`STYLE=`*string*	×	×	✓	×	×	✓	×	×	✓
`TITLE=`*string*	×	×	✓	×	×	×	×	×	✓

BODY

Defines the beginning and end of the body section of the page. **ALL**.

Attributes	2.0	3.2	4.0	N2	N3	N4	IE2	IE3	IE4
`<event_name>=script_code`	×	×	✓	×	×	✓	×	×	✓
`ALINK=color`	×	✓	D	✓	✓	✓	×	✓	✓
`BACKGROUND=`*string*	×	✓	D	✓	✓	✓	✓	✓	✓
`BGCOLOR=color`	×	✓	D	✓	✓	✓	✓	✓	✓
`BGPROPERTIES=FIXED`	×	×	×	×	×	×	✓	✓	✓
`BOTTOMMARGIN=number`	×	×	×	×	×	×	×	×	✓
`CLASS=classname`	×	×	✓	×	×	✓	×	✓	✓
`DIR=LTR|RTL`	×	×	✓	×	×	×	×	×	×
`ID=`*string*	×	×	✓	×	×	✓	×	✓	✓
`LANG=language_type`	×	×	✓	×	×	×	×	×	✓
`LANGUAGE=JAVASCRIPT|JSCRIPT|VBSCRIPT|VBS`	×	×	×	×	×	×	×	×	✓
`LEFTMARGIN=number`	×	×	×	×	×	×	✓	✓	✓
`LINK=color`	×	✓	D	✓	✓	✓	✓	✓	✓
`RIGHTMARGIN=number`	×	×	×	×	×	×	×	×	✓
`SCROLL=YES|NO`	×	×	×	×	×	×	×	×	✓
`STYLE=`*string*	×	×	✓	×	×	✓	×	✓	✓
`TEXT=color`	×	✓	D	✓	✓	✓	✓	✓	✓
`TITLE=`*string*	×	×	✓	×	×	×	×	×	✓
`TOPMARGIN=number`	×	×	×	×	×	×	✓	✓	✓
`VLINK=color`	×	✓	D	✓	✓	✓	✓	✓	✓

BR

Inserts a line break. **ALL.**

Attributes	2.0	3.2	4.0	N2	N3	N4	IE2	IE3	IE4
`CLASS=classname`	×	×	✓	×	×	✓	×	✓	✓
`CLEAR=ALL|LEFT|RIGHT|NONE`	×	✓	D	✓	✓	✓	✓	✓	✓
`ID=`*string*	×	×	✓	×	×	✓	×	×	✓
`LANGUAGE=JAVSCRIPT|JSCRIPT|VBSCRIPT|VBS`	×	×	×	×	×	×	×	×	✓
`STYLE=`*string*	×	×	×	×	×	✓	×	×	✓
`TITLE=`*string*	×	×	✓	×	×	×	×	×	✓

BUTTON

Renders an HTML button, the enclosed text used as the button's caption. **HTML 4.0, IE4.**

Attributes	2.0	3.2	4.0	N2	N3	N4	IE2	IE3	IE4
`<event_name>=script_code`	×	×	✓	×	×	×	×	×	✓
`ACCESSKEY=ley_character`	×	×	✓	×	×	×	×	×	✓
`CLASS=classname`	×	×	✓	×	×	×	×	×	✓
`DATAFLD=column_name`	×	×	×	×	×	×	×	×	✓
`DATAFORMATAS=HTML|TEXT`	×	×	×	×	×	×	×	×	✓
`DATASRC=id`	×	×	×	×	×	×	×	×	✓
`DIR=LTR|RTL`	×	×	✓	×	×	×	×	×	×
`DISABLED`	×	×	✓	×	×	×	×	×	✓
`ID=`*string*	×	×	✓	×	×	×	×	×	✓
`LANG=language_type`	×	×	✓	×	×	×	×	×	✓
`LANGUAGE=JAVASCRIPT|JSCRIPT|VBSCRIPT|VBS`	×	×	×	×	×	×	×	×	✓
`NAME=`*string*	×	×	✓	×	×	×	×	×	×
`STYLE=`*string*	×	×	✓	×	×	×	×	×	✓
`TABINDEX=number`	×	×	✓	×	×	×	×	×	×
`TITLE=`*string*	×	×	✓	×	×	×	×	×	✓
`TYPE=BUTTON|RESET|SUBMIT`	×	×	✓	×	×	×	×	×	✓
`VALUE=`*string*	×	×	✓	×	×	×	×	×	×

CAPTION

Specifies a caption to be placed next to a table. **ALL except HTML 2.0.**

Attributes	2.0	3.2	4.0	N2	N3	N4	IE2	IE3	IE4
`<event_name>=script_code`	×	×	✓	×	×	×	×	×	✓
`ALIGN=TOP|BOTTOM|LEFT|RIGHT`	×	✓	D	✓	✓	✓	✓	✓	✓
`CLASS=classname`	×	×	✓	×	×	✓	×	×	✓
`DIR=LTR|RTL`	×	×	✓	×	×	×	×	×	×
`ID=`*string*	×	×	✓	×	×	✓	×	×	✓
`LANG=language_type`	×	×	✓	×	×	×	×	×	✓
`LANGUAGE=JAVASCRIPT|JSCRIPT|VBSCRIPT|VBS`	×	×	×	×	×	×	×	×	✓
`STYLE=`*string*	×	×	✓	×	×	✓	×	×	✓
`TITLE=`*string*	×	×	✓	×	×	×	×	×	✓
`VALIGN=BOTTOM|TOP`	×	×	×	×	×	✓	✓	✓	✓

CENTER

Causes enclosed text and other elements to be centered on the page. **HTML 3.2, N2, N3, N4, IE2, IE3, IE4, deprecated in HTML 4.0.**

Attributes	2.0	3.2	4.0	N2	N3	N4	IE2	IE3	IE4
`<event_name>=script_code`	×	×	×	×	×	×	×	×	✓
`CLASS=classname`	×	×	×	×	×	✓	×	×	✓
`ID=`*string*	×	×	×	×	×	✓	×	×	✓
`LANG=language_type`	×	×	×	×	×	×	×	×	✓
`LANGUAGE=JAVASCRIPT|JSCRIPT|VBSCRIPT|VBS`	×	×	×	×	×	×	×	×	✓
`STYLE=`*string*	×	×	×	×	×	✓	×	×	✓
`TITLE=`*string*	×	×	×	×	×	×	×	×	✓

CITE

Renders text in italics. **ALL.**

Attributes	2.0	3.2	4.0	N2	N3	N4	IE2	IE3	IE4
`<event_name>=script_code`	×	×	✓	×	×	×	×	×	✓
`CLASS=classname`	×	×	✓	×	×	✓	×	×	✓
`DIR=LTR|RTL`	×	×	✓	×	×	×	×	×	×
`ID=`*string*	×	×	✓	×	×	✓	×	×	✓
`LANG=language_type`	×	×	✓	×	×	×	×	×	✓
`LANGUAGE=JAVASCRIPT|JSCRIPT|VBSCRIPT|VBS`	×	×	×	×	×	×	×	×	✓
`STYLE=`*string*	×	×	✓	×	×	✓	×	×	✓
`TITLE=`*string*	×	×	✓	×	×	×	×	×	✓

CODE

Renders text as a code sample in a fixed width font. **ALL.**

Attributes	2.0	3.2	4.0	N2	N3	N4	IE2	IE3	IE4
<event_name>=script_code	×	×	✓	×	×	×	×	×	✓
CLASS=classname	×	×	✓	×	×	✓	×	×	✓
DIR=LTR|RTL	×	×	✓	×	×	×	×	×	×
ID=*string*	×	×	✓	×	×	✓	×	×	✓
LANG=language_type	×	×	✓	×	×	×	×	×	✓
LANGUAGE=JAVASCRIPT|JSCRIPT|VBSCRIPT|VBS	×	×	×	×	×	×	×	×	✓
STYLE=*string*	×	×	✓	×	×	✓	×	×	✓
TITLE=*string*	×	×	✓	×	×	×	×	×	✓

COL

Used to specify column based defaults for a table. **HTML 4.0, IE3, IE4.**

Attributes	2.0	3.2	4.0	N2	N3	N4	IE2	IE3	IE4
<event_name>=script_code	×	×	✓	×	×	×	×	✓	×
ALIGN=CENTER|LEFT|RIGHT|JUSTIFY|CHAR	×	×	✓	×	×	×	×	✓	✓
CHAR=*string*	×	×	✓	×	×	×	×	×	×
CHAROFF=*string*	×	×	✓	×	×	×	×	×	×
CLASS=classname	×	×	✓	×	×	×	×	×	✓
DIR=LTR|RTL	×	×	✓	×	×	×	×	×	×
ID=*string*	×	×	✓	×	×	×	×	×	✓
SPAN=number	×	×	✓	×	×	×	×	✓	✓
STYLE=*string*	×	×	✓	×	×	×	×	×	✓
TITLE=*string*	×	×	✓	×	×	×	×	×	✓
VALIGN=BOTTOM|MIDDLE|TOP|BASELINE	×	×	✓	×	×	×	×	×	✓
WIDTH=number	×	×	✓	×	×	×	×	×	✓

COLGROUP

Used as a container for a group of columns. **HTML 4.0, IE3, IE4.**

Attributes	2.0	3.2	4.0	N2	N3	N4	IE2	IE3	IE4
<event_name>=script_code	×	×	✓	×	×	×	×	×	×
ALIGN=CENTER|LEFT|RIGHT|JUSTIFY|CHAR	×	×	✓	×	×	×	×	✓	✓
CHAR=*string*	×	×	✓	×	×	×	×	×	×
CHAROFF=*string*	×	×	✓	×	×	×	×	×	×

Attributes	2.0	3.2	4.0	N2	N3	N4	IE2	IE3	IE4
CLASS=classname	×	×	✓	×	×	×	×	×	✓
DIR=LTR|RTL	×	×	✓	×	×	×	×	×	×
ID=*string*	×	×	✓	×	×	×	×	×	✓
SPAN=number	×	×	✓	×	×	×	×	✓	✓
STYLE=*string*	×	×	✓	×	×	×	×	×	✓
TITLE=*string*	×	×	✓	×	×	×	×	×	✓
VALIGN=BOTTOM|MIDDLE|TOP|BASELINE	×	×	✓	×	×	×	×	✓	✓
WIDTH=number	×	×	✓	×	×	×	×	✓	✓

COMMENT

Denotes a comment that will not be displayed. **HTML 4.0, IE2, IE3, deprecated in IE4**.

Attributes	2.0	3.2	4.0	N2	N3	N4	IE2	IE3	IE4
ID=*string*	×	×	×	×	×	×	×	×	✓
LANG=language_type	×	×	×	×	×	×	×	×	✓
TITLE=*string*	×	×	×	×	×	×	×	×	✓

DD

The definition of an item in a definition list, usually indented from other text. **ALL**.

Attributes	2.0	3.2	4.0	N2	N3	N4	IE2	IE3	IE4
<event_name>=script_code	×	×	✓	×	×	×	×	×	✓
CLASS=classname	×	×	✓	×	×	✓	×	✓	✓
DIR=LTR|RTLR	×	×	✓	×	×	×	×	×	×
ID=*string*	×	×	✓	×	×	✓	×	✓	✓
LANG=language_type	×	×	✓	×	×	×	×	×	✓
LANGUAGE=JAVASCRIPT|JSCRIPT|VBSCRIPT|VBS	×	×	×	×	×	×	×	×	✓
STYLE=*string*	×	×	✓	×	×	✓	×	✓	✓
TITLE=*string*	×	×	✓	×	×	×	×	×	✓

DEL

Indicates a section of the document that has been deleted since a previous version. **HTML 4.0, IE4**.

Attributes	2.0	3.2	4.0	N2	N3	N4	IE2	IE3	IE4
`<event_name>=script_code`	×	×	✓	×	×	×	×	×	✓
`CITE=url`	×	×	✓	×	×	×	×	×	×
`CLASS=classname`	×	×	✓	×	×	×	×	×	✓
`DATETIME=date`	×	×	✓	×	×	×	×	×	×
`DIR=LTR|RTL`	×	×	✓	×	×	×	×	×	×
`ID=`*string*	×	×	✓	×	×	×	×	×	✓
`LANG=language_type`	×	×	✓	×	×	×	×	×	✓
`LANGUAGE=JAVASCRIPT|JSCRIPT|VBSCRIPT|VBS`	×	×	×	×	×	×	×	×	✓
`STYLE=`*string*	×	×	✓	×	×	×	×	×	✓
`TITLE=`*string*	×	×	✓	×	×	×	×	×	✓

DFN

The defining instance of a term. **ALL except HTML 2.0.**

Attributes	2.0	3.2	4.0	N2	N3	N4	IE2	IE3	IE4
`<event_name>=script_code`	×	×	✓	×	×	×	×	×	✓
`CLASS=classname`	×	×	✓	×	×	✓	×	×	✓
`DIR=LTR|RTL`	×	×	✓	×	×	×	×	×	×
`ID=`*string*	×	×	✓	×	×	✓	×	×	✓
`LANG=language_type`	×	×	✓	×	×	×	×	×	✓
`LANGUAGE=JAVASCRIPT|JSCRIPT|VBSCRIPT|VBS`	×	×	×	×	×	×	×	×	✓
`STYLE=`*string*	×	×	✓	×	×	✓	×	×	✓
`TITLE=`*string*	×	×	✓	×	×	×	×	×	✓

DIR

Renders text so that it appears like a directory-style file listing. **ALL, except deprecated in HTML 4.0.**

Attributes	2.0	3.2	4.0	N2	N3	N4	IE2	IE3	IE4
`<event_name>=script_code`	×	×	D	×	×	×	×	×	✓
`CLASS=classname`	×	×	D	×	×	✓	×	×	✓
`COMPACT`	✓	✓	D	×	×	✓	×	✓	×
`DIR=LTR|RTL`	×	×	D	×	×	×	×	×	×
`ID=`*string*	×	×	D	×	×	✓	×	×	✓
`LANG=language_type`	×	×	D	×	×	×	×	×	✓
`LANGUAGE=JAVASCRIPT|JSCRIPT|VBSCRIPT|VBS`	×	×	×	×	×	×	×	×	✓

Attributes	2.0	3.2	4.0	N2	N3	N4	IE2	IE3	IE4
STYLE=*string*	×	×	D	×	×	✓	×	×	✓
TITLE=*string*	×	×	×	×	×	✓	×	×	×
TYPE=CIRCLE|DISC|SQUARE	×	×	×	×	×	✓	×	×	×

DIV

Defines a container section within the page, and can hold other elements. **ALL except HTML 2.0.**

Attributes	2.0	3.2	4.0	N2	N3	N4	IE2	IE3	IE4
<event_name>=script_code	×	×	✓	×	×	×	×	×	✓
ALIGN=CENTER|LEFT|RIGHT	×	✓	D	✓	✓	✓	×	✓	✓
CLASS=classname	×	×	✓	×	×	✓	×	✓	✓
DATAFLD=column_name	×	×	×	×	×	×	×	×	✓
DATAFORMATAS=HTML|TEXT	×	×	×	×	×	×	×	×	✓
DATASRC=id	×	×	×	×	×	×	×	×	✓
DIR=LTR|RTL	×	×	✓	×	×	×	×	×	×
ID=*string*	×	×	✓	×	×	✓	×	✓	✓
LANG=language_type	×	×	✓	×	×	×	×	×	✓
LANGUAGE=JAVASCRIPT|JSCRIPT|VBSCRIPT|VBS	×	×	×	×	×	×	×	×	✓
NOWRAP	×	×	×	×	×	✓	×	✓	×
STYLE=*string*	×	×	✓	×	×	✓	×	×	✓
TITLE=*string*	×	×	✓	×	×	×	×	×	✓

DL

Denotes a definition list. **ALL.**

Attributes	2.0	3.2	4.0	N2	N3	N4	IE2	IE3	IE4
<event_name>=script_code	×	×	✓	×	×	×	×	×	✓
CLASS=classname	×	×	✓	×	×	✓	×	✓	✓
COMPACT	✓	✓	D	×	×	✓	×	✓	×
DIR=LTR|RTL	×	×	✓	×	×	×	×	×	×
ID=*string*	×	×	✓	×	×	✓	×	✓	✓
LANG=language_type	×	×	✓	×	×	×	×	×	✓
LANGUAGE=JAVASCRIPT|JSCRIPT|VBSCRIPT|VBS	×	×	×	×	×	×	×	×	✓
STYLE=*string*	×	×	✓	×	×	✓	×	✓	✓
TITLE=*string*	×	×	✓	×	×	×	×	×	✓

DT

Denotes a definition term within a definition list. **ALL.**

Attributes	2.0	3.2	4.0	N2	N3	N4	IE2	IE3	IE4
`<event_name>=script_code`	×	×	✓	×	×	×	×	×	✓
`CLASS=classname`	×	×	✓	×	×	✓	×	×	✓
`DIR=LTR|RTL`	×	×	✓	×	×	×	×	×	×
`ID=`*string*	×	×	✓	×	×	✓	×	×	✓
`LANG=language_type`	×	×	✓	×	×	×	×	×	✓
`LANGUAGE=JAVASCRIPT|JSCRIPT|VBSCRIPT|VBS`	×	×	×	×	×	×	×	×	✓
`STYLE=`*string*	×	×	✓	×	×	✓	×	×	✓
`TITLE=`*string*	×	×	✓	×	×	×	×	×	✓

EM

Renders text as emphasized, usually in italics. **ALL.**

Attributes	2.0	3.2	4.0	N2	N3	N4	IE2	IE3	IE4
`<event_name>=script_code`	×	×	✓	×	×	×	×	×	✓
`CLASS=classname`	×	×	✓	×	×	✓	×	×	✓
`DIR=LTR|RTL`	×	×	✓	×	×	×	×	×	×
`ID=`*string*	×	×	✓	×	×	✓	×	×	✓
`LANG=language_type`	×	×	✓	×	×	×	×	×	✓
`LANGUAGE=JAVASCRIPT|JSCRIPT|VBSCRIPT|VBS`	×	×	×	×	×	×	×	×	✓
`STYLE=`*string*	×	×	✓	×	×	✓	×	×	✓
`TITLE=`*string*	×	×	✓	×	×	×	×	×	✓

EMBED

Embeds documents of any type in the page, to be viewed in another suitable application. **N2, N3, N4, IE3, IE4.**

Attributes	2.0	3.2	4.0	N2	N3	N4	IE2	IE3	IE4
ALIGN=ABSBOTTOM|ABSMIDDLE|BASELINE|BOTTOM|LEFT|MIDDLE|RIGHT|TEXTTOP|TOP	×	×	×	×	×	✓	×	×	✓
ALT=text	×	×	×	×	×	×	×	×	✓
BORDER=number	×	×	D	×	×	✓	×	×	×
CLASS=classname	×	×	×	×	×	✓	×	×	✓
CODE=filename	×	×	×	×	×	×	×	×	✓
CODEBASE=url	×	×	×	×	×	×	×	×	✓
HEIGHT=number	×	×	×	✓	✓	✓	×	✓	✓
HIDDEN=*string*	×	×	×	×	×	✓	×	×	×
HSPACE=number	×	×	×	×	×	✓	×	×	✓
ID=*string*	×	×	×	×	×	✓	×	×	✓
NAME=*string*	×	×	×	✓	✓	✓	×	✓	✓
PALETTE=FOREGROUND|BACKGROUND	×	×	×	×	×	✓	×	✓	×
PLUGINSPAGE=*string*	×	×	×	×	×	✓	×	×	×
SRC=url	×	×	×	✓	✓	✓	×	✓	✓
STYLE=*string*	×	×	×	×	×	✓	×	×	✓
TITLE=*string*	×	×	×	×	×	×	×	×	✓
TYPE=*mime-type*	×	×	×	×	×	✓	×	×	×
UNITS=EN|EMS|PIXELS	×	×	×	×	×	✓	×	✓	✓
VSPACE=number	×	×	×	×	×	✓	×	×	✓
WIDTH=number	×	×	×	✓	✓	✓	×	✓	✓

FIELDSET

Draws a box around the contained elements to indicate related items. **HTML 4.0, IE4.**

Attributes	2.0	3.2	4.0	N2	N3	N4	IE2	IE3	IE4
<event_name>=script_code	×	×	✓	×	×	×	×	×	✓
ALIGN=CENTER|LEFT|RIGHT	×	×	×	×	×	×	×	×	✓
CLASS=classname	×	×	✓	×	×	×	×	×	✓
DIR=LTR|RTL	×	×	✓	×	×	×	×	×	×
ID=*string*	×	×	✓	×	×	×	×	×	✓
LANG=language_type	×	×	✓	×	×	×	×	×	✓
LANGUAGE=JAVASCRIPT|JSCRIPT|VBSCRIPT|VBS	×	×	×	×	×	×	×	×	✓

Attributes	2.0	3.2	4.0	N2	N3	N4	IE2	IE3	IE4
STYLE=*string*	×	×	✓	×	×	×	×	×	✓
TITLE=*string*	×	×	✓	×	×	×	×	×	✓

FONT

Specifies the font face, size, and color for rendering the text. **HTML 3.2, N2, N3, N4, IE2, IE3, IE4, deprecated in HTML 4.0.**

Attributes	2.0	3.2	4.0	N2	N3	N4	IE2	IE3	IE4
<event_name>=script_code	×	×	×	×	×	×	×	×	✓
CLASS=classname	×	×	D	×	×	✓	×	×	✓
COLOR=color	×	✓	D	✓	✓	✓	✓	✓	✓
DIR=LTR|RTL	×	×	D	×	×	×	×	×	×
FACE=font_family_name	×	×	D	×	✓	✓	✓	✓	✓
ID=*string*	×	×	D	×	×	✓	×	×	✓
LANG=language_type	×	×	D	×	×	×	×	×	✓
LANGUAGE=JAVASCRIPT|JSCRIPT|VBSCRIPT|VBS	×	×	×	×	×	×	×	×	✓
POINT-SIZE=*string*|number	×	×	×	×	×	✓	×	×	×
SIZE=number	×	✓	D	✓	✓	✓	✓	✓	✓
STYLE=*string*	×	×	D	×	×	✓	×	×	✓
TITLE=*string*	×	×	D	×	×	×	×	×	✓
WEIGHT=*string*|number	×	×	×	×	×	✓	×	×	×

FORM

Denotes a form containing controls and elements, whose values are sent to a server. ALL.

Attributes	2.0	3.2	4.0	N2	N3	N4	IE2	IE3	IE4
<event_name>=script_code	×	×	✓	×	×	✓	×	✓	✓
ACCEPT-CHARSET=*string*	×	×	✓	×	×	×	×	×	×
ACTION=*string*	✓	✓	✓	✓	✓	✓	✓	✓	✓
CLASS=classname	×	×	✓	×	×	✓	×	×	✓
DIR=LTR|RTL	×	×	✓	×	×	×	×	×	×
ENCTYPE=*string*	✓	✓	✓	✓	✓	✓	×	×	✓
ID=*string*	×	×	✓	×	×	✓	×	×	✓
LANG=language_type	×	×	✓	×	×	×	×	×	✓
LANGUAGE=JAVASCRIPT|JSCRIPT|VBSCRIPT|VBS	×	×	×	×	×	×	×	×	✓
METHOD=GET|POST	✓	✓	✓	✓	✓	✓	✓	✓	✓

Attributes	2.0	3.2	4.0	N2	N3	N4	IE2	IE3	IE4
NAME=*string*	×	×	×	×	×	✓	×	×	✓
STYLE=*string*	×	×	✓	×	×	✓	×	×	✓
TARGET=<window_name>|_parent|_blank|_top|_self	×	×	✓	✓	✓	✓	×	✓	✓
TITLE=*string*	×	×	✓	×	×	×	×	×	✓

FRAME

Specifies an individual frame within a frameset. **HTML 4.0, N2, N3, N4, IE3, IE4.**

Attributes	2.0	3.2	4.0	N2	N3	N4	IE2	IE3	IE4
<event_name>=script_code	×	×	×	×	×	✓	×	×	✓
ALIGN=CENTER|LEFT|RIGHT	×	×	×	×	×	✓	×	✓	×
BORDERCOLOR=color	×	×	×	×	✓	✓	×	×	✓
CLASS=classname	×	×	✓	×	×	✓	×	×	✓
DATAFLD=column_name	×	×	×	×	×	×	×	×	✓
DATASRC=id	×	×	×	×	×	×	×	×	✓
FRAMEBORDER=NO|YES|0|1	×	×	✓	×	✓	✓	×	✓	✓
ID=*string*	×	×	✓	×	×	✓	×	×	✓
LANG=language_type	×	×	×	×	×	×	×	×	✓
LANGUAGE=JAVASCRIPT|JSCRIPT|VBSCRIPT|VBS	×	×	×	×	×	×	×	×	✓
LONGDESC=url	×	×	✓	×	×	×	×	×	×
MARGINHEIGHT=number	×	×	✓	✓	✓	✓	×	✓	✓
MARGINWIDTH=number	×	×	✓	✓	✓	✓	×	✓	✓
NAME=*string*	×	×	✓	✓	✓	✓	×	✓	✓
NORESIZE=NORESIZE|RESIZE	×	×	✓	✓	✓	✓	×	✓	✓
SCROLLING=AUTO|YES|NO	×	×	✓	✓	✓	✓	×	✓	✓
SRC=url	×	×	✓	✓	✓	✓	×	✓	✓
STYLE=*string*	×	×	✓	×	×	×	×	×	✓
TITLE=*string*	×	×	✓	×	×	✓	×	×	✓

FRAMESET

Specifies a frameset containing multiple frames and other nested framesets. **HTML 4.0, N2, N3, N4, IE3, IE4**

Attributes	2.0	3.2	4.0	N2	N3	N4	IE2	IE3	IE4
<event_name>=script_code	×	×	✓	×	×	×	×	×	×
BORDER=number	×	×	D	×	✓	✓	×	×	✓

Attributes	2.0	3.2	4.0	N2	N3	N4	IE2	IE3	IE4
BORDERCOLOR=color	×	×	×	×	✓	✓	×	×	✓
CLASS=classname	×	×	✓	×	×	✓	×	×	✓
COLS=number	×	×	✓	✓	✓	✓	×	✓	✓
FRAMEBORDER=NO|YES|0|1	×	×	×	×	✓	✓	×	✓	✓
FRAMESPACING=number	×	×	×	×	×	×	×	✓	✓
ID=*string*	×	×	✓	×	×	✓	×	×	✓
LANG=language_type	×	×	×	×	×	×	×	×	✓
LANGUAGE=JAVASCRIPT|JSCRIPT|VBSCRIPT|VBS	×	×	×	×	×	×	×	×	✓
ROWS=number	×	×	✓	✓	✓	✓	×	✓	✓
STYLE=*string*	×	×	✓	×	×	×	×	×	✓
TITLE=*string*	×	×	✓	×	×	×	×	×	✓

HEAD

Contains tags holding unviewed information about the document. **ALL.**

Attributes	2.0	3.2	4.0	N2	N3	N4	IE2	IE3	IE4
CLASS=classname	×	×	×	×	×	✓	×	×	✓
DIR=LTR|RTL	×	×	✓	×	×	×	×	×	×
ID=*string*	×	×	×	×	×	✓	×	×	✓
LANG=language_type	×	×	✓	×	×	×	×	×	×
PROFILE=url	×	×	✓	×	×	×	×	×	×
TITLE=*string*	×	×	×	×	×	×	×	×	✓

Hn

The six elements (H1 to H6) render text as a range of heading styles. **ALL.**

Attributes	2.0	3.2	4.0	N2	N3	N4	IE2	IE3	IE4
<event_name>=script_code	×	×	✓	×	×	×	×	×	✓
ALIGN=CENTER|LEFT|RIGHT	×	✓	D	✓	✓	×	✓	✓	✓
CLASS=classname	×	×	✓	×	×	✓	×	×	✓
DIR=LTR|RTL	×	×	✓	×	×	×	×	×	×
ID=*string*	×	×	✓	×	×	✓	×	×	✓
LANG=language_type	×	×	✓	×	×	×	×	×	✓
LANGUAGE=JAVASCRIPT|JSCRIPT|VBSCRIPT|VBS	×	×	×	×	×	×	×	×	✓
STYLE=*string*	×	×	✓	×	×	✓	×	×	✓
TITLE=*string*	×	×	✓	×	×	×	×	×	✓

HR

Places a horizontal rule in the page. **ALL**.

Attributes	2.0	3.2	4.0	N2	N3	N4	IE2	IE3	IE4
`<event_name>=script_code`	×	×	✓	×	×	×	×	×	✓
`ALIGN=CENTER|LEFT|RIGHT`	×	✓	D	✓	✓	✓	✓	✓	✓
`CLASS=classname`	×	×	✓	×	×	✓	×	✓	✓
`COLOR=color`	×	×	×	×	×	×	✓	✓	✓
`DIR=LTR|RTL`	×	×	✓	×	×	×	×	×	×
`ID=`*string*	×	×	✓	×	×	✓	×	✓	✓
`LANG=language_type`	×	×	✓	×	×	×	×	×	✓
`LANGUAGE=JAVASCRIPT|JSCRIPT|VBSCRIPT|VBS`	×	×	×	×	×	×	×	×	✓
`NOSHADE`	×	✓	D	✓	✓	✓	✓	✓	✓
`SIZE=number`	×	✓	D	✓	✓	✓	✓	✓	✓
`SRC=url`	×	×	×	×	×	×	×	×	✓
`STYLE=`*string*	×	×	✓	×	×	✓	×	✓	✓
`TITLE=`*string*	×	×	✓	×	×	×	×	×	✓
`WIDTH=number`	×	✓	D	✓	✓	✓	✓	✓	✓

HTML

The outer tag for the page, which identifies the document as containing HTML elements. **ALL**.

Attributes	2.0	3.2	4.0	N2	N3	N4	IE2	IE3	IE4
`DIR=LTR|RTL`	×	×	✓	×	×	×	×	×	×
`LANG=language_type`	×	×	✓	×	×	×	×	×	×
`TITLE=`*string*	×	×	×	×	×	×	×	×	✓
`VERSION=url`	×	×	D	×	×	×	×	×	×

I

Renders text in an italic font where available. **ALL**.

Attributes	2.0	3.2	4.0	N2	N3	N4	IE2	IE3	IE4
`<event_name>=script_code`	×	×	✓	×	×	×	×	×	✓
`CLASS=classname`	×	×	✓	×	×	✓	×	×	✓
`DIR=LTR|RTL`	×	×	✓	×	×	×	×	×	×
`ID=`*string*	×	×	✓	×	×	✓	×	×	✓
`LANG=language_type`	×	×	✓	×	×	×	×	×	✓

Attributes	2.0	3.2	4.0	N2	N3	N4	IE2	IE3	IE4
LANGUAGE=JAVASCRIPT|JSCRIPT|VBSCRIPT|VBS	✗	✗	✗	✗	✗	✗	✗	✗	✓
STYLE=*string*	✗	✗	✓	✗	✗	✓	✗	✗	✓
TITLE=*string*	✗	✗	✓	✗	✗	✗	✗	✗	✓

IFRAME

Used to create in-line floating frames within the page. **HTML 4.0, IE3, IE4**

Attributes	2.0	3.2	4.0	N2	N3	N4	IE2	IE3	IE4
ALIGN=ABSBOTTOM|ABSMIDDLE|BASELINE|BOTTOM|LEFT|MIDDLE|RIGHT|TEXTTOP|TOP	✗	✗	D	✗	✗	✗	✗	✗	✓
BORDER=number	✗	✗	D	✗	✗	✗	✗	✗	✓
BORDERCOLOR=color	✗	✗	✗	✗	✗	✗	✗	✗	✓
CLASS=classname	✗	✗	✓	✗	✗	✗	✗	✗	✓
DATAFLD=column_name	✗	✗	✗	✗	✗	✗	✗	✗	✓
DATASRC=id	✗	✗	✗	✗	✗	✗	✗	✗	✓
FRAMEBORDER=NO|YES|0|1	✗	✗	✓	✗	✗	✗	✗	✗	✓
FRAMESPACING=number	✗	✗	✗	✗	✗	✗	✗	✗	✓
HEIGHT=number	✗	✗	✓	✗	✗	✗	✗	✗	✓
HSPACE=number	✗	✗	✗	✗	✗	✗	✗	✗	✓
ID=*string*	✗	✗	✓	✗	✗	✗	✗	✗	✓
LANG=language_type	✗	✗	✗	✗	✗	✗	✗	✗	✓
LANGUAGE=JAVASCRIPT|JSCRIPT|VBSCRIPT|VBS	✗	✗	✗	✗	✗	✗	✗	✗	✓
LONGDESC=url	✗	✗	✓	✗	✗	✗	✗	✗	✗
MARGINHEIGHT=number	✗	✗	✓	✗	✗	✗	✗	✗	✓
MARGINWIDTH=number	✗	✗	✓	✗	✗	✗	✗	✗	✓
NAME=*string*	✗	✗	✓	✗	✗	✗	✗	✗	✓
NORESIZE=NORESIZE|RESIZE	✗	✗	✗	✗	✗	✗	✗	✗	✓
SCROLLING=AUTO|YES|NO	✗	✗	✓	✗	✗	✗	✗	✗	✓
SRC=url	✗	✗	✓	✗	✗	✗	✗	✗	✓
STYLE=*string*	✗	✗	✓	✗	✗	✗	✗	✗	✓
TITLE=*string*	✗	✗	✓	✗	✗	✗	✗	✗	✓
VSPACE=number	✗	✗	✗	✗	✗	✗	✗	✗	✓
WIDTH=number	✗	✗	✓	✗	✗	✗	✗	✗	✓

ILAYER

Defines a separate area of the page as an inline layer that can hold a different page. **N4 only.**

<table>
<tr><th>Attributes</th><th>2.0</th><th>3.2</th><th>4.0</th><th>N2</th><th>N3</th><th>N4</th><th>IE2</th><th>IE3</th><th>IE4</th></tr>
<tr><td><event_name>=script_code</td><td>×</td><td>×</td><td>×</td><td>×</td><td>×</td><td>✓</td><td>×</td><td>×</td><td>×</td></tr>
<tr><td>ABOVE=object_id</td><td>×</td><td>×</td><td>×</td><td>×</td><td>×</td><td>✓</td><td>×</td><td>×</td><td>×</td></tr>
<tr><td>BACKGROUND=string</td><td>×</td><td>×</td><td>×</td><td>×</td><td>×</td><td>✓</td><td>×</td><td>×</td><td>×</td></tr>
<tr><td>BELOW=object_id</td><td>×</td><td>×</td><td>×</td><td>×</td><td>×</td><td>✓</td><td>×</td><td>×</td><td>×</td></tr>
<tr><td>BGCOLOR=color</td><td>×</td><td>×</td><td>D</td><td>×</td><td>×</td><td>✓</td><td>×</td><td>×</td><td>×</td></tr>
<tr><td>CLASS=classname</td><td>×</td><td>×</td><td>×</td><td>×</td><td>×</td><td>✓</td><td>×</td><td>×</td><td>×</td></tr>
<tr><td>CLIP=number[,number,number,number]</td><td>×</td><td>×</td><td>×</td><td>×</td><td>×</td><td>✓</td><td>×</td><td>×</td><td>×</td></tr>
<tr><td>ID=string</td><td>×</td><td>×</td><td>×</td><td>×</td><td>×</td><td>✓</td><td>×</td><td>×</td><td>×</td></tr>
<tr><td>LEFT=number</td><td>×</td><td>×</td><td>×</td><td>×</td><td>×</td><td>✓</td><td>×</td><td>×</td><td>×</td></tr>
<tr><td>NAME=string</td><td>×</td><td>×</td><td>×</td><td>×</td><td>×</td><td>✓</td><td>×</td><td>×</td><td>×</td></tr>
<tr><td>PAGEX=number</td><td>×</td><td>×</td><td>×</td><td>×</td><td>×</td><td>✓</td><td>×</td><td>×</td><td>×</td></tr>
<tr><td>PAGEY=number</td><td>×</td><td>×</td><td>×</td><td>×</td><td>×</td><td>✓</td><td>×</td><td>×</td><td>×</td></tr>
<tr><td>SRC=url</td><td>×</td><td>×</td><td>×</td><td>×</td><td>×</td><td>✓</td><td>×</td><td>×</td><td>×</td></tr>
<tr><td>STYLE=string</td><td>×</td><td>×</td><td>×</td><td>×</td><td>×</td><td>✓</td><td>×</td><td>×</td><td>×</td></tr>
<tr><td>TOP=number</td><td>×</td><td>×</td><td>×</td><td>×</td><td>×</td><td>✓</td><td>×</td><td>×</td><td>×</td></tr>
<tr><td>VISIBILITY=SHOW|HIDE|INHERIT</td><td>×</td><td>×</td><td>×</td><td>×</td><td>×</td><td>✓</td><td>×</td><td>×</td><td>×</td></tr>
<tr><td>WIDTH=number</td><td>×</td><td>×</td><td>×</td><td>×</td><td>×</td><td>✓</td><td>×</td><td>×</td><td>×</td></tr>
<tr><td>Z-INDEX=number</td><td>×</td><td>×</td><td>×</td><td>×</td><td>×</td><td>✓</td><td>×</td><td>×</td><td>×</td></tr>
</table>

IMG

Embeds an image or a video clip in the document. **Supported by ALL.**

<table>
<tr><th>Attributes</th><th>2.0</th><th>3.2</th><th>4.0</th><th>N2</th><th>N3</th><th>N4</th><th>IE2</th><th>IE3</th><th>IE4</th></tr>
<tr><td><event_name>=script_code</td><td>×</td><td>×</td><td>✓</td><td>×</td><td>×</td><td>✓</td><td>×</td><td>×</td><td>✓</td></tr>
<tr><td>ALIGN=BASBOTTOM|ABSMIDDLE|BASELINE|
BOTTOM|LEFT|MIDDLE|RIGHT|TEXTTOP|TOP</td><td>✓</td><td>✓</td><td>D</td><td>✓</td><td>✓</td><td>✓</td><td>✓</td><td>✓</td><td>✓</td></tr>
<tr><td>ALT=text</td><td>✓</td><td>✓</td><td>✓</td><td>✓</td><td>✓</td><td>✓</td><td>✓</td><td>✓</td><td>✓</td></tr>
<tr><td>BORDER=number</td><td>×</td><td>✓</td><td>D</td><td>✓</td><td>✓</td><td>✓</td><td>✓</td><td>✓</td><td>✓</td></tr>
<tr><td>CLASS=classname</td><td>×</td><td>×</td><td>✓</td><td>×</td><td>×</td><td>✓</td><td>×</td><td>✓</td><td>✓</td></tr>
<tr><td>CONTROLS</td><td>×</td><td>×</td><td>×</td><td>×</td><td>×</td><td>×</td><td>✓</td><td>✓</td><td>×</td></tr>
<tr><td>DATAFLD=column_name</td><td>×</td><td>×</td><td>×</td><td>×</td><td>×</td><td>×</td><td>×</td><td>×</td><td>✓</td></tr>
<tr><td>DATASRC=id</td><td>×</td><td>×</td><td>×</td><td>×</td><td>×</td><td>×</td><td>×</td><td>×</td><td>✓</td></tr>
<tr><td>DIR=LTR|RTL</td><td>×</td><td>×</td><td>✓</td><td>×</td><td>×</td><td>×</td><td>×</td><td>×</td><td>×</td></tr>
<tr><td>DYNSRC=string</td><td>×</td><td>×</td><td>×</td><td>×</td><td>×</td><td>×</td><td>✓</td><td>✓</td><td>✓</td></tr>
<tr><td>HEIGHT=number</td><td>×</td><td>✓</td><td>✓</td><td>✓</td><td>✓</td><td>✓</td><td>✓</td><td>✓</td><td>✓</td></tr>
<tr><td>HSPACE=number</td><td>×</td><td>✓</td><td>✓</td><td>✓</td><td>✓</td><td>✓</td><td>✓</td><td>✓</td><td>✓</td></tr>
<tr><td>ID=string</td><td>×</td><td>×</td><td>✓</td><td>×</td><td>×</td><td>✓</td><td>×</td><td>✓</td><td>✓</td></tr>
<tr><td>ISMAP</td><td>✓</td><td>✓</td><td>✓</td><td>✓</td><td>✓</td><td>✓</td><td>✓</td><td>✓</td><td>✓</td></tr>
<tr><td>LANG=language_type</td><td>×</td><td>×</td><td>✓</td><td>×</td><td>×</td><td>×</td><td>×</td><td>×</td><td>✓</td></tr>
</table>

Attributes	2.0	3.2	4.0	N2	N3	N4	IE2	IE3	IE4
LANGUAGE=JAVASCRIPT | JSCRIPT | VBSCRIPT | VBSVBSCRIPT | VBS	×	×	×	×	×	×	×	×	✓
LONGDESC=url	×	×	✓	×	×	×	×	×	×
LOOP=number	×	×	×	×	×	×	✓	✓	✓
LOWSRC=url	×	×	×	✓	✓	✓	×	×	✓
NAME=*string*	×	×	×	×	×	✓	×	×	✓
SRC=url	✓	✓	✓	✓	✓	✓	✓	✓	✓
START=number | *string*	×	×	×	×	×	×	✓	✓	×
STYLE=*string*	×	×	✓	×	×	✓	×	✓	✓
TITLE=*string*	×	×	✓	×	×	×	×	✓	✓
USEMAP=url	×	✓	✓	✓	✓	✓	✓	✓	✓
VSPACE=number	×	✓	✓	✓	✓	✓	✓	✓	✓
WIDTH=number	×	✓	✓	✓	✓	✓	✓	✓	✓

INPUT

Specifies a form input control, such as a button, text or check box. **Supported by ALL**.

Attributes	2.0	3.2	4.0	N2	N3	N4	IE2	IE3	IE4
<event_name>=script_code	×	×	✓	×	×	✓	×	✓	✓
ACCEPT=*string*	×	×	✓	×	×	×	×	×	×
ACCESSKEY=key_character	×	×	✓	×	×	×	×	×	✓
ALIGN=CENTER | LEFT | RIGHT	✓	✓	D	✓	✓	✓	✓	✓	✓
ALT=text	×	×	✓	×	×	×	×	×	×
CHECKED=FALSE | TRUE	✓	✓	✓	✓	✓	✓	✓	✓	✓
CLASS=classname	×	×	✓	×	×	✓	×	✓	✓
DATAFLD=column_name	×	×	×	×	×	×	×	×	✓
DATAFORMATAS=HTML | TEXT	×	×	×	×	×	×	×	×	✓
DATASRC=id	×	×	×	×	×	×	×	×	✓
DIR=LTR | RTL	×	×	✓	×	×	×	×	×	×
DISABLED	×	×	✓	×	×	×	×	×	✓
ID=*string*	×	×	✓	×	×	✓	×	✓	✓
LANG=language_type	×	×	✓	×	×	×	×	×	✓
LANGUAGE=JAVASCRIPT | JSCRIPT | VBSCRIPT | VBS	×	×	×	×	×	×	×	×	✓
MAXLENGTH=number	✓	✓	✓	✓	✓	✓	✓	✓	✓
NAME=*string*	✓	✓	✓	✓	✓	✓	✓	✓	✓
NOTAB	×	×	×	×	×	×	×	✓	×
READONLY	×	×	✓	×	×	×	×	×	✓
SIZE=number	✓	✓	✓	✓	✓	✓	✓	✓	✓

Attributes	2.0	3.2	4.0	N2	N3	N4	IE2	IE3	IE4
SRC=url	✓	✓	✓	✓	✓	×	✓	✓	✓
STYLE=*string*	×	×	✓	×	×	✓	×	✓	✓
TABINDEX=number	×	×	✓	×	×	×	×	✓	✓
TITLE=*string*	×	×	✓	×	×	×	×	✓	✓
TYPE=BUTTON|CHECKBOX|FILE|HIDDEN|IMAGE|PASSWORD|RADIO|RESET|SUBMIT|TEXT	✓	✓	✓	✓	✓	✓	✓	✓	✓
USEMAP=url	×	×	✓	×	×	×	×	×	×
VALUE=*string*	✓	✓	✓	✓	✓	✓	✓	✓	✓

INS

Indicates a section of the document that has been inserted since a previous version. **HTML 4.0, IE4.**

Attributes	2.0	3.2	4.0	N2	N3	N4	IE2	IE3	IE4
<event_name>=script_code	×	×	✓	×	×	×	×	×	✓
CITE=url	×	×	✓	×	×	×	×	×	×
CLASS=classname	×	×	✓	×	×	×	×	×	✓
DATETIME=date	×	×	✓	×	×	×	×	×	×
DIR=LTR|RTL	×	×	✓	×	×	×	×	×	×
ID=*string*	×	×	✓	×	×	×	×	×	✓
LANG=language_type	×	×	✓	×	×	×	×	×	✓
LANGUAGE=JAVASCRIPT|JSCRIPT|VBSCRIPT|VBS	×	×	×	×	×	×	×	×	✓
STYLE=*string*	×	×	✓	×	×	×	×	×	✓
TITLE=*string*	×	×	✓	×	×	×	×	×	✓

ISINDEX

Indicates the presence of a searchable index. **ALL. Deprecated in HTML 4.0.**

Attributes	2.0	3.2	4.0	N2	N3	N4	IE2	IE3	IE4
ACTION=*string*	×	×	×	✓	✓	✓	✓	✓	×
CLASS=classname	×	×	D	×	×	✓	×	×	✓
DIR=LTR|RTL	×	×	D	×	×	×	×	×	×
ID=*string*	×	×	D	×	×	✓	×	×	✓
LANG=language_type	×	×	D	×	×	×	×	×	✓
LANGUAGE=JAVASCRIPT|JSCRIPT|VBSCRIPT|VBS	×	×	×	×	×	×	×	×	✓
PROMPT=*string*	×	✓	D	✓	✓	✓	✓	✓	✓
STYLE=*string*	×	×	D	×	×	✓	×	×	✓
TITLE=*string*	×	×	D	×	×	×	×	×	×

KBD

Renders text in fixed-width font, as though entered on a keyboard. **ALL.**

Attributes	2.0	3.2	4.0	N2	N3	N4	IE2	IE3	IE4
`<event_name>=script_code`	✗	✗	✓	✗	✗	✗	✗	✗	✓
`CLASS=classname`	✗	✗	✓	✗	✗	✓	✗	✗	✓
`DIR=LTR|RTL`	✗	✗	✓	✗	✗	✗	✗	✗	✗
`ID=`*string*	✗	✗	✓	✗	✗	✓	✗	✗	✓
`LANG=language_type`	✗	✗	✓	✗	✗	✗	✗	✗	✓
`LANGUAGE=JAVASCRIPT|JSCRIPT|VBSCRIPT|VBS`	✗	✗	✗	✗	✗	✗	✗	✗	✓
`STYLE=`*string*	✗	✗	✓	✗	✗	✓	✗	✗	✓
`TITLE=`*string*	✗	✗	✓	✗	✗	✗	✗	✗	✓

KEYGEN

Used to generate key material in the page. **N2, N3, N4.**

Attributes	2.0	3.2	4.0	N2	N3	N4	IE2	IE3	IE4
`CHALLENGE=`*string*	✗	✗	✗	✗	✗	✓	✗	✗	✗
`CLASS=classname`	✗	✗	✗	✗	✗	✓	✗	✗	✗
`ID=`*string*	✗	✗	✗	✗	✗	✓	✗	✗	✗
`NAME=`*string*	✗	✗	✗	✗	✗	✓	✗	✗	✗

LABEL

Defines the text of a label for a control-like element. **HTML 4.0, IE4.**

Attributes	2.0	3.2	4.0	N2	N3	N4	IE2	IE3	IE4
`<event_name>=script_code`	✗	✗	✓	✗	✗	✗	✗	✗	✓
`ACCESSKEY=key_character`	✗	✗	✓	✗	✗	✗	✗	✗	✓
`CLASS=classname`	✗	✗	✓	✗	✗	✗	✗	✗	✓
`DATAFLD=column_name`	✗	✗	✗	✗	✗	✗	✗	✗	✓
`DATAFORMATAS=HTML|TEXT`	✗	✗	✗	✗	✗	✗	✗	✗	✓
`DATASRC=id`	✗	✗	✗	✗	✗	✗	✗	✗	✓
`DIR=LTR|RTL`	✗	✗	✓	✗	✗	✗	✗	✗	✗
`FOR=element_name`	✗	✗	✓	✗	✗	✗	✗	✗	✓
`ID=string`	✗	✗	✓	✗	✗	✗	✗	✗	✓
`LANG=language_type`	✗	✗	✓	✗	✗	✗	✗	✗	✓
`LANGUAGE=JAVASCRIPT|JSCRIPT|VBSCRIPT|VBS`	✗	✗	✗	✗	✗	✗	✗	✗	✓

Attributes	2.0	3.2	4.0	N2	N3	N4	IE2	IE3	IE4
STYLE=*string*	×	×	✓	×	×	×	×	×	✓
TITLE=*string*	×	×	✓	×	×	×	×	×	✓

LAYER

Defines a separate area of the page as a layer that can hold a different page. **N4 only**.

Attributes	2.0	3.2	4.0	N2	N3	N4	IE2	IE3	IE4
`<event_name>=script_code`	×	×	×	×	×	✓	×	×	×
`ABOVE=object_id`	×	×	×	×	×	✓	×	×	×
`BACKGROUND=`*string*	×	×	×	×	×	✓	×	×	×
`BELOW=object_id`	×	×	×	×	×	✓	×	×	×
`BGCOLOR=color`	×	×	D	×	×	✓	×	×	×
`CLASS=classname`	×	×	×	×	×	✓	×	×	×
`CLIP=number[,number,number,number]`	×	×	×	×	×	✓	×	×	×
`ID=`*string*	×	×	×	×	×	✓	×	×	×
`LEFT=number`	×	×	×	×	×	✓	×	×	×
`NAME=string`	×	×	×	×	×	✓	×	×	×
`PAGEX=number`	×	×	×	×	×	✓	×	×	×
`PAGEY=number`	×	×	×	×	×	✓	×	×	×
`SRC=url`	×	×	×	×	×	✓	×	×	×
`STYLE=`*string*	×	×	×	×	×	✓	×	×	×
`TOP=number`	×	×	×	×	×	✓	×	×	×
`VISIBILITY=SHOW|HIDE|INHERIT`	×	×	×	×	×	✓	×	×	×
`WIDTH=number`	×	×	×	×	×	✓	×	×	×
`Z-INDEX=number`	×	×	×	×	×	✓	×	×	×

LEGEND

Defines the title text to place in the 'box' created by a `FIELDSET` tag. **HTML 4.0, IE4**.

Attributes	2.0	3.2	4.0	N2	N3	N4	IE2	IE3	IE4
`<event_name>=script_code`	×	×	✓	×	×	×	×	×	✓
`ACCESSKEY=key_character`	×	×	✓	×	×	×	×	×	×
`ALIGN=BOTTOM|CENTER|LEFT|RIGHT|TOP`	×	×	D	×	×	×	×	×	✓
`CLASS=classname`	×	×	✓	×	×	×	×	×	✓
`DIR=LTR|RTL`	×	×	✓	×	×	×	×	×	×
`ID=`*string*	×	×	✓	×	×	×	×	×	✓

Attributes	2.0	3.2	4.0	N2	N3	N4	IE2	IE3	IE4
LANG=language_type	×	×	✓	×	×	×	×	×	✓
LANGUAGE=JAVASCRIPT|JSCRIPT|VBSCRIPT|VBS	×	×	×	×	×	×	×	×	✓
STYLE=*string*	×	×	✓	×	×	×	×	×	✓
TITLE=*string*	×	×	✓	×	×	×	×	×	✓
VALIGN=BOTTOM|TOP	×	×	×	×	×	×	×	×	✓

LI

Denotes one item within an ordered or unordered list. **ALL.**

Attributes	2.0	3.2	4.0	N2	N3	N4	IE2	IE3	IE4
<event_name>=script_code	×	×	✓	×	×	×	×	×	✓
CLASS=classname	×	×	✓	×	×	✓	×	✓	✓
DIR=LTR|RTL	×	×	✓	×	×	×	×	×	×
ID=string	×	×	✓	×	×	✓	×	✓	✓
LANG=language_type	×	×	✓	×	×	×	×	×	✓
LANGUAGE=JAVASCRIPT|JSCRIPT|VBSCRIPT|VBS	×	×	×	×	×	×	×	×	✓
STYLE=*string*	×	×	✓	×	×	✓	×	✓	✓
TITLE=*string*	×	×	✓	×	×	×	×	×	✓
TYPE=1|a|A|I|I|DISC|CIRCLE|SQUARE	×	✓	D	✓	✓	✓	✓	✓	✓
VALUE=*string*	×	✓	D	✓	✓	✓	✓	✓	✓

LINK

Defines a hyperlink between the document and some other resource. **HTML 2.0, 3.2 & 4.0, IE3, IE4.**

Attributes	2.0	3.2	4.0	N2	N3	N4	IE2	IE3	IE4
<event_name>=script_code	×	×	✓	×	×	×	×	×	×
CHARSET=charset	×	×	✓	×	×	×	×	×	×
CLASS=classname	×	×	✓	×	×	×	×	×	×
DIR=LTR|RTL	×	×	✓	×	×	×	×	×	×
DISABLED	×	×	×	×	×	×	×	×	✓
HREF=url	✓	✓	✓	✓	✓	✓	×	✓	✓
HREFLANG=langcode	×	×	✓	×	×	×	×	×	×
ID=*string*	×	×	✓	×	×	✓	×	×	✓
LANG=language_type	×	×	✓	×	×	×	×	×	✓
MEDIA=SCREEN|PRINT|PROJECTION|BRAILLE|SPEECH|ALL	×	×	✓	×	×	×	×	×	✓

Attributes	2.0	3.2	4.0	N2	N3	N4	IE2	IE3	IE4
METHODS=*string*	✓	×	×	×	×	×	×	×	×
REL=relationship	✓	✓	✓	✓	✓	✓	×	✓	✓
REV=relationship	✓	✓	✓	✓	✓	✓	×	✓	×
STYLE=*string*	×	×	✓	×	×	✓	×	×	×
TARGET=<window_name>|_parent|_blank|_tope|_self	×	×	✓	×	×	×	×	×	×
TITLE=*string*	✓	✓	✓	✓	✓	✓	×	✓	✓
TYPE=MIME-type	×	×	✓	×	×	✓	×	✓	✓
URN=*string*	✓	×	×	×	×	×	×	×	×

LISTING

Renders text in fixed-width type. Use **PRE** instead. **HTML 2.0, deprecated 3.2, supported IE2, IE3, IE4.**

Attributes	2.0	3.2	4.0	N2	N3	N4	IE2	IE3	IE4
<event_name>=script_code	×	×	×	×	×	×	×	×	✓
CLASS=classname	×	×	×	×	×	×	×	×	✓
ID=*string*	×	×	×	×	×	×	×	×	✓
LANG=language_type	×	×	×	×	×	×	×	×	✓
LANGUAGE=JAVASCRIPT|JSCRIPT|VBSCRIPT|VBS	×	×	×	×	×	×	×	×	✓
STYLE=*string*	×	×	×	×	×	×	×	×	✓
TITLE=*string*	×	×	×	×	×	×	×	×	✓

MAP

Specifies a collection of hot spots for a client-side image map. **ALL except HTML 2.0.**

Attributes	2.0	3.2	4.0	N2	N3	N4	IE2	IE3	IE4
<event_name>=script_code	×	×	×	×	×	×	×	×	✓
CLASS=classname	×	×	✓	×	×	✓	×	×	✓
ID=*string*	×	×	✓	×	×	✓	×	×	✓
LANG=language_type	×	×	×	×	×	×	×	×	✓
NAME=*string*	×	✓	✓	✓	✓	✓	✓	✓	✓
STYLE=*string*	×	×	✓	×	×	✓	×	×	✓
TITLE=*string*	×	×	✓	×	×	×	×	×	✓

MARQUEE

Creates a scrolling text marquee in the page. **IE2, IE3, IE4.**

<table>
<tr><th>Attributes</th><th>2.0</th><th>3.2</th><th>4.0</th><th>N2</th><th>N3</th><th>N4</th><th>IE2</th><th>IE3</th><th>IE4</th></tr>
<tr><td><event_name>=script_code</td><td>✗</td><td>✗</td><td>✗</td><td>✗</td><td>✗</td><td>✗</td><td>✗</td><td>✗</td><td>✓</td></tr>
<tr><td>ALIGN=TOP|MIDDLE|BOTTOM</td><td>✗</td><td>✗</td><td>✗</td><td>✗</td><td>✗</td><td>✗</td><td>✓</td><td>✓</td><td>✗</td></tr>
<tr><td>BEHAVIOR=ALTERNATE|SCROLL|SLIDE</td><td>✗</td><td>✗</td><td>✗</td><td>✗</td><td>✗</td><td>✗</td><td>✓</td><td>✓</td><td>✓</td></tr>
<tr><td>BGCOLOR=color</td><td>✗</td><td>✗</td><td>✗</td><td>✗</td><td>✗</td><td>✗</td><td>✓</td><td>✓</td><td>✓</td></tr>
<tr><td>CLASS=classname</td><td>✗</td><td>✗</td><td>✗</td><td>✗</td><td>✗</td><td>✗</td><td>✗</td><td>✗</td><td>✓</td></tr>
<tr><td>DATAFLD=column_name</td><td>✗</td><td>✗</td><td>✗</td><td>✗</td><td>✗</td><td>✗</td><td>✗</td><td>✗</td><td>✓</td></tr>
<tr><td>DATAFORMATAS=HTML|TEXT</td><td>✗</td><td>✗</td><td>✗</td><td>✗</td><td>✗</td><td>✗</td><td>✗</td><td>✗</td><td>✓</td></tr>
<tr><td>DATASRC=id</td><td>✗</td><td>✗</td><td>✗</td><td>✗</td><td>✗</td><td>✗</td><td>✗</td><td>✗</td><td>✓</td></tr>
<tr><td>DIRECTION=DOWN|LEFT|RIGHT|UP</td><td>✗</td><td>✗</td><td>✗</td><td>✗</td><td>✗</td><td>✗</td><td>✓</td><td>✓</td><td>✓</td></tr>
<tr><td>HEIGHT=number</td><td>✗</td><td>✗</td><td>✗</td><td>✗</td><td>✗</td><td>✗</td><td>✓</td><td>✓</td><td>✓</td></tr>
<tr><td>HSPACE=number</td><td>✗</td><td>✗</td><td>✗</td><td>✗</td><td>✗</td><td>✗</td><td>✓</td><td>✓</td><td>✓</td></tr>
<tr><td>ID=string</td><td>✗</td><td>✗</td><td>✗</td><td>✗</td><td>✗</td><td>✗</td><td>✗</td><td>✗</td><td>✓</td></tr>
<tr><td>LANG=language_type</td><td>✗</td><td>✗</td><td>✗</td><td>✗</td><td>✗</td><td>✗</td><td>✗</td><td>✗</td><td>✓</td></tr>
<tr><td>LANGUAGE=JAVASCRIPT|JSCRIPT|
VBSCRIPT|VBS</td><td>✗</td><td>✗</td><td>✗</td><td>✗</td><td>✗</td><td>✗</td><td>✗</td><td>✗</td><td>✓</td></tr>
<tr><td>LOOP=number</td><td>✗</td><td>✗</td><td>✗</td><td>✗</td><td>✗</td><td>✗</td><td>✓</td><td>✓</td><td>✓</td></tr>
<tr><td>SCROLLAMOUNT=number</td><td>✗</td><td>✗</td><td>✗</td><td>✗</td><td>✗</td><td>✗</td><td>✓</td><td>✓</td><td>✓</td></tr>
<tr><td>SCROLLDELAY=number</td><td>✗</td><td>✗</td><td>✗</td><td>✗</td><td>✗</td><td>✗</td><td>✓</td><td>✓</td><td>✓</td></tr>
<tr><td>STYLE=string</td><td>✗</td><td>✗</td><td>✗</td><td>✗</td><td>✗</td><td>✗</td><td>✗</td><td>✗</td><td>✓</td></tr>
<tr><td>TITLE=string</td><td>✗</td><td>✗</td><td>✗</td><td>✗</td><td>✗</td><td>✗</td><td>✗</td><td>✗</td><td>✓</td></tr>
<tr><td>TRUESPEED</td><td>✗</td><td>✗</td><td>✗</td><td>✗</td><td>✗</td><td>✗</td><td>✗</td><td>✗</td><td>✓</td></tr>
<tr><td>VSPACE=number</td><td>✗</td><td>✗</td><td>✗</td><td>✗</td><td>✗</td><td>✗</td><td>✓</td><td>✓</td><td>✓</td></tr>
<tr><td>WIDTH=number</td><td>✗</td><td>✗</td><td>✗</td><td>✗</td><td>✗</td><td>✗</td><td>✓</td><td>✓</td><td>✓</td></tr>
</table>

MENU

Renders the following block of text as individual items. Use lists instead. **ALL, deprecated in HTML 4.0.**

<table>
<tr><th>Attributes</th><th>2.0</th><th>3.2</th><th>4.0</th><th>N2</th><th>N3</th><th>N4</th><th>IE2</th><th>IE3</th><th>IE4</th></tr>
<tr><td><event_name>=script_code</td><td>✗</td><td>✗</td><td>D</td><td>✗</td><td>✗</td><td>✗</td><td>✗</td><td>✗</td><td>✓</td></tr>
<tr><td>CLASS=classname</td><td>✗</td><td>✗</td><td>D</td><td>✗</td><td>✗</td><td>✓</td><td>✗</td><td>✗</td><td>✓</td></tr>
<tr><td>COMPACT</td><td>✓</td><td>✓</td><td>D</td><td>✗</td><td>✗</td><td>✓</td><td>✗</td><td>✓</td><td>✗</td></tr>
<tr><td>ID=string</td><td>✗</td><td>✗</td><td>D</td><td>✗</td><td>✗</td><td>✓</td><td>✗</td><td>✗</td><td>✓</td></tr>
<tr><td>LANG=language_type</td><td>✗</td><td>✗</td><td>D</td><td>✗</td><td>✗</td><td>✗</td><td>✗</td><td>✗</td><td>✓</td></tr>
<tr><td>LANGUAGE=JAVASCRIPT|JSCRIPT|
VBSCRIPT|VBS</td><td>✗</td><td>✗</td><td>✗</td><td>✗</td><td>✗</td><td>✗</td><td>✗</td><td>✗</td><td>✓</td></tr>
</table>

Attributes	2.0	3.2	4.0	N2	N3	N4	IE2	IE3	IE4
STYLE=*string*	×	×	D	×	×	✓	×	×	✓
TITLE=*string*	×	×	D	×	×	×	×	×	✓
TYPE=CIRCLE|DISC|SQUARE	×	×	×	×	×	✓	×	×	×

META

Provides various types of unviewed information or instructions to the browser. **ALL.**

Attributes	2.0	3.2	4.0	N2	N3	N4	IE2	IE3	IE4
CHARSET=*string*	×	×	×	×	×	×	×	✓	×
CONTENT=metacontent	✓	✓	✓	✓	✓	✓	✓	✓	✓
DIR=LTR|RTL	×	×	✓	×	×	×	×	×	×
HTTP-EQUIV=*string*	✓	✓	✓	✓	✓	✓	✓	✓	✓
LANG=language_type	×	×	✓	×	×	×	×	×	×
NAME=metaname	✓	✓	✓	✓	✓	✓	×	✓	✓
SCHEME=*string*	×	×	✓	×	×	×	×	×	×
TITLE=*string*	×	×	×	×	×	×	×	×	✓
URL=url	×	×	×	×	×	×	×	✓	✓

MULTICOL

Used to define multiple column formatting. **N2, N3, N4.**

Attributes	2.0	3.2	4.0	N2	N3	N4	IE2	IE3	IE4
CLASS=classname	×	×	×	×	×	✓	×	×	×
COLS=number	×	×	×	×	✓	✓	×	×	×
GUTTER=number	×	×	×	×	✓	✓	×	×	×
ID=*string*	×	×	×	×	×	✓	×	×	×
STYLE=*string*	×	×	×	×	×	✓	×	×	×
WIDTH=number	×	×	×	×	✓	✓	×	×	×

NEXTID

Defines values used by text editing software when parsing or creating the document. **HTML 2.0 only.**

Attributes	2.0	3.2	4.0	N2	N3	N4	IE2	IE3	IE4
N=*string*	✓	×	×	×	×	×	×	×	×

NOBR

Renders text without any text wrapping in the page. **N2, N3, N4, IE2, IE3, IE4.**

Attributes	2.0	3.2	4.0	N2	N3	N4	IE2	IE3	IE4
ID=*string*	×	×	×	×	×	×	×	×	✓
STYLE=*string*	×	×	×	×	×	×	×	×	✓
TITLE=*string*	×	×	×	×	×	×	×	×	✓

NOEMBED

Defines the HTML to be displayed by browsers that do not support embeds. **N2, N3, N4.**

NOFRAMES

Defines the HTML to be displayed in browsers that do not support frames. **HTML 4.0, N2, N3, N3, IE3, IE4**

Attributes	2.0	3.2	4.0	N2	N3	N4	IE2	IE3	IE4
ID=*string*	×	×	×	×	×	×	×	×	✓
STYLE=*string*	×	×	×	×	×	×	×	×	✓
TITLE=*string*	×	×	×	×	×	×	×	×	✓

NOLAYER

Defines the part of a document that will be displayed in browsers that don't support layers. **N4.**

NOSCRIPT

Defines the HTML to be displayed in browsers that do not support scripting. **HTML 4.0, N3, N4, IE3, IE4.**

OBJECT

Inserts an object or other non-intrinsic HTML control into the page. **HTML 4.0, IE3, IE4.**

Attributes	2.0	3.2	4.0	N2	N3	N4	IE2	IE3	IE4
<event_name>=script_code	×	×	✓	×	×	×	×	×	✓
ACCESSKEY=key_character	×	×	×	×	×	×	×	×	✓
ALIGN=ABSBOTTOM | ABSMIDDLE | BASELINE | BOTTOM | LEFT | MIDDLE | RIGHT | TEXTTOP | TOP	✓	✓	D	×	×	×	×	✓	✓
ARCHIVE=urllist	×	×	✓	×	×	×	×	×	×

Attributes	2.0	3.2	4.0	N2	N3	N4	IE2	IE3	IE4
BORDER=number	✗	✗	D	✗	✗	✗	✗	✓	✗
CLASS=classname	✗	✗	✓	✗	✗	✗	✗	✗	✓
CLASSID=*string*	✗	✗	✓	✗	✗	✗	✗	✓	✓
CODE=filename	✗	✗	✗	✗	✗	✗	✗	✗	✓
CODEBASE=url	✗	✗	✓	✗	✗	✗	✗	✓	✓
CODETYPE=url	✗	✗	✓	✗	✗	✗	✗	✓	✓
DATA=*string*	✗	✗	✓	✗	✗	✗	✗	✓	✓
DATAFLD=column_name	✗	✗	✗	✗	✗	✗	✗	✗	✓
DATASRC=id	✗	✗	✗	✗	✗	✗	✗	✗	✓
DECLARE	✗	✗	✓	✗	✗	✗	✗	✓	✗
DIR=LTR|RTL	✗	✗	✓	✗	✗	✗	✗	✗	✗
HEIGHT=number	✗	✗	✓	✗	✗	✗	✗	✓	✓
HSPACE=number	✗	✗	✓	✗	✗	✗	✗	✓	✗
ID=*string*	✗	✗	✓	✗	✗	✗	✗	✗	✓
LANG=language_type	✗	✗	✓	✗	✗	✗	✗	✗	✓
LANGUAGE=JAVASCRIPT|JSCRIPT|VBSCRIPT|VBS	✗	✗	✗	✗	✗	✗	✗	✗	✓
NAME=*string*	✗	✗	✓	✗	✗	✗	✗	✓	✓
NOTAB	✗	✗	✗	✗	✗	✗	✗	✓	✗
SHAPES	✗	✗	✗	✗	✗	✗	✗	✓	✗
STANDBY=*string*	✗	✗	✓	✗	✗	✗	✗	✓	✗
STYLE=*string*	✗	✗	✓	✗	✗	✗	✗	✗	✓
TABINDEX=number	✗	✗	✓	✗	✗	✗	✗	✓	✓
TITLE=*string*	✗	✗	✓	✗	✗	✗	✗	✓	✓
TYPE=MIME-type	✗	✗	✓	✗	✗	✗	✗	✗	✗
USEMAP=url	✗	✗	✓	✗	✗	✗	✗	✓	✗
VSPACE=number	✗	✗	✓	✗	✗	✗	✗	✓	✗
WIDTH=number	✗	✗	✓	✗	✗	✗	✗	✓	✓

OL

Renders lines of text that have `<LI>` tags as an ordered list. **ALL.**

Attributes	2.0	3.2	4.0	N2	N3	N4	IE2	IE3	IE4
<event_name>=script_code	✗	✗	✓	✗	✗	✗	✗	✗	✓
CLASS=classname	✗	✗	✓	✗	✗	✓	✗	✗	✓
COMPACT	✓	✓	D	✓	✓	✓	✗	✓	✗
DIR=LTR|RTL	✗	✗	✓	✗	✗	✗	✗	✗	✗
ID=*string*	✗	✗	✓	✗	✗	✓	✗	✓	✓

Attributes	2.0	3.2	4.0	N2	N3	N4	IE2	IE3	IE4
LANG=language_type	×	×	✓	×	×	×	×	×	✓
LANGUAGE=JAVASCRIPT|JSCRIPT|VBSCRIPT|VBS	×	×	×	×	×	×	×	×	✓
START=number	×	✓	D	✓	✓	✓	✓	✓	✓
STYLE=*string*	×	×	✓	×	×	✓	×	✓	✓
TITLE=*string*	×	×	✓	×	×	×	×	×	✓
TYPE=1|a|A|I|I	×	✓	D	✓	✓	✓	✓	✓	✓

OPTGROUP

Creates a collapsible and hierarchical list of options

Attributes	2.0	3.2	4.0	N2	N3	N4	IE2	IE3	IE4
<event_name>=script_code	×	×	✓	×	×	×	×	×	×
CLASS=classname	×	×	✓	×	×	×	×	×	×
DISABLED	×	×	✓	×	×	×	×	×	×
DIR=LTR|RTL	×	×	✓	×	×	×	×	×	×
ID=*string*	×	×	✓	×	×	×	×	×	×
LABEL=*string*	×	×	✓	×	×	×	×	×	×
LANG=language_type	×	×	✓	×	×	×	×	×	×
STYLE=*string*	×	×	✓	×	×	×	×	×	×
TITLE=*string*	×	×	✓	×	×	×	×	×	×

OPTION

Denotes one choice in a **SELECT** drop-down or list element. **ALL.**

Attributes	2.0	3.2	4.0	N2	N3	N4	IE2	IE3	IE4
<event_name>=script_code	×	×	✓	×	×	×	×	×	✓
CLASS=classname	×	×	✓	×	×	✓	×	×	✓
DIR=LTR|RTL	×	×	✓	×	×	×	×	×	×
DISABLED	×	×	✓	✓	✓	×	×	×	×
ID=*string*	×	×	✓	×	×	✓	×	×	✓
LABEL=*string*	×	×	✓	×	×	×	×	×	×
LANG=language_type	×	×	✓	×	×	×	×	×	×
LANGUAGE=JAVASCRIPT|JSCRIPT|VBSCRIPT|VBS	×	×	×	×	×	×	×	×	✓
PLAIN	×	×	×	✓	✓	✓	×	×	×
SELECTED	✓	✓	✓	✓	✓	✓	✓	✓	✓
STYLE=*string*	×	×	✓	×	×	✓	×	×	×

Attributes	2.0	3.2	4.0	N2	N3	N4	IE2	IE3	IE4
TITLE=*string*	×	×	✓	×	×	×	×	×	×
VALUE=*string*	✓	✓	✓	✓	✓	✓	✓	✓	✓

P

Denotes a paragraph. The end tag is optional. **ALL.**

Attributes	2.0	3.2	4.0	N2	N3	N4	IE2	IE3	IE4
<event_name>=script_code	×	×	✓	×	×	×	×	×	✓
ALIGN=CENTER|LEFT|RIGHT	×	✓	D	✓	✓	✓	✓	✓	✓
CLASS=classname	×	×	✓	×	×	✓	×	✓	✓
DIR=LTR|RTL	×	×	✓	×	×	×	×	×	×
ID=*string*	×	×	✓	×	×	✓	×	✓	✓
LANG=language_type	×	×	✓	×	×	×	×	×	✓
LANGUAGE=JAVASCRIPT|JSCRIPT|VBSCRIPT|VBS	×	×	×	×	×	×	×	×	✓
STYLE=*string*	×	×	✓	×	×	✓	×	✓	✓
TITLE=*string*	×	×	✓	×	×	×	×	×	✓

PARAM

Used in an **OBJECT** or **APPLET** tag to set the object's properties. **ALL except HTML 2.0.**

Attributes	2.0	3.2	4.0	N2	N3	N4	IE2	IE3	IE4
DATAFLD=column_name	×	×	×	×	×	×	×	×	✓
DATAFORMATAS=HTML|TEXT	×	×	×	×	×	×	×	×	✓
DATASRC=id	×	×	×	×	×	×	×	×	✓
ID	×	×	✓	×	×	×	×	×	×
NAME=*string*	×	✓	✓	✓	✓	✓	×	✓	✓
TYPE=*string*	×	×	✓	×	×	×	×	✓	×
VALUE=*string*	×	✓	✓	✓	✓	✓	×	✓	✓
VALUETYPE=DATA|REF|OBJECT	×	×	✓	×	×	×	×	✓	×

PLAINTEXT

Renders text in fixed-width type without processing any tags it may contain. **Deprecated in HTML 2.0, 3.0, N2, N3 and N4, supported in IE2, IE3, IE4.**

Attributes	2.0	3.2	4.0	N2	N3	N4	IE2	IE3	IE4
<event_name>=script_code	×	×	×	×	×	×	×	×	✓
CLASS=classname	×	×	×	×	×	×	×	×	✓
ID=*string*	×	×	×	×	×	×	×	×	✓
LANG=language_type	×	×	×	×	×	×	×	×	✓
LANGUAGE=JAVASCRIPT|JSCRIPT|VBSCRIPT|VBS	×	×	×	×	×	×	×	×	✓
STYLE=*string*	×	×	×	×	×	×	×	×	✓
TITLE=*string*	×	×	×	×	×	×	×	×	✓

PRE

Renders text in fixed-width type. **ALL.**

Attributes	2.0	3.2	4.0	N2	N3	N4	IE2	IE3	IE4
<event_name>=script_code	×	×	✓	×	×	×	×	×	✓
CLASS=classname	×	×	✓	×	×	✓	×	×	✓
DIR=LTR|RTL	×	×	✓	×	×	×	×	×	×
ID=*string*	×	×	✓	×	×	✓	×	×	✓
LANG=language_type	×	×	✓	×	×	×	×	×	✓
LANGUAGE=JAVASCRIPT|JSCRIPT|VBSCRIPT|VBS	×	×	×	×	×	×	×	×	✓
STYLE=*string*	×	×	✓	×	×	✓	×	×	✓
TITLE=*string*	×	×	✓	×	×	×	×	×	✓
WIDTH=number	✓	✓	✓	✓	✓	✓	×	×	×

Q

A short quotation, such as the URL of the source document or a message. **HTML 4.0, IE4.**

Attributes	2.0	3.2	4.0	N2	N3	N4	IE2	IE3	IE4
<event_name>=script_code	×	×	✓	×	×	×	×	×	✓
CITE=url	×	×	✓	×	×	×	×	×	×
CLASS=classname	×	×	✓	×	×	×	×	×	✓
DIR=LTR|RTL	×	×	✓	×	×	×	×	×	×
ID=*string*	×	×	✓	×	×	×	×	×	✓
LANG=language_type	×	×	✓	×	×	×	×	×	✓
STYLE=*string*	×	×	✓	×	×	×	×	×	✓
TITLE=*string*	×	×	✓	×	×	×	×	×	✓

S

Renders text in strikethrough type. **Supported in HTML 3.2, N3, N4, IE2, IE3, IE4, deprecated in HTML 4.0.**

Attributes	2.0	3.2	4.0	N2	N3	N4	IE2	IE3	IE4
`<event_name>=script_code`	×	×	D	×	×	×	×	×	✓
`CLASS=classname`	×	×	D	×	×	✓	×	×	✓
`DIR=LTR|RTL`	×	×	D	×	×	×	×	×	×
`ID=`*string*	×	×	D	×	×	✓	×	×	✓
`LANG=language_type`	×	×	D	×	×	×	×	×	✓
`LANGUAGE=JAVASCRIPT|JSCRIPT|VBSCRIPT|VBS`	×	×	×	×	×	×	×	×	✓
`STYLE=`*string*	×	×	D	×	×	✓	×	×	✓
`TITLE=`*string*	×	×	D	×	×	×	×	×	✓

SAMP

Renders text as a code sample listing, usually in a smaller font. **ALL.**

Attributes	2.0	3.2	4.0	N2	N3	N4	IE2	IE3	IE4
`<event_name>=script_code`	×	×	✓	×	×	×	×	×	✓
`CLASS=classname`	×	×	✓	×	×	✓	×	×	✓
`DIR=LTR|RTL`	×	×	✓	×	×	×	×	×	×
`ID=`*string*	×	×	✓	×	×	✓	×	×	✓
`LANG=language_type`	×	×	✓	×	×	×	×	×	✓
`LANGUAGE=JAVASCRIPT|JSCRIPT|VBSCRIPT|VBS`	×	×	×	×	×	×	×	×	✓
`STYLE=`*string*	×	×	✓	×	×	✓	×	×	✓
`TITLE=`*string*	×	×	✓	×	×	×	×	×	✓

SCRIPT

Specifies a script for the page that will be interpreted by a script engine. **HTML 3.2, 4.0, N2, N3, N4, IE3, IE4.**

Attributes	2.0	3.2	4.0	N2	N3	N4	IE2	IE3	IE4
`ARCHIVE=url`	×	×	×	×	×	✓	×	×	×
`CHARSET=charset`	×	×	✓	×	×	×	×	×	×
`CLASS=classname`	×	×	×	×	×	✓	×	×	✓
`DEFER`	×	×	✓	×	×	×	×	×	×
`EVENT=<event_name>`	×	×	×	×	×	×	×	×	✓
`FOR=element_name`	×	×	×	×	×	×	×	×	✓

Attributes	2.0	3.2	4.0	N2	N3	N4	IE2	IE3	IE4
ID=*string*	×	×	×	×	×	✓	×	×	✓
LANGUAGE=JAVASCRIPT|JSCRIPT|VBSCRIPT|VBS	×	×	D	✓	✓	✓	×	✓	✓
SRC=url	×	×	✓	×	✓	✓	×	×	✓
STYLE=*string*	×	×	×	×	×	✓	×	×	✓
TITLE=*string*	×	×	×	×	×	×	×	×	✓
TYPE=*string*	×	×	✓	×	×	×	×	✓	✓

SELECT

Defines a list box or drop-down list. **ALL.**

Attributes	2.0	3.2	4.0	N2	N3	N4	IE2	IE3	IE4
<event_name>=script_code	×	×	✓	×	×	✓	×	×	✓
ACCESSKEY=key_character	×	×	×	×	×	×	×	×	✓
ALIGN=ABSBOTTOM|ABSMIDDLE|BASELINE|BOTTOM|LEFT|MIDDLE|RIGHT|TEXTTOP|TOP	×	×	×	×	×	×	×	×	✓
CLASS=classname	×	×	✓	×	×	✓	×	×	✓
DATAFLD=column_name	×	×	×	×	×	×	×	×	✓
DATASRC=id	×	×	×	×	×	×	×	×	✓
DIR=LTR|RTL	×	×	✓	×	×	×	×	×	×
DISABLED	×	×	✓	×	×	×	×	×	✓
ID=*string*	×	×	✓	×	×	✓	×	×	✓
LANG=language_type	×	×	✓	×	×	×	×	×	✓
LANGUAGE=JAVASCRIPT|JSCRIPT|VBSCRIPT|VBS	×	×	×	×	×	×	×	×	✓
MULTIPLE	✓	✓	✓	✓	✓	✓	✓	✓	✓
NAME=*string*	✓	✓	✓	✓	✓	✓	✓	✓	✓
SIZE=number	✓	✓	✓	✓	✓	✓	✓	✓	✓
STYLE=*string*	×	×	✓	×	×	✓	×	×	✓
TABINDEX=number	×	×	✓	×	×	×	×	×	✓
TITLE=*string*	×	×	✓	×	×	×	×	×	✓

SERVER

Used to run a Netscape LiveWire script. **N2, N3, N4.**

Attributes	2.0	3.2	4.0	N2	N3	N4	IE2	IE3	IE4
CLASS=classname	×	×	×	×	×	✓	×	×	×
ID=*string*	×	×	×	×	×	✓	×	×	×

SMALL

Specifies that text should be displayed with a smaller font than the current font. **HTML 3.2, 4.0, N2, N3, N4, IE3, IE4**.

Attributes	2.0	3.2	4.0	N2	N3	N4	IE2	IE3	IE4
`<event_name>=script_code`	×	×	✓	×	×	×	×	×	✓
`CLASS=classname`	×	×	✓	×	×	✓	×	×	✓
`DIR=LTR|RTL`	×	×	✓	×	×	×	×	×	×
`ID=`*string*	×	×	✓	×	×	✓	×	×	✓
`LANG=language_type`	×	×	✓	×	×	×	×	×	✓
`LANGUAGE=JAVASCRIPT|JSCRIPT|VBSCRIPT|VBS`	×	×	×	×	×	×	×	×	✓
`STYLE=`*string*	×	×	✓	×	×	✓	×	×	✓
`TITLE=`*string*	×	×	✓	×	×	×	×	×	✓

SPACER

Used to specify vertical and horizontal spacing of elements. **HTML 3.2, 4.0, N2, N3, N4, IE3, IE4**.

Attributes	2.0	3.2	4.0	N2	N3	N4	IE2	IE3	IE4
`ALIGN=ABSBOTTOM|ABSMIDDLE|BASELINE|BOTTOM|LEFT|MIDDLE|RIGHT|TEXTTOP|TOP`	×	×	×	×	✓	✓	×	×	×
`CLASS=classname`	×	×	×	×	×	✓	×	×	×
`HEIGHT=number`	×	×	×	×	✓	✓	×	×	×
`ID=`*string*	×	×	×	×	×	✓	×	×	×
`SIZE=number`	×	×	×	×	✓	✓	×	×	×
`STYLE=`*string*	×	×	×	×	×	✓	×	×	×
`TYPE=BLOCK|HORIZONTAL|VERTICAL`	×	×	×	×	✓	✓	×	×	×
`WIDTH=number`	×	×	×	×	✓	✓	×	×	×

SPAN

Used (with a style sheet) to define non-standard attributes for text on the page. **HTML 4.0, IE4**.

Attributes	2.0	3.2	4.0	N2	N3	N4	IE2	IE3	IE4
`<event_name>=script_code`	×	×	✓	×	×	×	×	×	✓
`CLASS=classname`	×	×	✓	×	×	✓	×	×	✓
`DATAFLD=column_name`	×	×	×	×	×	×	×	×	✓
`DATAFORMATAS=HTML|TEXT`	×	×	×	×	×	×	×	×	✓

Attributes	2.0	3.2	4.0	N2	N3	N4	IE2	IE3	IE4
DATASRC=id	×	×	×	×	×	×	×	×	✓
DIR=LTR|RTL	×	×	✓	×	×	×	×	×	×
ID=*string*	×	×	✓	×	×	✓	×	×	✓
LANG=language_type	×	×	✓	×	×	×	×	×	✓
LANGUAGE=JAVASCRIPT|JSCRIPT|VBSCRIPT|VBS	×	×	×	×	×	×	×	×	✓
STYLE=*string*	×	×	✓	×	×	✓	×	✓	✓
TITLE=*string*	×	×	✓	×	×	×	×	×	✓

STRIKE

Renders text in strikethrough type. **HTML 3.2, N3, N4, IE3, IE4, deprecated in HTML 4.0.**

Attributes	2.0	3.2	4.0	N2	N3	N4	IE2	IE3	IE4
<event_name>=script_code	×	×	D	×	×	×	×	×	✓
CLASS=classname	×	×	D	×	×	✓	×	×	✓
DIR=LTR|RTL	×	×	D	×	×	×	×	×	×
ID=*string*	×	×	D	×	×	✓	×	×	✓
LANG=language_type	×	×	D	×	×	×	×	×	✓
LANGUAGE=JAVASCRIPT|JSCRIPT|VBSCRIPT|VBS	×	×	×	×	×	×	×	×	✓
STYLE=*string*	×	×	D	×	×	✓	×	×	✓
TITLE=*string*	×	×	D	×	×	×	×	×	✓

STRONG

Renders text in bold face. **ALL.**

Attributes	2.0	3.2	4.0	N2	N3	N4	IE2	IE3	IE4
<event_name>=script_code	×	×	✓	×	×	×	×	×	✓
CLASS=classname	×	×	✓	×	×	✓	×	×	✓
DIR=LTR|RTL	×	×	✓	×	×	×	×	×	×
ID=*string*	×	×	✓	×	×	✓	×	×	✓
LANG=language_type	×	×	✓	×	×	×	×	×	✓
LANGUAGE=JAVASCRIPT|JSCRIPT|VBSCRIPT|VBS	×	×	×	×	×	×	×	×	✓
STYLE=*string*	×	×	✓	×	×	✓	×	×	✓
TITLE=*string*	×	×	✓	×	×	×	×	×	✓

STYLE

Specifies the style properties (i.e. the style sheet) for the page. **HTML 3.2, 4.0, N4, IE3, IE4.**

Attributes	2.0	3.2	4.0	N2	N3	N4	IE2	IE3	IE4
DIR=LTR|RTL	×	×	✓	×	×	×	×	×	×
DISABLED	×	×	×	×	×	×	×	×	✓
ID=*string*	×	×	×	×	×	✓	×	×	×
LANG=language_type	×	×	✓	×	×	×	×	×	×
MEDIA=SCREEN|PRINT|PROJECTION|BRAILLE|SPEECH|ALL	×	×	✓	×	×	×	×	×	✓
SRC=url	×	×	×	×	×	✓	×	×	×
TITLE=*string*	×	×	✓	×	×	×	×	✓	✓
TYPE=*string*	×	×	✓	×	×	✓	×	✓	✓

SUB

Renders text as a subscript using a smaller font than the current font. **HTML 3.2, 4.0, N2, N3, N4, IE3, IE4.**

Attributes	2.0	3.2	4.0	N2	N3	N4	IE2	IE3	IE4
<event_name>=script_code	×	×	✓	×	×	×	×	×	✓
CLASS=classname	×	×	✓	×	×	✓	×	×	✓
DIR=LTR|RTL	×	×	✓	×	×	×	×	×	×
ID=*string*	×	×	✓	×	×	✓	×	×	✓
LANG=language_type	×	×	✓	×	×	×	×	×	✓
LANGUAGE=JAVASCRIPT|JSCRIPT|VBSCRIPT|VBS	×	×	×	×	×	×	×	×	✓
STYLE=*string*	×	×	✓	×	×	✓	×	×	✓
TITLE=*string*	×	×	✓	×	×	×	×	×	✓

SUP

Renders text as a superscript using a smaller font than the current font. **HTML 3.2, 4.0, N2, N3, N4, IE3, IE4.**

Attributes	2.0	3.2	4.0	N2	N3	N4	IE2	IE3	IE4
`<event_name>=script_code`	×	×	✓	×	×	×	×	×	✓
`CLASS=classname`	×	×	✓	×	×	✓	×	×	✓
`DIR=LTR|RTL`	×	×	✓	×	×	×	×	×	×
`ID=`*string*	×	×	✓	×	×	✓	×	×	✓
`LANG=language_type`	×	×	✓	×	×	×	×	×	✓
`LANGUAGE=JAVASCRIPT|JSCRIPT|VBSCRIPT|VBS`	×	×	×	×	×	×	×	×	✓
`STYLE=`*string*	×	×	✓	×	×	✓	×	×	✓
`TITLE=`*string*	×	×	✓	×	×	×	×	×	✓

TABLE

Denotes a section of **<TR>** **<TD>** and **<TH>** tags organized into rows and columns. **ALL except HTML 2.0**.

Attributes	2.0	3.2	4.0	N2	N3	N4	IE2	IE3	IE4
`<event_name>=script_code`	×	×	✓	×	×	×	×	×	✓
`ALIGN=CENTER|LEFT|RIGHT`	×	✓	D	×	×	✓	✓	✓	✓
`BACKGROUND=`*string*	×	×	×	×	×	×	✓	✓	✓
`BGCOLOR=color`	×	×	D	×	✓	✓	✓	✓	✓
`BORDER=number`	×	✓	D	✓	✓	✓	×	✓	✓
`BORDERCOLOR=color`	×	×	×	×	×	×	✓	✓	✓
`BORDERCOLORDARK=color`	×	×	×	×	×	×	✓	✓	✓
`BORDERCOLORLIGHT=color`	×	×	×	×	×	×	✓	✓	✓
`CELLPADDING=number`	×	✓	✓	✓	✓	✓	×	✓	✓
`CELLSPACING=number`	×	✓	✓	✓	✓	✓	×	✓	✓
`CLASS=classname`	×	×	✓	×	×	✓	×	✓	✓
`CLEAR=ALL|LEFT|RIGHT|NONE`	×	×	×	×	×	×	×	✓	×
`DATAPAGESIZE=number`	×	×	×	×	×	×	×	×	✓
`DATASRC=id`	×	×	×	×	×	×	×	×	✓
`DIR=LTR|RTL`	×	×	✓	×	×	×	×	×	×
`FRAME=ABOVE|BELOW|BORDER|BOX|HSIDES|LHS|RHS|VOID|VSIDES`	×	×	✓	×	×	×	×	✓	✓
`HEIGHT=number`	×	×	×	✓	✓	✓	×	×	✓
`HSPACE=number`	×	×	×	×	×	✓	×	×	×
`ID=`*string*	×	×	✓	×	×	✓	×	✓	✓
`LANG=language_type`	×	×	✓	×	×	×	×	×	✓
`LANGUAGE=JAVASCRIPT|JSCRIPT|VBSCRIPT|VBS`	×	×	×	×	×	×	×	×	✓
`NOWRAP`	×	×	×	×	×	×	×	✓	×
`RULES=ALL|COLS|GROUPS|NONE|ROWS`	×	×	✓	×	×	×	×	✓	✓

Attributes	2.0	3.2	4.0	N2	N3	N4	IE2	IE3	IE4
SUMMARY	×	×	✓	×	×	×	×	×	×
STYLE=*string*	×	×	✓	×	×	✓	×	✓	✓
TITLE=*string*	×	×	✓	×	×	×	×	×	✓
VALIGN=BOTTOM|TOP	×	×	×	×	×	×	✓	✓	×
VSPACE=number	×	×	×	×	×	✓	×	×	×
WIDTH=number	×	✓	✓	✓	✓	✓	×	✓	✓

TBODY

Denotes a section of **<TR>** and **<TD>** tags forming the body of the table. **HTML 4.0, IE3, IE4**.

Attributes	2.0	3.2	4.0	N2	N3	N4	IE2	IE3	IE4
<event_name>=script_code	×	×	✓	×	×	×	×	×	✓
ALIGN=CENTER|LEFT|RIGHT|JUSTIFY|CHAR	×	×	✓	×	×	×	×	×	✓
BGCOLOR=color	×	×	D	×	×	×	×	×	✓
CHAR=*string*	×	×	✓	×	×	×	×	×	×
CHAROFF=*string*	×	×	✓	×	×	×	×	×	×
CLASS=classname	×	×	✓	×	×	×	×	✓	✓
DIR=LTR|RTL	×	×	✓	×	×	×	×	×	×
ID=*string*	×	×	✓	×	×	×	×	✓	✓
LANG=language_type	×	×	✓	×	×	×	×	×	✓
LANGUAGE=JAVASCRIPT|JSCRIPT|VBSCRIPT|VBS	×	×	×	×	×	×	×	×	✓
STYLE=*string*	×	×	✓	×	×	×	×	✓	✓
TITLE=*string*	×	×	✓	×	×	×	×	×	✓
VALIGN=BASELINE|BOTTOM|CENTER|TOP	×	×	✓	×	×	×	×	×	✓

TD

Specifies a cell in a table. **HTML 3.2, 4.0, N2, N3, N4, IE3, IE4.**

Attributes	2.0	3.2	4.0	N2	N3	N4	IE2	IE3	IE4
<event_name>=script_code	×	×	✓	×	×	×	×	×	✓
ABBR=*string*	×	×	✓	×	×	×	×	×	×
ALIGN=CENTER|LEFT|RIGHT|JUSTIFY|CHAR	×	✓	✓	✓	✓	✓	✓	✓	✓
AXIS=cellname	×	×	✓	×	×	×	×	×	×
BACKGROUND=*string*	×	×	×	×	×	×	✓	✓	✓
BGCOLOR=color	×	×	D	×	✓	✓	✓	✓	✓
BORDERCOLOR=color	×	×	×	×	×	×	✓	✓	✓
BORDERCOLORDARK=color	×	×	×	×	×	×	✓	✓	✓

Attributes	2.0	3.2	4.0	N2	N3	N4	IE2	IE3	IE4
BORDERCOLORLIGHT=color	×	×	×	×	×	×	✓	✓	✓
CHAR=*string*	×	×	✓	×	×	×	×	×	×
CHAROFF=*string*	×	×	✓	×	×	×	×	×	×
CLASS=classname	×	×	✓	×	×	✓	×	✓	✓
COLSPAN=number	×	✓	✓	✓	✓	✓	×	✓	✓
DIR=LTR|RTL	×	×	✓	×	×	×	×	×	×
HEADERS= *string*	×	×	✓	×	×	×	×	×	×
HEIGHT=number	×	✓	D	×	×	✓	×	✓	×
ID=*string*	×	×	✓	×	×	✓	×	✓	✓
LANG=language_type	×	×	✓	×	×	×	×	×	✓
LANGUAGE=JAVASCRIPT|JSCRIPT|VBSCRIPT|VBS	×	×	×	×	×	×	×	×	✓
NOWRAP	×	✓	D	✓	✓	✓	×	✓	✓
ROWSPAN=number	×	✓	✓	✓	✓	✓	×	✓	✓
SCOPE=ROW|COL|ROWGROUP|COLGROUP	×	×	✓	×	×	×	×	×	×
STYLE=*string*	×	×	✓	×	×	✓	×	✓	✓
TITLE=*string*	×	×	✓	×	×	×	×	×	✓
VALIGN=BASELINE|BOTTOM|CENTER|TOP	×	✓	✓	✓	✓	✓	×	✓	✓
WIDTH=number	×	✓	D	✓	✓	✓	×	✓	×

TEXTAREA

Specifies a multi-line text input control. **ALL**.

Attributes	2.0	3.2	4.0	N2	N3	N4	IE2	IE3	IE4
<event_name>=script_code	×	×	✓	×	×	✓	×	×	✓
ACCESSKEY=key_character	×	×	✓	×	×	×	×	×	✓
ALIGN=BASBOTTOM|ABSMIDDLE|BASELINE|BOTTOM|LEFT|MIDDLE|RIGHT|TEXTTOP|TOP	×	×	×	×	×	×	×	×	✓
CLASS=classname	×	×	✓	×	×	✓	×	×	✓
COLS=number	✓	✓	✓	✓	✓	✓	✓	✓	✓
DATAFLD=column_name	×	×	×	×	×	×	×	×	✓
DATASRC=id	×	×	×	×	×	×	×	×	✓
DIR=LTR|RTL	×	×	✓	×	×	×	×	×	×
DISABLED	×	×	✓	×	×	×	×	×	✓
ID=*string*	×	×	✓	×	×	✓	×	×	✓
LANG=language_type	×	×	✓	×	×	×	×	×	✓
LANGUAGE=JAVASCRIPT|JSCRIPT|VBSCRIPT|VBS	×	×	×	×	×	×	×	×	✓
NAME=*string*	✓	✓	✓	✓	✓	✓	×	✓	✓
READONLY	×	×	✓	×	×	×	×	×	✓

Attributes	2.0	3.2	4.0	N2	N3	N4	IE2	IE3	IE4
ROWS=number	✓	✓	✓	✓	✓	✓	✓	✓	✓
STYLE=*string*	×	×	✓	×	×	✓	×	×	✓
TABINDEX=number	×	×	✓	×	×	×	×	×	✓
TITLE=*string*	×	×	✓	×	×	×	×	×	✓
WRAP=PHYSICAL|VERTICAL|OFF	×	×	×	✓	✓	✓	×	×	✓

TFOOT

Denotes a set of rows to be used as the footer of a table. **HTML 4.0, IE3, IE4.**

Attributes	2.0	3.2	4.0	N2	N3	N4	IE2	IE3	IE4
<event_name>=script_code	×	×	✓	×	×	×	×	×	✓
ALIGN=CENTER|LEFT|RIGHT|JUSTIFY|CHAR	×	×	✓	×	×	×	×	×	✓
BGCOLOR=color	×	×	D	×	×	×	×	×	✓
CHAR=*string*	×	×	✓	×	×	×	×	×	×
CHAROFF=*string*	×	×	✓	×	×	×	×	×	×
CLASS=classname	×	×	✓	×	×	×	×	✓	✓
DIR=LTR|RTL	×	×	✓	×	×	×	×	×	×
ID=*string*	×	×	✓	×	×	×	×	✓	✓
LANG=language_type	×	×	✓	×	×	×	×	×	✓
LANGUAGE=JAVASCRIPT|JSCRIPT|VBSCRIPT|VBS	×	×	×	×	×	×	×	×	✓
STYLE=*string*	×	×	✓	×	×	×	×	✓	✓
TITLE=*string*	×	×	✓	×	×	×	×	×	✓
VALIGN=BASELINE|BOTTOM|CENTER|TOP	×	×	✓	×	×	×	×	×	✓

TH

Denotes a header row in a table. Contents are usually bold and centered within each cell. **HTML 3.2, 4.0, N2, N3, N4, IE2, IE3, IE4.**

Attributes	2.0	3.2	4.0	N2	N3	N4	IE2	IE3	IE4
<event_name>=script_code	×	×	✓	×	×	×	×	×	✓
ABBR=*string*	×	×	✓	×	×	×	×	×	×
ALIGN=CENTER|LEFT|RIGHT|JUSTIFY|CHAR	×	✓	✓	✓	✓	✓	✓	✓	✓
AXIS=cellname	×	×	✓	×	×	×	×	×	×
BACKGROUND=*string*	×	×	×	×	×	×	✓	✓	✓
BGCOLOR=color	×	×	D	×	✓	✓	✓	✓	✓
BORDERCOLOR=color	×	×	×	×	×	×	✓	✓	✓
BORDERCOLORDARK=color	×	×	×	×	×	×	✓	✓	✓
BORDERCOLORLIGHT=color	×	×	×	×	×	×	✓	✓	✓

Attributes	2.0	3.2	4.0	N2	N3	N4	IE2	IE3	IE4
CHAR=*string*	×	×	✓	×	×	×	×	×	×
CHAROFF=*string*	×	×	✓	×	×	×	×	×	×
CLASS=classname	×	×	✓	×	×	✓	×	✓	✓
COLSPAN=number	×	✓	✓	✓	✓	✓	×	✓	✓
DIR=LTR|RTL	×	×	✓	×	×	×	×	×	×
HEADERS= *string*	×	×	✓	×	×	×	×	×	×
HEIGHT=number	×	✓	D	×	×	✓	×	×	×
ID=*string*	×	×	✓	×	×	✓	×	✓	✓
LANG=language_type	×	×	✓	×	×	×	×	×	✓
LANGUAGE=JAVASCRIPT|JSCRIPT|VBSCRIPT|VBS	×	×	×	×	×	×	×	×	✓
NOWRAP	×	✓	D	✓	✓	✓	×	✓	✓
ROWSPAN=number	×	✓	✓	✓	✓	✓	×	✓	✓
SCOPE=ROW|COL|ROWGROUP|COLGROUP	×	×	✓	×	×	×	×	×	×
STYLE=*string*	×	×	✓	×	×	✓	×	✓	✓
TITLE=*string*	×	×	✓	×	×	×	×	×	✓
VALIGN=BASELINE|BOTTOM|CENTER|TOP	×	✓	✓	✓	✓	✓	✓	✓	✓
WIDTH=number	×	✓	D	✓	✓	✓	×	✓	×

THEAD

Denotes a set of rows to be used as the header of a table. **HTML 4.0, IE3, IE4.**

Attributes	2.0	3.2	4.0	N2	N3	N4	IE2	IE3	IE4
<event_name>=script_code	×	×	✓	×	×	×	×	×	✓
ALIGN=CENTER|LEFT|RIGHT|JUSTIFY|CHAR	×	×	✓	×	×	×	×	✓	✓
BGCOLOR=color	×	×	D	×	×	×	×	×	✓
CHAR=*string*	×	×	✓	×	×	×	×	×	×
CHAROFF=*string*	×	×	✓	×	×	×	×	×	×
CLASS=classname	×	×	✓	×	×	×	×	✓	✓
DIR=LTR|RTL	×	×	✓	×	×	×	×	×	×
ID=string	×	×	✓	×	×	×	×	✓	✓
LANG=language_type	×	×	✓	×	×	×	×	×	✓
LANGUAGE=JAVASCRIPT|JSCRIPT|VBSCRIPT|VBS	×	×	×	×	×	×	×	×	✓
STYLE=*string*	×	×	✓	×	×	×	×	✓	✓
TITLE=*string*	×	×	✓	×	×	×	×	×	✓
VALIGN=BASELINE|BOTTOM|CENTER|TOP	×	×	✓	×	×	×	×	✓	✓

TITLE

Denotes the title of the document and used in the browser's window title bar. **ALL.**

Attributes	2.0	3.2	4.0	N2	N3	N4	IE2	IE3	IE4
DIR=LTR|RTL	×	×	✓	×	×	×	×	×	×
ID=*string*	×	×	×	×	×	✓	×	×	✓
LANG=language.type	×	×	✓	×	×	×	×	×	×
TITLE=*string*	×	×	×	×	×	×	×	×	✓

TR

Specifies a row in a table. **HTML 3.2, 4.0, N2, N3, N4, IE3, IE4.**

Attributes	2.0	3.2	4.0	N2	N3	N4	IE2	IE3	IE4
<event_name>=script_code	×	×	✓	×	×	×	×	×	✓
ALIGN=CENTER|LEFT|RIGHT|JUSTIFY|CHAR	×	✓	✓	✓	✓	✓	✓	✓	✓
BACKGROUND=*string*	×	×	×	×	×	×	✓	×	×
BGCOLOR=color	×	×	D	×	✓	✓	✓	✓	✓
BORDERCOLOR=color	×	×	×	×	×	×	✓	✓	✓
BORDERCOLORDARK	×	×	×	×	×	×	✓	✓	✓
BORDERCOLORLIGHT=color	×	×	×	×	×	×	✓	✓	✓
CHAR=*string*	×	×	✓	×	×	×	×	×	×
CHAROFF=*string*	×	×	✓	×	×	×	×	×	×
CLASS=classname	×	×	✓	×	×	✓	×	✓	✓
DIR=LTR|RTL	×	×	✓	×	×	×	×	×	×
ID=*string*	×	×	✓	×	×	✓	×	✓	✓
LANG=language_type	×	×	✓	×	×	×	×	×	✓
LANGUAGE=JAVASCRIPT|JSCRIPT|VBSCRIPT|VBS	×	×	×	×	×	×	×	×	✓
NOWRAP	×	×	×	×	×	×	×	✓	×
STYLE=*string*	×	×	✓	×	×	✓	×	✓	✓
TITLE=*string*	×	×	✓	×	×	×	×	×	✓
VALIGN=BASELINE|BOTTOM|CENTER|TOP	×	✓	✓	✓	✓	✓	✓	✓	✓

TT

Renders text in fixed-width type. **ALL.**

Attributes	2.0	3.2	4.0	N2	N3	N4	IE2	IE3	IE4
`<event_name>=script_code`	×	×	✓	×	×	×	×	×	✓
`CLASS=classname`	×	×	✓	×	×	✓	×	×	✓
`DIR=LTR|RTL`	×	×	✓	×	×	×	×	×	×
`ID=`*string*	×	×	✓	×	×	✓	×	×	✓
`LANG=language_type`	×	×	✓	×	×	×	×	×	✓
`LANGUAGE=JAVASCRIPT|JSCRIPT|VBSCRIPT|VBS`	×	×	×	×	×	×	×	×	✓
`STYLE=`*string*	×	×	✓	×	×	✓	×	×	✓
`TITLE=`*string*	×	×	✓	×	×	×	×	×	✓

U

Renders text underlined. **HTML 3.2, N3, N4, IE2, IE3, IE4, deprecated in HTML 4.0.**

Attributes	2.0	3.2	4.0	N2	N3	N4	IE2	IE3	IE4
`<event_name>=script_code`	×	×	D	×	×	×	×	×	✓
`CLASS=classname`	×	×	D	×	×	✓	×	×	✓
`DIR=LTR|RTL`	×	×	D	×	×	×	×	×	×
`ID=`*string*	×	×	D	×	×	✓	×	×	✓
`LANG=language_type`	×	×	D	×	×	×	×	×	✓
`LANGUAGE=JAVASCRIPT|JSCRIPT|VBSCRIPT|VBS`	×	×	×	×	×	×	×	×	✓
`STYLE=`*string*	×	×	D	×	×	✓	×	×	✓
`TITLE=`*string*	×	×	D	×	×	×	×	×	✓

UL

Renders lines of text which have **<LI>** tags as a bulleted list. **ALL.**

Attributes	2.0	3.2	4.0	N2	N3	N4	IE2	IE3	IE4
`<event_name>=script_code`	×	×	✓	×	×	×	×	×	✓
`CLASS=classname`	×	×	✓	×	×	✓	×	✓	✓
`COMPACT`	✓	✓	D	✓	✓	✓	×	✓	×
`DIR=LTR|RTL`	×	×	✓	×	×	×	×	×	×
`ID=`*string*	×	×	✓	×	×	✓	×	✓	✓
`LANG=language_type`	×	×	✓	×	×	×	×	×	✓
`LANGUAGE=JAVASCRIPT|JSCRIPT|VBSCRIPT|VBS`	×	×	×	×	×	×	×	×	✓
`STYLE=`*string*	×	×	✓	×	×	✓	×	✓	✓

Attributes	2.0	3.2	4.0	N2	N3	N4	IE2	IE3	IE4
TITLE=*string*	×	×	✓	×	×	×	×	×	✓
TYPE=CIRCLE|DISC|SQUARE	×	✓	✓	✓	✓	✓	×	×	✓

VAR

Renders text as a small fixed-width font. **HTML 2.0, 3.2, 4.0, IE2, IE3, IE4**.

Attributes	2.0	3.2	4.0	N2	N3	N4	IE2	IE3	IE4
<event_name>=script_code	×	×	✓	×	×	×	×	×	✓
CLASS=classname	×	×	✓	×	×	×	×	×	✓
DIR=LTR|RTL	×	×	✓	×	×	×	×	×	×
ID=*string*	×	×	✓	×	×	×	×	×	✓
LANG=language_type	×	×	✓	×	×	×	×	×	✓
LANGUAGE=JAVASCRIPT|JSCRIPT|VBSCRIPT|VBS	×	×	×	×	×	×	×	×	✓
STYLE=*string*	×	×	✓	×	×	×	×	×	✓
TITLE=*string*	×	×	✓	×	×	×	×	×	✓

WBR

Inserts a soft line break in a block of **NOBR** text. **N2, N3, N4, IE3, IE4.**

Attributes	2.0	3.2	4.0	N2	N3	N4	IE2	IE3	IE4
CLASS=classname	×	×	×	×	×	✓	×	×	✓
ID=*string*	×	×	×	×	×	✓	×	×	✓
LANGUAGE=JAVASCRIPT|JSCRIPT|VBSCRIPT|VBS	×	×	×	×	×	×	×	×	✓
STYLE=*string*	×	×	×	×	×	✓	×	×	✓
TITLE=*string*	×	×	×	×	×	×	×	×	✓

XMP

Renders text in fixed-width typeface, as used for example code. Use **PRE** or **SAMP** instead. **HTML 2.0, N2, N3, N4, IE3, IE4, deprecated in HTML 3.2.**

Attributes	2.0	3.2	4.0	N2	N3	N4	IE2	IE3	IE4
<event_name>=script_code	×	×	×	×	×	×	×	×	✓
CLASS=classname	×	×	×	×	×	✓	×	×	✓
ID=*string*	×	×	×	×	×	✓	×	×	✓
LANG=language_type	×	×	×	×	×	×	×	×	✓

Attributes	2.0	3.2	4.0	N2	N3	N4	IE2	IE3	IE4
`LANGUAGE=JAVASCRIPT|JSCRIPT|VBSCRIPT|VBS`	✗	✗	✗	✗	✗	✗	✗	✗	✓
`STYLE=`*string*	✗	✗	✗	✗	✗	✓	✗	✗	✓
`TITLE=`*string*	✗	✗	✗	✗	✗	✗	✗	✗	✓

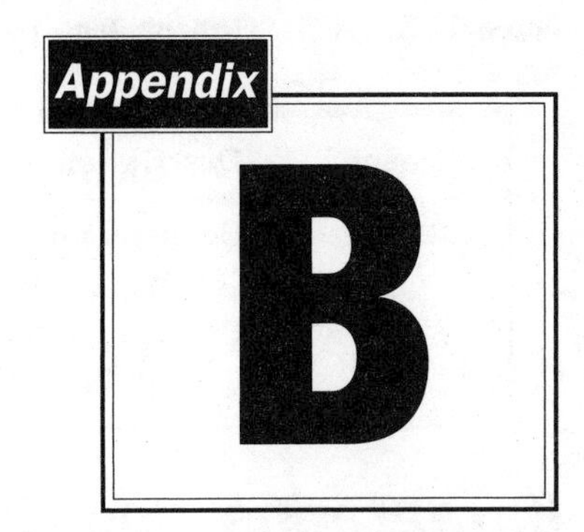

HTML Element Tags by Category

In this section, we've listed all the HTML element tags, and divided them up by category. When you know what you want to do, but aren't sure which tag you need, just look in the appropriate table then refer back to Appendix A to get a list of the appropriate attributes that this element supports.

Document Structure

Element	Description
<!-- -->	Denotes a comment that is ignored by the HTML parser.
<!DOCTYPE>	Declares the type and content format of the document.
<BDO>	Turns off the bi-directional rendering algorithm for selected fragments of text.
<BODY>	Defines the beginning and end of the body section of the page.
<COMMENT>	Denotes a comment that will not be displayed.
<DEL>	Indicates a section of the document that has been deleted since a previous version.
<DIV>	Defines a container section within the page, and can hold other elements.
<HEAD>	Contains tags holding unviewed information about the document.
<HTML>	The outer tag for the page, which identifies the document as containing HTML elements.
<INS>	Indicates a section of the document that has been inserted since a previous version.
<ISINDEX>	Indicates the presence of a searchable index.
<KEYGEN>	Used to generate key material in the page.
<META>	Provides various types of unviewed information or instructions to the browser.

Element	Description
<NEXTID>	Defines values used by text editing software when parsing or creating the document.
<SPAN>	Used (with a style sheet) to define non-standard attributes for text on the page.

Paragraphs and Document Layout

Element	Description
 	Inserts a line break.
<CENTER>	Causes enclosed text and other elements to be centered on the page.
<Hn>	The six elements <H1> to <H6> render text as a range of heading styles.
<HR>	Places a horizontal rule in the page.
<MULTICOL>	Used to define multiple column formatting.
<NOBR>	Renders text without any text wrapping in the page.
<P>	Denotes a paragraph. The end tag is optional.
<SPACER>	Used to specify vertical and horizontal spacing of elements.
<WBR>	Inserts a soft line break in a block of <NOBR> text.

Text and Font Styles

Element	Description
<ABBR> <ACRONYM>	Indicates a sequence of characters that compose an acronym (e.g., "WWW").
<ADDRESS>	Specifies information such as address, signature and authorship.
<B>	Renders text in boldface where available.
<BASEFONT>	Sets the base font values to be used as the default font when rendering text.
<BIG>	Renders text in a relatively larger font than the current font.
<BLINK>	Causes the text to flash on and off within the page.
<BLOCKQUOTE>	Denotes a quotation in text, usually a paragraph or more.
<CITE>	Cites text by rendering it in italics.
<CODE>	Renders text as a code sample in a fixed width font.
<EM>	Renders text as emphasized, usually in italics.
<FONT>	Specifies the font face, size, and color for rendering the text.

Element	Description
<I>	Renders text in an italic font where available.
<KBD>	Renders text in fixed-width font.
<LISTING>	Renders text in fixed-width type.
<MARQUEE>	Creates a scrolling text marquee in the page.
<PLAINTEXT>	Renders text in fixed-width type without processing any tags it may contain.
<PRE>	Renders text in fixed-width type.
<S>	Renders text in strikethrough type.
<SAMP>	Renders text as a code sample listing.
<SMALL>	Specifies that text should be displayed with a smaller font than the current font.
<STRIKE>	Renders text in strikethrough type.
<STRONG>	Renders text in bold face.
<STYLE>	Specifies the style properties (i.e. the style sheet) for the page.
<SUB>	Renders text as a subscript using a smaller font than the current font.
<SUP>	Renders text as a superscript using a smaller font than the current font.
<TT>	Renders text in fixed-width type.
<U>	Renders text underlined.
<VAR>	Renders text as a small fixed-width font.
<XMP>	Renders text in fixed-width typeface, as used for example text.

Lists and Definitions

Element	Description
<DD>	The definition of an item in a definition list, usually indented from other text.
<DIR>	Renders text as a directory-style file listing.
<DL>	Denotes a definition list.
<DFN>	The defining instance of a term.
<DT>	Denotes a definition term within a definition list.
<LI>	Denotes one item within an ordered or unordered list.
<MENU>	Renders the following block of text as individual items.
<OL>	Renders lines of text that have **<LI>** tags as an ordered list.
<UL>	Renders lines of text which have **<LI>** tags as a bulleted list.

Links to Other Documents and Resources

Element	Description
<A>	Defines a hypertext link. The **HREF** or the **NAME** attribute must be specified.
<AREA>	Specifies the shape of a "hot spot" in a client-side image map .
<BASE>	Specifies the document's base URL.
<LINK>	Defines a hyperlink between the document and some other resource.
<MAP>	Specifies a collection of hot spots for a client-side image map
<Q>	The URL of the source document or message used as a quotation in this page.

Graphics, Objects and Multimedia

Element	Description
<APPLET>	Places a Java Applet or other executable content in the page.
<BGSOUND>	Specifies a background sound to be played while the page is loaded.
<EMBED>	Embeds documents of any type in the page, to be viewed in another suitable application.
<IMG>	Embeds an image or a video clip in the document.
<NOEMBED>	Defines the HTML to be displayed by browsers that do not support embeds.
<OBJECT>	Inserts an object or other non-intrinsic HTML control into the page.
<PARAM>	Used in an **<OBJECT>** or **<APPLET>** tag to set the object's properties.

Forms, Controls and Scripting

Element	Description
<BUTTON>	Renders an HTML button, the enclosed text used as the button's caption.
<FIELDSET>	Draws a box around the contained elements to indicate related items.
<FORM>	Denotes a form containing controls and elements, whose values are sent to a server.
<INPUT>	Specifies a form input control, such as a button, text or check box.

Element	Description
<LABEL>	Defines the text of a label for a control-like element.
<LEGEND>	Defines the title text to place in the 'box' created by a <FIELDSET> tag.
<NOSCRIPT>	Defines the HTML to be displayed in browsers that do not support scripting.
<OPTION>	Denotes one choice in a <SELECT> drop-down or list element.
<OPTGROUP>	Allows authors to group choices into a hierarchy.
<SCRIPT>	Specifies a script for the page that will be interpreted by a script engine.
<SELECT>	Defines a list box or drop-down list.
<SERVER>	Used to run a Netscape LiveWire script.
<TEXTAREA>	Specifies a multi-line text input control.

HTML Tables

Element	Description
<CAPTION>	Specifies a caption to be placed next to a table.
<COL>	Used to specify column based defaults for a table.
<COLGROUP>	Used as a container for a group of columns.
<TABLE>	Denotes a section of <TR> <TD> and <TH> tags organized into rows and columns.
<TBODY>	Denotes a section of <TR> and <TD> tags forming the body of the table.
<TD>	Specifies a cell in a table.
<TFOOT>	Denotes a set of rows to be used as the footer of a table.
<TH>	Denotes a header row in a table. Contents are centered within each cell and are bold.
<THEAD>	Denotes a set of rows to be used as the header of a table.
<TITLE>	Denotes the title of the document, and used in the browser's window title bar.
<TR>	Specifies a row in a table.

Frames and Layers

Element	Description
<FRAME>	Specifies an individual frame within a frameset.
<FRAMESET>	Specifies a frameset containing multiple frames and other nested framesets.
<IFRAME>	Used to create in-line floating frames within the page.
<ILAYER>	Defines a separate area of the page as an inline layer that can hold a different page.
<LAYER>	Defines a separate area of the page as a layer that can hold a different page.
<NOFRAMES>	Defines the HTML to be displayed in browsers that do not support frames.
<NOLAYER>	Defines the part of a document that will be displayed in browsers that don't support layers.

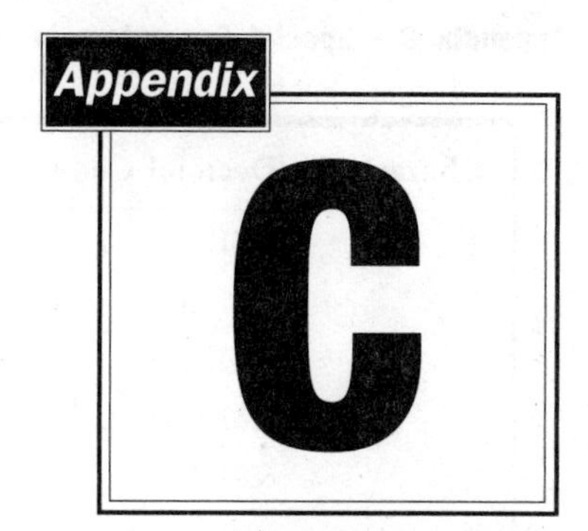

Special Characters in HTML

The following table gives you the codes you need to insert special characters into your HTML documents. Some characters have their own mnemonic names—for example, the registered trademark character can be written in HTML as ®. Where there is no mnemonic name, you can insert the character simply by including its decimal code.

Character	Decimal Code	HTML	Description
"	"	"	Quotation mark
&	&	&	Ampersand
<	<	<	Less than
>	>	>	Greater than
			Non-breaking space
¡	¡	¡	Inverted exclamation
¢	¢	¢	Cent sign
£	£	£	Pound sterling
¤	¤	¤	General currency sign
¥	¥	¥	Yen sign
¦	¦	¦	Broken vertical bar
§	§	§	Section sign
¨	¨	¨	Diæresis/umlaut
©	©	©	Copyright
ª	ª	ª	Feminine ordinal
«	«	«	Left angle quote,
¬	¬	¬	Not sign
-			Soft hyphen
®	®	®	Registered trademark
¯	¯	¯	Macron accent
°	°	°	Degree sign

Character	Decimal Code	HTML	Description
±	±	±	Plus or minus
^{2}	²	²	Superscript two
^{3}	³	³	Superscript three
´	´	´	Acute accent
µ	µ	µ	Micro sign
¶	¶	¶	Paragraph sign
·	·	·	Middle dot
¸	¸	¸	Cedilla
^{1}	¹	¹	Superscript one
º	º	º	Masculine ordinal
»	»	»	Right angle quote
¼	¼	¼	Fraction one quarter
½	½	½	Fraction one half
¾	¾	¾	Fraction three-quarters
¿	¿	¿	Inverted question mark
À	À	À	Capital A, grave accent
Á	Á	Á	Capital A, acute accent
Â	Â	Â	Capital A, circumflex
Ã	Ã	Ã	Capital A, tilde
Ä	Ä	Ä	Capital A, diæresis / umlaut
Å	Å	Å	Capital A, ring
Æ	Æ	Æ	Capital AE, ligature
Ç	Ç	Ç	Capital C, cedilla
È	È	È	Capital E, grave accent
É	É	É	Capital E, acute accent
Ê	Ê	Ê	Capital E, circumflex
Ë	Ë	Ë	Capital E, diæresis / umlaut
Ì	Ì	Ì	Capital I, grave accent
Í	Í	Í	Capital I, acute accent
Î	Î	Î	Capital I, circumflex
Ï	Ï	Ï	Capital I, diæresis /umlaut
Ð	Ð	Ð	Capital Eth, Icelandic
Ñ	Ñ	Ñ	Capital N, tilde
Ò	Ò	Ò	Capital O, grave accent
Ó	Ó	Ó	Capital O, acute accent
Ô	Ô	Ô	Capital O, circumflex
Õ	Õ	Õ	Capital O, tilde

Character	Decimal Code	HTML	Description
Ö	Ö	Ö	Capital O, diæresis / umlaut
×	×	×	Multiplication sign
Ø	Ø	Ø	Capital O, slash
Ù	Ù	Ù	Capital U, grave accent
Ú	Ú	Ú	Capital U, acute accent
Û	Û	Û	Capital U, circumflex
Ü	Ü	Ü	Capital U, diæresis / umlaut
Ý	Ý	Ý	Capital Y, acute accent
Þ	Þ	Þ	Capital Thorn, Icelandic
ß	ß	ß	German sz
à	à	à	Small a, grave accent
á	á	á	Small a, acute accent
â	â	â	Small a, circumflex
ã	ã	ã	Small a, tilde
ä	ä	ä	Small a, diæresis / umlaut
å	å	å	Small a, ring
æ	æ	æ	Small ae ligature
ç	ç	ç	Small c, cedilla
è	è	è	Small e, grave accent
é	é	é	Small e, acute accent
ê	ê	ê	Small e, circumflex
ë	ë	ë	Small e, diæresis / umlaut
ì	ì	ì	Small i, grave accent
í	í	í	Small i, acute accent
î	î	î	Small i, circumflex
ï	ï	ï	Small i, diæresis / umlaut
ð	ð	ð	Small eth, Icelandic
ñ	ñ	ñ	Small n, tilde
ò	ò	ò	Small o, grave accent
ó	ó	ó	Small o, acute accent
ô	ô	ô	Small o, circumflex
õ	õ	õ	Small o, tilde
ö	ö	ö	Small o, diæresis / umlaut
÷	÷	÷	Division sign
ø	ø	ø	Small o, slash
ù	ù	ù	Small u, grave accent
ú	ú	ú	Small u, acute accent

Character	Decimal Code	HTML	Description
û	û	û	Small u, circumflex
ü	ü	ü	Small u, diæresis / umlaut
ý	ý	ý	Small y, acute accent
þ	þ	þ	Small thorn, Icelandic
ÿ	ÿ	ÿ	Small y, diæresis / umlaut

Remember, if you want to show HTML code in a browser, you have to use the special character codes for the angled brackets in order to avoid the browser interpreting them as start and end of tags.

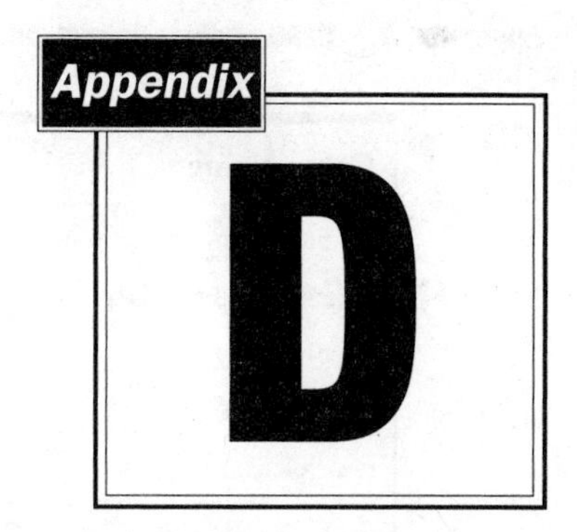

HTML Color Names and Values

Colors Sorted by Name

Color Name	Value	IE4 Color Constant
aliceblue	F0F8FF	htmlAliceBlue
antiquewhite	FAEBD7	htmlAntiqueWhite
aqua	00FFFF	htmlAqua
aquamarine	7FFFD4	htmlAquamarine
azure	F0FFFF	htmlAzure
beige	F5F5DC	htmlBeige
bisque	FFE4C4	htmlBisque
black	000000	htmlBlack
blanchedalmond	FFEBCD	htmlBlanchedAlmond
blue	0000FF	htmlBlue
blueviolet	8A2BE2	htmlBlueViolet
brown	A52A2A	htmlBrown
burlywood	DEB887	htmlBurlywood
cadetblue	5F9EA0	htmlCadetBlue
chartreuse	7FFF00	htmlChartreuse
chocolate	D2691E	htmlChocolate
coral	FF7F50	htmlCoral
cornflowerblue	6495ED	htmlCornflowerBlue
cornsilk	FFF8DC	htmlCornsilk
crimson	DC143C	htmlCrimson
cyan	00FFFF	htmlCyan
darkblue	00008B	htmlDarkBlue

Color Name	Value	IE4 Color Constant
darkcyan	008B8B	htmlDarkCyan
darkgoldenrod	B8860B	htmlDarkGoldenRod
darkgray	A9A9A9	htmlDarkGray
darkgreen	006400	htmlDarkGreen
darkkhaki	BDB76B	htmlDarkKhaki
darkmagenta	8B008B	htmlDarkMagenta
darkolivegreen	556B2F	htmlDarkOliveGreen
darkorange	FF8C00	htmlDarkOrange
darkorchid	9932CC	htmlDarkOrchid
darkred	8B0000	htmlDarkRed
darksalmon	E9967A	htmlDarkSalmon
darkseagreen	8FBC8F	htmlDarkSeaGreen
darkslateblue	483D8B	htmlDarkSlateBlue
darkslategray	2F4F4F	htmlDarkSlateGray
darkturquoise	00CED1	htmlDarkTurquoise
darkviolet	9400D3	htmlDarkViolet
deeppink	FF1493	htmlDeepPink
deepskyblue	00BFFF	htmlDeepSkyBlue
dimgray	696969	htmlDimGray
dodgerblue	1E90FF	htmlDodgerBlue
firebrick	B22222	htmlFirebrick
floralwhite	FFFAF0	htmlFloralWhite
forestgreen	228B22	htmlForestGreen
fuchsia	FF00FF	htmlFuchsia
gainsboro	DCDCDC	htmlGainsboro
ghostwhite	F8F8FF	htmlGhostWhite
gold	FFD700	htmlGold
goldenrod	DAA520	htmlGoldenRod
gray	808080	htmlGray
green	008000	htmlGreen
greenyellow	ADFF2F	htmlGreenYellow
honeydew	F0FFF0	htmlHoneydew
hotpink	FF69B4	htmlHotPink
indianred	CD5C5C	htmlIndianRed
indigo	4B0082	htmlIndigo
ivory	FFFFF0	htmlIvory
khaki	F0E68C	htmlKhaki

Color Name	Value	IE4 Color Constant
lavender	E6E6FA	htmlLavender
lavenderblush	FFF0F5	htmlLavenderBlush
lawngreen	7CFC00	htmlLawnGreen
lemonchiffon	FFFACD	htmlLemonChiffon
lightblue	ADD8E6	htmlLightBlue
lightcoral	F08080	htmlLightCoral
lightcyan	E0FFFF	htmlLightCyan
lightgray	D3D3D3	htmlLightGray
lightgreen	90EE90	htmlLightGreen
lightpink	FFB6C1	htmlLightPink
lightsalmon	FFA07A	htmlLightSalmon
lightseagreen	20B2AA	htmlLightSeaGreen
lightskyblue	87CEFA	htmlLightSkyBlue
lightslategray	778899	htmlLightSlateGray
lightsteelblue	B0C4DE	htmlLightSteelBlue
lightyellow	FFFFE0	htmlLightYellow
lime	00FF00	htmlLime
limegreen	32CD32	htmlLimeGreen
linen	FAF0E6	htmlLinen
magenta	FF00FF	htmlMagenta
maroon	800000	htmlMaroon
mediumaquamarine	66CDAA	htmlMediumAquamarine
mediumblue	0000CD	htmlMediumBlue
mediumorchid	BA55D3	htmlMediumOrchid
mediumpurple	9370DB	htmlMediumPurple
mediumseagreen	3CB371	htmlMediumSeaGreen
mediumslateblue	7B68EE	htmlMediumSlateBlue
mediumspringgreen	00FA9A	htmlMediumSpringGreen
mediumturquoise	48D1CC	htmlMediumTurquoise
mediumvioletred	C71585	htmlMediumVioletRed
midnightblue	191970	htmlMidnightBlue
mintcream	F5FFFA	htmlMintCream
mistyrose	FFE4E1	htmlMistyRose
moccasin	FFE4B5	htmlMoccasin
navajowhite	FFDEAD	htmlNavajoWhite
navy	000080	htmlNavy
oldlace	FDF5E6	htmlOldLace

Color Name	Value	IE4 Color Constant
olive	808000	htmlOlive
olivedrab	6B8E23	htmlOliveDrab
orange	FFA500	htmlOrange
orangered	FF4500	htmlOrangeRed
orchid	DA70D6	htmlOrchid
palegoldenrod	EEE8AA	htmlPaleGoldenRod
palegreen	98FB98	htmlPaleGreen
paleturquoise	AFEEEE	htmlPaleTurquoise
palevioletred	DB7093	htmlPaleVioletRed
papayawhip	FFEFD5	htmlPapayaWhip
peachpuff	FFDAB9	htmlPeachPuff
peru	CD853F	htmlPeru
pink	FFC0CB	htmlPink
plum	DDA0DD	htmlPlum
powderblue	B0E0E6	htmlPowderBlue
purple	800080	htmlPurple
red	FF0000	htmlRed
rosybrown	BC8F8F	htmlRosyBrown
royalblue	4169E1	htmlRoyalBlue
saddlebrown	8B4513	htmlSaddleBrown
salmon	FA8072	htmlSalmon
sandybrown	F4A460	htmlSandyBrown
seagreen	2E8B57	htmlSeaGreen
seashell	FFF5EE	htmlSeashell
sienna	A0522D	htmlSienna
silver	C0C0C0	htmlSilver
skyblue	87CEEB	htmlSkyBlue
slateblue	6A5ACD	htmlSlateBlue
slategray	708090	htmlSlateGray
snow	FFFAFA	htmlSnow
springgreen	00FF7F	htmlSpringGreen
steelblue	4682B4	htmlSteelBlue
tan	D2B48C	htmlTan
teal	008080	htmlTeal
thistle	D8BFD8	htmlThistle
tomato	FF6347	htmlTomato
turquoise	40E0D0	htmlTurquoise

Color Name	Value	IE4 Color Constant
violet	EE82EE	htmlViolet
wheat	F5DEB3	htmlWheat
white	FFFFFF	htmlWhite
whitesmoke	F5F5F5	htmlWhiteSmoke
yellow	FFFF00	htmlYellow
yellowgreen	9ACD32	htmlYellowGreen

Colors Sorted by Group

Color Name	Value	IE4 Color Constant
Blues		
azure	F0FFFF	htmlAzure
aliceblue	F0F8FF	htmlAliceBlue
lavender	E6E6FA	htmlLavender
lightcyan	E0FFFF	htmlLightCyan
powderblue	B0E0E6	htmlPowderBlue
lightsteelblue	B0C4DE	htmlLightSteelBlue
paleturquoise	AFEEEE	htmlPaleTurquoise
lightblue	ADD8E6	htmlLightBlue
blueviolet	8A2BE2	htmlBlueViolet
lightskyblue	87CEFA	htmlLightSkyBlue
skyblue	87CEEB	htmlSkyBlue
mediumslateblue	7B68EE	htmlMediumSlateBlue
slateblue	6A5ACD	htmlSlateBlue
cornflowerblue	6495ED	htmlCornflowerBlue
cadetblue	5F9EA0	htmlCadetBlue
indigo	4B0082	htmlIndigo
mediumturquoise	48D1CC	htmlMediumTurquoise
darkslateblue	483D8B	htmlDarkSlateBlue
steelblue	4682B4	htmlSteelBlue
royalblue	4169E1	htmlRoyalBlue
turquoise	40E0D0	htmlTurquoise
dodgerblue	1E90FF	htmlDodgerBlue
midnightblue	191970	htmlMidnightBlue
aqua	00FFFF	htmlAqua
cyan	00FFFF	htmlCyan

Color Name	Value	IE4 Color Constant
darkturquoise	00CED1	htmlDarkTurquoise
deepskyblue	00BFFF	htmlDeepSkyBlue
darkcyan	008B8B	htmlDarkCyan
blue	0000FF	htmlBlue
mediumblue	0000CD	htmlMediumBlue
darkblue	00008B	htmlDarkBlue
navy	000080	htmlNavy
Greens		
mintcream	F5FFFA	htmlMintCream
honeydew	F0FFF0	htmlHoneydew
greenyellow	ADFF2F	htmlGreenYellow
yellowgreen	9ACD32	htmlYellowGreen
palegreen	98FB98	htmlPaleGreen
lightgreen	90EE90	htmlLightGreen
darkseagreen	8FBC8F	htmlDarkSeaGreen
olive	808000	htmlOlive
aquamarine	7FFFD4	htmlAquamarine
chartreuse	7FFF00	htmlChartreuse
lawngreen	7CFC00	htmlLawnGreen
olivedrab	6B8E23	htmlOliveDrab
mediumaquamarine	66CDAA	htmlMediumAquamarine
darkolivegreen	556B2F	htmlDarkOliveGreen
mediumseagreen	3CB371	htmlMediumSeaGreen
limegreen	32CD32	htmlLimeGreen
seagreen	2E8B57	htmlSeaGreen
forestgreen	228B22	htmlForestGreen
lightseagreen	20B2AA	htmlLightSeaGreen
springgreen	00FF7F	htmlSpringGreen
lime	00FF00	htmlLime
mediumspringgreen	00FA9A	htmlMediumSpringGreen
teal	008080	htmlTeal
green	008000	htmlGreen
darkgreen	006400	htmlDarkGreen
Pinks and Reds		
lavenderblush	FFF0F5	htmlLavenderBlush
mistyrose	FFE4E1	htmlMistyRose

Color Name	Value	IE4 Color Constant
pink	FFC0CB	htmlPink
lightpink	FFB6C1	htmlLightPink
orange	FFA500	htmlOrange
lightsalmon	FFA07A	htmlLightSalmon
darkorange	FF8C00	htmlDarkOrange
coral	FF7F50	htmlCoral
hotpink	FF69B4	htmlHotPink
tomato	FF6347	htmlTomato
orangered	FF4500	htmlOrangeRed
deeppink	FF1493	htmlDeepPink
fuchsia	FF00FF	htmlFuchsia
magenta	FF00FF	htmlMagenta
red	FF0000	htmlRed
salmon	FA8072	htmlSalmon
lightcoral	F08080	htmlLightCoral
violet	EE82EE	htmlViolet
darksalmon	E9967A	htmlDarkSalmon
plum	DDA0DD	htmlPlum
crimson	DC143C	htmlCrimson
palevioletred	DB7093	htmlPaleVioletRed
orchid	DA70D6	htmlOrchid
thistle	D8BFD8	htmlThistle
indianred	CD5C5C	htmlIndianRed
mediumvioletred	C71585	htmlMediumVioletRed
mediumorchid	BA55D3	htmlMediumOrchid
firebrick	B22222	htmlFirebrick
darkorchid	9932CC	htmlDarkOrchid
darkviolet	9400D3	htmlDarkViolet
mediumpurple	9370DB	htmlMediumPurple
darkmagenta	8B008B	htmlDarkMagenta
darkred	8B0000	htmlDarkRed
purple	800080	htmlPurple
maroon	800000	htmlMaroon
Yellows		
ivory	FFFFF0	htmlIvory
lightyellow	FFFFE0	htmlLightYellow

Color Name	Value	IE4 Color Constant
yellow	FFFF00	htmlYellow
floralwhite	FFFAF0	htmlFloralWhite
lemonchiffon	FFFACD	htmlLemonChiffon
cornsilk	FFF8DC	htmlCornsilk
gold	FFD700	htmlGold
khaki	F0E68C	htmlKhaki
darkkhaki	BDB76B	htmlDarkKhaki
Beiges and Browns		
snow	FFFAFA	htmlSnow
seashell	FFF5EE	htmlSeashell
papayawhite	FFEFD5	htmlPapayaWhite
blanchedalmond	FFEBCD	htmlBlanchedAlmond
bisque	FFE4C4	htmlBisque
moccasin	FFE4B5	htmlMoccasin
navajowhite	FFDEAD	htmlNavajoWhite
peachpuff	FFDAB9	htmlPeachPuff
oldlace	FDF5E6	htmlOldLace
linen	FAF0E6	htmlLinen
antiquewhite	FAEBD7	htmlAntiqueWhite
beige	F5F5DC	htmlBeige
wheat	F5DEB3	htmlWheat
sandybrown	F4A460	htmlSandyBrown
palegoldenrod	EEE8AA	htmlPaleGoldenRod
burlywood	DEB887	htmlBurlywood
goldenrod	DAA520	htmlGoldenRod
tan	D2B48C	htmlTan
chocolate	D2691E	htmlChocolate
peru	CD853F	htmlPeru
rosybrown	BC8F8F	htmlRosyBrown
darkgoldenrod	B8860B	htmlDarkGoldenRod
brown	A52A2A	htmlBrown
sienna	A0522D	htmlSienna
saddlebrown	8B4513	htmlSaddleBrown
Whites and Grays		
white	FFFFFF	htmlWhite
ghostwhite	F8F8FF	htmlGhostWhite

Color Name	Value	IE4 Color Constant
whitesmoke	F5F5F5	htmlWhiteSmoke
gainsboro	DCDCDC	htmlGainsboro
lightgray	D3D3D3	htmlLightGray
silver	C0C0C0	htmlSilver
darkgray	A9A9A9	htmlDarkGray
gray	808080	htmlGray
lightslategray	778899	htmlLightSlateGray
slategray	708090	htmlSlateGray
dimgray	696969	htmlDimGray
darkslategray	2F4F4F	htmlDarkSlateGray
black	000000	htmlBlack

Colors Sorted by Depth

Color Name	Value	IE4 Color Constant
white	FFFFFF	htmlWhite
ivory	FFFFF0	htmlIvory
lightyellow	FFFFE0	htmlLightYellow
yellow	FFFF00	htmlYellow
snow	FFFAFA	htmlSnow
floralwhite	FFFAF0	htmlFloralWhite
lemonchiffon	FFFACD	htmlLemonChiffon
cornsilk	FFF8DC	htmlCornsilk
seashell	FFF5EE	htmlSeashell
lavenderblush	FFF0F5	htmlLavenderBlush
papayawhip	FFEFD5	htmlPapayaWhip
blanchedalmond	FFEBCD	htmlBlanchedAlmond
mistyrose	FFE4E1	htmlMistyRose
bisque	FFE4C4	htmlBisque
moccasin	FFE4B5	htmlMoccasin
navajowhite	FFDEAD	htmlNavajoWhite
peachpuff	FFDAB9	htmlPeachPuff
gold	FFD700	htmlGold
pink	FFC0CB	htmlPink
lightpink	FFB6C1	htmlLightPink
orange	FFA500	htmlOrange

Color Name	Value	IE4 Color Constant
lightsalmon	FFA07A	htmlLightSalmon
darkorange	FF8C00	htmlDarkOrange
coral	FF7F50	htmlCoral
hotpink	FF69B4	htmlHotPink
tomato	FF6347	htmlTomato
orangered	FF4500	htmlOrangeRed
deeppink	FF1493	htmlDeepPink
fuchsia	FF00FF	htmlFuchsia
magenta	FF00FF	htmlMagenta
red	FF0000	htmlRed
oldlace	FDF5E6	htmlOldLace
linen	FAF0E6	htmlLinen
antiquewhite	FAEBD7	htmlAntiqueWhite
salmon	FA8072	htmlSalmon
ghostwhite	F8F8FF	htmlGhostWhite
mintcream	F5FFFA	htmlMintCream
whitesmoke	F5F5F5	htmlWhiteSmoke
beige	F5F5DC	htmlBeige
wheat	F5DEB3	htmlWheat
sandybrown	F4A460	htmlSandyBrown
azure	F0FFFF	htmlAzure
honeydew	F0FFF0	htmlHoneydew
aliceblue	F0F8FF	htmlAliceBlue
khaki	F0E68C	htmlKhaki
lightcoral	F08080	htmlLightCoral
palegoldenrod	EEE8AA	htmlPaleGoldenRod
violet	EE82EE	htmlViolet
darksalmon	E9967A	htmlDarkSalmon
lavender	E6E6FA	htmlLavender
lightcyan	E0FFFF	htmlLightCyan
burlywood	DEB887	htmlBurlywood
plum	DDA0DD	htmlPlum
gainsboro	DCDCDC	htmlGainsboro
crimson	DC143C	htmlCrimson
palevioletred	DB7093	htmlPaleVioletRed
goldenrod	DAA520	htmlGoldenRod
orchid	DA70D6	htmlOrchid

Color Name	Value	IE4 Color Constant
thistle	D8BFD8	htmlThistle
lightgray	D3D3D3	htmlLightGray
tan	D2B48C	htmlTan
chocolate	D2691E	htmlChocolate
peru	CD853F	htmlPeru
indianred	CD5C5C	htmlIndianRed
mediumvioletred	C71585	htmlMediumVioletRed
silver	C0C0C0	htmlSilver
darkkhaki	BDB76B	htmlDarkKhaki
rosybrown	BC8F8F	htmlRosyBrown
mediumorchid	BA55D3	htmlMediumOrchid
darkgoldenrod	B8860B	htmlDarkGoldenRod
firebrick	B22222	htmlFirebrick
powderblue	B0E0E6	htmlPowderBlue
lightsteelblue	B0C4DE	htmlLightSteelBlue
paleturquoise	AFEEEE	htmlPaleTurquoise
greenyellow	ADFF2F	htmlGreenYellow
lightblue	ADD8E6	htmlLightBlue
darkgray	A9A9A9	htmlDarkGray
brown	A52A2A	htmlBrown
sienna	A0522D	htmlSienna
yellowgreen	9ACD32	htmlYellowGreen
darkorchid	9932CC	htmlDarkOrchid
palegreen	98FB98	htmlPaleGreen
darkviolet	9400D3	htmlDarkViolet
mediumpurple	9370DB	htmlMediumPurple
lightgreen	90EE90	htmlLightGreen
darkseagreen	8FBC8F	htmlDarkSeaGreen
saddlebrown	8B4513	htmlSaddleBrown
darkmagenta	8B008B	htmlDarkMagenta
darkred	8B0000	htmlDarkRed
blueviolet	8A2BE2	htmlBlueViolet
lightskyblue	87CEFA	htmlLightSkyBlue
skyblue	87CEEB	htmlSkyBlue
gray	808080	htmlGray
olive	808000	htmlOlive
purple	800080	htmlPurple

Color Name	Value	IE4 Color Constant
maroon	800000	htmlMaroon
aquamarine	7FFFD4	htmlAquamarine
chartreuse	7FFF00	htmlChartreuse
lawngreen	7CFC00	htmlLawnGreen
mediumslateblue	7B68EE	htmlMediumSlateBlue
lightslategray	778899	htmlLightSlateGray
slategray	708090	htmlSlateGray
olivedrab	6B8E23	htmlOliveDrab
slateblue	6A5ACD	htmlSlateBlue
dimgray	696969	htmlDimGray
mediumaquamarine	66CDAA	htmlMediumAquamarine
cornflowerblue	6495ED	htmlCornflowerBlue
cadetblue	5F9EA0	htmlCadetBlue
darkolivegreen	556B2F	htmlDarkOliveGreen
indigo	4B0082	htmlIndigo
mediumturquoise	48D1CC	htmlMediumTurquoise
darkslateblue	483D8B	htmlDarkSlateBlue
steelblue	4682B4	htmlSteelBlue
royalblue	4169E1	htmlRoyalBlue
turquoise	40E0D0	htmlTurquoise
mediumseagreen	3CB371	htmlMediumSeaGreen
limegreen	32CD32	htmlLimeGreen
darkslategray	2F4F4F	htmlDarkSlateGray
seagreen	2E8B57	htmlSeaGreen
forestgreen	228B22	htmlForestGreen
lightseagreen	20B2AA	htmlLightSeaGreen
dodgerblue	1E90FF	htmlDodgerBlue
midnightblue	191970	htmlMidnightBlue
aqua	00FFFF	htmlAqua
cyan	00FFFF	htmlCyan
springgreen	00FF7F	htmlSpringGreen
lime	00FF00	htmlLime
mediumspringgreen	00FA9A	htmlMediumSpringGreen
darkturquoise	00CED1	htmlDarkTurquoise
deepskyblue	00BFFF	htmlDeepSkyBlue
darkcyan	008B8B	htmlDarkCyan
teal	008080	htmlTeal

Color Name	Value	IE4 Color Constant
green	008000	htmlGreen
darkgreen	006400	htmlDarkGreen
blue	0000FF	htmlBlue
mediumblue	0000CD	htmlMediumBlue
darkblue	00008B	htmlDarkBlue
navy	000080	htmlNavy
black	000000	htmlBlack

The VBScript Language

Array Handling

Dim—declares an array variable. This can be static with a defined number of elements or dynamic and can have up to 60 dimensions.
ReDim—used to change the size of an array variable which has been declared as dynamic.
Preserve—keyword used to preserve the contents of an array being resized. If you need to use this then you can only re-dimension the rightmost index of the array.

```
Dim strEmployees ()
ReDim strEmployees (9,1)

strEmployees (9,1) = "Phil"

ReDim strEmployees (9,2)              'loses the contents of element (9,1)
strEmployees (9,2) = "Paul"

ReDim Preserve strEmployees (9,3)    'preserves the contents of (9,2)
strEmployees (9,3) = "Smith"
```

LBound—returns the smallest subscript for the dimension of an array. Note that arrays always start from the subscript zero so this function will always return the value zero.
UBound—used to determine the size of an array.

```
Dim strCustomers (10, 5)
intSizeFirst = UBound (strCustomers, 1)       'returns SizeFirst = 10
intSizeSecond = UBound (strCustomers, 2)      'returns SizeSecond = 5
```

The actual number of elements is always one greater than the value returned by `UBound` because the array starts from zero.

Assignments

`Let`—used to assign values to variables (optional).
`Set`—used to assign an object reference to a variable.

```
Let intNumberOfDays = 365

Set txtMyTextBox = txtcontrol
txtMyTextBox.Value = "Hello World"
```

Constants

`Empty`—an empty variable is one that has been created but not yet assigned a value.
`Nothing`—used to remove an object reference.

```
Set txtMyTextBox = txtATextBox        'assigns object reference
Set txtMyTextBox = Nothing            'removes object reference
```

`Null`—indicates that a variable is not valid. Note that this isn't the same as `Empty`.
`True`—indicates that an expression is true. Has numerical value –1.
`False`—indicates that an expression is false. Has numerical value 0.

Error constant:

Constant	Value
`vbObjectError`	&h80040000

System Color constants:

Constant	Value	Description
`vbBlack`	`&h00`	Black
`vbRed`	`&hFF`	Red
`vbGreen`	`&hFF00`	Green
`vbYellow`	`&hFFFF`	Yellow
`vbBlue`	`&hFF0000`	Blue
`vbMagenta`	`&hFF00FF`	Magenta
`vbCyan`	`&hFFFF00`	Cyan
`vbWhite`	`&hFFFFFF`	White

Comparison constants:

Constant	Value	Description
`vbBinaryCompare`	0	Perform a binary comparison.
`vbTextCompare`	1	Perform a textual comparison.
`vbDatabaseCompare`	2	Perform a comparison based upon information in the database where the comparison is to be performed.

Date and Time constants:

Constant	Value	Description
`VbSunday`	1	Sunday
`vbMonday`	2	Monday
`vbTuesday`	3	Tuesday
`vbWednesday`	4	Wednesday
`vbThursday`	5	Thursday
`vbFriday`	6	Friday
`vbSaturday`	7	Saturday
`vbFirstJan1`	1	Use the week in which January 1 occurs (default).
`vbFirstFourDays`	2	Use the first week that has at least four days in the new year.
`vbFirstFullWeek`	3	Use the first full week of the year.
`vbUseSystem`	0	Use the format in the regional settings for the computer.
`vbUseSystemDayOfWeek`	0	Use the day in the system settings for the first weekday.

Date Format constants:

Constant	Value	Description
`vbGeneralDate`	0	Display a date and/or time in the format set in the system settings. For real numbers display a date and time. For integer numbers display only a date. For numbers less than 1, display time only.

Table continued on following page

Constant	Value	Description
vbLongDate	1	Display a date using the long date format specified in the computers regional settings.
vbShortDate	2	Display a date using the short date format specified in the computers regional settings.
vbLongTime	3	Display a time using the long time format specified in the computers regional settings.
vbShortTime	4	Display a time using the short time format specified in the computers regional settings.

File Input/Output constants:

Constant	Value	Description
ForReading	1	Open a file for reading only.
ForWriting	2	Open a file for writing. If a file with the same name exists, its previous one is overwritten.
ForAppending	8	Open a file and write at the end of the file.

String constants:

Constant	Value	Description
vbCr	Chr(13)	Carriage return only
vbCrLf	Chr(13) & Chr(10)	Carriage return and linefeed (Newline)
vbLf	Chr(10)	Line feed only
vbNewLine	-	Newline character as appropriate to a specific platform
vbNullChar	Chr(0)	Character having the value 0
vbNullString	-	String having the value zero (not just an empty string)
vbTab	Chr(9)	Horizontal tab

Tristate constants:

Constant	Value	Description
`TristateTrue`	-1	True
`TristateFalse`	0	False
`TristateUseDefault`	-2	Use default setting

VarType constants:

Constant	Value	Description
`vbEmpty`	0	Un-initialized (default)
`vbNull`	1	Contains no valid data
`vbInteger`	2	Integer subtype
`vbLong`	3	Long subtype
`vbSingle`	4	Single subtype
`vbDouble`	5	Double subtype
`vbCurrency`	6	Currency subtype
`vbDate`	7	Date subtype
`vbString`	8	String subtype
`vbObject`	9	Object
`vbError`	10	Error subtype
`vbBoolean`	11	Boolean subtype
`vbVariant`	12	Variant (used only for arrays of variants)
`vbDataObject`	13	Data access object
`vbDecimal`	14	Decimal subtype
`vbByte`	17	Byte subtype
`vbArray`	8192	Array

Control Flow

`For...Next`–executes a block of code a specified number of times.

```
Dim intSalary (10)
For intCounter = 0 to 10
   intSalary (intCounter) = 20000
Next
```

`For Each...Next Statement`–repeats a block of code for each element in an array or collection.

```
For Each Item In Request.QueryString("MyControl")
  Response.Write Item & "<BR>"
Next
```

`Do...Loop`—executes a block of code while a condition is true or until a condition becomes true.

```
Do While strDayOfWeek <> "Saturday" And strDayOfWeek <> "Sunday"
   MsgBox ("Get Up! Time for work")
   ...
Loop

Do
   MsgBox ("Get Up! Time for work")
   ...
Loop Until strDayOfWeek = "Saturday" Or strDayOfWeek = "Sunday"
```

`If...Then...Else`—used to run various blocks of code depending on conditions.

```
If intAge < 20 Then
   MsgBox ("You're just a slip of a thing!")
ElseIf intAge < 40 Then
   MsgBox ("You're in your prime!")
Else
   MsgBox ("You're older and wiser")
End If
```

`Select Case`—used to replace `If...Then...Else` statements where there are many conditions.

```
Select Case intAge
Case 21,22,23,24,25,26
   MsgBox ("You're in your prime")
Case 40
   MsgBox ("You're fulfilling your dreams")
Case 65
   MsgBox ("Time for a new challenge")
End Select
```

Note that `Select Case` can only be used with precise conditions and not with a range of conditions.

`While...Wend`—executes a block of code while a condition is true.

```
While strDayOfWeek <> "Saturday" AND strDayOfWeek <> "Sunday"
   MsgBox ("Get Up! Time for work")
   ...
Wend
```

Functions

VBScript contains several functions that can be used to manipulate and examine variables. These have been subdivided into the general categories of:

 Conversion Functions

 Date/Time Functions

- Math Functions
- Object Management Functions
- Script Engine Identification Functions
- String Functions
- Variable Testing Functions

For a full description of each function, and the parameters it requires, see the VBScript Help file. This is installed by default in your **Docs/ASPDocs/VBS/VBScript** subfolder of your IIS installation directory.

Conversion Functions

These functions are used to convert values in variables between different types:

Function	Description
Asc	Returns the numeric ANSI code number of the first character in a string.
AscB	As above, but provided for use with byte data contained in a string. Returns result from the first byte only.
AscW	As above, but provided for Unicode characters. Returns the **Wide** character code, avoiding the conversion from Unicode to ANSI.
Chr	Returns a string made up of the ANSI character matching the number supplied.
ChrB	As above, but provided for use with byte data contained in a string. Always returns a single byte.
ChrW	As above, but provided for Unicode characters. Its argument is a **Wide** character code, thereby avoiding the conversion from ANSI to Unicode.
CBool	Returns the argument value converted to a **Variant** of subtype **Boolean**.
CByte	Returns the argument value converted to a **Variant** of subtype **Byte**.
CDate	Returns the argument value converted to a **Variant** of subtype **Date**.
CDbl	Returns the argument value converted to a **Variant** of subtype **Double**.
CInt	Returns the argument value converted to a **Variant** of subtype **Integer**.
CLng	Returns the argument value converted to a **Variant** of subtype **Long**
CSng	Returns the argument value converted to a **Variant** of subtype **Single**

Table continued on following page

Function	Description
`CStr`	Returns the argument value converted to a `Variant` of subtype `String`.
`Fix`	Returns the integer (whole) part of a number.
`Hex`	Returns a string representing the hexadecimal value of a number.
`Int`	Returns the integer (whole) portion of a number.
`Oct`	Returns a string representing the octal value of a number.
`Round`	Returns a number rounded to a specified number of decimal places.
`Sgn`	Returns an integer indicating the sign of a number.

Date/Time Functions

These functions return date or time values from the computer's system clock, or manipulate existing values:

Function	Description
`Date`	Returns the current system date.
`DateAdd`	Returns a date to which a specified time interval has been added.
`DateDiff`	Returns the number of days, weeks, or years between two dates.
`DatePart`	Returns just the day, month or year of a given date.
`DateSerial`	Returns a `Variant` of subtype `Date` for a specified year, month, and day.
`DateValue`	Returns a `Variant` of subtype `Date`.
`Day`	Returns a number between `1` and `31` representing the day of the month.
`Hour`	Returns a number between `0` and `23` representing the hour of the day.
`Minute`	Returns a number between `0` and `59` representing the minute of the hour.
`Month`	Returns a number between `1` and `12` representing the month of the year.
`MonthName`	Returns the name of the specified month as a string.
`Now`	Returns the current date and time.
`Second`	Returns a number between `0` and `59` representing the second of the minute.
`Time`	Returns a `Variant` of subtype `Date` indicating the current system time.

Function	Description
`TimeSerial`	Returns a `Variant` of subtype `Date` for a specific hour, minute, and second.
`TimeValue`	Returns a `Variant` of subtype `Date` containing the time.
`Weekday`	Returns a number representing the day of the week.
`WeekdayName`	Returns the name of the specified day of the week as a string.
`Year`	Returns a number representing the year.

Math Functions

These functions perform mathematical operations on variables containing numerical values:

Function	Description
`Atn`	Returns the arctangent of a number.
`Cos`	Returns the cosine of an angle.
`Exp`	Returns `e` (the base of natural logarithms) raised to a power.
`Log`	Returns the natural logarithm of a number.
`Randomize`	Initializes the random-number generator.
`Rnd`	Returns a random number.
`Sin`	Returns the sine of an angle.
`Sqr`	Returns the square root of a number.
`Tan`	Returns the tangent of an angle.

Object Management Functions

These functions are used to manipulate objects, where applicable:

Function	Description
`CreateObject`	Creates and returns a reference to an ActiveX or OLE Automation object.
`GetObject`	Returns a reference to an ActiveX or OLE Automation object.
`LoadPicture`	Returns a picture object.

Script Engine Identification

These functions return the version of the scripting engine:

Function	Description
ScriptEngine	A string containing the major, minor, and build version numbers of the scripting engine.
ScriptEngineMajorVersion	The major version of the scripting engine, as a number.
ScriptEngineMinorVersion	The minor version of the scripting engine, as a number.
ScriptEngineBuildVersion	The build version of the scripting engine, as a number.

String Functions

These functions are used to manipulate string values in variables:

Function	Description
Filter	Returns an array from a string array, based on specified filter criteria.
FormatCurrency	Returns a string formatted as currency value.
FormatDateTime	Returns a string formatted as a date or time.
FormatNumber	Returns a string formatted as a number.
FormatPercent	Returns a string formatted as a percentage.
InStr	Returns the position of the first occurrence of one string within another.
InStrB	As above, but provided for use with byte data contained in a string. Returns the byte position instead of the character position.
InstrRev	As InStr, but starts from the end of the string.
Join	Returns a string created by joining the strings contained in an array.
LCase	Returns a string that has been converted to lowercase.
Left	Returns a specified number of characters from the left end of a string.
LeftB	As above, but provided for use with byte data contained in a string. Uses that number of bytes instead of that number of characters.
Len	Returns the length of a string or the number of bytes needed for a variable.
LenB	As above, but is provided for use with byte data contained in a string. Returns the number of bytes in the string instead of characters.
LTrim	Returns a copy of a string without leading spaces.

Function	Description
`Mid`	Returns a specified number of characters from a string.
`MidB`	As above, but provided for use with byte data contained in a string. Uses that numbers of bytes instead of that number of characters.
`Replace`	Returns a string in which a specified substring has been replaced with another substring a specified number of times.
`Right`	Returns a specified number of characters from the right end of a string.
`RightB`	As above, but provided for use with byte data contained in a string. Uses that number of bytes instead of that number of characters.
`RTrim`	Returns a copy of a string without trailing spaces.
`Space`	Returns a string consisting of the specified number of spaces.
`Split`	Returns a one-dimensional array of a specified number of substrings.
`StrComp`	Returns a value indicating the result of a string comparison.
`String`	Returns a string of the length specified made up of a repeating character.
`StrReverse`	Returns a string in which the character order of a string is reversed.
`Trim`	Returns a copy of a string without leading or trailing spaces.
`UCase`	Returns a string that has been converted to uppercase.

Variable Testing Functions

These functions are used to determine the type of information stored in a variable:

Function	Description
`IsArray`	Returns a **`Boolean`** value indicating whether a variable is an array.
`IsDate`	Returns a **`Boolean`** value indicating whether an expression can be converted to a date.
`IsEmpty`	Returns a **`Boolean`** value indicating whether a variable has been initialized.
`IsNull`	Returns a **`Boolean`** value indicating whether an expression contains no valid data

Table continued on following page

Function	Description
`IsNumeric`	Returns a **Boolean** value indicating whether an expression can be evaluated as a number.
`IsObject`	Returns a **Boolean** value indicating whether an expression references a valid ActiveX or OLE Automation object.
`VarType`	Returns a number indicating the subtype of a variable.

Variable Declarations

`Dim`—declares a variable.

Error Handling

`On Error Resume Next`—indicates that if an error occurs, control should continue at the next statement.
`Err`—this is the error object that provides information about run-time errors.

Error handling is very limited in VBScript and the **`Err`** object must be tested explicitly to determine if an error has occurred.

Input/Output

This consists of **`Msgbox`** for output and **`InputBox`** for input:

MsgBox

This displays a message, and can return a value indicating which button was clicked.

```
MsgBox "Hello There",20,"Hello Message","c:\windows\MyHelp.hlp",123
```

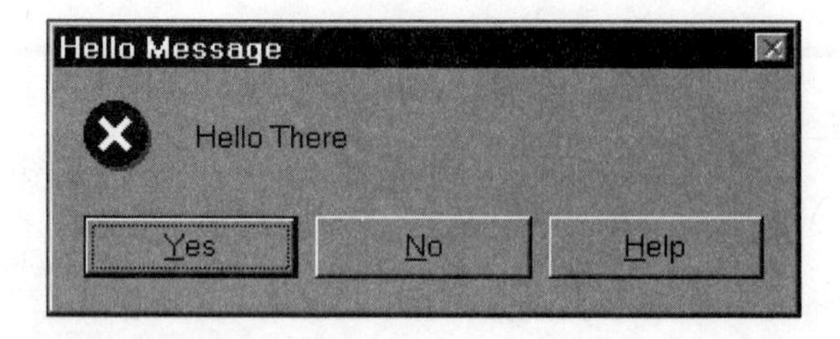

The parameters are:
`"Hello There"`—this contains the text of the message and is obligatory.
`20`—this determines which icon and buttons appear on the message box.

`"Hello Message"`—this contains the text that will appear as the title of the message box.
`"c:\windows\MyHelp.hlp"`—this adds a Help button to the message box and determines the help file that is opened if the button is clicked.
`123`–this is a reference to the particular help topic that will be displayed if the Help button is clicked.

The value of the icon and buttons parameter is determined using the following tables:

Constant	Value	Buttons
`vbOKOnly`	0	OK
`vbOKCancel`	1	OK Cancel
`vbAbortRetryIngnore`	2	Abort Retry Ignore
`vbYesNoCancel`	3	Yes No Cancel
`vbYesNo`	4	Yes No
`vbRetryCancel`	5	Retry Cancel
`vbDefaultButton1`	0	The first button from the left is the default.
`vbDefaultButton2`	256	The second button from the left is the default.
`vbDefaultButton3`	512	The third button from the left is the default.
`vbDefaultButton4`	768	The fourth button from the left is the default.

Constant	Value	Description	Icon
`vbCritical`	16	Critical Message	
`vbQuestion`	32	Questioning Message	
`vbExclamation`	48	Warning Message	
`vbInformation`	64	Informational Message	

Constant	Value	Description
vbApplicationModal	0	Just the application stops until user clicks a button.
vbSystemModal	4096	Whole system stops until user clicks a button.

To specify which buttons and icon are displayed you simply add the relevant values. So, in our example we add together **4 + 16** to display the Yes and No buttons, with Yes as the default, and to show the **Critical** icon.

You can determine which button the user clicked by assigning the return code of the **MsgBox** function to a variable:

```
intButtonClicked = MsgBox ("Hello There",35,"Hello Message")
```

Notice that brackets enclose the **MsgBox** parameters when used in this format. The following table determines the value assigned to the variable **intButtonClicked**:

Constant	Value	Button Clicked
vbOK	1	OK
vbCancel	2	Cancel
vbAbort	3	Abort
vbRetry	4	Retry
vbIgnore	5	Ignore
vbYes	6	Yes
vbNo	7	No

InputBox

This accepts text entry from the user and returns it as a string.

```
strTextEntered = InputBox ("Please enter your name","Login","John Smith",500, 500)
```

"Please enter your name"—this is the prompt displayed in the input box.
"Login"—this is the text displayed as the title of the input box.
"John Smith"—this is the default value displayed in the input box.
500—specifies the x position of the input box.
500—specifies the y position of the input box.

As with the **MsgBox** function, you can also specify a help file and topic to add a Help button to the input box.

Procedures

`Call`—optional method of calling a subroutine.
`Function`—used to declare a function.
`Sub`—used to declare a subroutine.

Other Keywords

`Rem`—old style method of adding comments to code.
`Option Explicit`—forces you to declare a variable before it can be used.

Visual Basic Run-time Error Codes

The following error codes also apply to VBA code and many will not be appropriate to an application built completely around VBScript. However, if you have built your own components then these error codes may well be brought up when such components are used.

Code	Description
3	Return without GoSub
5	Invalid procedure call
6	Overflow
7	Out of memory
9	Subscript out of range
10	This array is fixed or temporarily locked
11	Division by zero
13	Type mismatch
14	Out of string space
16	Expression too complex
17	Can't perform requested operation
18	User interrupt occurred
20	Resume without error
28	Out of stack space
35	Sub or Function not defined
47	Too many DLL application clients
48	Error in loading DLL
49	Bad DLL calling convention
51	Internal error
52	Bad file name or number
53	File not found
54	Bad file mode
55	File already open
57	Device I/O error
58	File already exists
59	Bad record length
61	Disk full
62	Input past end of file
63	Bad record number
67	Too many files
68	Device unavailable
70	Permission denied
71	Disk not ready
74	Can't rename with different drive
75	Path/File access error
76	Path not found

Table continued on following page

Code	Description
322	Can't create necessary temporary file
325	Invalid format in resource file
380	Invalid property value
423	Property or method not found
424	Object required
429	OLE Automation server can't create object
430	Class doesn't support OLE Automation
432	File name or class name not found during OLE Automation operation
438	Object doesn't support this property or method
440	OLE Automation error
442	Connection to type library or object library for remote process has been lost. Press OK for dialog to remove reference.
443	OLE Automation object does not have a default value
445	Object doesn't support this action
446	Object doesn't support named arguments
447	Object doesn't support current locale setting
448	Named argument not found
449	Argument not optional
450	Wrong number of arguments or invalid property assignment
451	Object not a collection
452	Invalid ordinal
453	Specified DLL function not found

Code	Description
454	Code resource not found
455	Code resource lock error
457	This key is already associated with an element of this collection
458	Variable uses an OLE Automation type not supported in Visual Basic
481	Invalid picture
500	Variable is undefined
501	Cannot assign to variable
1001	Out of memory
1002	Syntax error
1003	Expected ':'
1004	Expected ';'
1005	Expected '('
1006	Expected ')'
1007	Expected ']'
1008	Expected '{'
1009	Expected '}'
1010	Expected identifier
1011	Expected '='
1012	Expected 'If'
1013	Expected 'To'
1014	Expected 'End'
1015	Expected 'Function'
1016	Expected 'Sub'
1017	Expected 'Then'
1018	Expected 'Wend'
1019	Expected 'Loop'
1020	Expected 'Next'
1021	Expected 'Case'
1022	Expected 'Select'
1023	Expected expression
1024	Expected statement
1025	Expected end of statement
1026	Expected integer constant

Code	Description
1027	Expected 'While' or 'Until'
1028	Expected 'While', 'Until' or end of statement
1029	Too many locals or arguments
1030	Identifier too long
1031	Invalid number
1032	Invalid character
1033	Un-terminated string constant
1034	Un-terminated comment
1035	Nested comment
1036	'Me' cannot be used outside of a procedure
1037	Invalid use of 'Me' keyword
1038	'loop' without 'do'
1039	Invalid 'exit' statement
1040	Invalid 'for' loop control variable
1041	Variable redefinition
1042	Must be first statement on the line
1043	Cannot assign to non-ByVal argument

For more information about VBScript, visit Microsoft's VBScript site at:

`http://www.microsoft.com/vbscript/us/techinfo/vbsdocs.htm`

JavaScript Reference

General Information

JavaScript is included in an HTML document with the **<SCRIPT>** tag. Here's an example:

```
<HTML>
<HEAD>

<!-- wrap script in comments
<SCRIPT LANGUAGE = "JavaScript">
script code goes here
</SCRIPT>
-->

</HEAD>
<BODY>
HTML goes here
</BODY>
</HTML>
```

The following points should be kept in mind when programming in JavaScript:

- The main core of your JavaScript code should be put in the <HEAD> section of the document. This ensures that all the code has been loaded before an attempt is made to execute it. "On-the-fly" scripts that generate HTML at specific parts of the document can be placed exactly as required.
- The script code should be wrapped in a comment tag, as this stops older (non-JavaScript) browsers from trying to read the code.
- JavaScript is case-sensitive.
- In Javascript, semicolons (;) are used to separate statements when they are on the same line. If the statements are not on the same line, semicolons are optional.

New in JavaScript Version 1.2

The changes to the language that appear in version 1.2 are:

- The statement **`new Array(`***value***`)`** creates a new array with the first element (indexed zero) set to the specified value. You can create a new array with several elements by listing them in the brackets separated by commas, using **`new Array(`***value0*, *value1*, *value2*, **`...)`**.
- The **`Number`** object now returns **`NaN`** (not a number) if a string being converted is not a legal number, rather than an error.
- The equality operators `==` and `!=` no longer try and convert the values to the same type before comparison. They are just compared 'as is'.
- The new **`break`** and **`continue`** statements can be used to jump out of a loop or other construct, and continue execution at a specific line:

```
while (count < 4)
{
  if (anothervalue == 2 ) break skipitall;
  somevalue = somevalue + anothervalue;
}
skipitall :
//execution continues here outside the loop
```

```
while (count < 4)
{
  if (anothervalue == 2 ) continue skipit;
  somevalue = somevalue + anothervalue;
  skipit :
  //execution continues here within the loop
}
```

- JavaScript now contains the **`do..while`** construct and the **`switch`** construct:

```
do
  somevalue = somevalue + anothervalue;
while (anothervalue != 2 );
```

```
switch (language)
{
  case "Java" :
    alert("One program for all.");
    break;
  case "C" :
    alert("Speed is king.");
    break;
  case "VB" :
    alert("Anyone can do it.");
}
```

- The **`String`** object has three new methods, **`charCodeAt`**, **`fromCharCode`**, and **`substr`**. **`charCodeAt`** returns the ASCII code of the character at the specified position, **`fromCharCode`** constructs a string from a comma-separated list of ASCII code values, and **`substr`** returns a specified number of characters from a string:

```
MyString = "ABCDE";
alert(MyString.charCodeAt(2))    // produces 66 (decimal).
```

```
MyString.fromCharCode(65, 66, 67)    // returns "ABC"
```

```
MyString = "ABCDE";
MyString.substr(2, 5)    // returns "BCD"
```

Other changes are:

- the **substring** method no longer swaps over the indexes when the first is greater than the second
- the **sort** method now works on all platforms and converts undefined elements to null and sorts them to the top of the array
- the **split** method now removes more than one white-space character when splitting a string
- the **toString** method now converts the object or array into a string literal

Values

JavaScript recognizes the following data types:

- **strings**—"Hello World"
- **numbers**—both integers (86) and decimal values (86.235)
- **boolean**—true or false

A null (*no value*) value is assigned with the keyword **null**.

JavaScript also makes use of 'special characters' in a similar way to the C++ programming language:

Character	Function
\n	newline
\t	tab
\f	form feed
\b	backspace
\r	carriage return

You may 'escape' other characters by preceding them with a backslash (\), to prevent the browser from trying to interpret them. This is most commonly used for quotes and backslashes, or to include a character by using its octal (base 8) value:

```
document.write("This shows a \"quote\" in a string.");
document.write("This is a backslash: \\");
document.write("This is a space character: \040.");
```

Variables

JavaScript is a **loosely typed** language. This means that variables do not have an explicitly defined variable type. Instead, every variable can hold values of various types. Conversions between types are done automatically when needed, as this example demonstrates:

```
x = 55;      // x is assigned to be the integer 55
y = "55"; // y is assigned to be the string "55"
y = '55';    // an alternative using single quotes

z = 1 + y;
<!-- even though y is a string, it will be automatically
 converted to the appropriate integer value so that 1 may
 be added to it. -->

document.write(x);
<!-- the number 55 will be written to the screen. Even
 though x is an integer and not a string, Javascript will
 make the  necessary conversion for you. -->

n = 3.14159;  // assigning a real (fractional) number
n = 0546;     // numbers starting 0 assumed to be octal
n = 0xFFEC;   // numbers starting 0x assumed to be hex
n = 2.145E-5; // using exponential notation
```

Variable names must start with either a letter or an underscore. Beyond the first letter, variables may contain any combination of letters, underscores, and digits. JavaScript is case sensitive, so `this_variable` is not the same as `This_Variable`.

Variables do not need to be declared before they are used. However, you may use the `var` keyword to explicitly define a variable. This is especially useful when there is the possibility of conflicting variable names. When in doubt, use `var`.

```
var x = "55";
```

Assignment Operators

The following operators are used to make assignments in JavaScript:

Operator	Example	Result
=	x = y	x equals y
+=	x += y	x equals x plus y
-=	x -= y	x equals x minus y
*=	x *= y	x equals x multiplied by y
/=	x /= y	x equals x divided by y
%=	x %= y	x equals x modulus y

Each operator assigns the value on the right to the variable on the left.

```
x = 100;
y = 10;
x += y;  // x now is equal to 110
```

Equality Operators

Operator	Meaning
==	is equal to
!=	is not equal to
>	is greater than
>=	is greater than or equal to
<	is less than
<=	is less than or equal to

Other Operators

Operator	Meaning
+	Addition
-	Subtraction
*	Multiplication
/	Division
%	Modulus
++	Increment
--	Decrement
-	Unary Negation

<table>
<tr><th>Operator</th><th>Meaning</th></tr>
<tr><td>& or AND</td><td>Bitwise AND</td></tr>
<tr><td>| or OR</td><td>Bitwise OR</td></tr>
<tr><td>^ or XOR</td><td>Bitwise XOR</td></tr>
<tr><td><<</td><td>Bitwise left shift</td></tr>
<tr><td>>></td><td>Bitwise right shift</td></tr>
<tr><td>>>></td><td>Zero-fill right shift</td></tr>
<tr><td>&&</td><td>Logical AND</td></tr>
<tr><td>||</td><td>Logical OR</td></tr>
<tr><td>!</td><td>Not</td></tr>
</table>

String Operators

Operator	Meaning
+	Concatenates strings, so `"abc" + "def"` is `"abcdef"`
>	Compare strings in a case-sensitive way. A string is 'greater' than
>=	another based on the Latin ASCII code values of the characters,
<	starting from the left of the string. So `"DEF"` is greater than `"ABC"`
<=	and `"DEE"`, but less than `"abc"`.

Comments

Operator	Meaning
`// a comment`	A single line comment
`/* this text is a multi-line comment */`	A multi-line comment

Input/Output

In JavaScript, there are three different methods of providing information to the user, and getting a response back.

Alert

This displays a message with an OK button.

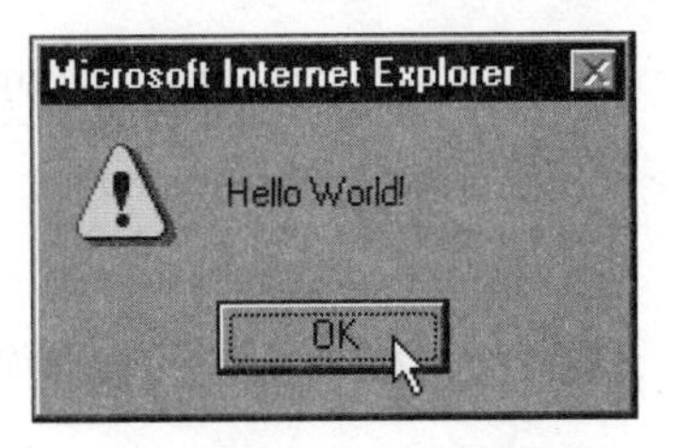


```
alert("Hello World!");
```

Confirm

Displays a message with both an OK and a Cancel button. True is returned if the OK button is pressed, and false is returned if the Cancel button is pressed.

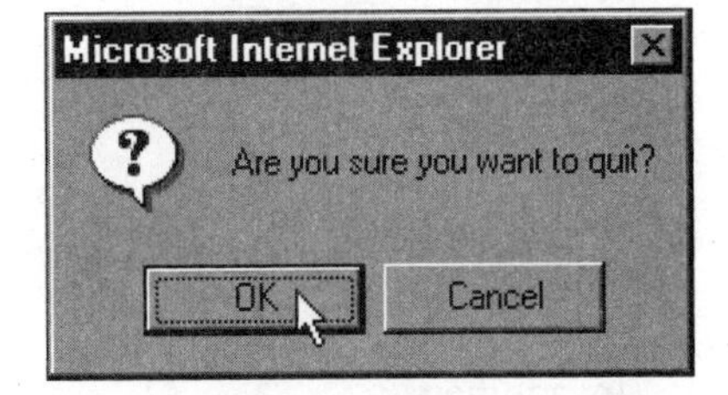


```
confirm("Are you sure you want to quit?");
```

Prompt

Displays a message and a text box for user input. The first string argument forms the text that is to be displayed above the text box. The second argument is a string, integer, or property of an existing object, which represents the default value to display inside the box. If the second argument is not specified, "<undefined>" is displayed inside the text box.

The string typed into the box is returned if the OK button is pressed. False is returned if the Cancel button is pressed

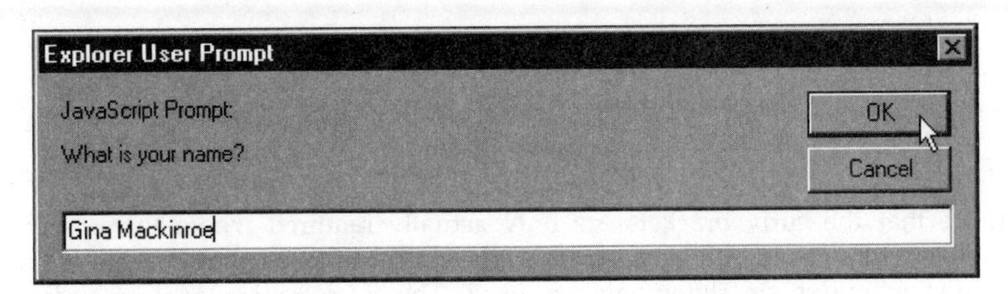


```
prompt("What is your name?", "");
```

Control Flow

There are two ways of controlling the flow of a program in JavaScript. The first involves **conditional** statements, which follow either one branch of the program or another. The second way is to use a **repeated iteration** of a set of statements.

Conditional Statements

JavaScript has one conditional statement:

`if..then..else`–used to run various blocks of code—depending on conditions. These statements have the following general form in JavaScript:

if (*condition*)
{
code to be executed if condition is true
}
else
{
code to be executed if condition is false
};

In addition:

- The `else` portion is optional.
- `if` statements may be nested.
- Multiple statements must be enclosed by braces.

Here is an example:

```
person_type = prompt("What are you ?", "");
if (person_type == "cat")
  alert("Here, have some cat food.")
else
{
  if (person_type == "dog")
    alert("Here, have some dog food.")
  else
  {
    if (person_type == "human")
      alert("Here have some, er, human food!");
  };
};
```

Notice that the curly brackets are only actually required where there is more than one statement within the block. Like many other constructs, they can be omitted where single statements are used. The final semi-colon is mandatory:

if (*condition*)
code to be executed if condition is true
else
code to be executed if condition is false;

Loop Statements

`for`–executes a block of code a specified number of times.

```
for (i = 0; i = 10; i++)
{
  document.write(i);
}
```

`while`—executes a block of code while a condition is true.

```
while (condition)
{
  statements to execute ...
}
```

`break`—will cause an exit from a loop regardless of the condition statement.

```
x = 0;
while (x != 10)
{
  n = prompt("Enter a number or 'q' to quit", "");
  if (n == "q")
  {
    alert("See ya");
    break;
  }
}
```

`continue`—will cause the loop to jump immediately back to the condition statement.

```
x = 0;
while (x != 1)
{
  if (!(confirm("Should I add 1 to n ?")))
  {
    continue;
    // the following x++ is never executed
    x++;
  }
x++;
}
alert("Bye");
```

Built-in Functions

JavaScript provides a number of built-in functions that can be accessed within code.

Function	Description
`escape(`*char*`)`	Returns a string of the form `%`*XX* where *XX* is the ASCII encoded value of *char*.
`eval(`*expression*`)`	Returns the result of evaluating the numeric expression *expression*
`isNaN(`*value*`)`	Returns a Boolean value of **`true`** if *value* is not a legal number.
`parseFloat(`*string*`)`	Converts *string* to a floating-point number.
`ParseInt(`*string*`, `*base*`)`	Converts *string* to an integer number with the base of *base*.
`typeOf(`*object*`)`	Returns the data type of *object* as a string, such as **`"boolean"`**, **`"function"`**, etc.

Built-in Objects

JavaScript provides a set of built-in data-type objects, which have their own set of properties, and methods—and which can be accessed with JavaScript code.

Array Object

The **`Array`** object specifies a method of creating arrays and working with them. To create a new array, use:

```
cats = new Array();     // create an empty array
cats = new Array(10);   // create an array of 10 items

// or create and fill an array with values in one go:
cats = new Array("Boo Boo", "Purrcila", "Sam", "Lucky");
```

Properties	Description
`length`	A read/write Integer value specifying the number of elements in the array.

Methods	Description
`join([`*string*`])`	Returns a string containing each element of the array, optionally separated with *string*.
`reverse()`	Reverses the order of the array.
`sort([`*function*`])`	Sorts the array, optionally based upon the results of a function specified by *function*.

Early versions of JavaScript had no explicit array structure. However, JavaScript's object mechanisms allow for easy creation of arrays:

```
function MakeArray(n)
{
  this.length = n;
  for (var i = 1; i <= n; i++)
    this[i] = 0;
  return this
}
```

With this function included in your script, you can create arrays with:

```
cats = new MakeArray(20);
```

You can then populate the array like this:

```
cats[1] = "Boo Boo";
cats[2] = "Purrcila";
cats[3] = "Sam";
cats[4] = "Lucky";
```

Boolean Object

The **`Boolean`** object is used to store simple yes/no, true/false values. To create a new Boolean object, use the syntax:

```
MyAnswer = new Boolean([value])
```

If ***`value`*** is **`0`**, **`null`**, omitted, or an empty string the new Boolean object will have the value **`false`**. All other values, *including the string* **`"false"`**, create an object with the value **`true`**.

Methods	Description
`toString()`	Returns the value of the Boolean as the string **`"true"`** or **`"false"`**.
`valueOf()`	Returns the primitive numeric value of the object for conversion in calculations.

Date Object

The **`Date`** object provides a method for working with dates and times inside of JavaScript. New instances of the **`Date`** object are invoked with:

```
newDateObject = new Date([dateInfo])
```

`dateInfo` is an optional specification for the date to set in the new object. If it is not specified, the current date and time are used. ***`dateInfo`*** can use any of the following formats:

milliseconds (*since midnight GMT on January 1st 1970*)
year, month, day (e.g. 1997, 0, 27 is 27th Jan 1997)
year, month, day, hours, minutes, seconds
month day, year hours:minutes:seconds
(e.g. September 23, 1997 08:25:30)

Methods	Description
`getDate()`	Returns the day of the month as an Integer between 1 and 31.
`getDay()`	Returns the day of the week as an Integer between 0 (Sunday) and 6 (Saturday).
`getHours()`	Returns the hours as an Integer between 0 and 23.
`getMinutes()`	Returns the minutes as an Integer between 0 and 59.
`getMonth()`	Returns the month as an Integer between 0 (January) and 11 (December).
`getSeconds()`	Returns the seconds as an Integer between 0 and 59.
`getTime()`	Returns the number of milliseconds between January 1, 1970 at 00:00:00 GMT and the current `Date` object as an Integer.
`getTimeZoneOffset()`	Returns the number of minutes difference between local time and GMT as an Integer.
`getYear()`	Returns the year (generally minus 1900 - i.e. only two digits) as an Integer.
`parse(`*dateString*`)`	Returns the number of milliseconds in a date string, since Jan. 1, 1970 00:00:00 GMT.
`setDate(`*dayValue*`)`	Sets the day of the month where *dayValue* is an Integer between 1 and 31.
`setHours(`*hoursValue*`)`	Sets the hours where *hoursValue* is an Integer between 0 and 59.
`setMinutes(`*minutesValue*`)`	Sets the minutes where *minutesValue* is an Integer between 0 and 59.
`setMonth(`*monthValue*`)`	Sets the month where *monthValue* is an Integer between 0 and 11.
`setSeconds(`*secondsValue*`)`	Sets the seconds where *secondsValue* is an Integer between 0 and 59.
`setTime(`*timeValue*`)`	Sets the value of a `Date` object where *timeValue* is and integer representing the number of milliseconds in a date string, since Jan. 1, 1970 00:00:00 GMT.
`setYear(`*yearValue*`)`	Sets the year where *yearValue* is an Integer (generally) greater than 1900.
`toGMTString()`	Converts a date from local time to GMT, and returns it as a string.
`toLocaleString()`	Converts a date from GMT to local time, and returns it as a string.
`UTC(`*year*`, `*month*`, `*day* `[,`*hrs*`] [,`*min*`] [,`*sec*`])`	Returns the number of milliseconds in a date object, since Jan. 1, 1970 00:00:00 Universal Coordinated Time (GMT).

Function Object

The **Function** object provides a mechanism for compiling JavaScript code as a function. A new function is invoked with the syntax:

```
functionName = new Function(arg1, arg2, ..., functionCode)
```

where ***arg1***, ***arg2***, etc. are the arguments for the function object being created, and ***functionCode*** is a string containing the body of the function. This can be a series of JavaScript statements separated by semi-colons.

Properties	Description
`arguments[]`	A reference to the **Arguments** array that holds the arguments that were provided when the function was called.
`caller`	Specifies the function that called the **Function** object.
`prototype`	Provides a way for adding properties to a **Function** object.

Arguments Object

The **Arguments** object is list (array) of arguments in a **Function** object.

Properties	Description
`length`	An Integer specifying the number of arguments provided to the function when it was called.

Math Object

Provides a set of properties and methods for working with mathematical constants and functions. Simply reference the **Math** object, then the method or property required:

```
MyArea = Math.PI * MyRadius * MyRadius;
MyResult = Math.floor(MyNumber);
```

Properties	Description
`E`	Euler's Constant *e* (the base of natural logarithms).
`LN10`	The value of the natural logarithm of 10.
`LN2`	The value of the natural logarithm of 2.
`LOG10E`	The value of the natural logarithm of E.
`LOG2E`	The value of the base 2 logarithm of E.
`PI`	The value of the constant π (pi).
`SQRT1_2`	The value of the square root of a half.
`SQRT`	The value of the square root of two.

Methods	Description
`abs(`*number*`)`	Returns the absolute value of *number*.
`acos(`*number*`)`	Returns the arc cosine of *number*.
`asin(`*number*`)`	Returns the arc sine of *number*.
`atan(`*number*`)`	Returns the arc tangent of *number*.
`atan2(`*x, y*`)`	Returns the angle of the polar coordinate of a point *x*, *y* from the *x*-axis.
`ceil(`*number*`)`	Returns the next largest Integer greater than *number*, i.e. rounds up.
`cos(`*number*`)`	Returns the cosine of *number*.
`exp(`*number*`)`	Returns the value of *number* as the exponent of *e*, as in e^{number}.
`floor(`*number*`)`	Returns the next smallest Integer less that *number*, i.e. rounds down.
`log(`*number*`)`	Returns the natural logarithm of *number*.
`max(`*num1, num2*`)`	Returns the greater of the two values *num1* and *num2*.
`min(`*num1, num2*`)`	Returns the smaller of the two values *num1* and *num2*.
`pow(`*num1, num2*`)`	Returns the value of *num1* to the power of *num2*.
`random()`	Returns a random number between 0 and 1.
`round(`*number*`)`	Returns the closest Integer to *number* i.e. rounds up *or* down to the nearest whole number.
`sin(`*number*`)`	Returns the sin of *number*.
`sqrt(`*number*`)`	Returns the square root of *number*.
`tan(`*number*`)`	Returns the tangent of *number*.

Number Object

The Number Object provides a set of properties that are useful when working with numbers:

```
MyArea = Math.PI * MyRadius * MyRadius;
MyResult = Math.floor(MyNumber);
```

Properties	Description
`MAX_VALUE`	The maximum numeric value represented in JavaScript (~1.79E+308).
`MIN_VALUE`	The minimum numeric value represented in JavaScript (~2.22E-308).
`NaN`	A value meaning 'Not A Number'.
`NEGATIVE_INFINITY`	A special value for negative infinity ("-Infinity").
`POSITIVE_INFINITY`	A special value for infinity ("Infinity").

Methods	Description
toString([*radix_base*]**)**	Returns the value of the number as a string to a radix (base) of 10, unless specified otherwise in *radix_base*.
valueOf()	Returns the primitive numeric value of the object.

String Object

The **String** object provides a set of methods for text manipulation. To create a new string object, the syntax is:

```
MyString = new String([value])
```

where ***value*** is the optional text to place in the string when it is created. If this is a number, it is converted into a string first.

Properties	Description
length	An Integer representing the number of characters in the string.

Methods	Description
anchor("*nameAttribute***")**	Returns the original string surrounded by **<A>** and **</A>** anchor tags, with the **NAME** attribute set to "*nameAttribute*".
big()	Returns the original string enclosed in **<BIG>** and **</BIG>** tags.
blink()	Returns the original string enclosed in **<BLINK>** and **</BLINK>** tags.
bold()	Returns the original string enclosed in **<B>** and **</B>** tags.
charAt(*index***)**	Returns the single character at position *index* within the **String** object.
fixed()	Returns the original string enclosed in **<TT>** and **</TT>** tags.
fontcolor("*color***")**	Returns the original string surrounded by **<FONT>** and **</FONT>** tags, with the **COLOR** attribute set to "*color*".
fontsize("*size***")**	Returns the original string surrounded by **<FONT>** and **</FONT>** anchor tags, with the **SIZE** attribute set to "*size*".
indexOf(*searchValue* [,*fromIndex*]**)**	Returns first occurrence of the string *searchValue* starting at index *fromIndex*.
italics()	Returns the original string enclosed in **<I>** and **</I>** tags.

Methods	Description
`lastIndexOf(`*searchValue* `[,`*fromIndex*`])`	Returns the index of the last occurrence of the string *searchValue*, searching backwards from index *fromIndex*.
`link("`*hrefAttribute*`")`	Returns the original string surrounded by **<A>** and **</A>** link tags, with the **HREF** attribute set to "*hrefAttribute*".
`small()`	Returns the original string enclosed in **<SMALL>** and **</SMALL>** tags.
`split(`*separator*`)`	Returns an array of strings created by separating the **String** object at every occurrence of *separator*.
`strike()`	Returns the original string enclosed in **<STRIKE>** and **</STRIKE>** tags.
`sub()`	Returns the original string enclosed in **_{** and **}** tags.
`substring(`*indexA*`,` *indexB*`)`	Returns the sub-string of the original **String** object from the character at *indexA* up to and including the one **before** the character at *indexB*.
`sup()`	Returns the original string enclosed in **^{** and **}** tags.
`toLowerCase()`	Returns the original string with all the characters converted to lowercase.
`toUpperCase()`	Returns the original string with all the characters converted to uppercase.

Reserved Words

The following are reserved words that can't be used for function, method, variable, or object names. Note that while some words in this list are not currently used as JavaScript keywords, they have been reserved for future use.

```
abstract    else        int         super
boolean     extends     interface   switch
break       false       long        synchronized
byte        final       native      this
case        finally     new         throw
catch       float       null        throws
char        for         package     transient
class       function    private     true
const       goto        protected   try
continue    if          public      typeof
default     implements  reset       var
delete      import      return      void
do          in          short       while
double      instanceof  static      with
```

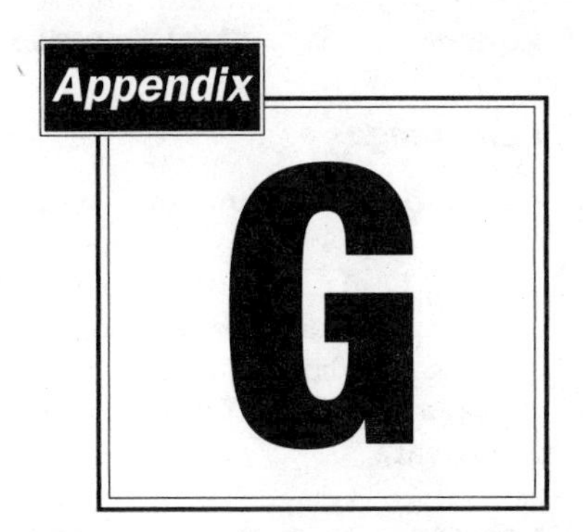

Style Sheet Properties

Over 70 Cascading Style Sheets properties are used in the major browsers. Most of them are in the CSS1 recommendations, but a few have only recently been introduced in the CSS2 public drafts. We've broken up the properties into several major 'groups' and listed which are new in CSS2. We've listed all the properties below (by group), with some of the crucial information for each. We start with a summary of the units of measurement.

Units of Measurement

There are two basic categories of unit: relative and absolute (plus percentages). As a general rule, relative measures are preferred, as using absolute measures requires familiarity with the actual mechanism of display (e.g. what kind of printer, what sort of monitor, etc.).

Relative Units

Values: `em`, `en`, `ex`, `px`

`em`, `en` and `ex` are typographic terms, and refer to the sizes of other characters on display.
`px` refers to a measurement in screen pixels, which is generally only meaningful for display on computer monitors and depends on the user's display resolution setting.
In IE4, `em` and `ex` are the same as `pt`, and `en` is the same as `px`.

Absolute Units

Values: `in`, `cm`, `mm`, `pt`, `pc`

`in` gives the measurement in inches, `cm` gives it in centimetres, `mm` in millimetres, `pt` is in typeface points (72 to an inch), and `pc` is in picas (1 pica equals 12 points). These units are generally only useful when you know what the output medium is going to be, since browsers are allowed to approximate if they must.

Percentage

Values:	Numeric

This is given as a number (with or without a decimal point), and is relative to a length unit (which is usually the font size of the current element). You should note that child elements will inherit the computed value, not the percentage value (so a child will not be 20% of the parent, it will be the same size as the parent).

Listing of Properties

There follows a listing of all the properties for use in Dynamic HTML, together with their JavaScript Style Sheet equivalent, the equivalent scripting property in IE4, possible values, defaults, and other useful information. The properties are divided up into categories—**font** properties, **color** and **background** properties, **text** properties, **size** and **position** properties, **printing** properties, **filter** properties and **other** properties.

Font Properties

font

JSS Equivalent:	not supported
IE4 Scripting Property:	`font`
Values:	`<font-size>`, `[/<line-height>]`, `<font-family>`
Default:	Not defined
Applies to:	All elements
Inherited:	Yes
Percentage?:	Only on `<font-size>` and `<line-height>`

This allows you to set several font properties all at once, with the initial values being determined by the properties being used (e.g. the default for `font-size` is different to the default for `font-family`). This property should be used with multiple values separated by spaces, or a comma if specifying multiple font-families.

font-family

JSS Equivalent:	`fontFamily`
IE4 Scripting Property:	`fontFamily`
Values:	Name of a font family (e.g. New York) or a generic family (e.g. Serif)
Default:	Set by browser
Applies to:	All elements
Inherited:	Yes
Percentage?:	No

You can specify multiple values in order of preference (in case the browser doesn't have the font you want). To do so, simply specify them and separate multiple values with commas. You should end with a generic font-family (allowable values would then be **serif**, **sans-serif**, **cursive**, **fantasy**, or **monospace**). If the font name has spaces in it, you should enclose the name in quotation marks.

font-size

JSS Equivalent:	`fontSize`
IE4 Scripting Property:	`fontSize`
Values:	`<absolute>`, `<relative>`, `<length>`, `<percentage>`
Default:	`medium`
Applies to:	All elements
Inherited:	Yes
Percentage?:	Yes, relative to parent font size

The values for this property can be expressed in several ways:

- Absolute size: legal values are **xx-small**, **x-small**, **small**, **medium**, **large**, **x-large**, **xx-large**
- Relative size: values are **larger**, **smaller**
- Length: values are in any unit of measurement, as described at the beginning of this Section.
- Percentage: values are a percentage of the parent font size

font-style

JSS Equivalent:	`fontStyle`
IE4 Scripting Property:	`fontStyle`
Values:	`normal`, `italic`, or `oblique`
Default:	`normal`
Applies to:	All elements
Inherited:	Yes
Percentage?:	No

This is used to apply styling to your font—if a pre-rendered font is available (e.g. New York Oblique) then that will be used if possible. If not, the styling will be applied electronically.

font-variant

JSS Equivalent:	not supported
IE4 Scripting Property:	`fontVariant`
Values:	`normal`, `small-caps`
Default:	`normal`
Applies to:	All elements
Inherited:	Yes
Percentage?:	No

Normal is the standard appearance, and is therefore set as the default. **Small-caps** uses capital letters that are the same size as normal lowercase letters.

font-weight

JSS Equivalent:	`fontWeight`
IE4 Scripting Property:	`fontWeight`
Values:	`normal`, `bold`, `bolder`, `lighter`—or numeric values from 100 to 900
Default:	`normal`
Applies to:	All elements
Inherited:	Yes
Percentage?:	No

Specifies the 'boldness' of text, which is usually expressed by stroke thickness. If numeric values are used, they must proceed in 100-unit increments (e.g. 250 isn't legal). **`400`** is the same as **`normal`**, and **`700`** is the same as **`bold`**.

Color and Background Properties

color

JSS Equivalent:	`color`
IE4 Scripting Property:	`color`
Values:	Color name or RGB value
Default:	Depends on browser
Applies to:	All elements
Inherited:	Yes
Percentage?:	No

Sets the text color of any element. The color can be specified by name (e.g. green) or by RGB-value. The RGB value can be expressed in several ways; in hex—"#FFFFFF", by percentage—"80%, 20%, 0%", or by value—"255,0,0".

background

JSS Equivalent:	not supported
IE4 Scripting Property:	`background`
Values:	`transparent`, `<color>`, `<URL>`, `<repeat>`, `<scroll>`, `<position>`
Default:	`transparent`
Applies to:	All elements
Inherited:	No
Percentage?:	Yes, will refer to the dimension of the element itself

Specifies the background of the document. **`Transparent`** is the same as no defined background. You can use a solid color, or you can specify the URL for an image to be used. The URL can be absolute or relative, but must be enclosed in parentheses and immediately preceded by **`url`**:

```
BODY { background: url(http://foo.bar.com/image/small.gif) }
```

It is possible to use a color and an image, in which case the image will be overlaid on top of the color. The color can be a single color, or two colors that will be blended together. Images can have several properties set:

- `<repeat>` can be **repeat**, **repeat-x** (where **x** is a number), **repeat-y** (where **y** is a number) and **no-repeat**. If no repeat value is given, then **repeat** is assumed.
- `<scroll>` determines whether the background image will remain fixed, or scroll when the page does. Possible values are **fixed** or **scroll**.
- `<position>` specifies the location of the image on the page. Values are by percentage (horizontal, vertical), by absolute distance (in a unit of measurement, horizontal then vertical), or by keyword (values are **top**, **middle**, **bottom**, **left**, **center**, **right**)

It is also possible to specify different parts of the background properties separately using the next five properties:

background-attachment

JSS Equivalent:	not supported
IE4 Scripting Property:	`backgroundAttachment`
Values:	`fixed`, `scroll`
Default:	`scroll`
Applies to:	All elements
Inherited:	No
Percentage?:	No

Determines whether the background will remain fixed, or scroll when the page does.

background-color

JSS Equivalent:	`backgroundColor`
IE4 Scripting Property:	`backgroundColor`
Values:	`transparent`, `<color>`
Default:	`transparent`
Applies to:	All elements
Inherited:	No
Percentage?:	No

Sets a color for the background. This can be a single color, or two colors blended together. The colors can be specified by name (e.g. green) or by RGB-value (which can be stated in hex "#FFFFFF", by percentage "80%, 20%, 0%", or by value "255,0,0"). The syntax for using two colors is:

```
BODY { background-color: red / blue }
```

background-image

JSS Equivalent:	`backgroundImage`
IE4 Scripting Property:	`backgroundImage`
Values:	`<URL>`, `none`
Default:	`none`
Applies to:	All elements
Inherited:	No
Percentage?:	No

You can specify the URL for an image to be used as the background. The **URL** can be absolute or relative, but must be enclosed in parentheses and immediately preceded by `url`:

background-position

JSS Equivalent:	not supported
Scripting Properties:	**backgroundPosition, backgroundPositionX, backgroundPositionY**
Values:	**<position> <length> top, center, bottom, left, right.**
Default:	**top, left**
Applies to:	All elements
Inherited:	No
Percentage?:	No

Specifies the initial location of the background image on the page using two values, which are defined as a percentage (horizontal, vertical), an absolute distance (in a unit of measurement, horizontal then vertical), or using two of the available keywords.

background-repeat

JSS Equivalent:	not supported
IE4 Scripting Property:	**backgroundRepeat**
Values:	**repeat, repeat-x, repeat-y, no-repeat.**
Default:	**repeat**
Applies to:	All elements
Inherited:	No
Percentage?:	No

Determines whether the image is repeated to fill the page or element. If **repeat-x** or **repeat-y** are used, the image is repeated in only one direction. The default is to repeat the image in both directions.

Text Properties

letter-spacing

JSS Equivalent:	not supported
IE4 Scripting Property:	**letterSpacing**
Values:	**normal, <length>**
Default:	**normal**
Applies to:	All elements
Inherited:	Yes
Percentage?:	No

Sets the distance between letters. The length unit indicates an addition to the default space between characters. Values, if given, should be in units of measurement.

line-height

JSS Equivalent: `lineHeight`
IE4 Scripting Property: `lineHeight`
Values: `<number>`, `<length>`, `<percentage>`, `normal`
Default: Depends on browser
Applies to: All elements
Inherited: Yes
Percentage?: Yes, relative to the font-size of the current element

Sets the height of the current line. Numerical values are expressed as the font size of the current element multiplied by the value given (for example, 1.2 would be valid). If given by length, a unit of measurement must be used. Percentages are based on the font-size of the current font size, and should normally be more than 100%.

list-style

JSS Equivalent: not supported
IE4 Scripting Property: `listStyle`
Values: `<keyword>`, `<position>`, `<url>`
Default: Depends on browser
Applies to: All elements
Inherited: Yes
Percentage?: No

Defines how list items are displayed. Can be used to set all the properties, or the individual styles can be set independently using the following styles.

list-style-image

JSS Equivalent: not supported
IE4 Scripting Property: `listStyleImage`
Values: `none`, `<url>`
Default: `none`
Applies to: All elements
Inherited: Yes
Percentage?: No

Defines the URL of an image to be used as the 'bullet' or list marker for each item in a list.

list-style-position

JSS Equivalent: not supported
IE4 Scripting Property: `listStylePosition`
Values: `inside`, `outside`
Default: `outside`
Applies to: All elements
Inherited: Yes
Percentage?: No

Indicates if the list marker should be placed indented or extended in relation to the list body.

list-style-type

JSS Equivalent:	`listStyleType`
IE4 Scripting Property:	`listStyleType`
Values:	`none`, `circle`, `disk`, `square`, `decimal`, `lower-alpha`, `upper-alpha`, `lower-roman`, `upper-roman`
Default:	`disk`
Applies to:	All elements
Inherited:	Yes
Percentage?:	No

Defines the type of 'bullet' or list marker used to precede each item in the list.

text-align

JSS Equivalent:	`textAlign`
IE4 Scripting Property:	`textAlign`
Values:	`left`, `right`, `center`, `justify`
Default:	Depends on browser
Applies to:	All elements
Inherited:	Yes
Percentage?:	No

Describes how text is aligned within the element. Essentially replicates the `<DIV ALIGN=>` tag.

text-decoration

JSS Equivalent:	`textDecoration`
Scripting Properties:	`textDecoration`, `textDecorationLineThrough`, `textDecorationUnderline`, `textDecorationOverline`
Values:	`none`, `underline`, `overline`, `line-through`
Default:	`none`
Applies to:	All elements
Inherited:	No
Percentage?:	No

Specifies any special appearance of the text. Open to extension by vendors, with unidentified extensions rendered as an underline. This property is not inherited, but will usually span across any 'child' elements.

text-indent

JSS Equivalent:	`textIndent`
IE4 Scripting Property:	`textIndent`
Values:	`<length>`, `<percentage>`
Default:	Zero
Applies to:	All elements
Inherited:	Yes
Percentage?:	Yes, refers to width of parent element

Sets the indentation values, in units of measurement, or as a percentage of the parent element's width.

text-transform

JSS Equivalent: `textTransform`
IE4 Scripting Property: `textTransform`
Values: `capitalize`, `uppercase`, `lowercase`, `none`
Default: `none`
Applies to: All elements
Inherited: Yes
Percentage?: No

- `capitalize` will set the first character of each word in the element as uppercase.
- `uppercase` will set every character in the element in uppercase.
- `lowercase` will place every character in lowercase.
- `none` will neutralize any inherited settings.

vertical-align

JSS Equivalent: `verticalAlign`
IE4 Scripting Property: `verticalAlign`
Values: `baseline`, `sub`, `super`, `top`, `text-top`, `middle`, `bottom`, `text-bottom`, `<percentage>`
Default: `baseline`
Applies to: Inline elements
Inherited: No
Percentage?: Yes, will refer to the line-height itself

Controls the vertical positioning of any affected element.

- `baseline` sets the alignment with the base of the parent.
- `middle` aligns the vertical midpoint of the element with the baseline of the parent plus half of the vertical height of the parent.
- `sub` makes the element a subscript.
- `super` makes the element a superscript.
- `text-top` aligns the element with the top of text in the parent element's font.
- `text-bottom` aligns with the bottom of text in the parent element's font.
- `top` aligns the top of the element with the top of the tallest element on the current line.
- `bottom` aligns with the bottom of the lowest element on the current line.

Size and Border Properties

These values are used to set the characteristics of the layout 'box' that exists around elements. They can apply to characters, images, and so on.

border-top-color, border-right-color, border-bottom-color, border-left-color, border-color

JSS Equivalent: `borderColor`—rest unsupported
Scripting Properties: `borderTopColor`, `borderRightColor`, `borderBottomColor`, `borderLeftColor`, `borderColor`
Values: `<color>`
Default: `<none>`
Applies to: Block and replaced elements
Inherited: No
Percentage?: No

Sets the color of the four borders. By supplying the URL of an image instead, the image itself is repeated to create the border.

border-top-style, border-right-style, border-bottom-style, border-left-style, border-style

JSS Equivalent: `borderStyle`–rest unsupported
Scripting Properties: `borderTopStyle`, `borderRightStyle`, `borderBottomStyle`, `borderLeftStyle`, `borderStyle`
Values: `none`, `solid`, `double`, `groove`, `ridge`, `inset`, `outset`
Default: `none`
Applies to: Block and replaced elements
Inherited: No
Percentage?: No

Sets the style of the four borders.

border-top, border-right, border-bottom, border-left, border

JSS Equivalent: not supported
Scripting Properties: `borderTop`, `borderRight`, `borderBottom`, `borderLeft`, `border`
Values: `<border-width>`, `<border-style>`, `<color>`
Default: `medium`, `none`, `<none>`
Applies to: Block and replaced elements
Inherited: No
Percentage?: No

Sets the properties of the border element (box drawn around the affected element). Works roughly the same as the margin settings, except that it can be made visible.

`<border-width>` can be `thin`, `medium`, `thick`, or as a unit of measurement.

- `<border-style>` can be **none**, **solid**.

The color argument is used to fill the background of the element while it loads, and behind any transparent parts of the element. By supplying the URL of an image instead, the image itself is repeated to create the border. It is also possible to specify values for attributes of the border property separately using the **border-width**, **border-style** and **border-color** properties.

border-top-width, border-right-width, border-bottom-width, border-left-width, border-width

JSS Equivalent:	`borderTopWidth`, `borderRightWidth`, `borderBottomWidth`, `borderLeftWidth`, `borderWidths()`
Scripting Properties:	`borderTopWidth`, `borderRightWidth`, `borderBottomWidth`, `borderLeftWidth`, `borderWidth`
Values:	`thin`, `medium`, `thick <length>`
Default:	`medium`
Applies to:	Block and replaced elements
Inherited:	No
Percentage?:	No

Sets the width of the border for the element. Each side can be set individually, or the **border-width** property used to set all of the sides. You can also supply up to four arguments for the border-width property to set individual sides, in the same way as with the **margin** property.

clear

JSS Equivalent:	`clear`
IE4 Scripting Property:	`clear`
Values:	`none`, `both`, `left`, `right`
Default:	`none`
Applies to:	All elements
Inherited:	No
Percentage?:	No

Forces the following elements to be displayed below an element which is aligned. Normally, they would wrap around it.

clip

JSS Equivalent:	not supported
IE4 Scripting Property:	`clip`
Values:	`rect(<top>, <right>, <bottom>, <left>)`, `auto`
Default:	`auto`
Applies to:	All elements
Inherited:	No
Percentage?:	No

Controls which part of an element is visible. Anything that occurs outside the clip area is not visible.

display

JSS Equivalent: `display`
IE4 Scripting Property: `display`
Values: `""`, `none`
Default: `""`
Applies to: All elements
Inherited: No
Percentage?: No

This property indicates whether an element is rendered. If set to `none` the element is not rendered, if set to `""` it is rendered.

float

JSS Equivalent: `align`
IE4 Scripting Property: `styleFloat`
Values: `none`, `left`, `right`
Default: `none`
Applies to: `DIV`, `SPAN` and replaced elements
Inherited: No
Percentage?: No

Causes following elements to be wrapped to the left or right of the element, rather than being placed below it.

height

JSS Equivalent: `height`
Scripting Properties: `height`, `pixelHeight`, `posHeight`
Values: `auto`, `<length>`
Default: `auto`
Applies to: `DIV`, `SPAN` and replaced elements
Inherited: No
Percentage?: No

Sets the vertical size of an element, and will scale the element if necessary. The value is returned as a string including the measurement type (`px`, `%`, etc.). To retrieve the value as a number, query the `posHeight` property.

left – New in CSS2

JSS Equivalent: not supported
Scripting Properties: `left, pixelLeft, posLeft`
Values: `auto`, `<length>`, `<percentage>`
Default: `auto`
Applies to: All elements
Inherited: No
Percentage?: Yes, refers to parent's width

Sets or returns the left position of an element when displayed in 2D canvas mode, allowing accurate placement and animation of individual elements. The value is returned as a string including the measurement type (`px`, `%`, etc.). To retrieve the value as a number, query the `posLeft` property.

margin-top, margin-right, margin-bottom, margin-left, margin

JSS Equivalent:	`marginTop, marginRight, marginBottom, marginLeft, margins()`
Scripting Properties:	`marginTop, marginRight, marginBottom, marginLeft, margin`
Values:	`auto`, `<length>`, `<percentage>`
Default:	Zero
Applies to:	Block and replaced elements
Inherited:	No
Percentage?:	Yes, refers to parent element's width

Sets the size of margins around any given element. You can use **`margin`** as shorthand for setting all of the other values (as it applies to all four sides). If you use multiple values in **`margin`** but use less than four, opposing sides will try to be equal. These values all set the effective minimum distance between the current element and others.

overflow – New in CSS2

JSS Equivalent:	not supported
IE4 Scripting Property:	`overflow`
Values:	`none`, `clip`, `scroll`
Default:	`none`
Applies to:	All elements
Inherited:	No
Percentage?:	No

This controls how a container element will display its content if this is not the same size as the container.

- **`none`** means that the container will use the default method. For example, as in an image element, the content may be resized to fit the container.
- **`clip`** means that the contents will not be resized, and only a part will be visible.
- **`scroll`** will cause the container to display scroll bars so that the entire contents can be viewed by scrolling.

padding-top, padding-right, padding-bottom, padding-left, padding

JSS Equivalent:	`paddingTop`, `paddingRight`, `paddingBottom`, `paddingLeft`, `paddings()`
Scripting Properties:	`paddingTop`, `paddingRight`, `paddingBottom`, `paddingLeft`, `padding`
Values:	`auto`, `<length>`, `<percentage>`
Default:	`Zero`
Applies to:	Block and replaced elements
Inherited:	No
Percentage?:	Yes, refers to parent element's width

Sets the distance between the content and border of an element. You can use **padding** as shorthand for setting all of the other values (as it applies to all four sides). If you use multiple values in **padding** but use less than four, opposing sides will try to be equal. These values all set the effective minimum distance between the current element and others.

position – New in CSS2

JSS Equivalent: not supported
IE4 Scripting Property: **position**
Values: **absolute**, **relative**, **static**
Default: **relative**
Applies to: All elements
Inherited: No
Percentage?: No

Specifies if the element can be positioned directly on the 2-D canvas.

- **absolute** means it can be fixed on the background of the page at a specified location, and move with it.
- **static** means it can be fixed on the background of the page at a specified location, but not move when the page is scrolled.
- **relative** means that it will be positioned normally, depending on the preceding elements.

top – New in CSS2

JSS Equivalent: not supported
Scripting Properties: **top, pixelTop, posTop**
Values: **auto**, **<percentage>**, **<length>**
Default: **auto**
Applies to: All elements
Inherited: No
Percentage?: Yes, refers to parent's width

Sets or returns the vertical position of an element when displayed in 2-D canvas mode, allowing accurate placement and animation of individual elements. Value is returned as a string including the measurement type (**px**, **%**, etc.). To retrieve the value as a number, query the **posTop** property.

visibility – New in CSS2

JSS Equivalent: not supported
IE4 Scripting Property: **visibility**
Values: **visible**, **hidden**, **inherit**
Default: **inherit**
Applies to: All elements
Inherited: No
Percentage?: No

Allows the element to be displayed or hidden on the page. Elements which are hidden still take up the same amount of space, but are rendered transparently.

Can be used to dynamically display only one of several overlapping elements

- **`visible`** means that the element will be visible.
- **`hidden`** means that the element will not be visible.
- **`inherit`** means that the element will only be visible when its parent or container element is visible.

white-space

JSS Equivalent:	`whiteSpace`
IE4 Scripting Property:	not supported
Values:	`<length>,<percentage>`
Default:	`Zero`
Applies to:	Block-level elements
Inherited:	No
Percentage?:	Yes, refers to parent's width

Sets the spacing between elements. Using a <percentage> value will base the spacing on the parent element or default spacing for that element.

width

JSS Equivalent:	`width`
Scripting Properties:	`width, pixelWidth, posWidth`
Values:	`auto`, `<length>`, `<percentage>`
Default:	`auto`, except for any element with an intrinsic dimension
Applies to:	`DIV`, `SPAN` and replaced elements
Inherited:	No
Percentage?:	Yes, refers to parent's width

Sets the horizontal size of an element, and will scale the element if necessary. The value is returned as a string including the measurement type (**`px`**, `%`, etc.). To retrieve the value as a number, query the **`posWidth`** property.

z-index – New in CSS2

JSS Equivalent:	not supported
IE4 Scripting Property:	`zIndex`
Values:	`<number>`
Default:	Depends on the HTML source
Applies to:	All elements
Inherited:	No
Percentage?:	No

Controls the ordering of overlapping elements, and defines which will be displayed 'on top'. Positive numbers are above the normal text on the page, and negative numbers are below. Allows a 2.5-D appearance by controlling the layering of the page's contents.

Printing Properties

page-break-after

JSS Equivalent: not supported
IE4 Scripting Property: `pageBreakAfter`
Values: `<auto>`, `<always>`, `<left>`, `<right>`
Default: `<auto>`
Applies to: All elements
Inherited: No
Percentage?: No

Controls when to set a page break and on what page the content will resume, i.e. either the left or the right.

page-break-before

JSS Equivalent: not supported
IE4 Scripting Property: `pageBreakBefore`
Values: `<auto>`, `<always>`, `<left>`, `<right>`
Default: `<auto>`
Applies to: All elements
Inherited: No
Percentage?: No

Controls when to set a page break and on what page the content will resume, i.e. either the left or the right.

Other Properties

cursor

JSS Equivalent: not supported
IE4 Scripting Property: `cursor`
Values: `auto`, `crosshair`, `default`, `hand`, `move`, `e-resize`, `ne-resize`, `nw-resize`, `n-resize`, `se-resize`, `sw-resize`, `s-resize`, `w-resize`, `text`, `wait`, `help`
Default: `auto`
Applies to: All elements
Inherited: No
Percentage?: No

Specifies the type of cursor the mouse pointer should be.

IE4 Unsupported CSS Properties

Internet Explorer 4 doesn't support the following CSS properties:

- `word-spacing`
- `!important`
- `first-letter pseudo`
- `first-line pseudo`
- `white-space`

Navigator 4 Unsupported CSS Properties

Navigator 4 doesn't support the following CSS properties:

- `word-spacing`
- `!important`
- `first-letter pseudo`
- `first-line pseudo`
- `font`
- `font-variant`
- `letter-spacing`
- `list-style-image,list-style-position,list-style`
- `background-attachment,background-position,background-repeat,background`
- `border-top-color,border-right-color,border-left-color,border-bottom-color`
- `border-top-style,border-left-style,border-right-style,border-bottom-style`
- `border-top,border-right,border-bottom,border-left,border`
- `clip`
- `overflow`
- `left`
- `position`
- `top`
- `visibility`
- `z-index`
- `page-break-after`
- `page-break-before`

- cursor
- @import

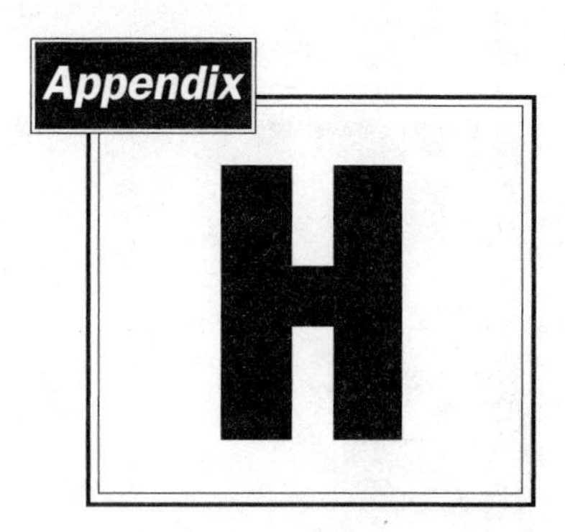

Support and Errata

One of the most irritating things about any programming book can be when you find that a bit of code you've just spent an hour typing simply doesn't work. You check it a hundred times to see if you've set it up correctly and then you notice the spelling mistake in the variable name on the book page. Grrrr! Of course, you can blame the authors for not taking enough care and testing the code, the editors for not doing their job properly, or the proofreaders for not being eagle-eyed enough, but this doesn't get around the fact that mistakes do happen.

We try hard to ensure no mistakes sneak out into the real world, but we can't promise you that this book is 100% error free. What we can do is offer the next best thing by providing you with immediate support and feedback from experts who have worked on the book and try to ensure that future editions eliminate these gremlins. The following section will take you step by step through how to post errata to our web site to get that help:

- Finding a list of existing errata on the web site
- Adding your own errata to the existing list
- What happens to your errata once you've posted it (why doesn't it appear immediately?)

and how to mail a question for technical support:

- What your e-mail should include
- What happens to your e-mail once it has been received by us

Finding an Errata on the Web Site

Before you send in a query, you might be able to save time by finding the answer to your problem on our web site, **`http:\\www.wrox.com`**. Each book we publish has its own page and its own errata sheet. You can get to any book's page by using the drop down list box on our web site's welcome screen.

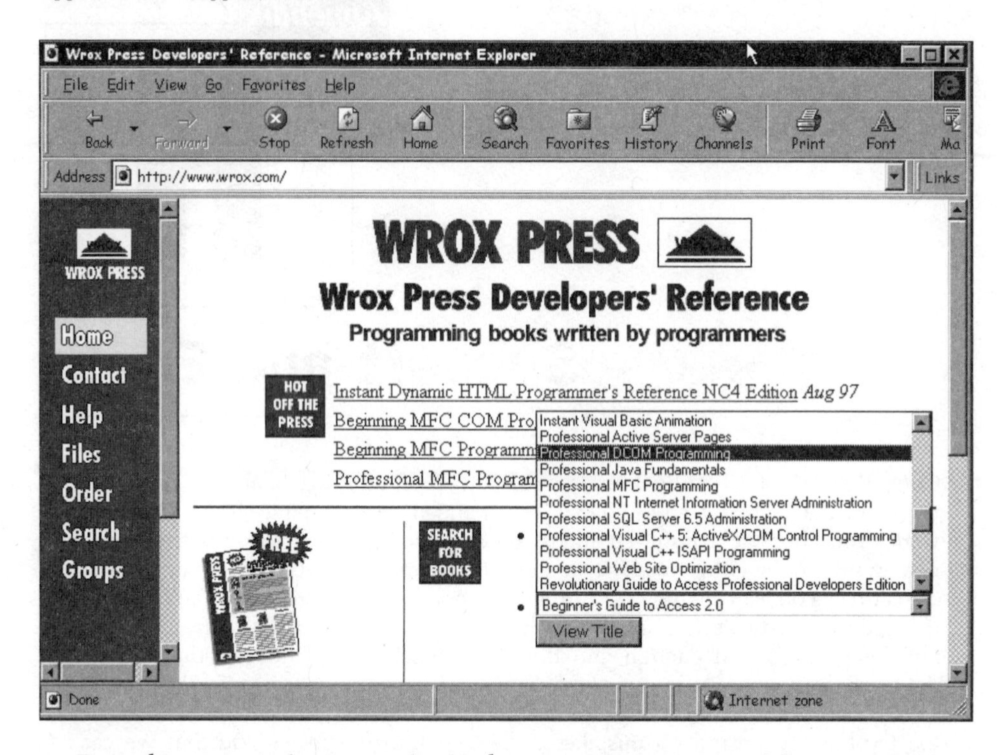

From this you can locate any book's home page on our site. Select your book and click View Title to get the individual title page:

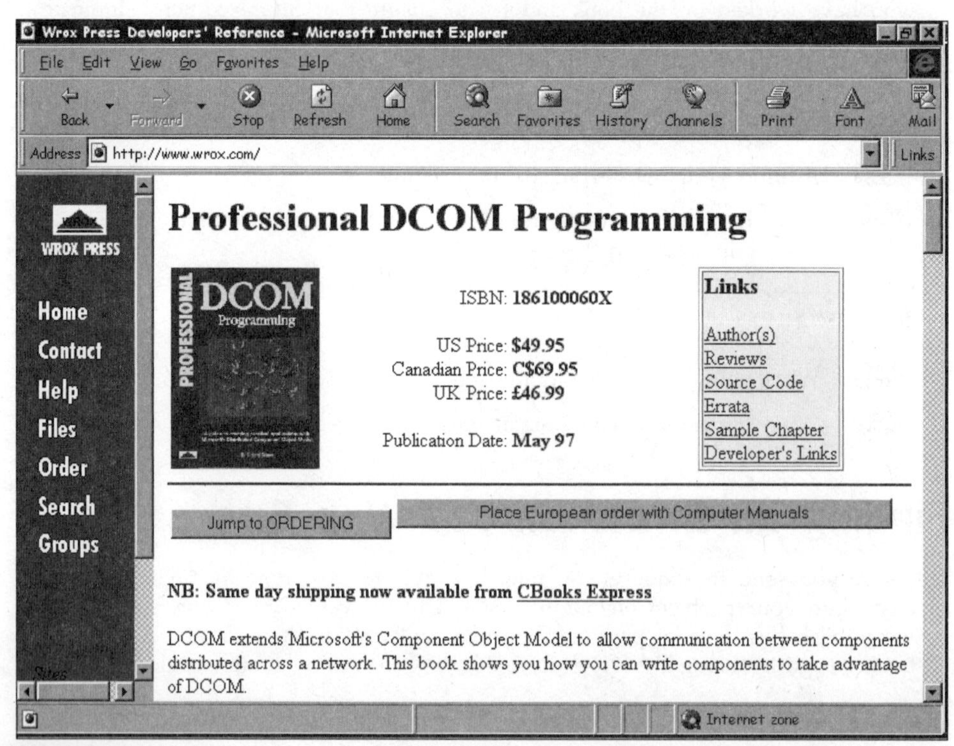

Each book has a set of links. If you click on the Errata link, you'll immediately be transported to the errata sheet for that book:

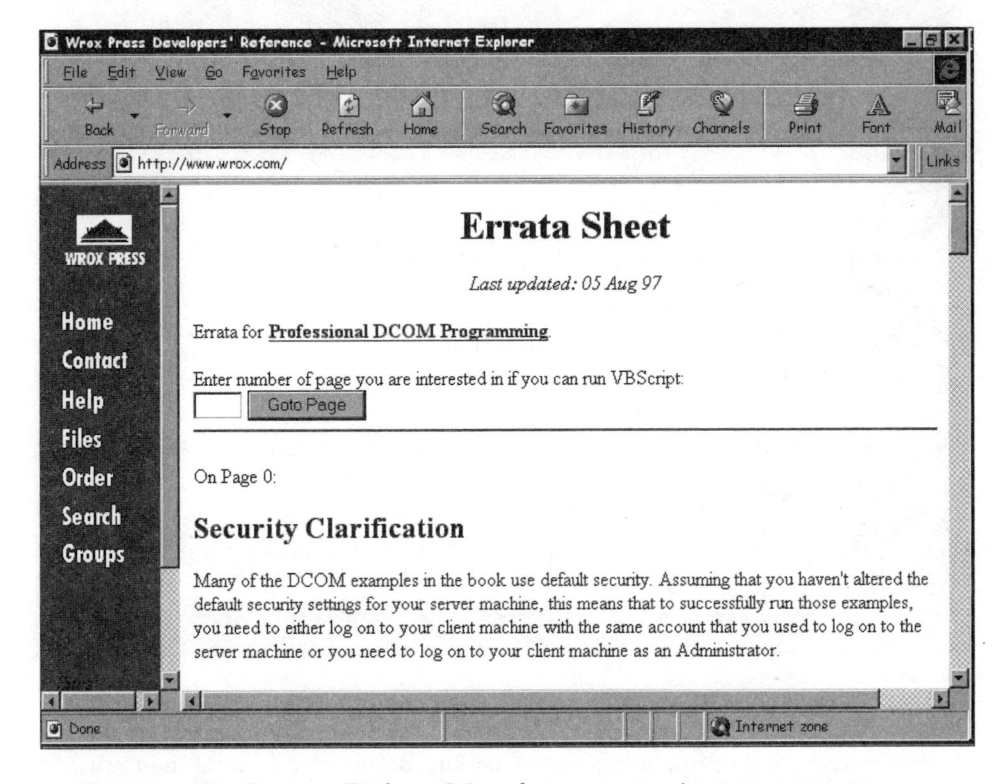

If you're using Internet Explorer 3.0 or later, you can jump to errors more quickly using the text box provided. The errata lists are updated on daily basis, ensuring that you always have the most up-to-date information on bugs and errors.

Adding an Errata to the Sheet Yourself

It's always possible that you may not find your error listed, in which case you can enter details of the fault yourself. It might be anything from a spelling mistake to a faulty piece of code in a book. Sometimes you'll find useful hints that aren't really errors on the listing. By entering errata you may save another reader some hours of frustration and, of course, you will be helping us to produce even higher quality information. We're very grateful for this sort of guidance and feedback. Here's how to do it:

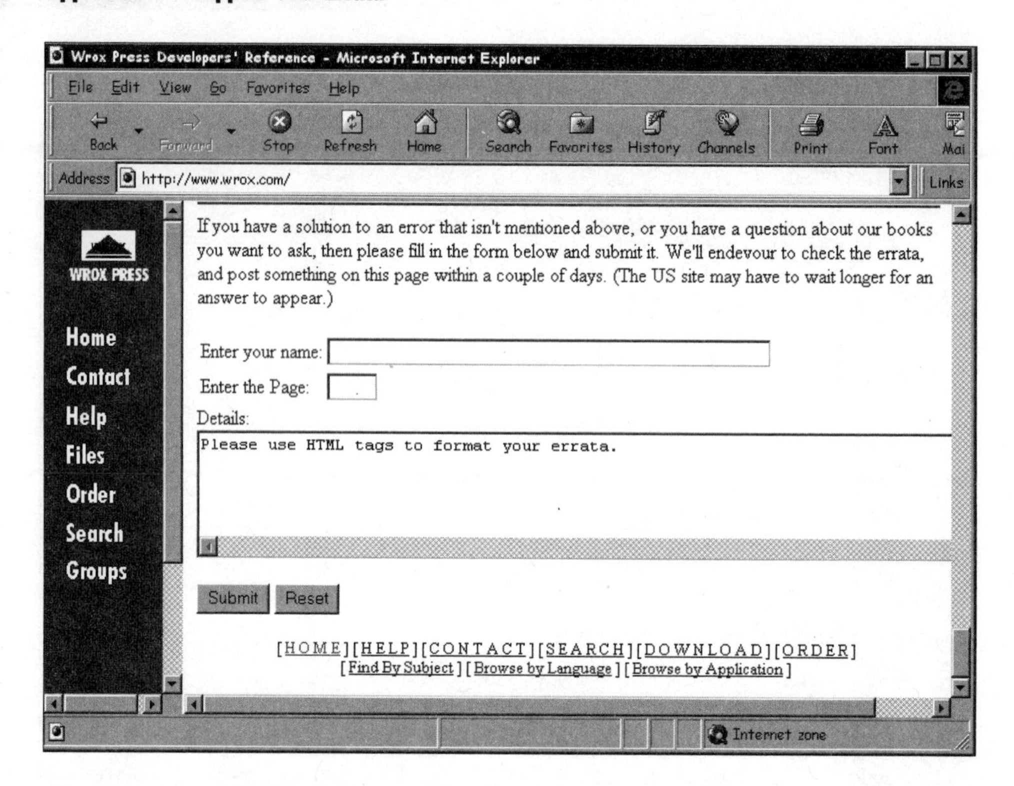

Find the errata page for the book, then scroll down to the bottom of the page, where you will see a space for you to enter your name (and e-mail address for preference), the page the errata occurs on and details of the errata itself. The errata should be formatted using HTML tags - the reminder for this can be deleted as you type in your error.

Once you've typed in your message, click on the Submit button and the message is forwarded to our editors. They'll then test your submission and check that the error exists, and that any suggestions you make are valid. Then your submission, together with a solution, is posted on the site for public consumption. Obviously this stage of the process can take a day or two, but we will endeavor to get a fix up sooner than that.

E-mail Support

If you wish to directly query a problem in the book with an expert who knows the book in detail then e-mail `support@wrox.com`, with the title of the book and the last four numbers of the ISBN in the Subject field of the e-mail. A typical e-mail should include the following things:

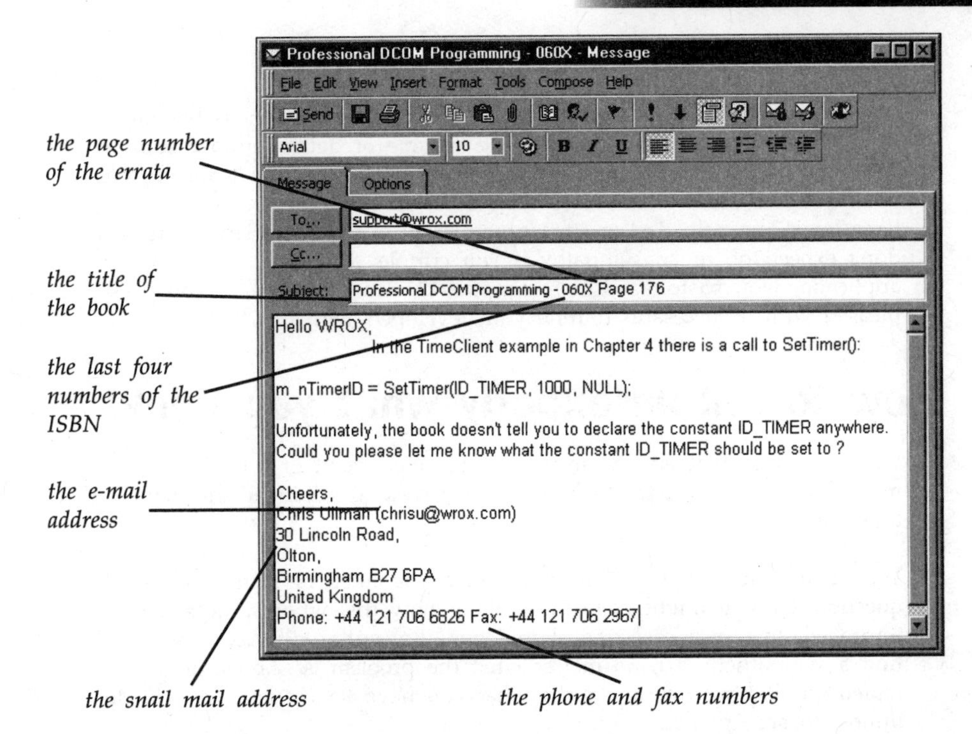

We won't send you junk mail. We need details to help save your time and ours. If we need to replace a disk or CD we'll be able to get it to you straight away. When you send an e-mail it will go through the following chain of support;

Customer Support

Your message is delivered to one of our customer support staff who are the first people to read it. They have files on the most frequently asked questions and will answer anything immediately. They answer general questions about the books and web site.

Editorial

Deeper queries are forwarded on the same day to the technical editor responsible for that book. They have experience with the programming language or particular product and are able to answer detailed technical questions on the subject. Once an issue has been resolved, the editor can post the errata to the web site.

The Author(s)

Finally, in the unlikely event that the editor can't answer your problem, he/she will forward the request to the author. We try to protect the author from any distractions from writing. However, we are quite happy to forward specific requests to them. All Wrox authors help with the support on their books. They'll mail the customer and editor with their response, and again, all readers should benefit.

What we can't answer

Obviously with an ever growing range of books and an ever-changing technology base, there is an increasing volume of data requiring support. While we endeavor to answer all questions about a book, we can't answer bugs in your own programs that you've adapted from our code. So, while you might have loved the help desk system examples in our Active Server Pages book, don't expect too much sympathy if you cripple your company with a live application you customized from chapter 12. But do tell us if you're especially pleased with a successful routine you developed with our help.

How to tell us exactly what you think!

We understand that errors can destroy the enjoyment of a book and can cause many wasted and frustrated hours, so we seek to minimize the distress that they can cause.

You might just wish to tell us how much you liked or loathed the book in question. Or you might have ideas about how this whole process could be improved. In which case you should e-mail `feedback@wrox.com`. You'll always find a sympathetic ear, no matter what the problem is. Above all you should remember that we do care about what you have to say and we will do our utmost to act upon it.

Index

Symbols

A

B

D

E

F

G

H

I

J

L

O

P

Q

R

S

T

U

V

W

ASP Today

www.asptoday.com

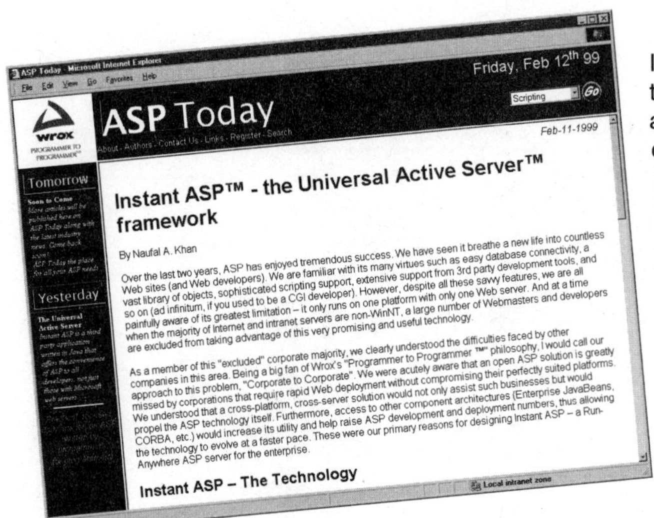

It's not easy keeping up to date with what's hot and what's not in the ever-changing world of internet development. Even if you stick to one narrow topic like ASP, trawling through the mailing lists each day and finding new and better code is still a twenty-four-seven job. Which is where we come in.

You already know Wrox Press from its series of titles on ASP and its associated technologies. We realise that we can't bring out a book everyday to keep you all up to date, so from March 1, we're starting a brand new website at www.asptoday.com which will do all the hard work for you. Every week you'll find new tips, tricks and techniques for you to try out and test in your development, covering ASP components, ADO, RDS, ADSI, CDO, Security, Site Design, BackOffice, XML and more. Look out also for bug alerts when they're found and fixes when they're available.

We hope that you won't be shy in telling us what you think of the site and the content we put on it either. If you like what you'll see, we'll carry on as we are, but if you think we're missing something, then we'll address it accordingly. If you've got something to write, then do so and we'll include it. We're hoping our site will become a global effort by and for the entire ASP community.

In anticipation,
Dan Maharry, ASPToday.com